Greenhill Books

1813: LEIPZIG
Napoleon and the Battle of the Nations

1813: LEIPZIG

Napoleon and the Battle of the Nations

by Digby Smith

Greenhill Books, London

Stackpole Books, Pennsylvania

1813: Leipzig – Napoleon and the Battle of the Nations
first published 2001 by Greenhill Books, Lionel Leventhal Limited, Park House,
1 Russell Gardens, London NW11 9NN
and
Stackpole Books, 5067 Ritter Road, Mechanicsburg, PA 17055, USA

British Library Cataloguing in Publication Data
Smith, Digby
1813: Leipzig: Napoleon and the Battle of the Nations
1. Leipzig, Battle of, 1813
I. Title   II. Eighteen thirteen
940.2'7

ISBN 1-85367-435-4

Library of Congress Cataloging-in-Publication Data available

Typeset by DP Photosetting, Aylesbury, Bucks
Printed and bound in Great Britain by CPD (Wales), Ebbw Vale

Contents

List of Illustrations and Maps

8   *List of Illustrations and Maps*

MAPS

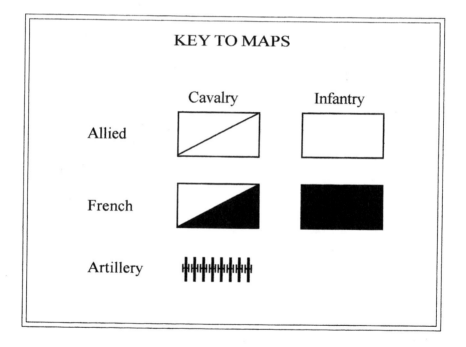

KEY TO MAPS

	Cavalry	Infantry
Allied		
French		
Artillery		

Acknowledgements

Over the years, many people have been of great assistance by pointing me in the right direction for the best and most reliable data on those aspects of military history which particularly interest me. And yet, despite researching and collecting for over thirty years, there remain vast areas of Napoleonic military history about which I find I know virtually nothing.

Of particular help in the preparation of this book were Jörg Titze of Leipzig, who was kind enough to accompany me all over the battlefield, and to provide me with his very detailed account of the defection of the Saxons on 18 October; Nickolas E. Sebrimatov and Frederic Feather; Görun Frielund; Markus Gärtner, who once again allowed me free rein in his library and made many helpful suggestions; and Jonathan North, who provided some of the dramatic eyewitness accounts.

As regards the original sources utilised here, quite the most unreliable is Colonel Marcellin de Marbot's memoirs. His veracity borders on that of the notorious *Bulletins* of the *Grande Armée*. He is nevertheless included because of his distinctly racy style and his ability to introduce a note of light relief – once one is aware of his shortcomings. At the other end of the scale is *Vor Leipzig 1813*, an excellent collection of eyewitness accounts of these momentous events, produced by the government of the German Democratic Republic in 1988, shortly before the collapse of the Berlin Wall.

Digby Smith, 2001

Introduction

At the base of the gargantuan monument to the Battle of the Nations in Leipzig is a small military museum. It contains some of the most interesting and well-preserved artefacts of the Saxon army that I have ever seen, plus many other rare items from the battle including Poniatowski's saddle and shabraque. The monument itself is located just south of the old exhibition ground on Carl-Hampel-Platz. It is possible to climb to the top, offering excellent panoramic views of the city and the southern battlefield.

The gatehouse of the manor at Dölitz has also been converted into a museum, containing many dioramas of parts of the battle. It is well-preserved, and well worth a visit. When I visited the battlefield in 1999 the gatehouse in Markkleeberg was being renovated, and I believe the plan is to open another museum of the battle here. The archives of the city of Leipzig itself also contain much material relating to the battle, and to the events of 1813 as a whole.

In the period 1861–4, Doctor Apel placed a series of forty-four small stone monuments around the battlefield, most of which still exist today. Each is coded and contains information as to which division or corps stood on that spot on which day of the battle, and gives the strength of the formation. There are many other monuments on the field apart from Doctor Apel's. One of the most impressive is the Russian church on the Semmelweis-Strasse, between the Friedenspark and the old exhibition ground in the Thonberg district in the centre of the city. Do go in, it is well worth a visit.

Unfortunately, much of the south-western portion of the battlefield has fallen victim to opencast lignite mining, and the northern sector is completely built over. The eastern and south-eastern parts are still much as they were, however, and merit a visit, but good preparatory reading will allow the visitor to reap the largest rewards.

Chapter 1

The Road to Leipzig

The effects of the Russian campaign

Napoleon lost most of the *Grande Armée* which he had led into Russia in 1812, including nearly all of his artillery and cavalry. The casualties suffered in this catastrophic campaign had begun to reach serious proportions long before the effects of 'General Winter' came into play. Most of his corps were already down to fifty per cent of their start-out strengths by as early as mid August, although the well-supplied Imperial Guard did not decline to this level until the end of September.

All the contestants suffered under the harsh winter conditions, but loss of life in the *Grande Armée* – through starvation, disease, and cold – rose dramatically during the retreat. Luckily for Napoleon, Kutusov had immense respect for his qualities as a commander, and his pursuit of the invaders was never energetic. The Russian high command also badly bungled their chances of trapping the French at the Beresina, and Victor's spirited resistance there saved thousands of lives for the Emperor. Once the last of the invaders had been expelled from the 'Holy soil of Russia' pursuit by the Russian army slackened markedly. Nevertheless, casualties within the *Grande Armée* amounted to a staggering ninety per cent of its strength, although many cadres of officers and NCOs must be subtracted from this figure, having been sent back to their depots in France in the course of the campaign as their men dwindled away from starvation and sickness.

Hoping to return and reconquer the area, Napoleon left considerable garrisons in various fortresses in Poland as he withdrew: 30,000 men in Danzig, and 5,000 each in Glogau, Küstrin, Modlin, and Thorn. This politico-strategic decision robbed him of 50,000 veteran troops – many of them admittedly sick – while the Allies, though they had to leave blockading forces at these places, could often deploy fairly raw militia for this task, enabling them to free their own first-line troops for more demanding duties in the field.

The military landscape was changed dramatically by Napoleon's defeat, which sent deep shock waves through Europe's political alliances. Diplomatic activity was furious in the early part of 1813 as all parties explored possible new alliances in the aftermath of the *Grande Armée*'s destruction. Meanwhile, apart from minor probing raids deep into northern Germany by light forces consisting mostly of cavalry, there was no military activity until April. By this time Russia and Prussia were allied against France and the Confederation of the Rhine, Austria was neutral, and Britain was pouring money and equipment into the coffers and depots of Napoleon's enemies via the Baltic.[1]

---

[1] The energies devoted by the various states to the rebuilding of their armies, and the results of their efforts, are reviewed in detail in chapter 2.

On 4 March, Prince Eugene – who had taken over command of the remnants of the *Grande Armée* in Napoleon's absence – evacuated Berlin, abandoned the line of the Oder, and fell back to Leipzig and the line of the Elbe. The following month, the protagonists closed with one another on the Elbe and minor actions increased in frequency and intensity. May saw the first serious combats, with Napoleon's victory at Lützen (Gross-Görschen) on the 2nd and again at Bautzen and Wurschen on the 20th–21st. The Russo-Prussian allies were forced back into Silesia; they were in trouble and desperately needed a chance to regroup and to rethink their strategy if they were to avoid destruction. Barclay de Tolly, the Russian commander, was even prepared to abandon the Prussians and withdraw to Warsaw. Napoleon, too, needed time to consolidate his position and to digest the new formations and reinforcement drafts which were coming up from France. Consequently he proposed an armistice, and, after negotiations at Poischwitz, a cease-fire came into effect on 4 June.

Another factor which had persuaded Napoleon to propose the armistice was the concentration of Schwarzenberg's as yet neutral Austrian corps on the lower River Eger in Bohemia, on the southern flank of the French army. If Napoleon attempted to invade Silesia to finish off the Russo-Prussians, he could be exposed to a serious threat from this quarter.

The cessation of military activity made way for more frantic diplomacy – between Austria and Saxony, between Austria and Bavaria, between France and Austria, and between Britain and the Allies. In northern Europe this led to Austria's recruitment to the coalition of Russia, Prussia, and Sweden against France, the Confederation of the Rhine, and Denmark. In the south, meanwhile, the Duke of Wellington's allied armies thrust across the Bidassoa into France, and Austria wrestled with Prince Eugene in northern Italy.

Austria had joined the Allies by the Treaty of Reichenbach, which was signed on 27 June 1813. The preceding day, in the Marcolini palace in Dresden, Napoleon had uttered that famous phrase to the Austrian Chancellor, Prince Metternich: 'What are the lives of 200,000 men to me?'; at which Metternich had cried: 'Open the doors and windows, so that Europe may hear these words!'[2] On 11 August, Austria gave notice to Napoleon that

---

[2] This account of the interview is taken from *1813–1815 Österreich in den Befreiungskriegen-Die Politik Metternichs*, p. 112. However, Grabowski, one of Napoleon's orderly officers and – naturally – a great admirer of his, was in an adjoining room at this point, and claims that the Emperor never said these words, Grabowski attributes the quotation to Thiers, who, he says, invented it and inserted it in volume XVI of his *Histoire du Consulat de l'Empire*. Grabowski cites as additional evidence the fact that Napoleon's *Memoires*, written years later on St Helena, did not contain this phrase. But Napoleon's *Memoires* contain (and omit or alter) many things, such as that he lost the battle of Leipzig because 'the entire Saxon army, with 60 guns, which occupied a vital sector of our front, went over to the enemy and turned these guns on us.' The reader shall see further on just how accurate this claim was, and will be able to judge for himself the overall veracity of the Emperor's *Memoires*. (*Contd on next page*)

the armistice would end and that she would enter the war against France. The king of Saxony, however, whose country was firmly in Napoleon's grip, could not bring himself to move to the Allied side and returned to his unhappy country when hostilities recommenced.

The Trachenberg plan

The enlistment of Austria to the Allied cause in July altered the balance of power in Germany considerably in their favour, and even before the month of June was out Radetzky, the Austrian Chief of Staff, had formulated the strategic concept which was to guide the Allies to victory at Leipzig. It was simple: 'Act offensively against an inferior foe; act defensively against a superior foe'. Prinz Schwarzenberg, the Allied supreme commander, underlined the importance of this strategy, warning against underestimating the threat posed by Napoleon, and against taking risks if there were better and safer ways to achieve the agreed aim. He estimated that:

> In his position, Napoleon must wish to fight a major battle as soon as possible, for his forces will weaken every day as ours grow stronger. We, now difficult to unite, must not allow this battle to take place until all conditions point to the fact that we will win it.
>
> In order to create this opportunity, the French army must be weakened by marches and minor actions. This can be facilitated by assembling our armies in three masses: one each in Bohemia, Silesia and the Mark,[3] but it will only succeed if we adhere to the iron law that that army which is being attacked by Napoleon withdraws, and the other two armies quickly assault him in flank and rear and thus draw him away from the first.
>
> This continuous advancing and withdrawing must tire him more than the three and must give them the opportunity to fall on and destroy the enemy force opposing them.
>
> When these losses have sufficiently weakened the enemy, we will be able to push him back from the Elbe and against the Saale and here, possibly in the area of Leipzig, we can offer him battle with our united forces and fate will take care of the rest.

On 9 July 1813 the Czar, the king of Prussia, and the crown prince of Sweden met at Trachenberg (now Zmigrod in Poland), north of Breslau in Silesia. On the 11th a council of war took place at which Crown Prince Bernadotte, von Suchtelen, von Stedingk, von Knesebeck, Prince Wolkonsky, and

---

Grabowski adds that Napoleon, having exhausted his patience with Metternich, went up to him in a rage, made a sharp movement with his hand which knocked Metternich's hat from his hand, and shouted: 'Well, Metternich, tell me how is England paying you to betray me?' Metternich did not answer but silently picked up his hat, gave a frosty bow, and left the room.
[3] Brandenburg in Prussia.

General von Toll were present. This meeting resulted in the plan which von Toll presented to the Czar, the king of Prussia, and Bernadotte on the 12th. Although no copy of the original document is known to exist, von Toll's memoirs contain this version:

> The main Allied forces must always concentrate against the enemy's main body.
>
> This means that:
>
> 1. Those corps which are operating against the flanks and rear of the enemy will always take the shortest line towards the enemy line of operations.
>
> 2. The Allied main body will take up a position which will allow it to oppose the enemy whichever way he turns. The bastion of Bohemia seems to lend itself to this plan.

This was von Toll's account of the birth of the winning strategy for the 1813 campaign. There is, however, another version. On 31 May 1813, Prinz Schwarzenberg and Radetzky went to Prague and met with the mortally wounded von Scharnhorst, Blücher's chief of staff, who was in hospital there, and the principles of the 'Trachenberg' plan were the result of the discussion between these three men that day. Bearing in mind the great mental powers of von Scharnhorst and his grasp of strategic principles, this version of events seems much more credible.

Radetzky at once set to work to transform the concept into a viable military operation. It was to prove an unqualified success, and Napoleon apparently never fully realised that he was being so thoroughly manipulated. In accordance with the plan's strategy, the Allied armies were divided into three groups, one each in Bohemia, Silesia, and North Germany. The 150,000-strong Russo-Prussian army in Silesia was to leave 50,000 men in the province, while the 100,000 men of its main body were to advance through Landshut and Glatz to Jungbunzlau and Budin at the end of the armistice, there joining up with 120,000 Austrians to form the main Allied army which was to act offensively. Crown Prince Bernadotte was to set 15–20,000 men of his army to observe the French and Danes in Hamburg and Lübeck and the remaining 70,000 were to concentrate around Treuenbrietzen, about fifty kilometres south-west of Berlin at the crossing of the modern B2 and B102 roads. The Army of Bohemia was to operate according to circumstances – that is to say, always to confront the enemy's main body, be it in Silesia, Saxony, or Bavaria. The Army of Silesia was to avoid a general action unless all advantages were on its side. If it was to advance to the Elbe, it was to cross this river between Torgau and Dresden and unite with Bernadotte's army to form a mass of 120,000 men. If, however, the Army of Bohemia had to be reinforced before the union of these two armies, the Army of Silesia would march on Bohemia. The Army of the North was to advance on the Elbe at the end of the armistice, cross this river between Torgau and Magdeburg, and advance on Leipzig. The Allied plan closed with the sentence: 'All Allied armies will act offensively; the enemy camp is their target.'

Radetzky's plan estimated the available Allied forces at 405,000 men (including 40,000 in Italy), and Napoleon's at 430–450,000, made up as follows:

Main army under Napoleon	190,000[4]
Prince Eugene in Italy and Illyria	60,000
Corps at Munich	40–50,000
Augereau's corps near Würzburg	40–50,000
Davout on the lower Elbe	20,000
Danish corps	10,000
Garrisons in the fortresses on the Elbe	70,000

He assumed that Napoleon would concentrate his army on the Elbe so as to be able to deliver a decisive blow as soon as the armistice was over, to destroy the infant alliance. This blow would have to be struck at the Austrian army in Bohemia, as this was on his right flank and threatened his communications with the Rhine. If Napoleon struck into Bohemia, he would simultaneously secure his right flank and take possession of a fertile area as yet untouched by the war, capable of supporting his armies for some time. If this first operation proved successful, he could then support Augereau and Wrede in their advance down the Danube valley, which would aid in turn the advance of Prince Eugene from Italy into Steiermark. Should Eugene be able to advance into the Danube valley and unite with the Franco-Bavarians, their combined forces would far outnumber the Austrian corps of Reuss and Hiller and would be able to threaten Vienna – much as in 1805 and 1809. Napoleon could undertake his thrust into Bohemia in the confident knowledge that the fortified line of the Elbe would protect his rear.

Any other operations against the Armies of the North or of Silesia would bring him large tracts of land but no real strategic advantage, for the further he advanced northwards or eastwards from the Elbe, the greater was the Army of Bohemia's threat to his lines of communication to the Rhine. An operation across the Oder and on to the Vistula, on the other hand, would relieve his troops in the fortresses there but would weaken his army without achieving a decisive victory. Almost certainly the Allies would evacuate or destroy any magazines in his path and take up a position on his right flank in Bohemia, and thus pen him into the exhausted area between the Oder and the Vistula. The Austrian planners were therefore unanimous that all military logic pointed to Napoleon striking at the Army of Bohemia as a first step in any new campaign. The other possibilities – strikes against Berlin or Silesia – were thought to be much less likely.

The anticipated French lunge at Bohemia was to be answered by twin advances on Dresden by Blücher and Bernadotte, while the Austrian army would withdraw south and avoid battle. Radetzky thus planned to hold the Army of Bohemia strictly on the defensive initially, and to have the other two

---

[4] As we know, he had 380,000.

Allied armies ready to launch aggressive attacks on the enemy's flank and rear to draw Napoleon away from Bohemia when he attacked.

Prinz Schwarzenberg agreed entirely with the concepts of his chief of staff, both on this matter and in the strategy of avoiding any major battle until the enemy had been considerably weakened, while still exploiting any opportunity which might present itself. This was the only possible way to combat an enemy of Napoleon's calibre. Until that final, decisive battle could be fought under the most favourable circumstances, the three Allied armies must remain isolated around Napoleon's periphery and seek to wear his army down by causing him to march and counter-march in the exhausted Saxon wilderness.

The details of the plan having been worked out, they were sent to the Czar in the hands of *Oberst* Latour, who had been fully briefed. Among other things, the plan called for Wittgenstein's Russian corps to be placed under Schwarzenberg's command and to march at once to join him in Bohemia. Once the Russians informed the Austrians of the exact strength of this corps, arrangements would be made to provide food and forage for it on the Austrian army scale. It would be treated exactly as if it were part of the Austrian army.

As it would be difficult for the northern Allied armies to force their way over the central section of the River Elbe, the Austrians suggested that they cross the river upstream in Bohemia. For this purpose, fortified bridges existed at Leimeritz, Raudnitz, and Melnik, north of Prague. If a pontoon bridge was needed, the Austrians had one available in Raudnitz, which would be placed at the Czar's disposal. The Czar willingly entered into the spirit of this offer and initially wanted to send 115,000 men down into Budin, on the right bank of the Eger in Bohemia, by 20 August. Welcome as these reinforcements would have been, the move was not possible because there was insufficient transport in north-eastern Bohemia to move the necessary supplies to feed this many men and horses. The Austrian Commissary General for Bohemia could only provide bread for 90,000 men and forage for 25,000 horses, and only for twenty days. The Kaiser therefore suggested that initially only 70,000 Russian troops should enter Bohemia, while the other 45,000 should remain in Silesia until sufficient logistical arrangements could be made to support them in their area of operations.

Accordingly, on 27 July, in the Austrian headquarters in Lieben, *Feldmarschall-Leutnants* Radetzky and Prohaska reached agreement with the Russian General Quartermaster Diebitsch and General Intendant Bachmanoff that I and II Russian Corps under Wittgenstein and Kleist's II Prussian Corps should cross the Bohemian border on 11 August in four columns on the roads from Landshut, Neurode, and Glatz in Silesia. Eight days later, the Russo-Prussian guards and reserves should follow in two columns on the roads from Trautenau via Neu-Paka and from Braunau via Pölitz and Gross-Skalitz. In this manner their supplies could be guaranteed by the Austrian authorities. Schwarzenberg for his part guaranteed, under all conditions, to have concentrated the Army of Bohemia by 9 August in the area of Holau, Hühnerwasser, and Hirschberg, with his headquarters in Mscheno, between Prague and Leipa to the north. This would protect the Allied assembly point from any danger from the French around Dresden and would threaten any advance these hostile forces might make eastwards into the Lausitz area during the move. The Czar agreed to all these proposals.

Apparently, Napoleon had a copy of the entire Allied plan in his hands shortly after it was completed, obtained by the Saxon War Minister for a bribe of 250 Gold Napoleons. The Emperor's fatefully overconfident reaction to it was: 'The Allies will certainly make mistakes and then we will fall on them and destroy them.'

In the meantime he took advantage of the security provided by the armistice to take a secret trip lasting eight days, to meet the Empress Marie Louise in Mainz and to attend to various political matters. He left Dresden early on the morning of 25 July, accompanied only by Berthier, Rustan, a master of horse, two ADCs, and some orderly officers and pages, and returned via Bamberg and Plauen on 2 August. During his absence Caulaincourt represented his interests at the Congress of Prague, and the Emperor's staff enjoyed a welcome rest.

The end of the armistice

When the Armistice of Poischwitz was terminated on 17 August, Napoleon had 420,000 men concentrated on the Elbe, 380,000 of whom were available for field operations. His lines of communication from Leipzig back to France ran through Naumburg, Erfurt, Kassel, and Mainz, while those in North Germany ran eastwards from Wesel fortress on the lower Rhine, through Hanover, to Hamburg and Magdeburg. The Allies had 750,000 men in the field, 520,000 of them – later rising to 580,000 – in Germany. Of these, 90,000 were assembled around the fortresses still held by the French, 30,000 were held ready against Bavaria, and 50,000 were in Italy. On the line of the Elbe, the French-held towns of Dresden, Königstein, Lilienstein, Meissen, Pirna, and Sonnstein were fortified, in addition to Magdeburg and Torgau. A new road was built from Lilienstein to Stolpen, twenty kilometres to the north, to ease any French advance in the direction of Bautzen.

Still convinced that the Allied coalition might fall apart if he could seize the Prussian capital, on 15 August Napoleon appointed Marshal Ney commander of the 'Army of the Bober' with the aim of thrusting towards Berlin. Ney's army consisted of his own III Corps and those of Macdonald (XI), Lauriston (V), Marmont (VI), and Sebastiani (II Cavalry Corps). The capture of Berlin at this juncture would have had much less impact on affairs than in the past, however, as all government functions had been moved east into Silesia, as had such national treasures as were left after the French visitations of 1806–12. The protection of Berlin was the responsibility of Bernadotte's Army of the North, but Napoleon did not expect any serious threat from his ex-comrade. When asked what Bernadotte would do, he said: 'He will mark time.'

The Emperor's usual confidence and decisiveness was strangely lacking at this point. Having expounded his plan to his marshals, he took the amazing step of asking their opinions of it. Marshal Marmont commented that splitting the *Grande Armée* into two separate entities was risky and that 'I greatly fear lest on the day which Your Majesty gains a great victory, and believes you have won a decisive battle, you may learn that you have lost two.'

On 17 August Napoleon left Dresden with VIII Corps and the Guard (60,000 men) and advanced eastwards to Reichenbach to join up with Ney's 120,000 men. Left behind in the Dresden area was Saint-Cyr, with 25,000 men. Next day, Napoleon continued on to Görlitz. Here he heard that Wittgenstein, with 40,000 men, had moved south to enter Bohemia, and that the Austrians had crossed to the left bank of the Elbe for an unknown destination. Still hoping for a quick and decisive victory, Napoleon turned south to catch Wittgenstein if he could. On the 19th he passed through Zittau and pushed on as far as Gabel (now Jablonne, in the Czech Republic) with the intention of clarifying what enemy forces were to his front. Here he learned that the Army of Bohemia had moved to the west though Prague and that it had been joined by 40,000 Russians and Prussians. (In fact this information was wrong, the true figure being 120,000.) From this intelligence, Napoleon wrongly deduced that the Army of Silesia (now 100,000-strong) had about 200,000 men and that this must be his primary target before he turned on Schwarzenberg. This was his first serious miscalculation of the Leipzig campaign, and vividly illustrates the problems caused to commanders in the field by the 'fog of war'.

Despite the advice of his staff, Blücher, hearing in mid-August that the French had entered neutral territory, crossed the demarcation line from Silesia on the 14th in violation of the terms of the armistice and advanced slowly westwards, reaching the Bunzlau area on the 20th, having covered seventy kilometres in seven days. Due to the terrible weather, and a failure in his food supplies, the morale of the Army of Silesia had plummeted; much of the *Landwehr* just went off home to dry out and get something to eat. Yorck had a flaming row with Blücher on the operation and handed in his resignation; it was rejected.

The French and Prussian armies groped their way towards one another in the area of Bunzlau (now Boleslawiec, on Route E 40 in Poland, where it crosses the River Bober – now the Bobr). The clash at Löwenberg (Lwowek Slaski) on the Bober on 21 August was broken off by Blücher very quickly, as soon as he learned that Napoleon was present. He withdrew rapidly to Goldberg (Zlotoryja), twenty kilometres east of the Bober, and on the 24th was at Jaür (Jawor) on the Wütende Neisse River – now the Wysa Szalona – south of Liegnitz (Legnica).

The Prussian *Landwehr* received their baptism of fire at Löwenberg. The Schweidnitz battalion braved canister fire and threw the enemy back at the point of the bayonet. They were only taken out of the line when they ran out of ammunition, and when they marched past Yorck he had his line regiments present arms to them. Blücher wrote: 'At first it was only so-so with the

Landwehr battalions, but now that they've had a good taste of powder, they're as good as the line battalions.' Napoleon, however, had a very different opinion of them. When he saw some captured *Landwehr*, he wrote: 'The enemy infantry is absolutely wretched; this encourages me.'

Blücher had planned a grand strategic coup at Löwenberg, but the Russian Generals Langeron and Sacken failed him. Blücher wrote to Hardenberg: 'I intend to clear Silesia very soon. The enemy has lost a lot of people; I cannot give you our exact losses yet, but in view of our advantages, they are not large. The Russians have lost over 2,000 dead and wounded in Langeron's corps; I don't know what Sacken has lost. I am tired and can write no more.' Blücher resolved to spend as much time as possible with Langeron in future in order to improve their co-operation.

The next actions of the campaign centred on Dresden, the Saxon capital. Napoleon's entire campaign suffered from his fixation that this city must be held at all costs – a radical change in his strategy, which usually centred on the enemy's army rather than on static defences. Towards the end of the armistice he said: 'What is important to me is to avoid being cut off from Dresden and the Elbe, I will care little if I am cut off from France.'

On 22 August the Allies achieved a minor victory at Pirna (Goldberg), as the Army of Bohemia emerged from the Erzgebirge mountains and moved up on Dresden. The weather had been dreadfully wet for days, and their progress through the hills was very slow. On the 22nd, however, Napoleon had received news from Dresden that the city was being threatened by the Allied advance. He left the chase of Blücher to Macdonald with the 90,000 men of III, V, and XI Corps and II Cavalry Corps; removed Ney and his corps from the Army of the Bober (which he placed under Oudinot's command), and marched to the rescue of Dresden. The Trachenberg plan was beginning to work.

When Ney left the Army of the Bober he took his III Corps with him, but this was a misunderstanding of Napoleon's order: the corps should have been sent to reinforce Macdonald. It therefore had to be redirected, and did not reach Bunzlau until the evening of the 25th.

On the 23rd, Oudinot clashed with von Bülow's and Tauentzien's Prussian corps of the Army of the North at Gross-Beeren, only seventeen kilometres south of Berlin. Bernadotte, true to his credo of keeping out of harm's way, was some considerable distance away from this location with the Russian and Swedish corps of his army. Thanks to the firm fighting spirit of von Bülow and his men Oudinot was nevertheless defeated, losing over 5,300 men, fourteen guns, and fifty-eight ammunition waggons; von Bülow lost 1,700 men. Oudinot fell back south-west to Wittenberg on the Elbe, which he reached at the end of August. Berlin was saved, no thanks to the Crown Prince of Sweden.

Saint-Cyr's patrols had detected the advance north through the Erzgebirge of the forward elements of the Army of Bohemia and it soon became clear that the Allies would swamp the garrison of Dresden by sheer weight of numbers. Accordingly, he had sent the urgent call for aid to Napoleon which the latter had received on 22 August. The Russian vanguard of the Army of Bohemia closed up to the south of Dresden on the 23rd and drove in the French outposts, but did nothing else. Next day saw only occasional skirmishing as the Prussian and Russian contingents continued to trudge in through the rain. At ten o'clock in the morning on the 25th the Allied monarchs and their staffs assembled on the heights of Räcknitz (now swallowed up in the suburb of Mockritz), from where the weakness of the Dresden garrison was evident. The Czar and General Moreau wanted to assault at once to exploit their advantage, but Schwarzenberg insisted that they wait until the next day, by when the Austrian army would have come in from the Erzgebirge. The Allies were to pay a very high price for this delay.

Between 23 and 26 August, Napoleon, the Guard, and Marmont's VI Corps marched over 140 kilometres in very bad conditions to come to Dresden's aid. Napoleon's arrival in the threatened city had an electrifying effect on the morale of the garrison. As Yorck von Wartenburg later wrote: 'I know of no example in war which furnishes clearer evidence of how the numbers and morale of troops, important features as they are, may be so overmatched by the weight of one person of genius.'

At Dresden, the pendulum of the fortunes of war swung hard in favour of the Emperor, who made fullest use of the twenty-four hours that Schwarzenberg had given him and very convincingly won a two-day battle fought on 26–7 August, pushing the shaken Army of Bohemia back south, into the mountains and away from its allies. The Austro-Russians lost 23,000 men, forty guns, and fifteen colours, the last being from Metzko's division, which was surrounded and captured by Murat's cavalry on the west wing of the field. Napoleon's losses were estimated at 10,000.

***

Despite this early setback in the campaign, the Allied leaders kept their heads and stuck to the Trachenberg plan. Meanwhile, Blücher persisted in his offensive strategy in Silesia. Hearing that Macdonald had halted at the Katzbach river, he saw a chance to strike at the Army of the Bober when it over-extended itself on 26 August, and inflicted a stinging defeat on the French in the battle of the Katzbach. The rain was so heavy here that muskets would not fire and all melees were fought with butt and bayonet. As the French advanced over the swollen Katzbach, Blücher sent an ADC to Yorck telling him to count the enemy as they crossed the river and to let across only as many men as he could beat. Yorck retorted: 'Oh yes? Well you ride over and count them yourself! In this rain I can't even count my own fingers!' Macdonald lost 30,000 men, 105 guns (thirty-six in the battle, the rest in the mud of the retreat), 300 ammunition waggons, and two eagles. Ney's III Corps took no part in the battle. Sacken had excelled himself in the action; Langeron had not.

Next day, the 27th, there followed the clash at Hagelberg (Lübnitz), where General Baron Girard's 10th Division, III Corps, was very badly mauled by a Russo-Prussian corps from the Army of the North. Also on the 27th, and the

28th, the French I Corps under Vandamme bested the Russian II Corps under Duke Eugen von Württemberg at Pirna, near Dresden, but casualties were light on both sides.

The clash at Plagwitz (known to the French as the River Bober), which took place on the 29th on the river of that name, was a more serious affair in which Puthod's isolated 17th Division of V Corps was trapped against the flooded river and effectively destroyed by *Generalmajor* Prince Scherbatoff's VI Corps and Baron Korff's I Cavalry Corps. Puthod and over 3,000 of his men were captured, as were all sixteen guns and three eagles, before the French finally capitulated. Russian losses were light.

On the 28th the Emperor had left Dresden with the Guard and advanced south towards the Bohemian mountains to join the other French corps chasing the battered Army of Bohemia. He marched via Freiberg and Frauenstein but then, having received reports from his corps commanders, convinced himself that all adequate measures were well in hand to ensure the destruction of the enemy and that he could devote himself to other matters. Accordingly, he said to Count Lobau: '*Eh bien – je ne vois plus rien – faites retourner la vielle garde a Dresde! La jeune garde restera ici au bivouac!*' ('Well, I see nothing – have the Old Guard return to Dresden! The Young Guard will bivouac here!') And he climbed into his coach and returned to the Saxon capital. This failure to press the pursuit of the defeated Allies was to have catastrophic consequences for his fortunes two days later.

When, on 29 August, Napoleon received news of Girard's defeat at Hagelsberg, of Bernadotte's advance on Wittenberg, and of Macdonald's withdrawal to Görlitz, he decided to interpose himself between Bernadotte and Blücher and marched off from Dresden to Hoyerswerda, sixty kilometres to the north-east. However, on hearing that Macdonald would have to withdraw from Görlitz the Emperor turned south and marched to Bautzen to engage Blücher, who arrived at Bautzen, fifty kilometres east of Dresden, on 1 September, but retreated as soon as the French main body came up.

Meanwhile, in the wet hills and valleys of the Bohemian mountains, a further blow to Napoleon's fortunes was unfolding. This was the battle fought on 29–30 August at Kulm in the hills of the Erzgebirge, where Vandamme's isolated I Corps, pursuing the defeated Allies south from the field of Dresden and far ahead of any other French formation, was almost destroyed. Vandamme himself was captured, as were three of his generals. Of his 37,000 men, 5,000 were killed and wounded and a further 10,000 captured. Twenty-one guns, 200 ammunition waggons, all the baggage, two eagles, and three colours were also taken. Allied losses were 12,000. It was here that General Kleist won his title 'von Nollendorf' (a village in the area) when he burst into Vandamme's rear in a surprise thrust from the north. Had Napoleon and the Guard pushed on on the 28th as he originally intended, or had Saint-Cyr pushed on at a faster pace, it would have been Kleist and not Vandamme who would have been defeated.

Baron von Odeleben, a Saxon colonel attached to Napoleon's headquarters, described the depressed silence which pervaded there when news of this latest catastrophe arrived in Dresden. 'From Napoleon's cabinet we heard that Vandamme himself was to blame for this disaster. He was too greedy for fame and had advanced too far and without taking adequate care. He was only intended to have secured the passes out of the mountains to protect Dresden from another raid and to allow Napoleon to march against Berlin.'

Napoleon was indeed keen to make yet another thrust at Berlin, but a further cry for help from Saint-Cyr in Dresden caused him to abandon this plan and to turn back south on 6 September, the same day which witnessed the next event in his ongoing tale of woe: the defeat at Dennewitz – known to the French as Jüterbog – of Marshal Ney's intended thrust at Berlin. Here, just sixty kilometres south-west of the Prussian capital, General von Bülow's III Prussian Corps of the Army of the North almost single-handedly defeated Ney's 45,000 men, killing and wounding 6,500, capturing 13,500, and taking fifty-four guns, 300 ammunition waggons, and four colours, for a loss of just over 6,000 killed and wounded. Ney himself wrote that he had been 'utterly defeated'. His beaten army fled forty kilometres in two days, back to Torgau on the Elbe.

There followed minor French victories at Dohna and Pirna on the Elbe about eight kilometres south-east of Dresden on 8 September, following which, on the 10th, Schwarzenberg took post in an extremely strong position on the heights of Aussig (now Usti on Route 30 in the Czech Republic, just north of the River Elbe/Labe), in the Bohemian Erzgebirge. In view of his generals' recent defeats Napoleon did not feel strong enough to assault this, and after vainly waiting three days in the inhospitable hills for the Allies to make a mistake he withdrew to make another lunge at Blücher in the Bautzen area. Once again the Prussian commander evaded his blow and the Emperor returned to Dresden.

Strangely enough, during the armistice Napoleon had shown none of his characteristic, professional interest in the Erzgebirge mountains and their limited passes between Saxony and Bohemia, and it was not until 9 September that he left Dresden to investigate this barrier. Initially he refused to accept that the mountains formed a major obstacle, but after spending five days fruitlessly probing in the directions of Teplitz and Nollendorf he returned to Peterswalde on the 15th, making only two further attempts – on the 16th and 18th – before finally abandoning the area and returning to Dresden on the 18th.

On 17 September there had been another minor Allied victory in the clash at Teplitz in the Erzgebirge, about fifty-five kilometres south of Dresden, as Napoleon tried a southern dash to catch the isolated Army of Bohemia and to destroy it before Blücher or Bernadotte could come to the rescue and snap at his heels.

Blücher, meanwhile, had been ordered to close up to, and operate with, the Army of the North against the enemy's lines of communication towards Erfurt. The army of Bohemia would advance north to tackle the rear of Napoleon's force about Dresden from the south. To counter these moves,

Napoleon left Macdonald's XI Corps on the right bank of the Elbe at Dresden, and sent III Corps to Meissen (about twenty-six kilometres downstream from Dresden) to cover his left flank, and XI Corps to Wurzen on the Mulde, twenty-six kilometres east of Leipzig. Ney, with IV and VII Corps and Arrighi's cavalry corps, was forward and to the left of Wurzen, while Murat, with II, V, and VIII Corps, covered the right flank towards the Erzgebirge. Mortier's Guard, the new I Corps, and XIV Corps were around Dippoldiswalde and Pirna, covering the road from Teplitz and Nollendorf. Napoleon and the rest of the Guard were in Dresden.

On 26 September, with the three Allied armies closing in around him, his men reduced to 300,000 and exhausted by the continual marching and counter-marching with nothing to show for it, Napoleon took the unpalatable decision to abandon the right bank of the Elbe. Radetzky's plan was working perfectly. Murat crossed the river at Meissen, having made his demonstration at Bischoffswerda. The Emperor ordered a scorched earth policy to be applied to the already-ruined eastern bank. All cattle were to be driven off, the woods burned, fruit trees cut down, and any sources of food, shelter, and fodder destroyed. The area was to be transformed into a wasteland. Luckily, however, his corps commanders mostly ignored these draconian instructions.

From 26 September to 6 October, Napoleon stayed in Dresden.

On 28 September an Allied pinprick was successfully delivered by the *Streifkorps* of Thielmann, Platoff, and Mensdorff, at Altenburg, forty kilometres south of Leipzig, where Lefebvre-Desnouëttes, with 6,500 men and twelve guns, was ambushed and lost 2,100 men, five guns, and three standards. The Allied *Streifkorps* lost just 200 killed and wounded.

On the same day, Blücher and Schwarzenberg began their agreed advances that were to culminate in the Battle of the Nations. Bernadotte was dragged unwillingly along behind Blücher. This was also the day on which Baron von Odeleben observed in Dresden that it became evident that Napoleon was no longer dictating events on the battlefield; he had clearly lost the initiative and was merely reacting to Allied moves. He remained in the city, bored and restless, inspecting the defences, or alone in his cabinet, waiting for the Allies to commit the inevitable slip which he believed would deliver them into his hands.

On 3 October Blücher forced the crossing of the Elbe at Wartenburg, about 100 kilometres downstream from Dresden. Here, General Yorck's I Prussian Corps defeated Bertrand's IV Corps to force its way south over the river. This was the Trachenberg plan in action. Yorck's I Corps lost sixty-seven officers and 1,548 men killed, wounded, and missing; the French lost 900 killed and wounded, and 1,000 captured, along with thirteen guns and eighty ammunition waggons. Bertrand withdrew southwards on Leipzig.

Whilst Bernadotte and his Army of the North dithered indecisively around Dessau (on the Mulde and Elbe between Magdeburg and Wartenburg), Blücher crossed the Elbe to drive south on Leipzig, join up with the Army of Bohemia, and offer battle to Napoleon.

On 8 October, Bavaria joined the Allies by the Treaty of Ried and an Austro-Bavarian corps was formed in Bavaria to operate against Napoleon's lines of communication back through Mainz.

Meanwhile, Napoleon had learned of Blücher's Elbe crossing on the 5th, and also of the Prussian commander's successful union with the Army of the North, which had at last begun to move south up the Mulde towards Leipzig. He also heard that Ney had retreated and that the Army of Bohemia was at Chemnitz, only sixty kilometres west of Dresden and 100 kilometres south-east of Leipzig.

***

On the afternoon of the 6th, Saint-Cyr had a long conversation with Napoleon in Dresden, during which the Emperor expounded various strategic possibilities, but stressed the vital importance of holding the city. It was to be the pivot of his future operations. Saint-Cyr was not convinced of its value, but Napoleon was so adamant about holding it that he did not dare to contradict him.

At midnight the same day, Napoleon sent for Saint-Cyr again. He had received news of Ney and had altered his plans. He now aimed to abandon Dresden, to take the entire garrison with him into the field and to crush Bernadotte and Blücher. Saint-Cyr recorded the Emperor's reasoning behind this sudden and radical change of strategic policy as follows:

> I shall certainly fight a battle. If I win, I shall surely regret not having all my troops under my hand. If, on the contrary, I suffer a reverse, in leaving you here you will be of no service to me in the battle and you will be hopelessly lost.
>
> Moreover, what is Dresden worth today? It can no longer be the pivot of the operations of the army, which, owing to the exhaustion of the surrounding country, cannot subsist here.
>
> This city cannot even be considered as a great depot, for you would find in it subsistence for a few days only.
>
> There are in Dresden 12,000 sick who will die since they are the residue of the 60,000 who have entered the hospitals since the commencement of the campaign.
>
> Add to this that the season is advancing, and that the Elbe, once frozen over, no longer offers a position.
>
> I wish to take up another position for the winter, refusing my right on Erfurt, and extending my centre along the Saale, which is a good position in all seasons, because the heights of my left bank are always excellent for defence.
>
> I shall rest my left on Magdeburg, and that city will become for me of greater importance than Dresden.

After elaborating on the strengths of the defences of Magdeburg, Napoleon continued:

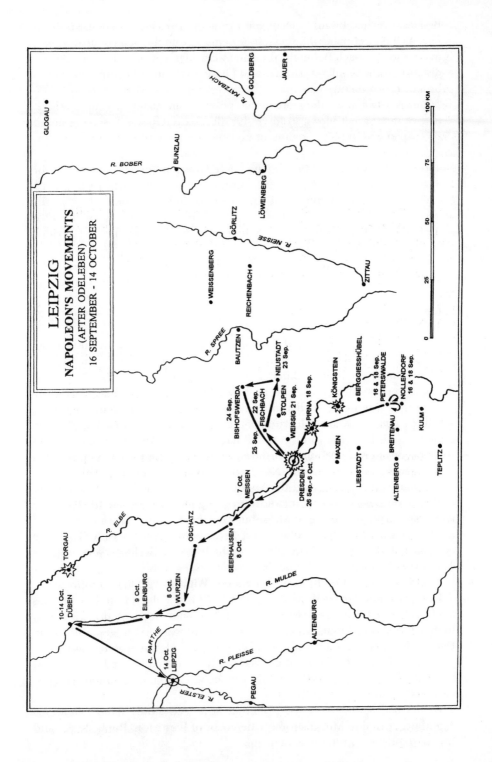

LEIPZIG
NAPOLEON'S MOVEMENTS
(AFTER ODELEBEN)
16 SEPTEMBER - 14 OCTOBER

Besides, I repeat, I want to change my position; Dresden is too near Bohemia. As soon as I make the smallest movement from the neighbourhood of
the city to approach Bohemia, the enemy's armies, having only a very short
distance to cover, will return to it, and I have no chance of cutting them off
by moving on their rear.

Finally, by adopting the more distant position I am going to occupy, I wish
to give them great blows; to force the Allied sovereigns to a solid peace,
putting an end to the calamities of Europe.

But twelve hours later, after he had left Dresden for the last time, the
Emperor's strategic thinking made another 180-degree turn, tossing over-
board all the valid arguments of the previous night. At one o'clock in the
afternoon of 7 October, in Meissen, twenty-six kilometres down the Elbe
from Dresden, Napoleon wrote to Saint-Cyr telling him that he had decided
to hold on to Dresden after all. Convoys of supplies were to be sent there, the
defences were to be strengthened, the wounded and sick evacuated. The
Emperor hoped for an early battle and was advancing to the north-west.
Napoleon thus robbed himself of two corps (I and XIV) for the forthcoming
battle of Leipzig, and these two corps were subsequently 'hopelessly lost', just
as he had so accurately predicted.

This very uncharacteristic dithering of the Emperor is some indication,
perhaps, of his increasingly confused state of mind during this campaign.

In the hope of finding Blücher at Wittenberg on the Elbe, Napoleon
advanced northwards. With him he had III, IV, VI, VII, and IX Corps, the
Guard, and Dombrowski's division. I Cavalry Corps was covering his left wing
south of Delitzsch. Blücher learned of the peril that was approaching the very
same day. His first reaction was to fall back north to Wartenburg, where his
supply trains were, but then he resolved to adhere to his instructions to act in
concert with the Army of the North, and on 9 October made his famous
'flank march' westwards, over the Mulde, to Halle on the Saale. Next day, he
took post on Bernadotte's left (southern) wing near Zörbig, the troops of the
two Allied armies meeting at Merseburg on the 11th. Bernadotte remained
in the area of Köthen, Alsleben, and Petersberg until the 16th. The Elbe
crossings at Dessau and Wittenberg – which led to Berlin – were held by
Tauentzien's corps and Thümen's division respectively.

Napoleon's intended blow on Blücher at Wittenberg fell on empty air.

Dombrowski relieved Wittenberg on the 12th, by which time Blücher was
at Halle, with Bernadotte to his north, and Napoleon had reshuffled his army
to face the major threats which he now thought were to his west and south.
But he had lost contact with Blücher's army and this worried him considerably. He was also under the misapprehension that Bernadotte was now
north of the Elbe, towards Berlin, whereas he was actually at Rothenburg, just
east of the Saale.

In the south, the Army of Bohemia advanced slowly from Chemnitz-
Altenburg, pushing Murat's force (the corps of Lauriston, Poniatowski, and
Victor) before them towards Leipzig.

At this point in the campaign, Schwarzenberg, with 220,000 men, stood against the 80–90,000 of Murat and Saint-Cyr, while the 160,000 of the Armies of the North and of Silesia opposed the 70,000 of Ney and Marmont. Napoleon, in the centre, had 90–100,000 men.

***

On 10 October there occurred the actions at Naumburg and Stössen; minor French victories over the Austrians as Augereau's IX Corps, advancing from Spain through Bayreuth up to Leipzig, brushed aside a weak Allied blocking force. On the 14th came the more substantial clash at Liebertwolkwitz, which was a drawn match between Murat's cavalry and that of the Allies.

From 10–14 October Napoleon stayed in the moated castle of Düben on the River Mulde, about thirty-four kilometres north of Leipzig. Baron von Odeleben recounts that they must have been the most irksome days that the Emperor had passed in many years.

> I saw the Emperor there, anxiously awaiting news from the Elbe, sitting idly on a sofa in his cabinet before a great table, on which lay a piece of white paper on which he doodled large, Gothic letters. His geographer, D'Albe, and another official – also idle – were with him in a corner of the room. Such rare moments of his career deserve to be recorded.

At last, on the 14th, news of Schwarzenberg's advance on Leipzig from Bohemia interrupted his torpor. At three o'clock in the morning Berthier received the Emperor's instructions to order the corps of the *Grande Armée* to concentrate on Leipzig. Napoleon raced south to reinforce Murat, and the stage was set for the great battle.

Significantly enough, although Napoleon now knew where the Army of Bohemia was, his lack of cavalry meant that he had lost sight of the Armies of Silesia and of the North. Blücher's eruption in his rear at Möckern on the 16th was to be a great, and unpleasant, surprise. As he himself said: 'A good general may be beaten, but he should never be surprised.'

Chapter 2

The Protagonists

The French Army

The catastrophic losses of his Russian adventure had meant that Napoleon required, in effect, a new army. True, the top echelon of officers was virtually intact and remained much as it had been in 1811, but only a small percentage of men below the rank of colonel had survived. All the artillery, baggage vehicles and draught horses, all the ammunition, engineering and bridging equipment, muskets, sabres, lances, pistols, ammunition pouches, uniforms, packs, boots, hats and helmets, saddlery and horse furniture – literally everything – had been lost, and needed to be replaced quickly. The same was true of such of his allies' contingents as had been in the central body of the *Grande Armée* at Moscow and on the northern flank at Polotsk – II and VI Corps. The Prussian corps which had fought in Latvia had managed to survive pretty much intact, but these assets were no longer at Napoleon's disposal; they had changed sides. Of the corps on the southern flank, the Austrians were also intact, but on the sidelines (and in July 1813 would likewise desert to the Allied cause), while the Saxons of VII Corps had suffered heavily in the later stages of the retreat. Thus most of the contingents of the Confederation of the Rhine were in the same state as the French army.

In September 1812 the Emperor had conscripted all the men liable for military service that year. However, being aware already that his needs in 1813 were likely to be just as immense as those in hand for the Russian campaign, he persuaded the French Senate to agree to bring forward the enlistment of 120,000 men from the classes of 1813, a number which was subsequently increased to 137,000. Consequently when he returned to Paris in December 1812 following the Russian debacle, these men were already in the depots, though they were still far from being trained, equipped, or ready for field service.

Much earlier, on 13 March 1812, Napoleon had organised the National Guard for the defence of France during his absence in Russia. This was not liable for service beyond the frontier and was organised departmentally into military divisions. National Guardsmen were divided into three *bans* or classes: the 1*er ban* comprised those men aged twenty to twenty-six of the conscription classes of 1807–12 who had not already been called up for military service; the 2*e ban*, physically fit men aged twenty-six to forty; and the 3*e ban*, physically fit men aged forty to sixty.

The decree ordering the establishment of the National Guard called for eighty-four (originally 100) cohorts to be raised at once from the 1*er ban*, a total later increased to eighty-eight cohorts. Each cohort consisted of six companies of 140 men, a depot company, and a company of 100 men.

Officers were provided by retired army officers and National Guardsmen who had served with the active army. Each cohort had a paper strength of 1,080 all ranks, which gave a theoretical strength of 91,000 for the first eighty-four cohorts; in actual fact, they reached only about 78,000.

On 11 January 1813 the Senate agreed that the National Guard cohorts should be transferred into the regular army. They were grouped into twenty-two new regiments (the 135e–156e *Ligne*), each of four field battalions of six companies and a depot battalion of four companies. The artillery units were likewise reorganised into three artillery *régiments à la suite*, which do not seem to have seen action, while one artillery company was retained with each of the new infantry regiments.

Also on 11 January, the Senate authorised the 'levy of the four classes' of 100,000 men of the conscription years of 1809–12, and directed that 150,000 men of the conscription class of 1814 should be earmarked for future military service. They were not called up immediately, as the training, feeding, housing, equipping, and clothing of so many men at the same time would have brought about the collapse of the depot organisation.

At the same time, Napoleon persuaded the departments and major cities to raise, clothe, arm, mount, and equip some 15–20,000 cavalry, while the 134e *Ligne* (two battalions) and the 37e *Légère* (four battalions) infantry regiments were raised from the Municipal Guards of Paris and of the Departmental Capitals respectively. The navy, blockaded in its harbours by Britain's Royal Navy, provided 8,000 men, who formed four regiments of *Artillerie de la Marine* or 'Naval Artillery' (which were, in fact, infantry). To these regiments were added 4,000 conscripts of the year 1813. Many units and cadres were also recalled from Spain, which made the Allies' task of liberating that unhappy country much easier.

On 3 April the Senate provided yet more men: 80,000 from the 1er ban of the National Guard; 90,000 from the conscription class of 1814; and 10,000 mounted men of the *Gardes d'Honneur* – sons of the better-off, who provided their own horses, uniforms and equipment and served with the Imperial Guard.

By means of this frantic and creative innovation some 656,000 new recruits were raised, of whom only the Municipal Guard and the naval contingent – some 13,000 men in all – had prior military experience. A further 30,000 men were called up in August 1813 and 240,000 more in October, but these took no part in the year's fighting.

The strength and physical stamina of the young conscripts, and consequently the quality of their regiments, left much to be desired; they could not march like the veterans, fell easy prey to sickness, and the standard of their training when they left the depots in the spring of 1813 was frighteningly low. The ability of battalions to manoeuvre was poor, and many recruits could not even load their muskets. When the reinforcement drafts marched to the front, carts had to follow them to pick up the footsore and the exhausted. The 'Naval Artillery', however, made excellent infantry.

The availability of sufficient good quality officers had proved another great difficulty. Veteran NCOs were therefore commissioned and young officer cadets were rushed into service, while others were transferred from units which had wasted away to skeleton strength in Spain.

The thirty-six French infantry regiments which had served in I–IV Corps in Russia were brought up to a strength of four battalions each, and the three veteran line regiments which were in Italy – the 13*e* (five battalions), the 23*e* (four battalions), and the 101*e* (three battalions) – were brought up into Germany.

Apart from the various depot battalions, there were also in France 100 cadre battalions of regiments serving in Spain and Illyria. These were pumped up to strength with new recruits and grouped together in twos and threes to form *Régiments de Ligne* if they all came from the same regiment, or *Régiments Provisoires* if the battalions were grouped together from different parent regiments.

From these polyglot units the following 'Corps of Observation' were formed:

– *The Imperial Guard.* The survivors from Russia were to form one division, to be reinforced with 3,000 veterans drawn from Spain. To these were to be added three divisions of the Young Guard, to be concentrated at Mainz. These soldiers were all conscripts.

– *I Corps* under Vandamme. Sixty-four battalions.

– *II Corps* under Victor. Forty-eight battalions.

– *The Elbe* (later V Corps) under Lauriston. To assemble at Magdeburg by 15 March. These forty-eight battalions were all drawn from National Guard cohorts.

– *1st of the Rhine* (later III Corps) under Ney. Sixty battalions, to assemble around Mainz during March.

– *Italy* (later IV and XII Corps) under Bertrand. Fifty-four battalions.

– *2nd of the Rhine* (later VI Corps) under Marmont. Fifty battalions, to assemble around Mainz during March and April. In fact, the fourth division was not ready until late May.

– *VII Corps.* Durutte's division, with two Saxon divisions to be added later.

– Two further corps to be formed around Mainz. These would not be ready until late August.

As regards cavalry, about 9–10,000 cavalrymen had trekked out of Russia, but the vast majority of these were without horses. It was decided to reconstitute the Guard cavalry completely and to reorganise the cavalry of the line (fifty-two regiments) into two corps under Latour-Maubourg and Sebastiani, while a third corps under Arrighi was to be built up around one squadron drawn from each of the regiments in Spain. A fourth was later also formed, and the Poles provided a fifth. Eventually, by the battle of Lützen, 11,000 French and 4,000 allied cavalry were put into the field, but they were outnumbered by about two or three to one. This total of 15,000 later rose to 25,000.

The difficulties of supplying cavalry remounts were immense, and the horsemanship and animal care were of such a low standard that many German regiments reported that it was possible to smell French cavalry from some way off if you were downwind of it, from the stench of the suppurating sores on their horses' backs where they had been rubbed by ill-fitting saddles. The lack of sufficient high-quality cavalry was to be Napoleon's major disadvantage in this campaign. Apart from the poor quality and limited numbers of its own horses, the standard of the artillery was, by contrast, very good.

In addition to the French army and those of the allied states of the Confederation of the Rhine, there was also the army of the Grand Duchy of Warsaw, consisting of V Corps (fourteen battalions), which did not join the *Grande Armée* until the armistice; Dombrowski's division; and IV (Polish) Cavalry Corps (twenty-four squadrons). Italian and Neapolitan contingents also served in Saxony.

***

So much for the materiel. But whereas the physical side of the army improved somewhat as the campaign commenced, its psychological well-being did not seem to follow this trend. Morale was initially very good among the new, mainly young, recruits, but later in the campaign it all too often proved to be of a very fragile nature. It would be true to say, in fact, that Napoleon had forged a serviceable but somewhat brittle weapon with which to fight this critically important campaign.

Captain Coignet recalls in his *Notebooks* that French morale was low even just after the victory at Dresden on 27 August. He heard many officers – on Napoleon's staff – blaspheming against the Emperor ('He's a ******* who will bring us all to ruin'): 'I was petrified to hear such remarks, and said to myself, "We are done for!" The next day I ventured to say to General Monthion "I believe our place is not here any longer. We should head for the Rhine by forced marches" '; to which Monthion replied: 'I approve of your idea, but the Emperor is obstinate and nobody can make him listen to reason.'

Another indicator of how brittle French morale had become may be found in the remark of a sergeant of dragoons on 12 October: 'I tell you one thing: in a month we will be back on the banks of the Rhine. The vengeance of the nations we have conquered, trampled upon and plundered will invade France in order to make a wilderness of the country. To prevent this happening is the only reason a right-minded Frenchman can have for bearing arms.'

Marmont (whose memoirs have been characterised by some as being unreliable) recalled that he met with Napoleon in Düben before the battle:

> One no longer recognised Napoleon during this campaign. I had a long talk with him in Düben, and I have never forgotten this conversation. . . . On my return from a reconnaissance to Bitterfeld and having made my report to the Emperor, I had just gone to bed when he sent for me. He spoke of his position and the different courses open to him. I insisted for all I was worth on the course of action which alone could save him. In my view his only

means of safety at the moment was to leave the battlefields of Bohemia, since earlier on he had been unwilling to conquer it, and quit the defiles which had been so fatal for him. He could not bring himself voluntarily to abandon Leipzig. He did not foresee that, a week later, he would be forced to do so, under very different auspices, amid disasters and confusion which accomplished his ruin. On the contrary, he was making preparations to go and do battle under the walls of this town. I discussed with him in detail the disadvantages of choosing such a battle at the far end of a funnel, with horrible defiles which were long and easy to block. But he replied with these memorable words which indicate the illusions he was still harbouring: 'I shall fight only as and when I feel inclined. They will never venture to attack me.'

On 10 January 1814 Wellington wrote to Lord Bathurst on this topic: 'It has always occurred to me that if Bonaparte had not placed himself in a position that every other officer would have avoided, and had not remained in it longer than was consistent with any notions of prudence, he would have retired in such a state, that the Allies could not have ventured to approach the Rhine.'

The Austrian Army

Sir Charles Stewart was present when the Czar, the Kaiser, and the king of Prussia reviewed an Austrian corps near Prague on 19 August; it included ninety-one battalions and fifty squadrons. This is what he had to say:

> The composition of this army was magnificent, although I perceived a great many recruits: still, the system that reigned throughout, and the military air that marked the soldier, especially the Hungarian, must ever fix it in my recollection as the finest army on the continent. The Russians may possess a more powerful soldiery, of greater physical strength and hardihood, but they cannot equal the Austrians in discipline or military maintien. The general officers of the latter are of a superior class: and the army has a fine ton in all its departments. To see one Austrian and one Hungarian regiment is to see the whole army: for a complete equality and uniformity reign throughout; and they have no constant changes of uniform and equipment: their movement was beautifully correct, and the troops seemed formed in the most perfect order. Twenty-four squadrons of cuirassiers and sixteen of hussars deserved to be particularly noticed. The artillery seemed less well appointed; and the ammunition waggons and horses for their guns and train were of an inferior description to those of the Russians (whose artillery horses are perfect); but the officers and men are scientific and expert and the artillery is not to be judged by its appearance.

By the terms of the Peace of Schönbrunn, which had followed the disastrous 1809 campaign, Austria had lost extremely large areas of its empire and was completely cut off from the sea, and thus from all direct contact with Britain. The treaty also imposed an immediate fine of 30 million

Francs, with a further 55 million to be paid to France in instalments, and Austria's army was limited to 150,000 men under arms. The huge arsenal in Vienna was emptied, its guns, vehicles, and ammunition being taken to France.

The massive fines left Austria close to bankruptcy, and Graf Wallis, its finance minister, hacked mercilessly into the defence budget to save money: one particular request for maintenance funds of 500,000 Gulden to replace worn-out clothing and shoes was reduced to 30,000 Gulden. The country's military storehouses were soon exhausted, and *Feldmarschall-Leutnant* Graf Radetzky remarked in later years that 'Wallis caused as much damage to the Austrian army as did Napoleon!'

By a treaty ratified in Vienna on 25 March 1812, Austria had agreed to provide a corps of 30,000 men under Schwarzenberg to aid the French invasion of Russia. This corps fought on the southern flank of the *Grande Armée* in Wolhynia and the Ukraine and consequently escaped the catastrophe which engulfed Napoleon's main force.

As early as November 1812 Russia began to send out diplomatic feelers to Austria to test its resolve, and suggested a pact against France. Initial reactions to the proposal were very cool, Austria having already paid a very high price for its several attempts to defeat the French during the last twenty years. In addition the pitiful state of its army prevented it from becoming involved in any immediate campaign. However, when Napoleon wrote to the Kaiser on 14 December asking for a new corps of 60,000 men, Franz prevaricated. In January 1813 the Russian state councillor Anstett arrived in Schwarzenberg's headquarters to propose a Russo-Austrian armistice. Schwarzenberg relayed the proposal to Vienna, and Metternich, the Austrian Chancellor, did not hesitate to approve it. It was ratified on 30 January, and preparations were simultaneously put in hand to mobilise 100,000 men. On 3 February the Austrian ambassador to France, Graf Bubna, announced to Napoleon that Austria was now neutral and would act as a negotiator between the warring parties. Napoleon inevitably saw through the ploy at once, but there was little that he could do about it at that moment. Consequently on 30 June the secret Treaty of Reichenbach was signed between France and Austria by which Napoleon accepted Austria's mediation with Russia and Prussia.

***

Since late 1809 each of the German regiments in the Austrian army had been reduced to two battalions, each of six companies of 50 men, and the third or depot battalions had been disbanded. Only the Hungarian battalions retained the older establishment strength of 120 men to a company. Jäger battalions were reduced from six companies to just two.

The situation was equally bleak in the cavalry. Heavy regiments were reduced from six squadrons to four, light regiments from eight squadrons to six, and these were only their theoretical paper establishments: in reality, the situation was much worse, due to lack of funds.

There were shortages of every item of equipment. The depots were empty, and there were no reserves. The military contractors, who had now been awaiting payment from the cash-strapped government for years, were unwilling to undertake new orders until the outstanding debts had been cleared. In 1810 *Feldmarschall-Leutnant* Graf Bellegarde, president of the *Hofkriegsrat* (the Court Council of War), estimated the minimum necessary budget for the army to be 92.16 million Gulden; he was given only 54 million. In an attempt to alleviate this situation the government issued bonds (*Antizipationsscheine*) early in 1813, which raised an additional 45 million Gulden. Difficulties were also encountered when it came to filling the army's ranks. Only in Austria proper was conscription possible. In Hungary the agreement of its parliament had to be obtained, whilst in Sieben-bürgen and the military border area towards Turkey great restraint had to be exercised in order to contain the Turks.

At the beginning of May 1813 the Kaiser authorised the formation of an army of 120,000 men in Bohemia, comprising eighty battalions of infantry, ninety-eight squadrons of cavalry, and thirty-one artillery batteries with 220 guns. It was based on *Feldmarschall* Graf Kollowrat's corps of twenty-two infantry battalions, thirty-four cavalry squadrons and sixty-two guns, already present in the province.

Of course, there were additional threats to Austria from outside Saxony. Prince Eugene de Beauharnais was forming an army in Italy, and the Bavarians were also rearming. It was therefore necessary to raise two further corps to counter these enemies, one against Bavaria under Prince Reuss, consisting of forty-three infantry battalions and forty-four cavalry squadrons, and the other, of thirty-one battalions and forty squadrons under *Feldzeug-meister* Hiller, to counter the threat from Italy.

In June the order went out to mobilise the *Landwehr* – lightly-armed, 'second-class' men, raised for territorial defence in times of emergency; one month later 50,000 were under arms.

At the end of April 1813 the Austrian army (including depots, garrisons, troops in Italy, etc) consisted of 194 battalions of infantry, 264 squadrons of cavalry, and 180 companies of artillery, a total of 199,000 men and 28,618 horses. By the beginning of the autumn campaign these figures had increased slightly, and were deployed as follows:

The Army of Bohemia	127,435 men
Meerveldt's corps in Theresienstadt	11,641 men
Hiller's corps and the garrisons of Prague, Königgrätz, and Josephstadt	27,514 men
Feldzeugmeister Reuss' army between the Enns and the Traun rivers	30,079 men
Total	*233,226 men*

By the end of December 1813 the Austrian Army's strength stood at 398 battalions of infantry, 371 squadrons of cavalry, and 220 artillery companies, a total of 547,994 men and 61,057 horses.

The Prussian Army

Under the terms of the Treaty of Tilsit of 8 September 1808, Prussia's army had been limited to 42,000 men. By dint of much creative thinking, however, Scharnhorst and other members of the Prussian General Staff had invented the Krümper system by which each regiment called up a certain number of recruits, gave them basic military training, and then discharged them again in order to call up and train another batch, so that the 42,000 ceiling imposed by Napoleon was never exceeded. By this means a pool of trained men was formed, and in 1813 these were formed into fifty-two infantry battalions in a very short time.

In 1812 Napoleon had demanded a corps of 20,000 men from Prussia, to operate on his northern flank as part of Macdonald's X Corps during the invasion of Russia. The regiments mobilised for this campaign were all (except the Leib-Regiment) 'composite' units, each consisting of infantry battalions and cavalry squadrons drawn from two parent regiments. In this way the invaluable training experience of service in the field was imparted to twice as many regiments as actually participated in the campaign.

Thanks to the radical social and military reforms carried out in Prussia by Freiherr von Stein on the one hand and by Blücher, Scharnhorst, von Gneisenau, von Boyen and their contemporaries on the other, all traces of the bad habits of the old army of 1806 had been ruthlessly eradicated. A new spirit of fiery patriotism inspired much of the nation and thus the army, and this was fuelled by a deep-seated hatred of the French. Physical punishment in the army was abolished except for the most serious offences, and the social standing of the military was elevated from its earlier lowly position. Almost the entire nation supported the war effort – women even donated their jewellery, and received in return similar items made in wrought and cast iron (surviving museum examples bear witness to the very high standards of artistry reached by the craftsmen). 'I gave my gold for iron' became a proud boast among Prussian women in the period 1813–15.

After Yorck's defection from Macdonald's corps in the Convention of Tauroggen on 30 December 1812, Prussia fielded an army of about 33,000 men. This was rapidly raised to 56,000. A royal decree of 3 February 1813 – and another dated the 9th – called for volunteers (*Freiwillige-Jäger*) from the middle and upper classes. These were to be aged between seventeen and twenty-four. They had to clothe and equip themselves, but were assured of preferential career treatment after the war. Companies of such volunteers were attached to most line infantry and cavalry regiments, and totalled 5,000 infantry, 3,000 cavalry, and 500 artillery and engineers. They could select which regiment they wished to serve in and after having completed basic training they could elect their own officers. This great latitude led to some Jäger detachments being quite weak while popular regiments, like the guards, eventually had five companies. Enthusiasm for military service was not universal, however, and conscription was introduced by the royal decree of 9 February. Remarkably, all this took place despite the fact that, until 4

March 1813, Prince Eugene still occupied Berlin, while much of the west of Prussia was still under French control.

The *Landwehr* was created by a royal decree of 17 March 1813, the same day that King Friedrich Wilhelm issued his call to the nation to rise up in arms against France in his '*An Mein Volk*' declaration. The Prussian *Landwehr* was based on the Austrian model of 1809. Service within it was obligatory for all able-bodied men aged between eighteen and forty-five, although substitutes could be provided on payment of a fee. Theoretically the *Landwehr* were to be used only for home defence purposes within the frontiers of Prussia, but in practice they were used exactly as if they were regulars. Initially only 20,000 were raised, armed with French muskets gathered up by the Russians as they pursued the disintegrating *Grande Armée* out of Russia. Their uniforms had to be provided by the municipalities, which led to many unfortunates marching off to war in terribly poor quality clothing which quickly fell apart. They had only one pair of shoes, which often fit badly and were frequently torn off in deep mud, leaving many soldiers barefoot for much of the campaign.

Landwehr troops consisted of both infantry and cavalry, with officers drawn from various sources. Some were veteran officers unemployed since the collapse of 1806, while others were invalids, *Freiwillige-Jäger* volunteers, or were transferred from line regiments. Although initially organised into their own brigades, during the Armistice of Poischwitz the *Landwehr* were broken up and the battalions were distributed among regular formations. This was partly to combat desertion, which was particularly high (29,000) in the early weeks of the 1813 campaign, when the worst Allied defeats took place. Of course, the *Landwehr* were in no way equal to experienced line regiments, but their quality improved rapidly in the hard school of war.

The quality of the equipment and weapons of the rapidly-expanded Prussian army often left much to be desired – as was true of all the armies which fought in the 1813 campaign. Much support was provided, financially and in kind, by Britain, several Prussian regiments being dressed in British uniforms. Muskets were of assorted origins – two Prussian models, one Austrian, the British Tower pattern (of which 113,000 were eventually supplied) and, later, French items taken on the battlefield. Initially the situation was so chaotic that many regiments had several different weapons of varying calibres, which made ammunition resupply a nightmare. During the armistice the opportunity was taken to exchange weapons between units, in order to achieve uniformity within each regiment. Even basic, simple items such as flints for firearms were in such short supply that the Berlin porcelain factory was ordered to manufacture substitutes.

In December 1812 eight 'Militia' battalions were raised by General von Bülow in East Prussia; on 15 January 1813 Yorck raised four East Prussian Reserve Battalions, three Lithuanian Füsilier Battalions, and eight Pommeranian Reserve Battalions. On 1 February it was decreed that each Grenadier Battalion should form one Reserve Battalion and each line infantry battalion should form two. On 27 March the king decreed the raising of National Cavalry Regiments in East Prussia, Pommerania, and Silesia. During the armistice all of these reserve battalions were taken from their parent regiments. Several were disbanded and the men used to bring the old regiments up to strength, while the Brandenburg Infantry Regiment Nr 12 and twelve Reserve Infantry Regiments were formed from the others. (These twelve Reserve regiments became the 13th–24th Prussian infantry regiments on 25 March 1815.)

The following free corps were also raised:

Lützow's – three infantry battalions, five cavalry squadrons, eight guns; these later became the 25th Prussian Infantry Regiment and the 6th Ulans.

The Elbe Regiment – two infantry battalions; these later became the 26th Prussian Infantry Regiment.

Hellwig's – a company of Jägers and three squadrons of cavalry; these later became part of the 27th Prussian Infantry Regiment and part of the 7th Ulans.

Von Reiche's Ausländer Jäger-Battalion; this later became part of the 27th Prussian Infantry Regiment.

Schill's – two squadrons of cavalry; this later became part of the 7th Ulans.

By 16 March 1813 – the day hostilities were declared – Prussia had raised the following troops:

The field army, infantry and cavalry – 1,776 officers, 66,963 men, 20,105 horses, 213 guns.
Train, technical and medical services – 2,643 men and 3,625 horses.
Second line troops – 615 officers, 32,642 men, 650 horses and 56 guns.
Garrison troops – 398 officers, 22,277 men, 1,743 horses.

By June 1813 Prussia had 113,381 infantry, 19,248 cavalry, 16,187 gunners and 1,305 pioneers in the field. In addition to this, there were 120,504 *Landwehr* organised in 149 infantry battalions and 113 cavalry squadrons. By 10 August these figures had risen to:

Infantry			
	Line	90 battalions	72,130 men
	Reserve and Garrison	39 battalions	31,838 men
	Jägers and *Freikorps*	8 battalions	11,153 men
	Landwehr	151 battalions	109,120 men
	Total	288 battalions	224,241 men
Cavalry	Line and National Cavalry		
	regiments	89 squadrons	13,375 men
	Reserve	22 squadrons	3,389 men
	Jägers and *Freikorps*	23 squadrons	3,064 men
	Landwehr	113 squadrons	10,952 men
	Totals	247 squadrons	30,780 men
Artillery	Field	50 batteries	8,749 men
	Fortress and siege	33 companies	6,566 men
Technical troops		567 field pioneers, 738 fortress pioneers	

At the start of the autumn campaign Prussia fielded the following troops:

With the Army of Bohemia		49,300 men
In the Army of Silesia		37,000 men
With the Army of the North		73,000 men
	Total	*159,300 men*

The Russian Army

Lieutenant-General Sir Charles Stewart had this to say on the Russian army:

> It was impossible not to observe that the state of the Russian army was, at this period, somewhat on the decline, from the incredible fighting and hardships which it had gone through during two campaigns. The battalions were so weak, that three or four scarcely formed a regiment, and seldom exceeded 250-300 men. The cavalry was fine and commanding. The horses, subsisting in a country abounding with forage, were in good condition.
>
> The regular heavy cavalry are undoubtedly very fine; the men gigantic, the horses good, the equipment superior and in perfect condition. The light cavalry are less striking in point of horses and general appearance, but some of the hussars and lancers are good. The artillery seems particularly fine and well appointed. The horses of the brigades belonging to the guards are more round, compact, and perfect than those in any other service.
>
> There is, however, a wide difference between the staple of the Russian army and the Emperor's guards. The latter are very select, both cavalry and infantry; nothing indeed, can be superior. The grenadiers of the guard are generally very tall men. The cuirassiers are equally large and stout. The discipline and well-dressed state of these men are very imposing. The whole appearance of a Russian army denotes hardihood and bravery, inured to any privations. They subsist well on black bread: few cattle are seen following the army. Their commissaries have little to do; and the great burden of managing the commissariat, which is so irksome a task to a British commander on service, seems perfectly light and easy to a Russian chief.
>
> Before I dismiss this hasty sketch of the Russian army, I cannot, as a military man, refrain from offering some remarks upon the enormous, unnecessary attirail [gear] by which it is attended. The numerous baggages, waggons of all descriptions, etc exceed belief; and no general officer has less than eighteen or twenty orderlies, cavalry and infantry, which always follow him. In fact, I am persuaded the men out of the ranks, and the followers and military attendants in a Russian army, amount at least to one-fifth of the total number.

However, Colonel Sir Neil Campbell's view regarding the quality of the Russian officer corps was that:

> The officers who possess education are so few in proportion to the whole number in the army that they are to be found only in the Guards, on the

Staff and in a few of the favourite regiments of cavalry. The staff officers are generally ten times as numerous as those attached to the generals of other nations; and the whole of them, excepting the chief, spend their days for the most part in eating and drinking, gambling and sleeping – all these operations too being performed in the same room, and by parties relieving each other!

Apart from the guard and line troops, there were the numerous Cossack regiments and the Baschkirs from the steppes of Central Asia. The armament and discipline of such light cavalry meant that they could not be used on the battlefield as line cavalry were – the Baschkirs were armed with bows and arrows, for instance. However, they were valuable both as scouts and, especially, as weapons of terror. They were utterly savage in appearance, and such was the reputation attributed to them by French survivors of the 1812 campaign that their mere proximity often caused panic in isolated or unsteady units.

In February 1813 there were not more than 110,000 Russians pursuing the French. These comprised 70,000 infantry, 30,000 cavalry (including Cossacks and Baschkirs) and 10,000 artillery and engineers. An imperial decree of 5 February ordered the raising of a reserve army of 163 infantry battalions, ninety-two cavalry squadrons and thirty-seven artillery batteries in the area around Bialystock. As with all attempts to conjure effective armies out of nothing in no time at all, the building of this force made painfully slow progress but, by August, Bennigsen's Reserve Army of Poland fielded thirty-four battalions of infantry, forty-one squadrons of cavalry, nine Cossack *pulks* (regiments) and twelve artillery batteries, and totalled 34,000 men and 134 guns. The rest of the new troops had meanwhile been integrated into the veteran formations of the other Russian armies.

At the start of the autumn campaign Russia fielded the following troops:

With the Army of Bohemia		77,200 men
In the Army of Silesia		62,200 men
With the Army of the North		30,500 men
	Total	*169,900 men*

The Swedish Army

In July, at the invitation of General Karl Johann Adlercreutz, Sir Charles Stewart reviewed a corps of 10,000 Swedish soldiers and recorded his impressions:

The appearance of the troops, collectively, was good; individually, they had not the air, the gait, or dress of disciplined soldiers: neither the old troops or new levies were steady under arms: their clothes were ill made; and their appearance, after seeing the Russians and the Prussians, was unprepossessing. However, I must do them justice to admit, that their performance in the field exceeded my anticipations. Their guards and artillery were composed of the choice of their men; and throughout, the composition of the Swedish soldiery was respectable.

The regiments exercised and moved on the French system of tactics: they were generally loose in their formations and had not that celerity which counterbalances the other fault. I saw four brigades of artillery – two were mounted, and two were called artillerie assise – carrying the cannoniers: this was formerly the practice in the Austrian service, but was abolished there, and should be everywhere, as it is disadvantageous when guns are to move rapidly on bad ground: these were of iron, and seemed to be particularly inefficient; the carriages, and everything relating to equipment, were very far behind those of the present day, and those in other armies.

I saw four cavalry regiments, two of hussars, one of heavy cavalry and one of chasseurs à cheval. The Swedish horse is not a good animal, having a very short neck, and an immense thick cart hind-quarter: he may endure fatigue, but in point of appearance and movement he is a sorry exhibition. There were, however, some few tolerable foreign horses in their cavalry; but in their exercise they were infinitely below par: nor, indeed, is it to be wondered at, as I understand few regiments of cavalry in Sweden are ever kept together. Proprietors of certain estates were obliged to keep a man and a horse for the government, equipped to serve in the cavalry, and to find them in everything. They had little opportunity of exercise, or being assembled: so that this arm, which required the most constant practice and vigilant attention to bring it to perfection, was very much in arrears in Sweden.

The Swedish army was a mixture of two different types of regiments. There were those that were permanently embodied – the *Varrade* – and included the guards, the grenadier regiments, the Mörner Hussars, the Narike-Varmland Jägers, the three artillery regiments, and the fortress troops, as well as a small corps of engineer officers; while the rest of the army was made up of part-time militia regiments – the *Indelta*. The latter units had a small, permanent cadre of officers, NCOs and soldiers, but the bulk of the men were called in for annual training for just four weeks each spring. This would account for the rather amateur performance which Sir Charles Stewart observed. The army had no permanent sapper or bridging organisation, detachments drawn from the infantry being placed under engineer officers to perform these functions in time of war.

The foot artillery pieces were three-, six- and twelve-pounder cannon and $5\frac{1}{2}$-inch howitzers. The horse artillery used six-pounder cannon and eight-pounder howitzers.

Schwarzenberg's problems

In September, the Allied commander Schwarzenberg wrote of his multinational command:

It really is inhuman what I have to tolerate and put up with, surrounded as I am by weaklings, fools of all kinds, eccentric project-makers, intriguers, blockheads, gossips, fault-finders. More than once I have felt in danger of being overwhelmed . . . The Czar is good but weak; the king [of Prussia] is a rough, coarse, unfeeling fellow who to me is as loathsome as the poor, brave Prussians are pleasant and estimable.

To his Kaiser, he wrote: 'The Czar puts me in such a state of confusion that I am often obliged, on irrefutable grounds, to give way on major issues. All this makes it almost impossible for me to answer to the immensely important outcome of our undertaking.' Just how impossible Schwarzenberg's task could be may be illustrated by the following anecdote related in Aster:[5]

On the evening of the 28th September, following the Allied defeat in the battle of Dresden, Schwarzenberg, Radetzky and a Russian identified only as T———l were planning the routes to be used by the Allied corps on their withdrawal south onto Teplitz in Bohemia. The Austrian corps were using the road through Dippoldiswalde and one Russian corps was on the Peterswalde road. T———l urged that Barclay's corps should use the Dippoldiswalde road but Schwarzenberg and Radetzky argued that he must go through Peterswalde as the single Russian corps there[6] would be too weak to stand up to Vandamme's corps if it caught up with it; anyway, the Dippoldiswalde road was full. There was an argument but eventually T———l gave in.

Before the Austrian dragoon officer rode off to carry the order to Barclay, T———l asked that he should also carry a note from him to Barclay. Graf C.M., one of Schwarzenberg's Adjutants, saw this and became suspicious; he read the unsigned, pencilled note. On one side it said (in French) 'Please send me a map of the Kulm area.' On the other side was more writing, but in Russian which he could not read. He took the note to Radetzky and explained his concern. Radetzky took it to T———l and asked him what the Russian sentence meant; T———l replied that it was just a personal message for Barclay, so it was sent off to him together with the order to march by Peterswalde.

At 9 o'clock on the morning of the 29th August, Schwarzenberg and his staff were in Dippoldiswalde when a large column of Russian troops appeared from the direction of Maxen led by Barclay de Tolly.

The nonplussed Schwarzenberg asked Barclay: 'Your Excellency, what are you doing here? Did you not receive an order to march via Peterswalde?'

Barclay: 'Yes, Your Highness! But later I received an instruction from headquarters that it would be better for me to march via Dippoldiswalde and as His Majesty, Czar Alexander, has given me permission to act as I deem best, I followed this instruction!'

In disobeying Schwarzenberg's order, Barclay had left one of the better roads to Teplitz open to the enemy who may well have used it to get there first with potentially disastrous consequences for the Allies.

Schwarzenberg sent for General T———l, who said he knew nothing of any

---

[5] Aster, p. 83.
[6] Ostermann's II Corps.

such arrangement between the Czar, and Barclay deserved to have his head placed at his feet.

Graf C.M. recovered the pencilled note in Russian that had been delivered to Barclay and had it translated by one of the Austrian liaison officers in the joint headquarters. It read: '*Die Strasse auf Dippoldiswalde dürfte für Sie jedenfalls die bessere sein. Ich würde dahin marschieren.*' ('The road through Dippoldiswalde will definitely be the better one for you. I would march there.')

Due to the Allied victory at Kulm on 30th September, Schwarzenberg hushed up the incident. So we have the incredible situation that the orders issued by the Supreme Allied Commander were regarded by his powerful allies as a basis for discussion only, and may be circumvented with impunity if thought fit. Not only this, but the Russians did not even bother to tell Schwarzenberg that they intended to ignore his order. The utter chaos that may well have resulted from this childish attitude may easily be imagined.

The author of the note was not identified.

The identities of 'T——l' and 'Graf C.M.' are not revealed by Aster, but the former was most probably Major-General Baron Toll, the Russian liaison officer in Schwarzenberg's headquarters, who was frequently a thorn in the side of the Austrian commander and his staff. 'C.M.' would seem to have been *Rittmeister* Clam-Martinie.

Chapter 3

Prelude to Battle

The enemies close up

Edouard von Löwenstern, a lieutenant and ADC to Peter Alexejewitsch Graf
Pahlen, commander of the Russian cavalry division with Wittgenstein in the
Army of Bohemia, provides the following personal account of the opening
stages of the Allied advance into Saxony:

> We crossed the border from Austria into Saxony at Reitzenhain.[7] The Graf
> and his entire suite lodged themselves on the local magistrate. A well filled
> table, good wine, white bed sheets and friendly, helpful people showed us
> that we were in Germany. We were in enemy territory, thus forage was taken
> where we found it. The strict discipline and the many imperial commissars
> that we had found in Bohemia were popular with nobody; now we were all
> happy and in good spirits.
>
> In Gössnitz[8] we bumped into the Krakau Cossacks;[9] we flew at them, cut
> them up and – as they were badly mounted – captured some sixty of them.
> We followed the fleeing Krakaür and soon met French cavalry. The skirmish
> went on until dark; Banasch was wounded in the toes and Deljanow on the
> foot. Five hussars from the *Leibeskadron* were captured. Two squadrons of the
> Sumy Hussars were detached to Grossstöbnitz to take an enemy war chest
> and other requisitions but they did not get anything. We stayed the night in
> Gössnitz.
>
> Pahlen was lodged with a good, upright man, who did him the honour of
> walking before him with a basket of flowers which he strewed in his path; our
> Graf walked on roses and forget-me-nots! We were attracted by the baskets of
> wine which seemed to wink at us from the corner. The table there groaned
> with food and we fell upon both food and wine with the same enthusiasm
> with which we had fallen on the Krakaürs a few hours before.
>
> We drove Poniatowski's corps out of Altenburg and regaled ourselves with
> a fine luncheon in the Hôtel de Gotha that we found there. Our boldness
> dictated that Pahlen and not Poniatowski should dine there.
>
> Several good friends were gathered around a pastry stall in the market
> with bottles of champagne in their hands, so I went and joined them. The
> drinking went on at a great pace and soon I had drunk so much that all of
> Altenburg seemed to be dancing in a ring around me.

---

[7] Now on the B174 road.
[8] South of Altenburg, on the B93.
[9] The Krakus, Polish light horse, newly raised and serving with Krasinski's 27th
Division, VIII Corps.

At this moment, just as I downed a cup of champagne, I was summoned to the Graf. I went to him and held myself as firmly upright as I could; awaiting his orders. Either he could not, or would not see what a state I was in; however, he sent me off to *Hetman* Graf Platoff[10] with important despatches.

The hard ride and the fresh air soon sobered me up and I found the old *Hetman* some hours from Altenburg. He turned me around very swiftly and sent me back. That same evening, I was sent to the town hall to arrange billets for our command but this job was soon done with as we were moved out that night to Windischleuba. We stayed here a couple of days. General Rüdiger, with the Grodno Hussars and Grekoff's Cossacks, was sent to Frohburg. Graf Wittgenstein came to Altenburg.

That night, the enemy attacked our outposts. After we had almost been captured due to the carelessness of our guide, we got to Frohburg. You could only make out the combatants by the light of the flashes of the pistols and carbines. Pahlen had dismounted and gone into a farm house; I and some others followed him. A lance tip smashing through a window alarmed us and we rushed out again and mounted up.

The enemy was in hot pursuit of the Jaroslaw Cossacks; two squadrons of hussars threw the enemy out of the place again with bloody heads. This night adventure cost us five officers.

At four in the afternoon, we left Windischleuba and advanced through the pretty Altenburg countryside, which I remember because of the distinctive national costume. That night we reached Borna.

Poniatowski's corps had thrown out picquets on this side of the town; we occupied the marketplace and the suburb with the 25th *Jägers* under the brave Colonel Witoschkin. The Sumy Hussars also went into bivouac in the town after having had a stiff fight at the Elster crossing.

Budberg rode into the town hall in order to get us something to eat; he was soon back, at a light trot, leading one of the councillors by his pigtail. This worthy carried a large basket of food and champagne under his arm. At midnight Graf Wittgenstein arrived and stopped off at the doctor's house briefly before leaving Borna again.

After a good supper and a lot of wine, Budberg and I went into a small shop where we had spotted a light. The shopkeeper had a great shock when his door flew open and we went in. 'What do you sell?' 'Tobacco,' came the answer. I laid in a small supply of cigars and tobacco; we had some champagne and toasted the French, who had some patrols out in the area. Budberg stayed there and I went back to my old blacksmith to sleep it off.

Next morning we were all mounted up and ready for combat. The army of Prince Poniatowski, the King of Naples and Marshal Victor was defiling on the road from Frohburg to Leipzig. Pahlen satisfied himself with bombarding this column with artillery and sending out his flankeurs. The French camped on the far side of a small river in Gösterwitz [?]; we bivouacked

---

[10] Commander of the Don Cossack Corps, Army of Bohemia.

between Borna and the enemy. We were soaked by heavy showers. After two days, the French slipped quietly away during the night. We followed on their heels and stopped in Espenhain ... Our outposts were continually bickering.

A view from the French side has been left to us by Colonel de Saint-Chamans of the 7*e* Chasseurs à Cheval:

I was ordered to present myself at Freistadt, a small town in Silesia occupied by my regiment. My regiment was in Sebastiani's II Cavalry Corps and, as I had known this general when he had been colonel of my regiment, we got on very well. He commanded some ninety squadrons and thirty guns; my regiment was part of Exelman's 4th Light Cavalry Division.

This cavalry appeared to be very good but, as was once said about the Great Condé's army, it needed to mature. Indeed, neither the men nor the horses had ever been to war; the former were twenty years old, the latter were four. It was said that they were chickens mounted on colts.

The troops very much wanted to face the enemy, but this sentiment fell apart as soon as they began to feel the fatigues of life on campaign. The infantry were in much the same state; they were brave but had little staying power.

Motivated by French honour and enthusiasm, we had carried the day at Lützen and Bautzen and should have called a halt there. These victories had been enough to secure a glorious peace. Then we should have pulled our troops back to the Rhine, placed them in camps, like that at Boulogne for two years. After that we could have dictated our will to Europe as we had done of old.

On 28th September the Emperor passed my regiment in review. Our state was dire and he seemed to recognise this. He praised us and made a number of complimentary remarks. My regiment numbered some 300 men; five weeks previously it had had twice that number. Generals Sebastiani and Exelmans eulogised about the regiment's performance.

I presented to the Emperor those officers that I felt deserved promotion to captain, lieutenant, and then presented a number of young men whom I thought would make excellent second-lieutenants.

'I don't need these young ones,' he told me warmly, 'show me some veterans of '93.'

I didn't quite understand and stood there in confusion.

'Yes, show me some veterans of '93.'

I turned and brought forward some old sergeants, as incapable as they were ancient. He charmed them without questioning them. Just as well, for if they had to answer his questions they would probably have uttered some nonsense and shown the Emperor the error of his ways!

After the promotions he declared that he wanted to award the Legion of Honour and that I was to prepare a list of deserving individuals.

On 5th September we found ourselves following an enemy formation. I had gone on ahead with my skirmishers to reconnoitre the terrain and to see whether or not we should launch a charge on the enemy. At the entrance to the Reichenbach defile I noticed a regiment of hussars coming up on our flank. 'They are Prussians!' I said to Dubois, my adjutant, who was with me.

'No colonel, they are French!' he replied. 'They must have come up another way and are coming over to support us.'

I repeated my fear that they were Prussians; he was equally sure that they were French. All the time they came closer. Suddenly, when they were only eighty paces away, a dozen of them broke away from the main body and came on ahead.

'Look, they are Prussians!' I shouted to Dubois. I wrenched my horse around just as he cried out to them 'Don't shoot, we are French!' He had barely uttered these words when they opened fire with their carbines. A ball went through my colback and another struck me in the lower abdomen and almost knocked me out of my saddle. I managed to tell Dubois to fall back as I was wounded.

We regained our own ranks and the enemy fell back. Lavoestine, Sebastiani's ADC, came up and helped me off my horse. Later, the surgeon examined me and found that the ball had hit my pocket watch which had absorbed much of the impact and had driven a part of the watch into my abdomen. This caused me tremendous pain and vomiting. However, after a little time I felt sufficiently well to resume command of my regiment. I would have preferred to rest, but I knew that my chasseurs thought me dead, which had affected their morale and endangered them, so I felt that my place was at their head.[11]

Thursday 14 October: Liebertwolkwitz

On the evening of 13 October, Murat aimed to withdraw northwards over the Parthe and to stand between Leipzig and Taucha. In doing this he would have given up the best terrain for the forthcoming battle and exposed Leipzig itself to attack. As soon as he heard this, Napoleon sent an aide, Major Baron Gourgaud, to stop him. Gourgaud found Murat already withdrawing and delivered the Emperor's message; Murat then turned back and took post on the slight but dominating heights between Markkleeberg and Liebertwolkwitz. The fields of fire from here were superb; the rear and lateral communications very good. Murat's right wing was on the Pleisse/Elster swamps. His dispositions were as follows: right wing (Markkleeberg–Dölitz–Lössnig–Connewitz): Kaminiecki's Division of Poniatowski's VIII Corps (Dombrowski's Division was at Wittenberg) – 5,400 infantry, 600 cavalry, thirty guns; between Markkleeberg and Wachau: Victor's II Corps (15,000 infantry, thirty-eight guns); then Lauriston's V Corps (12,000 infantry, 700 cavalry, fifty-three guns) from Wachau to Liebertwolkwitz.

---

[11] Colonel de Saint-Chamans returned to duty so quickly that his wound was not reported and so was not included in Martinien's casualty lists, although one other officer of the 7*e* is recorded to have been wounded here this day.

Liebertwolkwitz, 14 October

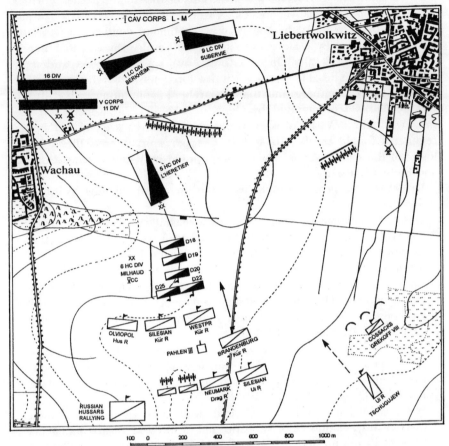

PRUSSIAN TROOPS = GM von ROEDER'S CAV; GM PRINZ AUGUST v PREUSSEN
ALL FROM LG v KLEIST'S (PRUSSIAN) CORPS

RUSSIAN CAVALRY = COUNT PAHLEN'S CAV DIV

At Holzhausen, as reserve, was a division of the Young Guard. Further back, at Thonberg, was Augereau's IX Corps (9,500 men), which had just arrived from Spain. With Augereau was Milhaud's 6th Heavy Cavalry Division, followed by L'Heretier's 5th Heavy Cavalry Division and Berckheim's 1st Light Cavalry Division (of I Cavalry Corps), commanded by General Pajol. This 4,000-strong cavalry force was set behind V Corps between the Galgenberg and the Monarchenhügel (Monarch's Hill). IV Cavalry Corps (commanded by General Sokolnicki, as Kellermann was sick) was behind VIII Corps at Markkleeberg. These French and Polish regiments fought on 14, 16 and 18 October and suffered the heaviest losses of the *Grande Armée*. They were opposed by Wittgenstein's Russians and Kleist's Prussians.

Dr Seyfert, the vicar of Taucha, recounts the ensuing combat as follows:

On the 14th, Wittgenstein had Prince Gortschakoff's I Corps, Prince Eugen von Württemberg's II Corps and General Pahlen III's Cavalry Corps (Illowaiski's Cossacks, the Hussar Brigades of General Rüdiger and Colonel Schufanoff and General Lisanewitsch's Ulan Brigade). Kleist's III (Prussian) Corps consisted of four infantry brigades and General Röder's Reserve Cavalry Brigade. The Allies had about 6,000 cavalry, 20,000 infantry and 48 guns on the field by the end of the day; they were opposed by about 7,000 cavalry, 32,400 infantry, and 121 guns.

First contact was between Illowaiski's Cossacks and the French cavalry of L'Heritier and Subervie near Liebertwolkwitz. The newly arrived dragoons from Spain were distinctive in their brown greatcoats which had been made up in Spain.

Between 9 and 10 o'clock Pajol withdrew into the main French position between Wachau and Liebertwolkwitz and the forward French Tirailleurs evacuated Gross-Pössna and fell back to Liebertwolkwitz. Pahlen advanced on Magdeborn; Klenau arrived in Gross-Pössna at 9 o'clock. *Feldmarschall-Leutnant* Mohr takes Gross-Pössna.

Pahlen had expected to snatch an early victory but was overthrown; the Isum and Grodno Hussars were driven off in confusion. General Pahlen sent to Kleist for help; before the Prussian cavalry arrived, Prince Eugen's Russian infantry came up by Güldengossa.

On the left wing at Aünhain were Illowaiski's three Cossack *Pulks* and the Guards Hussar Regiment; on the right wing, on the meadows north-east of Güldengossa, were the Lubny and Olviopol Hussar Regiments. In the second line were the Tschugujeff Ulans. In the Allied centre on the heights north of Güldengossa was the Sumy Hussar Regiment and a Russian horse artillery battery. This battery fired on the French cavalry; two of the enemy regiments charged the battery, which only just managed to limber up and escape in time. The Sumy Hussars counter-attacked but were outnumbered and had to flee into Güldengossa.

At this point, the Prussian Neumark Dragoons arrived; Pahlen greeted them with 'Just get at them, we'll overthrow them at once!' The Prussians answered: 'None of us is scared!' and charged forward together with the Russians. The fight was hectic, bitter.

Murat now threw in Milhaud's Dragoons with L'Heretier's and Subervie's men in second and third lines. Five thousand cavalry advanced in an apparently invincible mass. Milhaud's division was deployed as follows: at the front of the column were the 22e and 25e Dragoons, beside one another and in line abreast; behind them rode the 20e, 19e and 18e, each in line abreast. At this critical point, General Röder came up with the Brandenburg and Silesian Kürassiers; the heavy French phalanx was hit in right flank. Due to their close formation, most of the French troopers could not use their weapons and the whole mass was pushed back to Wachau.

There, however, the three Prussian Kürassier regiments were confronted by French infantry and surrounded by the enemy's hussars and Chasseurs à Cheval.

There was no plan, the regiments were thrown into the melee as they came up. It was chaos, friend and foe mixed together. The fight was so intense that often the exhausted men and horses rested close to one another before starting to fight again. Gradually, after a hard fight, the Prussians were beaten back and were taken up by the Neumark Dragoons.

Murat was in the thick of it. Distinguished by high ostrich plumes in his hat, and a gold-embroidered velvet costume, he came very close to being captured. Sources differ as to which officer it was that nearly took him. Some say it was *Leutnant* von der Lippe of the Neumark Dragoons; Dr Zelle (p.394) states that it was Major von Bredow of the Brandenburg Kürassiers. Whoever it was was close behind Murat at one pont, shouting 'Halt, König, halt!' when Murat's Master of Horse shot him down from behind.

On the evening of the 13th of October, Klenau had been at Borna, Lausigk, and Pomssen. On the 14th, Klenau's main body got to Threna. Here he received Wittgensteins's order to take Liebertwolkwitz and to push on to take Murat's cavalry in the left flank. Klenau hurried on and, at 11:30, his IR Erzherzog Karl Nr 3 assaulted Liebertwolkwitz. Klenau had sent his fifteen squadrons of cavalry under General Desfours from Threna on to Güldengossa to support his allies; they arrived in the nick of time at 12:30.

At 1400 hrs Murat concentrated his cavalry for another assault. Milhaud's Spanish veterans were again at the head of the column, L'Heretier's dragoons behind them, then Subervie and then Berckheim. The assault went due south.

Like a great, shining snake, the massive column of horsemen burst out of the smoke and bore down on the Allies.

As the Russian Adjutant Molostwoff said: 'All shrank back from this glistening vision which embodied for us the magic that surrounded Napoleon's brows. The mass of riders, with the sun glancing from their weapons and helmets, formed one huge, endless column which crushed all before it and hit the Prussians particularly hard.' But the fire of the four Russian and Prussian horse artillery batteries on the heights north of Güldengossa [the 7th, 8th, 10th Prussian and 7th Russian] hit the front and right flank of the column and ripped its head apart, stopping it in its tracks. Seizing the opportunity, the Russian hussars, with the Prussian Ulans and the Brandenburg Kürassiers, charged into the disorganised front ranks. At the same time, Desfours led the fresh Austrian cavalry [Kaiser Kürassiers, O'Reilly and Hohenzollern Chevaulégers, and Ferdinand Hussars] into the melee. They advanced from the bend in the Güldengossa–Liebertwolkwitz road and ploughed into the left flank of the closely-packed enemy column. This completed the confusion of Milhaud's division and threw them back onto L'Heretier's men. In a few minutes Murat's great column burst apart in all directions in panic and fled the field.

They could only be rallied at Probstheida, some 4 km to the north. It was about four o'clock.

At the same time that the Austrian cavalry launched their charge against Murat's column, the Austrian infantry attacked Liebertwolkwitz. The IR Erzherzog Karl under Colonel von Salis advanced from Niederholz via Gross-Pössna against the eastern side of the village; they were soon involved in heavy fighting with Maison's Division, which defended the place stubbornly from house to house. At about 1400 hrs the Austrians had taken the stone-walled *Gottesacker* [churchyard] after a bloody combat. Maison, aware of the vital nature of the position, counter-attacked with the 153*e Ligne* and drove the Austrians out of the *Gottesacker*. The Austrians regrouped and assaulted again with General Splenyi's brigade [the Württemberg and Lindenau regiments] and a battalion of the Wallachisch-Illyrisches Grenz IR and retook the cemetery. Maison threw in reinforcements [the 152*e* and 154*e*] and wrested the disputed point back. It was about five o'clock.

The fighting was so violent that no quarter was given. The Austrians were pushed back against the wall around the cemetery gate, which opened inwards; the crush was so great that they could not defend themselves. Next day witnesses found rows of dead Austrians, leaning against one another, skewered to the wall by bayonets.

The Austrian assault on Liebertwolkwitz from the south was supported by General Paumgarten's brigade from the area of the Kolmberg to the east. This thrust got as far as Pössgraben, where it was halted by the fire of a French battery deployed to the north of Liebertwolkwitz. There was no further action on this wing of the field today.

The situation was very different on the western flank, up against the River Pleisse. Here General Illowaiski's Cossacks and von Rüdiger's Grodno Hussars advanced north from Aünhain on the gap between Markkleeberg on the eastern bank of the river and Wachau about 1,200 metres to the east. Poniatowski threw his entire cavalry force against them and the heavily outnumbered Russians fell back south to Cröbern.

Now it was the turn of the Prussians. General von Mutius, with the six squadrons of the Silesian *Landwehr* Cavalry Regiment, charged the western wing of the Polish cavalry line and, supported by some of Russian General Helfreich's Jägers, drove them back into their main position. The fire of a powerful French battery, deployed on the heights east of Wachau, stopped any further Allied advance in this sector. It was now about six o'clock, and Prinz Schwarzenberg, who had arrived on the scene, ordered the action to be broken off.

There was little further offensive action by the French and Poles either, as General Duka's 3rd Kürassier Division had now arrived from Störmthal via Güldengossa at Cröbern, on the Pleisse, to reinforce Illowaiski and Rüdiger. A stalemate ensued.

Losses suffered by the French during the action comprised about 1,500 killed and wounded, and 1,000 captured. General Bertrand was among the wounded. The Allies lost the Russian Lieutenant-General Dokturoff and Major-General Nikitin killed, 2,500 officers and men killed and wounded, and 500 captured. The Silesian Kürassiers lost fourteen officers and 164 men, the Brandenburgers six officers and forty-five men, the East Prussians ten officers and fifty-two men, the Silesian Ulans ten men, the Neumark Dragoons about fifty men. The Austrian cavalry lost about seventy men, all ranks. Klenau's infantry lost 867 killed and wounded and 134 captured in the bitter fighting in Liebertwolkwitz itself. According to Napoleon, the French lost only 400 to 500 men in all, whilst the Allies lost 1,200 prisoners and two guns, without counting their dead and wounded.

Thus ended the action of 14 October. Murat had achieved his given task of holding the dominant heights between Markkleeberg and Liebert-wolkwitz, but the costs had been heavy and most of these fell upon the precious cavalry of which Napoleon had so little. The fault for this was Murat's alone. The use of a closely-packed, heavy column of cavalry in the face of the close-range fire of four batteries of hostile artillery – which were allowed to operate without any attempted disruption from the French side – invited a costly defeat. The whole sorry episode demon-strated Murat's complete failure to co-ordinate the actions of the assets available to him. In some ways, it was a foretaste of the needless sacrifice of the French cavalry at Waterloo in 1815.

The Russian General von Toll judged Murat's influence on this clash, and his capabilities as a cavalry commander, as follows:

> This singular combat lasted so long thanks only to Murat's thoughtless pugnacity. We may mention here that the reputation of this theatrical monarch as a splendid cavalry commander, 'the Seydlitz of Napoleon's army', was undeserved and survived only because nobody could tell the truth about Napoleon's brother-in-law.
>
> Murat was completely incapable of leading large formations of cavalry. Generals commanding other army corps sought to hide their cavalry brigades from his view when he was in their vicinity, for if he was aware of them, it was quite likely that he would commandeer them and ruin them in some senseless brawl. If he was in command of large cavalry masses, he very easily lost control over them as he could only manage what went on in his immediate area. Men like Latour-Maubourg, Nansouty – and above all the

very capable Montbrun – knew how to look after themselves, especially when he was not in their vicinity to hinder their efforts.

This time he thought it fun to take command of the veteran dragoon regiments which had returned from Spain with Augereau and these worthy warriors upheld their reputations for sustained gallantry completely. This combat went much against the French however, mainly – as German officers related – due to the fact that their own horses were in much better condition than those of the French. This allowed them to mount charges late in the action with much the same power and energy as at the beginning; whereas the French dragoon mounts were blown and weak. Thus these capable, veteran dragoons, who had so much irreplaceable combat value, lost about a third of their strength including 500 captured.

Finally, Murat pulled them back under cover of the French batteries where Pahlen – who would willingly have broken off the fight earlier – could not follow them.

Edouard von Löwenstern, Pahlen's ADC, related how he saw the fight:

On 13th October, Graf Pahlen advanced with all his cavalry, reinforced by several Prussian regiments, to Cröbern. On the 14th October the Sumy and Lubno Hussars were the tête; they were followed by the East Prussian and Maerkisch Kürassiers and the Silesian Ulans. Right up front was the brave Markoff and his guns.

Scarcely had he unlimbered and begun to fire in earnest, than the enemy cavalry moved off towards the battery at a trot.

Not far from Güldengossa and the village of Liebertwolkwitz, we made contact with Marshal Augereau, who had led 10,000 dragoons up from Spain; fine, strong men on excellent Andalusian horses. With the sun glinting from their helmets and swords, this terrible phalanx approached us. Markoff received them with well-aimed fire.

The French deployed fifty paces from us and charged at us. Lances, sabres and swords clashed against one another; many were thrown from their mounts in the first shock and trampled underfoot. At one moment we were charging forward with a great Hurrah!, the next we were riding for our lives and the Hurrahs had become cries of fear. We overthrew them and were overthrown in our turn. To right and left, to front and rear, all we could see was our men and the enemy hacking and stabbing at one another, with neither side getting the upper hand. The Prussians remembered that this was the anniversary of Jena and fought like lions to wipe out that disgrace.

Graf Pahlen was always at the head of his regiments, between the cavalry lines of the enemy and his own side. He led the charges himself and directed the reserves. He was always in the thick of the fight, where it was most critical, with only a light riding whip in his hand; giving orders calmly.

If I had been an enthusiastic admirer of his in the past, I now had to honour and admire him even more. This was not the blood-crazed, berserk bravery of a Figner, or the half-mad courage of a Seslawin; this was the coolbloodedness and noble bravery of a great commander. This day alone must have made his reputation as an extraordinary general.

Both sides fought with great bitterness. The Prussian Kürassiers were already in possession of a French battery and were preparing to tow away some of the guns, when fresh troops came up to stop them.

A French officer on a grey, all on his own, rode up to the Graf with his sabre raised; '*F. . ., rendez vous!*' he shouted. A Sumy hussar lunged at him with his lance; the Frenchman turned his horse and tried to escape but was cut down before he reached his own lines.

As Graf Pahlen had received orders not to let himself be drawn into a serious fight, towards evening the two sides had pulled apart. Now the artillery started up again and continued to thunder until darkness fell.

The casualties of the day lay together: French, Russians and Prussians, covered with gaping wounds from the edged weapons. Our cavalry reformed and went into bivouac by Cröbern.

The East Prussian Kürassiers had covered themselves with glory.

The king of Naples had commanded the enemy cavalry and had made much use of General Pajol's dragoons, which had only come back from Spain in the summer under Marshal Augereau's command.

The French had learned to respect our cavalry again this day, and they did not dare to engage us in such large formations again on the following days of the battle.

This bloody melee cost the enemy well over 1,000 prisoners, including many officers, and about as many again dead. Our hussars had taken 518 men prisoner. We lost about as many dead as the enemy but lost no prisoners.

The Sumy Hussars lost eleven officers, including Schischkin, my old squadron commander, who lost a leg. Graf Ivan Pahlen received a pistol shot in the leg.

***

Ernst Maximilian Hermann von Gaffron (ennobled in 1840 as the Freiherr von Gaffron-Kunern), a *Portepee-Fähnrich* – officer aspirant in a Prussian cavalry regiment – in the Silesian Kürassiers, has left us his recollections of this dramatic day:

> The morning of the 14th October was cold and foggy; by midday the sun broke through and it became a little warmer. I went looking for our regimental commander, Major von Folgersberg, my faithful mentor and a friend of my father's, and found him lying on one of the regimental baggage carts, covered with a blanket and shaking with a violent fever. He had been feeling unwell for some days. He spoke to me in a weak voice. When I saw his condition, I told him that it was impossible for him to stay with the regiment. He answered me with a weak grin: 'You can't believe that I am going to leave the regiment now? We might be in a battle today or tomorrow. I am not going to give up the honour of commanding the regiment on such a day, even if it kills me!'

He would not be moved from his decision; I felt that I would probably do the same. He shook my hand firmly and spoke of my father, then we parted. I met him once more, in the middle of the battle; but these were the last words I heard him speak, apart from: 'March, march, charge!'

It must have been between 10 and 11 o'clock when an ADC galloped up and the order rang out: 'To your horses and mount!' We moved off but soon came the command: 'Trot!' We trotted for about an hour, at first in column, then in troops, across country. We then came to a bivouac site where the straw, huts and campfire embers told us that the French must have left the place only this morning. These traces, and our rapid trot, told us that we must be near the enemy.

Röder's cavalry [the three Kürassier regiments, the Silesian Ulans and the Neumark Dragoons – eighteen squadrons in all, as two squadrons of Ulans were detached – two horse artillery batteries, and some weak Volunteer Jäger detachments] had been placed under command of the Russian General Graf Pahlen. He also commanded the Russian Grodno and Sumy Hussars [twelve squadrons] and a Russian horse artillery battery and thus had thirty squadrons and three batteries.

The Russian General Graf Wittgenstein, who commanded our Army Detachment [the corps of Wittgenstein, Kleist and Klenau], had ordered a reconnaissance in strength on Liebertwolkwitz to clarify enemy dispositions on the far side of the Pleisse. Pahlen's cavalry was the advanced guard, of which the point was the Grodno Hussars and ourselves.

In order to gain the gentle heights of Wachau and Liebertwolkwitz, we had to pass through the defile of the pretty village of Cröbern, which lay in a shallow valley. This we did at a fast trot, with our carbines at the ready. As we passed through, I noticed the fine, friendly-looking manor house, which lay to one side and was a picture of peace and cosiness.

Once through the village, we at once went into a gallop, first in troops, then on a regimental frontage. We halted briefly, then came the call 'Trot' and we moved off smartly again.

A dark mass stood against us, to their right front shone the white tower of Liebertwolkwitz.[12] With my short-sightedness, I could not make out the details of the dark mass, but soon I saw the flashing of helmets and swords as they closed with us.

The signal 'Gallop' sounded, and now I could see the enemy squadron clearly. The regiment was going at such a pace that even before the command '*Marsch, marsch!*' came, a thunderous cheer broke from our ranks. Folgersberg, who was riding on the left wing of our squadron, raised his sword, his '*Marsch, marsch!*' was echoed in our hurrah and the trumpet signal. The French dragoons, whose moustachioed faces I could now clearly see, stopped, suddenly turned, and withdrew in good formation.

We soon caught up with them as they were only about twenty paces before us. The sight of the enemy cavalry had brought the regiment to boiling

---

[12] Which was occupied by French infantry.

point. This was the anniversary of Jena; that blot had to be wiped out! This was our first cavalry combat of the campaign; something we had been waiting for for a long time.

An ADC, who witnessed our charge, told me later that it was a splendid sight. First the fresh tempo of the trot – in a parade-ground dressing – then the full gallop, then the impact as we hit the enemy and swept them away as would a storm.

The enemy dragoons were from Milhaud's first rank. As far as I remember, the Grodno Hussars were first through the Cröbern defile, then our regiment, as we went straight into the attack, because I only recall seeing men of these two regiments. The Grodno Hussars were, as usual, brilliant in this combat. The other regiments followed us as quickly as they could clear the defile.

At the point at which we cheered in that charge, and we could see the whites of the Frenchmen's eyes, there was no stopping us. Every rider spurred his horse and sought to split a French skull.

Our dear commander Folgersberg rode in front of the interval between the 1st and 2nd Squadrons; I was on the right wing of the 4th Troop, 1st Squadron. As we cheered, I whooped with joy, gave my chestnut my spurs and was one of the first to reach the French, who turned about at this instant.

There was no order in the ranks anymore, everyone rode like the wind. I passed Folgersberg at about six paces distance as he rode his fine, great iron grey. He nodded and waved to me in a friendly, but warning manner. That was our farewell. As I broke forward out of the ranks of my troop, the faithful Czekyra, who rode behind me shouted: 'Gently, gently, *Herr Portepee-Fähnrich!*' But his warning fell on deaf ears.

The French dragoons retired before us, initially at a trot, then at a gallop, in good formation. We often heard the officers calling: '*Serrez les rangs!*' [close ranks] and in fact, they rode so closely together that at first we could not break their ranks, but stayed close on their heels and hacked at them as best we could. The horse-tail manes of their helmets, their broad, stout leather bandoliers and the rolled greatcoats, which they wore over their shoulders, protected them so well that they were pretty impervious to cuts, and our Silesians were not trained to thrust nor were our broad-bladed swords long enough to reach them.

Just hacking at the heads and backs of the enemy did not do much good; it was not until some of our cleverer men knocked some of them out of their saddles with well-aimed stabs or pistol shots, that we were able to make a gap in their phalanx. Finally, we managed to break into their ranks and they burst apart. As our regiment was now out of order, the combat developed into a series of small, fighting groups in which the French lost many men.

At this point in the battle, I bumped into my young comrade, Senft von Pilsach, who had been made *Portepee-Fähnrich* with me a few days ago. 'Well, Senft, today is a fine day!' I called out to him; he smiled and nodded to me. A few moments later, he sank to the ground, his skull split by an enemy sword.

We chased, and fought with, the enemy for a long while; we threw his first line back onto his second, and his second onto his third. Suddenly, the enemy's ranks broke apart in front of us; a battery of horse artillery had become jammed in the mess of the dragoons and was soon surrounded by our men. We cut down the gunners and the drivers, or forced the latter to turn the guns around. We had turned several of the guns around, and I was about to take them back with some of my comrades, drunk with the joy of victory and oblivious to what else was going on around me, when suddenly I heard: '*En avant, dragons, à bas ces foutous Prussiens!*' coming from all sides!

I then realised that I and about 20–30 Kürassiers in the captured battery were surrounded by hostile dragoons. A colonel of the enemy dragoons, a tall, handsome man on a large, English thoroughbred light chestnut, decked out in the finest equipment, called his dragoons together and charged us.

The captured guns were abandoned; our small group of Kürassiers would have to cut their way out. We had to try to go it alone as there was no chance of forming a tight group. Some Kürassiers were behind me; I heard one cry 'Jesus Maria!' as one of them was cut down.

Five or six dragoons were after me. I thought I was lost, but swore to try everything to escape. To my horror, my chestnut began to lose speed, be it due to fatigue or for some other reason, despite the fact that I was urging it on with my spurs and the flat of my sword. As I was wearing an officer-pattern greatcoat and cartouche, the dragoons thought that I was an officer and chased after me all the harder.

The ground that we rode over was unploughed, very wet and very hard-going for our horses. The I saw a narrow track of firm grass, just wide enough for one horse. I urged my horse onto it and thus was able to pull away from the dragoons, still wading through the mud to my flank. Two dragoons who had lost their horses appeared in front of me. There was nothing for it but to go straight at them! I bowled one of them over and I was through.

A closed line of cavalry was approaching me from the right. I took them for Prussians and rode towards them; then I saw that they were wearing bearskins so I turned off to the right. After a short while, I met a troop of Kürassiers who had gathered themselves around *Premierleutnant* von Poser, commander of the *Standartenzuges* [escort to the standard].

Here the remnants of the regiment gathered; a small group which was quickly organised into troops. We didn't have much of a rest; large groups of French cavalry appeared and came at us. We charged against them, but didn't stand much of a chance against their superior numbers, until suddenly the Neumark Dragoons hit the enemy in the flank. We now joined up with our dragoons and charged the enemy and threw them back into a deep, sunken lane where many men and horses fell and filled the ditch.

We now reformed line and stood at the ready. A heavy artillery duel now began. We were subjected to a lot of shot and shell. *Rittmeister* von Klöber – our squadron commander – was before the squadron, just by me, and was ordering the ranks, when a shell landed between us, exploded, and a piece broke his stirrup and cut the ball of his foot. The rest of us around him were covered with dirt. His horse, whose girth had been cut, went down.

We thought he was dead, but soon found his wound. We carried him to a covered cart just behind the regiment and he was taken back to Pegau. While he was still near the regiment, a cannonball went through the canvas roof of the cart and the Saxon driver at once whipped up his horses to get out of the danger zone.

Meanwhile, the other regiments of our corps had been involved in some splendid charges against the enemy. The fight raged back and forth. This was definitely one of the most bloody and interesting cavalry combats in military history. Our Neumark Dragoons were very distinguished. Our cavalry charges were so violent that we drove deep into the enemy cavalry formation. The king of Naples was at the point of being captured in one of the melees. It is not certain if it was *Leutnant* von Lippe of the Neumark Dragoons or Major von Bredow of the Brandenburg Kürassiers who challenged Murat to surrender. Some say that the man wore a helmet, in which case it was Bredow; others say that it was *Leutnant* von Lippe of the dragoons.[13]

In the chase after the beaten enemy, the latter came up on the left side of the king of Naples and shouted: 'Surrender, king!' At this moment, the king's Master of Horse, who reported the incident, stabbed the brave officer in the side with a stiletto and killed him.

The result of the bloody combat was that our thirty squadrons held the field against an enemy three times as strong and that the French withdrew as darkness fell. We had achieved the aim of the reconnaissance and now withdrew into a comfortable bivouac behind the Universitätsholz between Güldengossa and Störmthal.

The regiment had bought its glory at a very heavy price. Fourteen officers were dead, wounded or missing, over half of the total. About 200 men and horses were out of action. These figures show how much the officers had exposed themselves.

The regiment's heavy losses were due to the fact that it had followed the beaten foe too closely and too far and had left the other Allied regiments too far behind. We also became disorganised around the captured battery and got involved in too many individual combats.

The French took advantage of these circumstances and of their superior numbers, and attacked us in the left flank with two regiments of dragoons so that the regiment had to fight its way out in small groups, which cost us heavy casualties.

I was one of the last to rejoin the regiment, and several Kürassiers had

---

[13] Prussian dragoons wore shakos in 1813. The sources differ regarding which officer nearly captured Murat. Odeleben (p.329) states that it was probably von Lippe, but that Major von Waldow, *Rittmeister* von Waldow, and *Leutnant* B. Richthofen of the same regiment (1st Neumark Dragoons) were also killed here. Dr Zelle (p.394) states that it was Major von Bredow.

reported seeing me in the midst of the French and had reported me as dead or captured. They had given me up for lost, and my faithful old Czekyra had shed a tear or two over me. His joy, when he saw me on my exhausted chestnut was thus the greater.

***

A civilian eyewitness of the desperate fighting – an inhabitant of Liebert-wolkwitz – wrote down his own account of this, the first of many dreadful days for thousands in the Leipzig area:

At about ten in the morning three cannon shots were heard and panic at once broke out. The French officers who had billeted themselves in the village could not get their possessions onto their packhorses quickly enough. There was now no doubt as to what dreadful fate awaited us. It was a case of everyone for himself; no-one thought of anything but saving his own skin. No-one knew what to do or where to go; they were no longer safe in their own houses. A great number fled into the church as they hoped to be safe from the bullets behind the stout walls; others took refuge in their cellars.

At about midday, heavy artillery fire and musketry broke out close by. The panic among those in the church was heart-rending to see, particularly when the church doors were broken in and bullets smashed the windows. This increased when those who looked through the windows reported that the houses in the Windmühlengasse [Windmill Lane] were on fire.

It was at about 4 pm, when the French drove the Allies out of the village for the third time, that a French officer came into the church and (in German) expressed his amazement that anyone could have decided to take refuge in a building in the centre of a battle. Now, however, there was no immediate threat; if danger again threatened, he continued, he would let us know.

Half an hour later a soldier appeared and gave us this dreaded news. Shortly afterwards the church door burst open and cannonballs smashed into the walls. Everyone was terrified. At last, the daughter of the saddler Bothe gathered her courage and left the church to search for her mother. Alas, she found her, shot dead in her own garden.

As we looked out of the church we were confronted with scenes of horror. All around lay dead and dying; outside the churchyard, in the market, bitter hand-to-hand fighting was still going on. The burning houses lit the scene.

With only that which we had on our bodies, and with no idea of the fate of our friends and relatives, we fled from the village towards Leipzig. Behind us we saw how our homes were consumed, one by one, by the flames. From Thursday 14th to Sunday 17th, villages in the area burned; some due to artillery fire, some due to the carelessness of soldiers billeted in them. There was no-one to fight the flames as almost all inhabitants had fled from the battle zone.

During this time the French continued to plunder and to destroy; the church [in Liebertwolkwitz] was also looted down to the bare walls. The vestments, the pulpit, the altar, the baptismal font, the pews – all were stolen. The crucifix, the monstrance, the collection pouch and the church seal were taken as well.

***

The sounds of the sharp clash at Liebertwolkwitz were carried by the chill, southerly wind and were clearly audible in the city of Leipzig itself. Groups of wounded French soldiers and stragglers began to trickle in from the south and tension among the population rose as rumour and counter-rumour circulated with a speed that can only be achieved under such circumstances. The crowds passing through the city gates increased in size; excitement rose when orderlies arrived to announce the imminent arrival of the Emperor and the king of Saxony from Düben and Eilenburg respectively.

Napoleon arrived at the gates of Leipzig at noon, having left Düben at 7:00 am and having hurried over the last kilometres as soon as the sounds of battle reached him. He was accompanied by the usual escort of infantry and cavalry of the Imperial Guard. He rode through the Halle Gate without pausing, through the city, and out of the outer Grimma Gate. Here he halted and set up his personal headquarters with Berthier and Caulaincourt, on Rabensteinplatz, opposite the high court building. As the day was cold, the Emperor had a large fire lit to warm himself. Reports from Murat came in and were eagerly studied. As the noise of the cannonade increased, Napoleon sent orders off by courier to the corps coming in from the north, instructing them to speed up their march.

After a while the convoy of the king of Saxony approached from the direction of Taucha; They had left Eilenburg at 9:00 am and were escorted by part of the Saxon Leib-Grenadier-Garde, the Saxon Dragoons, and by some Polish Lancers. The king dismounted from his coach to greet the Emperor before the royal family took up residence in Thomas' house in the main market square (now Nr 2), where they stayed until 23 October, when they were taken away by the Allies as prisoners of war.

The 2nd Division of the Old Guard, commanded by Curial, arrived soon after the king, and marched straight on in the direction of the fighting; it reached Holzhausen by nightfall. For his part, Napoleon now rode on to Reudnitz and took up quarters in the house of the banker Vetter.

At 4:00 pm Friant's 1st Division of the Old Guard also arrived and went into bivouac to both sides of the Wurzen road between the city and the Kohlgärten. The night was very cold and it rained heavily in a driving wind. The sounds of combat gradually died out as night fell.

Although the dull thuds of the cannon had ceased there was no peace in and around Leipzig, as thousands of cold, hungry, tired troops trudged through the streets, eager only to stop marching and to find something to eat and somewhere to sleep. The houses, shops, barns, sheds and churches of the town and surrounding villages were soon packed tight; and still they came. The rumble of guns and waggons, the jingle of harness, the shouting, the cursing, the cries of the wounded were incessant from 4:00 pm on the

14th until well into the forenoon of the 15th, regiments spasmodically poured through the town with drums beating and trumpets braying.

To add to the chaos, thousands of destitute refugees, including children separated from their families, also streamed into the town, hoping to find shelter and food. Many French soldiers made the plight of these unfortunates even worse by robbing them violently of any foodstuffs or valuables that they had. And this was by no means all. The French army, well schooled in making itself at home at the expense of its reluctant hosts, robbed every building in the vicinity of anything made of wood, in order to make bivouac fires. Many timbered buildings were literally torn to pieces and nothing was left but heaps of bricks and wattle and daub. Many of the Allied forces, treating Saxony as enemy territory – which it was – acted in the same manner. Soon Leipzig was surrounded by a belt of light generated by thousands of campfires.

The *Grande Armée* passed through Leipzig during the 14th and 15th and took up position in an arc to the east of the city, stretching from Markkleeberg in the south through Wachau on the Pleisse, Liebertwolkwitz, the Kolmberg, Holzhausen, Zweinaundorf, Paunsdorf, Schönefeld and Eutritzsch to Möckern on the Elster, north of Leipzig. Bertrand's IV Corps was west of the city around Lindenau on the road to Weissenfels and Napoleon's major depot and fortress at Erfurt. Napoleon had thus elected to give battle to his superior enemies – whose conjunction he had, as yet, been unable to prevent – with a major obstacle (the broad, swampy, closely overgrown river beds of the Pleisse and the Elster) directly at his back, across his lines of communication. Only one bridge was available for his withdrawal, and even that was approachable only through the major defile of the city of Leipzig.

If Borodino and Waterloo were 'off days' for the Emperor due to illness, his decision to give battle at Leipzig was foolhardiness of the greatest magnitude, for which no excuse has yet been produced.

Not all of the *Grande Armée* was yet concentrated. Two divisions of the Young Guard under Oudinot were at Seehausen, and the rest, under Mortier, at Wiederitzsch. The Guard cavalry was at Taucha to the north-east, and Fournier's cavalry division was back at Düben, to guard its bridges over the Mulde. The remnants of the Bavarian contingent guarded the Mulde bridges at Eilenburg, and the Mulde bridge at Wurzen was guarded by a battalion of the Old Guard. Off to the north-east. Latour-Maubourg's I Cavalry Corps reached Stötteritz on the evening of the 14th; Sebastiani's II Cavalry Corps was at Güntheritz and Podelwitz. On 15 October Reynier's VII (Saxon) Corps and Dombrowski's division were still some way off at Pratau and Kemberg. As on the 14th, Murat commanded in the southern sector of the front.

Chapter 4

Friday 15 October

Napoleon's plans

Napoleon met Murat early on the 15th and received a full report of the previous day's fighting. At 10:00 am he set out with his usual suite to inspect the scene of the conflict – something he did whenever possible. When they reached Probstheida an extraordinary scene met their eyes. The entire village was awash with wet, white feathers: the French soldiers' trousers were in such a worn-out state that they had ripped up all the eiderdowns and mattresses that they could find in order to use the ticking to make replacements.

The ride continued south-east through Meusdorf and on to the Galgenberg between Wachau and Liebertwolkwitz, an insignificant but dominating hillock which afforded a good all-round view of the surrounding countryside. He could clearly see the positions of yesterday's clash and the newly occupied posts in Holzhausen and Baalsdorf to the north. The enemy outposts were barely a kilometre away to his south. In order to discover if the entire Army of Bohemia was concentrated before him, at 3:00 pm he sent two officers to examine the outposts. Their apparent motive would be to enquire if many French officers had been captured in yesterday's clash; they would then try to ascertain if Prinz Schwarzenberg was present. However, their true aim was guessed and no information was forthcoming.

On hearing this, Napoleon rode off west to Dölitz to confer with Poniatowski. Whilst there, he inspected the Polish positions and went on to the Pleisse, toured the various crossing points, ordered the remaining bridges (except that at Dölitz manor) broken and had the depth of the river taken at several points. He then rode back along the French positions to Holzhausen, where he met Curial with the 2nd Division of the Old Guard. One of the units of the division was the Saxon Leib-Grenadier-Garde battalion under Major von Dressler. The Emperor spoke to him, asking the strength of the battalion and its campaign history.

About 500 metres to the west, in Zuckelhausen, Napoleon found Augereau's IX Corps. An eyewitness recalled the event:

> At 5 pm we were aware of the sounds of marching men and the noise of thousands shouting. We quickly climbed the tower and saw, to our astonishment, a large part of the French army assembled by Seifertshain [east of Liebertwolkwitz] repeatedly shouting: '*Vive l'Empereur!*' as Napoleon rode into the village. We assumed that the village would be assaulted, but the mass of men marched back to Holzhausen. We later heard that the Emperor's arrival had caused the outburst and that three regiments [139*e*, 141*e* and 154*e*] had been presented with new eagles. As the last rays of the

setting sun dimmed we could still hear the receding thousands chanting *'Vive l'Empereur!'*

Having completed his reconnaissance, Napoleon dictated his orders for the following day's operations to Berthier:

1. Tell the Duc de Tarente [Marshal Macdonald] to march to Holzhausen and from there to Seifertshain where he will receive orders to outflank the enemy's right wing. I will be in Liebertwolkwitz at 6 am tomorrow morning.

    2. At 5 am tomorrow, Saturday, the Guard will march for Liebertwolkwitz; Sebastiani, with the II Cavalry Corps, will go to Holzhausen. The other corps, deployed in line, will stand-to at dawn.

    3. Tell the Prince de la Moskwa [Marshal Ney] to hold himself in the area of Leipzig, ready for battle. He will have Marmont's VI Corps, Bertrand's IV Corps, Souham's III Corps and Lorge's cavalry division under his orders. If, tomorrow the 16th, the Army of Silesia does not approach from the direction of Halle, Marshal Marmont will cross the Parthe by the bridges at Leipzig and deploy his three divisions in echelon between Leipzig and Liebertwolkwitz. It will be necessary for the Prince de la Moskwa to send peasants (either willingly or by force) together with soldiers who speak German – and who will also be dressed as peasants – in various directions.[14] He will send someone to the Leipzig planetarium, where a Saxon officer will be as an observer, each hour to bring a report of what can be seen.

    If enemy infantry is visible in the direction of Halle and Landsberg they are to be attacked with vigour with the aim of taking prisoners for interrogation.

With this plan, Napoleon intended Murat to hold the Army of Bohemia to his front, while Macdonald and his group (Augereau and the three cavalry corps of Latour-Maubourg, Pajol, and Sebastiani) outflanked their right wing. Marshal Ney's group (III and IV Corps, Dombrowski's division, and Arrighi's III Cavalry Corps) was to cover the main body from an attack from the north. The Guard and Marmont's corps, between Liebertwolkwitz and Probstheida, were the reserve, to be used as a battering ram against the weakest and unsteadiest point of the enemy line at the appropriate moment. He had concentrated about 110,000 men east of the Pleisse for his main stroke against the Army of Bohemia. To protect his northern flank, III, VI and VII Corps, Dombrowski's division, and III Cavalry Corps totalled a further 52,600 men and 206 guns. Due to the fact that he believed the threat of Blücher's Army of Silesia interfering with his planned destruction of the Army of Bohemia to be extremely remote, he was to pull III and VI Corps (30,200 men) down to the south to reinforce his master stroke. Bertrand's IV Corps at Lindenau had a further 6,000 infantry, 300 cavalry and thirty-three guns, and the Leipzig garrison was about 7,000 strong.

---

[14] An apparent, major defect of these orders is their failure to explain what the aim was of sending these patrols out, or to specify clearly in which directions and how far out they were to go, and to whom they were to report.

With his customary skill, Napoleon had thoroughly exploited the advantages of the interior lines on which he was operating. He hoped to be able to destroy the Army of Bohemia before the other two Allied armies arrived on the scene.

Perhaps the only criticism that could be levelled at these dispositions would be that Napoleon failed to occupy the Kolmberg (two kilometres east of Liebertwolkwitz), although this would have extended his front somewhat. In the event, Macdonald had to take this feature on the 16th anyway.

For the Allies, on their exterior lines, the task of successful, timely co-operation in the face of such a capable opponent was immeasurably more complex. The fact that there was not just *one* commander nor *one* agreed plan in the Allied camps made co-ordination even more difficult. Another negative factor was that the Allies' couriers had so much further to travel between armies than did those of the French.

The Allies' plans

There was no such unity of purpose in the Army of Bohemia's headquarters as existed within the *Grande Armée*. The Czar's ideas were different from those of the Allied armies' supreme commander, Prinz Schwarzenberg. Schwarzenberg had originally presented a plan which foresaw the main action taking place west of Leipzig; this was rejected. He then had it modified. The second concept, worked out by his Quarter Master General (the Saxon General von Langenau, who was now in Austrian service), intended to have Blücher's Army of Silesia in the north cross to the west side of the Elster to attack Napoleon's lines of communication from Leipzig back to Merseburg at Lindenau. This attack would be supported from the south by Gyulai's III (Austrian) Corps, Moritz Liechtenstein's 1st Light Division, and the *Streifkorps* of Thielmann and Mensdorff.

II (Austrian) Corps, together with the Russian and Prussian Guards and the Austrian Reserve, were to advance north between the Elster and Pleisse rivers and force the Pleisse crossing to the eastern bank at Connewitz. The corps of Kleist, Klenau and Wittgenstein were to stay on the east bank of the Pleisse and advance north from Cröbern, Güldengossa, Gross-Pössna and Seifertshain against Murat's force between Wachau and Liebertwolkwitz. This plan apparently allotted no immediate role to the Army of the North. That von Langenau – a Saxon, and one-time chief of staff of that kingdom's army – should suggest the advance of the Allied reserve through the swampy, closely overgrown belt of land between the two rivers is amazing. Any units which entered this area would become (as proved to be the case) totally isolated, and quite unable to influence the course of the main action on the eastern bank of the Pleisse.

This second plan extended the Allied armies over a distance of four *Meilen* (about thirty kilometres) in terrain cut by swampy, overgrown ground which would split their forces into two – even three – parts which had no communication with one another. Over 70,000 men were to be sent against the defile of Lindenau, which could easily be defended by a much smaller French force; over 50,000 men were to be locked up in the swamps between Elster and Pleisse to try to force the defile of Connewitz; which left only 72,000 men to face the enemy at Wachau, which was the very place at which it must have been expected that Napoleon's main body would be concentrated.

This plan provoked immediate opposition from the Russian high command, including Barclay de Tolly, Diebitsch, Jomini and Wolkonsky, who all demanded that the main body of the Allied armies should be concentrated on the open plain east of the Pleisse against Wachau. Schwarzenberg, however, had accepted that von Langenau, as ex-chief of staff of the Saxon army, must have the best knowledge of the local terrain and had full confidence in him. He insisted that von Langenau's plan be executed. Even the protestations of the Czar did not move him.

Finally, the Czar said: 'Very well field marshal, as you insist on it, you may do with the Austrian army as you wish, but as far as the troops of Grand Prince Constantine and Barclay are concerned, they will go onto the right bank of the Pleisse where they should be and nowhere else!'

So much for the unity of the Allied command.

Schwarzenberg was consequently obliged to concede and to redraft his plan. His third version was as follows.

The army of General von Blücher will leave Schkeuditz at 7 in the morning and march on Leipzig.

Count Gyulai, with the III Austrian Corps, Leichtenstein's light division and General Thielmann, will concentrate at 6 am at Markranstadt, attack the enemy before them and advance on Leipzig.

Count Meerveldt will be ready with the II Austrian Corps at 6 am at Zwenkau. He will be followed by the Army Reserve of the Crown Prince of Hessen-Homburg with Count Nostitz's cavalry division and the two divisions of Bianchi and Weissenwolf. This column, under command of the Crown Prince of Hessen-Homburg, will march on Connewitz and take the bridge and the village.

All columns on the right bank of the Pleisse will be commanded by the Russian General Barclay. Count Wittgenstein will attack the enemy to his front at 7 am with his own corps and those of [Generals] Klenau and Kleist and drive them back on Leipzig.

The Russian grenadier corps of [General] Rajewski and the 3rd Russian Kürassier Division [of General] Duka will form the Allied reserve on the right wing of the troops on the right bank of the Pleisse.

The I Austrian Corps of Count Colloredo[15] will advance out of Borna and will form Count Klenau's reserve.

---

[15] At this point Colloredo's corps was still at Penig, about fifty kilometres (or two days' march) to the south!

The Russian Reserve Army of General von Bennigsen will arrive in Colditz on 16 October and will advance in the direction of Grimma and Wurzen.[16]

If this revised plan was considerably better than the first two, it still clung to the assault on Connewitz through the swampy defile between the two rivers. In Schwarzenberg's headquarters they were convinced of the sure success of the left hook into the enemy flank through Connewitz, and to this end had left the bulk of the Austrian army (30,000 men) around Gautsch and Gross-Städteln, opposite Markkleeberg and between the Elster and the Pleisse. If the enemy could hold the defile at Connewitz, then Wittgenstein would have to fight the main battle at Wachau alone with his 72,000 men. His reserves (the 24,000 men of the guards and the Kürassiers) were at Rötha, seven to eight kilometres away to the south on the Pleisse.

But these defects were minor when compared with the grim fact that – with the exception of VII Corps – Napoleon had his forces already concentrated under his hand whilst the Allies were issuing operational instructions for the next morning to considerable portions of their armies which were not yet present and could not definitely arrive for about twenty-four hours at the very least. For them to remain, with their fragmented forces, closed up to an enemy under so competent and experienced a commander as Napoleon – and to expect that he would allow them to get away with such sloppy conduct unpunished – bordered on lunacy. No doubt, their dearest wish – to close with and destroy their hated foe here and now, before he had an opportunity to slip out of their grasp – blinded the Allied commanders to the risks they were taking. They probably survived their brash stupidity only because Napoleon – deprived of accurate intelligence by his lack of cavalry and an ineffective spy network – was unaware of the glittering prize that lay right beneath his nose.

From ten in the morning to five o'clock in the afternoon there were skirmishes between the outposts of Marmont's VI French Corps and the advanced guard of the Army of Silesia on the road from Halle to Leipzig. Blücher's army left Halle just before eleven o'clock. That night, Yorck's corps bivouacked around Schkeuditz, Langeron's at Wehlitzsch and Cursdorf, and Saint-Priest's around Lützschena. At seven in the evening Major von Klüx and a Prussian battalion drove the French out of Hainichen, Lützschena and Stahmeln as they closed on Möckern.

Blücher, whose headquarters was now in Grosskugel, had no information as to the exact strengths and locations of the enemy in his area, so he ordered a reconnaissance in the direction of Leipzig for the morning of 16 October.

***

Ernst Moritz Arndt (a Prussian patriot and later a famous author, who had been exiled at Napoleon's insistence and was now a major in the Prussian

---

[16] Bennigsen's army and Count Bubna's 2nd Light Division, marching west from Dresden, were still at Hubertusberg, Grimma (twenty kilometres away to the east), and Colditz (thirty-eight kilometres to the south-east).

artillery) paid a visit to Blücher's headquarters on the 15th and recorded his impressions:

> I rode to Blücher's headquarters and reported to Colonel von Gneisenau [Blücher's chief of staff]. He was most friendly towards me, shook my hand warmly and spoke of our times together in Kolberg [sic] and was very confident that the great decision would be achieved in the next few days.
>
> Gneisenau was filled with great friendliness and a simplicity of manner; compared to the ever-dissatisfied Yorck, he would always be a winner.
>
> On this same afternoon, I managed to see Blücher himself. He was exactly as I remembered him from the campaign on the Rhein in 1795 and later at Aurich, Münster, and in 1806. He shook my hand, called me his old *Kriegskamerad* and said that of all the officers present, we two must have known each other the longest.
>
> The fact that a bloody, decisive battle might be fought by his troops next day did not seem to trouble him one bit. He laughed and chatted as if we were going on an exercise in peacetime and not into a fight for life and death with Napoleon, the greatest commander of all time.
>
> All the while he puffed thick clouds of smoke from his pipe and took frequent glasses of good Bordeaux wine that had been looted from the equipage of a French general. He joked with the officers and soldiers of the passing Prussian troops.
>
> And how well and firmly the old boy sat his horse, how his dark eyes sparkled over his long white moustache and what a picture of undiminished youth he made, despite his iron grey hair.
>
> He did not seem to be worried in the slightest about the plan of campaign and I repeatedly heard him answer to queries: 'Gneisenau will certainly have thought of that.' 'The young scamp [Gneisenau] understands everything.' 'You'll have to ask Gneisenau, he knows best how it should be done because he's the cleverest of our crew here.'

***

On the 15th the Army of the North made an early start from Cöthen for Halle but, on Bernadotte's orders, stopped between Radegast, Zörbig and Wettin (on the modern B183) after a march of scarcely twenty kilometres; Bennigsen's Reserve Army advanced to Richtenhain near Hartha (on the B175) and Waldheim; Graf Colloredo's I (Austrian) Corps came up from Chemnitz to Penig (on the B95); and Bubna's 2nd Light Division advanced to Nossen at the junction of the B175 and B101.

During the night Napoleon sent couriers to the various corps commanders ordering them to hasten their marches for their respective positions in readiness for the forthcoming battle. II Cavalry Corps was to move from Güntheritz and Podelwitz to Holzhausen, and Delmas' division of III Corps from Düben to Holzhausen; III and VI Corps were held in contact with the Army of Silesia. VII Corps was to go from Düben via Eilenburg to Taucha, and XI Corps from Panitzsch to Holzhausen.

On the 15th, from his headquarters in Pegau (about eighteen kilometres south of Leipzig), Prinz Schwarzenberg wrote to his wife:

> I wanted to write to you yesterday, my Nani, I was drawn to you, but I could
> not. A few hours' sleep have restored me well; I need it because tomorrow is
> going to see a great battle on the plains of Leipzig. I have arranged with
> Blücher that he will advance from Merseburg and Halle on Leipzig, next to
> him will be Gyulai, who is concentrated at Lützen today.
>
> Meerveldt will attack up the road from Zwenkau towards Connewitz and
> will be supported by the Austrian Reserve Corps. The corps of Wittgenstein,
> Kleist and Klenau form the *corps de bataille* between the Pleise and the Parthe
> and will attack the enemy to their front. I have nominated the Russian
> grenadiers, Kürassiers, Horse and Footguards to be the reserve. Bennigsen,
> with 40,000 men, should come up to Grimma after leaving as many again to
> blockade Dresden. The Crown Prince [of Sweden] may or may not co-
> operate, we don't yet know; he is really a true Gascon; it is unfortunately true
> that fortune often favours the braggarts.
>
> What do you think of the Bavarian affair? I think it is one of the most
> important developments with regard to the opinion of the Germans. The
> keystone to the German rump confederation is broken, now the whole
> edifice must collapse . . .
>
> This battle must last for some days for the situation is unique and the
> outcome will have endless consequences.
>
> Some days ago, Metternich gave me the cross you will find in this letter
> and told me that his wife had given it to him and made him promise to
> persuade me to wear it as it would bring me the luck I will need. I do not
> want luck from it, it would be like robbing you . . .
>
> One of brave Blücher's ADCs has just told me that he is on his way as
> agreed and will arrive on time.

The spirit which permeated the Allied armies at this time can perhaps best be
shown in the Army Order of the Day which Schwarzenberg sent out the same
evening:

> Brave warriors! The most important phase of the holy struggle is at hand; the
> decisive hour has struck. Prepare yourselves for the battle! The band which
> unites great nations for a great purpose will be drawn tighter and tighter on
> the field of battle. Russians, Prussians, Austrians! You are fighting for the
> freedom of Europe, for the independence of your cause, for the immortality
> of your names! All for one, each one for all! With this noble, with this
> masculine call go into holy battle! Stay true to it in the decisive hour, and
> victory is yours!

Just how much of this passionate, high-minded exhortation the average
German or Russian squaddy – cold, hungry, wet, and homesick – could
understand may well be questioned, but the spirit of the Allied high command comes across very clearly indeed.

Uncharacteristically, Napoleon issued no exhortation to his troops.

Chapter 5

Saturday 16 October

The opposing deployments

The morning of Saturday the 16th saw the whole plain around Leipzig covered in a heavy, clinging, autumnal mist. The unfortunate inhabitants of the villages on the battlefield reported that they were surrounded by a deep, powerful, murmuring, grumbling drone, punctuated by occasional trumpet calls and the rolls of drums as the hugest concentration of military might yet seen in Europe lumbered into its pre-ordained positions to decide the fate of a continent, and perhaps of the entire world. The French divisional commander, Count Maison, greeted his cold and hungry men with the words: 'Children, today is France's last day, tonight we have to have won or to be all dead.'

Wittgenstein commanded the Allied forces in this sector. They moved into position on the morning of the battle as follows:

On the left wing, by Markkleeberg and against the Pleisse, was the 4th Column (8,400 men; Dr Zelle alleges 10,000) under Lieutenant-General von Kleist, consisting of Prinz August von Preussen's 12th Brigade and General Helfreich's 14th Russian Division. Kleist was supported by Major-General Lewaschoff's brigade of Duka's 3rd Kürassier Division.

To the east, north-east of Güldengossa, was the 3rd Column (11,000 men; Zelle says 10,000) under the Russian Lieutenant-General Prinz Eugen von Württemberg, with II Russian Corps and *Generalmajor* von Klüx's 9th Prussian Brigade.

Directly to the east was the 2nd Column (9,000 men; Zelle says 10,000) under Lieutenant-General Prince Gortschakoff, consisting of General Mesenzoff's 5th Russian Division, Pahlen's cavalry corps (reduced to twenty-two Russian squadrons, the Prussian Neumark Dragoons, and the Silesian Kürassiers from General von Röder's Reserve Cavalry Division, and Pirch's 10th Prussian Brigade, a total, according to Zelle, of about 3,000 sabres). These were drawn up north of Störmthal and Oberholz, south of Liebertwolkwitz, and west of the main road now called the Leipziger Strasse from that place south-east to Threna.

Incredible as it may seem, there was then a gap in the Allied line of about three kilometres. Napoleon was on the Galgenberg (just two kilometres west of Liebertwolkwitz) from nine o'clock onwards, and Marshal Mortier was in Liebertwolkwitz itself. That neither noticed this gap, which was only four kilometres from the village over the wide-open plain – defies belief. Be that as it may, despite the Allies once again leading with their chins and giving no heed to closing this vulnerable and potentially deadly hole in their line, Lady Luck was with them. No French commander appears to have noticed this golden opportunity or – if they did – none bothered to exploit it.

In the east, on the Allied right wing, was the 1st Column of General Count Klenau (27,300 men; Zelle says 23,000) consisting of IV Austrian Corps, Ziethen's 11th Prussian Brigade, and part of General von Röder's Reserve Cavalry Division. These were at Seifertshain and the heights north of Gross-Pössna and Fuchshain. Platoff's Cossacks were posted as flank guards east of Seifertshain.

Five kilometres south of the Allied left wing (about eighty minutes' march), in the area of Gruna-Magdeborn, was the 11,000-strong (14,000 according to Zelle) Reserve of Lieutenant-General Rajewski's VIII Corps, with the rest of Duka's 3rd Kürassier Division.

A further five kilometres to the south of Rajewski, west of the Pleisse and level with Rötha, was the 14,000-strong Russo-Prussian Guard corps.

As von Langenau had proposed, the Austrian corps of General Count von Meerveldt (15,000 men), General the Crown Prince of Hessen-Homburg (15,000 men), and General von Nostitz's cavalry, were west of the Pleisse in and around Zwenkau. Thus about twenty-five per cent of the Allied army on the southern front was locked up in a swampy defile and unable to participate in or influence the vital battle. It is amazing that suggestions of treason on von Langenau's part were not raised. Even so, Prinz Schwarzenberg's qualities as a commander must certainly be called into question in view of his insistence on adhering to a plan the defects of which had all been clearly and decisively pointed out to him by the Russians only the day before.

The total Allied forces available east of the Pleisse to face Napoleon's 138,000-strong army in that sector was thus only 71,800, and these were so widely scattered that only 61,800 were initially in direct contact with the enemy.

In contrast to these confused Allied bunglings, let us examine – and admire – Napoleon's tactical deployment. The Emperor's forces, well concentrated and all obedient to the will of this acknowledged martial genius, were distributed as follows.

All bridges over the river from Leipzig south to Cröbern had been broken. In the west, Lefol's weak, newly formed, independent division was at Connewitz on the Pleisse guarding the crossing there. Poniatowski's VIII Corps was still in the positions it had held on the 14th, from Dölitz through Markkleeberg. Victor's II Corps was also in its old position around Wachau, and Lauriston's V Corps extended from the Galgenberg to Liebertwolkwitz in the east. Kellermann's IV Cavalry Corps was east of Connewitz and north of Dösen; it was commanded during the battle by General Sokolnicki.

The four divisions of the Young Guard (Marshals Mortier and Oudinot) were north of V Corps between Liebertwolkwitz and Probstheida. Friant's division of the Old Guard and Nansouty's Guard cavalry were just to the north around Probstheida, with I and V Cavalry Corps (Latour-Maubourg and Pajol) just to the east of them. Curial's division of the Old Guard and Augereau's IX Corps were around Zuckelhausen, two kilometres east of

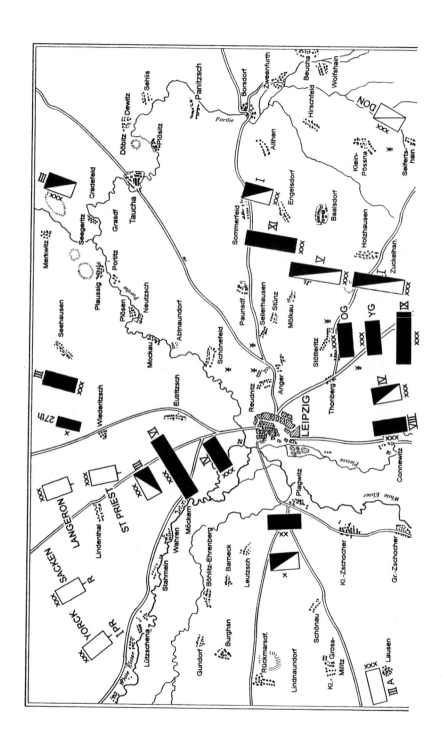

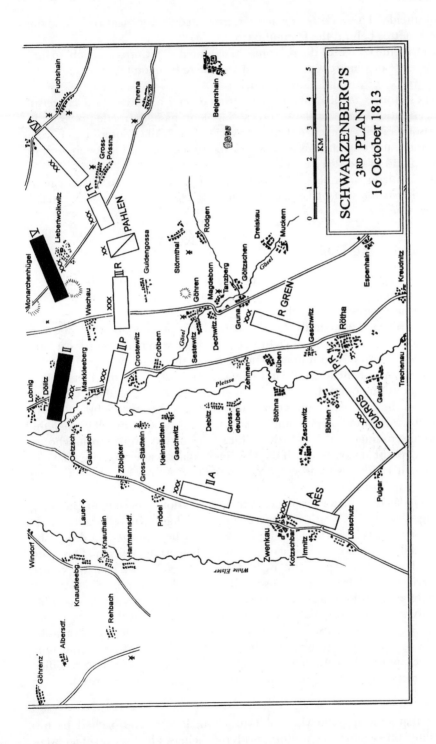

SCHWARZENBERG'S
3RD PLAN
16 October 1813

Probstheida. These corps formed a massive, central tactical reserve about 1,800 metres behind the front-line troops.

During the course of the morning, Macdonald's IX Corps and Sebastiani's II Cavalry Corps marched south from Taucha to form on the left wing of the Emperor's line around Holzhausen.

These forces totalled about 120,000 men on 14 October – a masterful concentration of the available forces. Napoleon had also made provision to garrison Leipzig, to allocate troops to ward off any Allied interference from the north and to guard his route of escape to the east, at Lindenau, west of Leipzig and of the River Elster.

If Napoleon may be criticised for having adopted a risky strategy in accepting battle east of Leipzig, his tactical dispositions were – as usual – virtually perfect.

Connewitz and Dölitz

Large areas of this part of the battlefield have been removed by opencast lignite mining since the end of the Second World War and several of the villages have vanished entirely.

Based on von Langenau's plan, Schwarzenberg planned to deliver a major thrust deep into Napoleon's right flank. As we have already seen, von Langenau should have had intimate knowledge of the close, swampy and overgrown nature of the strip of land between the Elster and the Pleisse. It is consequently incomprehensible why he should have suggested this course of action in the first place, and equally incomprehensible that Schwarzenberg should have insisted on pursuing it, particularly as he was himself leading the Austrian contingent through this difficult country en route to its chosen crossing point at Connewitz. If the Czar of Russia was able to divine that von Langenau's plan was a waste of time and men, why did Schwarzenberg cling to it so stubbornly?

But today the Allied supreme commander was doing more than one thing wrong. Today, the Allied supreme commander had achieved the unthinkable for any professional soldier. Not only had he managed to divide the main Allied field force in the face of the most dangerous tactician of his – and arguably any other – epoch, but he had also removed himself from the centre of gravity of the Allied army and isolated himself along with his chief of staff, most of his headquarters and over 28,000 men, in virtually inaccessible countryside out on one flank. Theoretically, command of the Allied troops on the right of the Pleisse consequently passed to Barclay de Tolly but, as he was in rear with the reserve, the burden fell to Wittgenstein. From nine o'clock onwards Czar Alexander was also present on the field and meddled in the tactical conduct of the battle – with surprisingly positive results.

***

Early that morning the vicar of Gautsch had been approached by two mounted officers in white uniforms with red facings, whom he assumed were

Saxons. Upon being asked by them if he were the vicar of the village, he replied that indeed he was. Imagine his surprise when they then responded with: 'You must come to Prinz Schwarzenberg, he wants a word with you.' He then had to trot along between them to the prince's location. Behind him rode a Cossack with a long beard and an even longer lance to ensure that he did not run away.

They met the prince, with his entire general staff, just to the north of Gautzsch. The prince asked the vicar, in a friendly manner, if he knew the way to Connewitz. When the vicar said yes, Schwarzenberg at once ordered his entourage (the vicar included) to start for that place. The horrified vicar protested that he was known personally to the French in Connewitz; if he appeared in the company of the Austrians and they had to beat a hasty retreat, he, as a pedestrian, would be left behind, and would be captured and shot as a spy. Schwarzenberg recognised his predicament and ordered that he be given a horse. With the vicar at his side, the Allied commander then set off for Connewitz at the head of his staff, all riding in column four abreast.

After passing through Ötzsch they reached the hamlet of Raschwitz on the left bank of the Pleisse, opposite Dölitz. Here the vicar declared that it would be dangerous to ride any further, as he knew that Prince Poniatowski's Poles were on the other side of the river, which could easily be waded at this point. However, his fears were disregarded by the Austrians and they rode on. At the end of the meadow they came to the so-called Teufelsloch (Devil's Hole), when suddenly shots rang out. The cavalcade at once set their spurs to their horses and retraced their steps to Gautzsch, where Schwarzenberg and several of his staff climbed the church tower to view the terrain. It was at this point that Colonel Wolzogen arrived with the Czar's urgent 'request' for assistance on the Allied main front.

Wolzogen may be regarded as the Russian equivalent to Marbot; always writing ripping yarns with himself as the inevitable hero. His account of events on this critical morning is as follows.

At 9 am the Czar arrived on the field and took up a position on the Wachtberg between Güldengossa and Göhren, about two kilometres behind Prinz Eugen's corps. Shortly afterwards Friedrich Wilhelm joined him, as did Kaiser Franz of Austria at about midday.[17] This slight hillock gave the three monarchs a good view over the southern battlefield. As Baron Wolzogen (then a colonel and present as an aide to Czar Alexander) recalled later in his memoirs, the Czar noticed the thick, dark masses of the French army ranged along the heights of Dösen, Wachau and Liebertwolkwitz and contrasted them with the obviously much smaller Allied columns in the foreground. The Allied columns were so far apart that they could not see one another, and thus each fought in isolation. There was no chance of mutual support or co-operation. Alexander turned to Wolzogen and asked if, in his opinion, the Allied assault would be successful. Wolzogen answered that

[17] This area has since been excavated away by the GDR government, to exploit the lignite deposits found there.

from what he could see, it was much more likely that the French would go over to the offensive and scatter the feeble Allied columns if they were not supported by strong reserves. 'But the Austrian main army is between the Pleisse and the Elster,' responded the Czar, 'and my guards and those of the king are still at Rötha!'

'Then,' said Wolzogen, to whom these odd dispositions were unknown, 'in this case we shall surely be crushed! How is it possible that such a large proportion of the army has been placed in the trap between two rivers where they are so surrounded with bushes and swamps that they cannot even see what is going on around them, let alone move freely about?'

The reliability of this tale cannot be determined; Wolzogen seems often to have been the Czar's saviour – at least by his own account. And if a Russian adjutant to the Czar, a stranger to Saxony, knew the ground in the area so intimately, how was it possible that von Langenau – a native of the kingdom – apparently did not?

'Schwarzenberg intends to advance through Connewitz, cut the French off from Leipzig and thus defeat them utterly,' said Alexander.

'That is absolutely impossible,' retorted Wolzogen, 'Leipzig is only half an hour from Connewitz and this space is too small for an outflanking manoeuvre to be considered. Anyway, the enemy would only need a few battalions along the embankment at Connewitz to defend it against a whole army. Even if the prince breaks through at Connwitz, he will be confronted by the French reserves which are there and will not be able to deploy. It is clear that this is a completely faulty disposition that can only be rectified by the rapid relocation of the Austrian reserves to the right bank of the Pleisse – if it is not already too late for that!'

Wolzogen's memoirs continue:

> The Czar was visibly shocked by what I had said and ordered me to ride at once to the prince, to explain this to him and to insist, in his name, that the Austrian reserves were to march at once.
>
> The Czar gave me an escort of his Cossacks and told me to use them to send him reports on the progress of the actions between the Pleisse and Elster and on the far side of the latter river and on the advance of Blücher's army.
>
> I was to remain between the two rivers.
>
> I thus rode through Cröbern to Gaschwitz, where it was only with the greatest difficulty, and with the help of my Cossacks, that we were able to find a ford across the Pleisse. At about ten-thirty I came across Prince Schwarzenberg and his chief of staff, General Count Radetzky, in front of Gautsch, and delivered the Czar's message.

Hearing Wolzogen – and now having seen the nature of the local ground for himself – Schwarzenberg responded: 'I have to fear myself that we won't break through at Connewitz.'

Radetzky added: 'Langenau is the only one who still clings on to this idea, which I didn't like right from the start. But now Your Excellency should not delay a minute to send off the Reserve, because they have an hour's march to get back to Gaschwitz; the crossing of the Pleisse will take two hours and then there will be another hour's march to Markkleeberg so that it will be about three o'clock before they will be able to support General Kleist, if – God forbid – he hasn't already been crushed.'

Schwarzenberg at once gave orders for the divisions of Bianchi and Weissenwolf to march with all speed for the threatened sector, to cross the Pleisse at Gaschwitz and Düben, and to advance on Markkleeberg. Count Nostitz's Kürassier division was to hurry on ahead of the infantry. Meerveldt's II Corps was left on the west bank of the Pleisse.

***

The main fighting on the Austrian side at Connewitz and Dölitz would be carried out by Longueville's 2nd Brigade of Lederer's Division (Regiments Bellegarde Nr 44 and Strauch Nr 24) and Klopstein's 1st Brigade (Regiments Wenzel Colloredo Nr 56 and Kaunitz Nr 20) of Alois Liechtenstein's Division. Mecsery's 2nd Brigade of Liechtenstein's Division would stay at Gautsch in reserve all day. Sorbenberg's 1st Brigade of Lederer's Division was sent north to Schleussig to make contact with Gyulai's III Corps at Lindenau. The action proceeded as follows.

Meerveldt's II Corps (the divisions of Alois Liechtenstein and Lederer) had led the way and advanced northwards from Gaschwitz at eight o'clock, marching to Gautsch and then eastwards on Connewitz. The terrain was so difficult that no artillery could be taken along. Until midday, the bulk of the 28,000 Austrians locked up in these swamps stood idly around whilst their comrades east of the Pleisse were fighting desperately against heavy odds.

The Austrian attack on Connewitz bridges was led by the Regiment Bellegarde Nr 44. The first bridge (over the old arm of the Pleisse) had been broken by the French, while the second – which led straight into the village itself – was about 400 metres from the first and had been blocked. Artillery covered the approaches, and the houses on the far bank were occupied in strength by skirmishers, whose fire kept the Austrians well back. The defenders were Lefol's March Division (four-and-a-half battalions and six guns), who had no trouble at all in keeping their attackers at bay, as the Austrians could only advance on a very narrow front.

Before long the Regiment Bellegarde had lost five officers and almost 200 men killed and wounded. The regiment behind it (Wenzel Colloredo Nr 56) fared little better; it had suffered heavy losses in the battle of Dresden and most of its men were fresh recruits, who were scarcely trained. The Austrians therefore looked for an alternative crossing point further upstream opposite Lössnig, but to no avail because of the swollen state of the river.

At last, seeing that he could achieve nothing here, Schwarzenberg ordered his troops to pull back and to keep the opposite bank under fire. Another attempt to cross the Pleisse would be made further upstream, at Dölitz.

Dölitz manor lies on the left bank of the Pleisse whilst the village lies on the right. A mill race runs through the manor courtyard, and between it and the

river stands a fortified gatehouse which offers an excellent defensive position
against any attack from the village itself. This sector of the line was held by
Poniatowski's Poles. He had put a small garrison into the manor and was so
confident that they could hold Dölitz that he had left the bridges over the
mill race and the river intact.

Captain Petzler stormed the manor with two companies of the 1st Battalion, Regiment Strauch Nr 24 of Longueville's brigade, and rapidly threw
the Poles out and back over both the mill race and the Pleisse. They quickly
reformed for a counter-attack, but in the meantime the Austrians had been
busy destroying what they could of the Pleisse bridge so that access over it was
already limited. Despite this, the Poles succeeded in retaking the gatehouse
after a stiff fight, but they could not push on across the mill race bridge.

By this time the Austrians had received reinforcements and their colonel –
Oberst Reisenfels – led them in a new charge which recovered the gatehouse.
Reisenfels was mortally wounded here. The situation now degenerated into
an infantry fire-fight across the river, with artillery support for the Poles from
the village and from the hill to its east, to which the Austrians could offer
nothing in return. The combat was so hot that the Regiment Strauch was
soon out of ammunition and was replaced by three companies of the Regiment Kaunitz Nr 20, who were also in action at Markkleeberg.

Meanwhile, the pointless squabble over the Pleisse at Connewitz went on,
with French and Austrian casualties mounting to no purpose. During the
afternoon General Longueville was shot from his horse and killed. Moving
north to disrupt the French withdrawal on Weissenfels on 19 October, *Feldmarschall-Leutnant* Bubna described the scene of this senseless slaughter:

> The French resistance here had been desperate; their bodies lay thickly in
> the rubble of the houses in the roads and among the barricades on the
> bridge. The road from the village [Connewitz] to the bridge was so thickly
> covered with their dead that no-one had had time to clear them away and
> the whole division just had to march over them. The other side of the bridge
> was no better and revealed a grisly sight. Many, many of our comrades had
> shed their blood here. The wood was full of our dead and on the bank of the
> Pleisse there were thick rows of our men who had died in a fire fight at
> twelve paces.

The situation at Dölitz improved for the Austrians at three o'clock, when they
at last managed to drag some guns up to the manor. These were quickly in
action, and soon the mill on the east bank was afire. This building had served
as a strongpoint for the Poles and when they were forced to evacuate it they
also had to abandon the meadows downstream.

It was now between four and five o'clock and the situation of the Franco-
Polish forces in this sector was becoming serious. The Austrian Reserve had
at last arrived to help Kleist, and Bianchi's division had taken Markkleeberg
from Semelle's 52*e* Division, which was forced to fall back north on Dölitz.
This division was taken under flanking fire from Meerveldt's II Corps on the
west bank of the Pleisse and was thrown into confusion.

Meerveldt – who was extremely short-sighted – mistook some of the enemy troops over the Pleisse for Prussians (they were in fact part of Curial's 2nd Division of the Old Guard) and thought that the time had at last come for him to cross the river and join his allies. He ordered an infantry bridge to be thrown over the Pleisse just upstream of Dölitz manor and rode over it with a few ADCs and orderlies. He got to within about twenty paces of the 'Allies' before they delivered a volley which brought down his horse. He was captured[18] (the ADC who came back over the river reported that he had been killed), and in his pocket was found a copy of the Allied plan of action for 17 October. The omniscient Wolzogen recounts that he had pleaded with von Meerveldt to leave this vital document with him before crossing the Pleisse, but that Meerveldt had refused to do so. On reporting Meerveldt's capture to the Czar next day, Wolzogen was promoted to major-general for his efforts in the Allied cause on the 16th.

Behind Curial's men there now appeared Souham's III Corps (the divisions of Brayer and Ricard), which had been transferred from the northern front via Eutritzsch, Schönefeld, Probstheida and Dösen. Although they had wasted hours in this endeavour – and their absence from the northern front had made Blücher's task of defeating Marmont that much easier – they were at least able to prop up this shaky portion of the southern front at a moment of crisis.

It was by now dark and Dölitz village remained in French hands. At eight o'clock that night the French made a last attempt to retake Dölitz manor, and the gatehouse was subjected to another hail of ball and canister, but the assault was beaten off by *Oberleutnant* Schindler of the Regiment Wenzel Colloredo; *Hauptmann* Pentz launched a counter-attack with the bayonet which drove the French back for the last time that day. Relative quiet then descended over this sector of the field.

***

The terrifying events of the day in Dölitz were reported by Justice Kurth and Assistant Justice Vollhardt:

> At three in the afternoon, the first Austrian cannon came up to the Pleisse from Raschwitz. The first shot hit the mill and ripped off a corner. As a result of the Austrian shells, the mill and the farm beside it went up in flames that evening. The retreating Poles set fire to several farms and houses in the area with bundles of blazing straw. A total of nine farms, together with all their outbuildings, four isolated barns, the mill and twelve houses were destroyed.
>
> The Poles tried to set fire to Dölitz manor house with artillery shells from a battery on the Kellerberg, but they failed because none of the shells exploded. All the rafters and tiles on the gatehouse were shot down.

---

[18] Grabowski states, on p.126 of his memoirs, that it was Pontiatowski's lancers who captured Meerveldt, and that Thiers, on p.565 of Vol XVI of his *Histoire*, is the source of this erroneous information; he in turn copied it from Faine.

The majority of the inhabitants of Dölitz had fled across the Pleisse before
the bridges were broken to take refuge in the woods of Ötzsch and Gautzsch,
where they bivouacked for several days. At ten o'clock in the evening more
of them, who had been hiding in the manor, also fled. The owner of the
manor, Major von Winkler, went with them, escorted by a sentry, over the
river via Raschwitz and Ötzsch to Gross-Städteln. Here, in the county farm of
Hohenthalschen, Major von Winkler's life was in danger. The Cossacks saw
his ribbon of the Saxon Order of St Heinrich and took him for an enemy
officer and threatened to shoot him. It was only thanks to the efforts of the
then vicar of Markkleeberg, Magistrate Kori, that his life was spared.

Other villagers, who had sought refuge in the mill, had to abandon it
when it caught fire. As they ran through the village the bullets whizzed
amongst them but no-one was hit. The refugees went to Engelsdorf.

Johann Gottfried Calov of Hintersass and his family stayed in Dölitz for the
whole of 16 October, despite the perilous situation there, which drove
them from one hiding place to another. At different times they sought
shelter in a house, then in a cellar, then behind a wall, and then in the
Schönkopf farm. Finally, because of the constant demands of the soldiery
(which they could not satisfy), and because of the fires which no-one tried
to put out, he fled with his wife, his seventy-one-year-old mother, and his
five children, of whom the oldest was six. They left Dölitz at three o'clock
in the morning and went to Leipzig, where they arrived at five o'clock.
They were often stopped by sentries on the way but, because of the children, they got through unharmed.

The vicar of Gautzsch, Dr Hentze, had this to say of his own experiences on
the 16th:

My home was Count Meerveldt's headquarters. Twenty-five hussars were
accommodated in my barn. Their task was to relay the observations of an
artillery officer up in the church tower to the commander. After Count
Meerveldt had lunched in my house, he went with an adjutant to Ötzsch to
reconnoitre the left bank of the Pleisse. Despite the cries of his escort, he
rode across to the other bank. There, he – who is short-sighted and somewhat deaf – was taken prisoner. Prince Alois Liechtenstein assumed command in his place. That evening, the general staff gathered in my house. I
was tending to a wounded officer in a room next to the parlour in which the
staff were meeting. When I finished, I went into the parlour; a small officer –
Prince Liechtenstein – approached me with the question: 'Who are you?'
When I answered: 'The owner of this house!' he said: 'Lucky for you,
because we are holding a council of war!'

There were 1,800 wounded in Gautzsch. As the church tower was being
used as an observation post, and as there were Austrian and Russian engineer officers there as well as several freemasons from Dölitz who were giving
information about the area, there were no wounded in the church.

That evening the school burned down; the inhabitants – together with
many others from the village – had fled into the woods. As there were so

many wounded in the village, Prince Liechtenstein ordered several of the hussars to act as the fire brigade.

General Sorbenburg (commander of the 1st Brigade of Lederer's division) reported as follows on the day's events at Schleussig:

> I placed myself by Schleussig with the rest of a battalion Kaunitz and two companies of Gradiskaner. One company was on the right bank of the Pleisse opposite the Brand-und-Spiess bridge. I sent out frequent patrols towards the suburbs and gardens of Leipzig. I was in close contact with Gyulai's III Corps and could clearly see his combat. On the enemy side I could see many campfires between Plagwitz and Lindenau.

Markkleeberg, the first phase: from dawn to eleven o'clock

Poniatowski was charged with the defence of this sector along the Pleisse. There were three bridges in Markkleeberg, two over the Pleisse – one between the manor and the schoolhouse and another, a few hundred metres to the south, on the road leading across the river towards the mill on the west bank – and the third to the west of the main course, crossing a minor channel on which the mill stood. On the afternoon of 13 October Poniatowski had ordered both the school bridge and the mill bridge to be broken, the villagers being forced to carry out the work. No guards were subsequently set on the bridges.

At the same time as the Prussians were advancing on Crostewitz, the 1st Battalion of the Austrian Regiment Kaunitz Nr 20 of Alois Liechtenstein's division of Meerveldt's II Corps, west of the Pleisse, floundered through the swamps and bushes and took possession of the unoccupied manor house of Markkleeberg, which lies on the west bank of the river. Their regimental commander, *Oberst* Lurem, was with them. They were accompanied by a battery of foot artillery and a light bridge, but due to terrain difficulties Lurem was forced to leave the guns and the other vehicles behind. His task was to establish contact with Kleist's Prussians on the east side of the river. He judged, however, that as no cavalry or artillery could be brought up, there was no hope of achieving anything significant, so he and the 1st Battalion's commander went back to their regiment and – incredibly – left their men in the manor to their own devices.

The manor complex comprised a moated quadrangle of buildings, with a solidly-built gatehouse in the eastern wall. From the gatehouse the road led over the moat bridge and past the church and vicarage to the partially-demolished school bridge over the Pleisse.

Following the departure of Lurem, the companies of *Oberleutnants* Hofmann and Weissvogel advanced beyond the church and, on their own initiative, repaired the unguarded school bridge and used it to cross to the east bank, where they took up positions at the schoolhouse. They totalled 160 men. At this point – for reasons which are not clear – Major Volny, from the

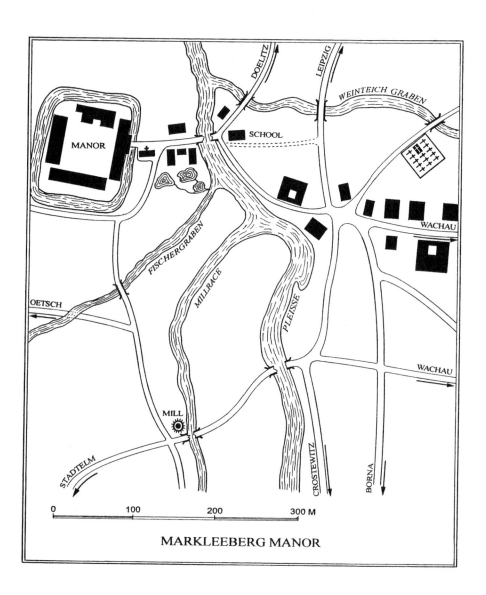

DOELITZ

LEIPZIG

WEINTEICH GRABEN

SCHOOL

MANOR

FISCHERGRABEN

OETSCH

MILLRACE

PLEISSE

WACHAU

WACHAU

MILL

STADTELM

CROSTEWITZ

BORNA

| 0 | 100 | 200 | 300 M |

MARKLEEBERG MANOR

Regiment Strauch Nr 24, arrived in the manor and took command of the 1st Battalion Kaunitz.

As soon as the French saw the Austrians at the schoolhouse, they reported this to Marshal Augereau. He at once ordered General Aylmard's 2*e* Brigade, 51*e* Division (34*e* and 35*e* Provisional Demi-Brigades) to counter-attack and crush this bridgehead. This brigade outnumbered the Austrian defenders by eight to one, and despite a heroic defence the latter were driven from the school and fell back over the Pleisse bridge, which they did not have time to destroy. The French followed.

The village schoolmaster, Christian David Schumann, had decided to stay in the schoolhouse with his family. They sought cover beneath the benches when bullets smashed through the walls from all directions, their panic rising to a peak when heavy pioneers' axes began to smash through the door. Voices from outside shouted: 'People, people, for God's sake get out of there or you're all dead, the house is going to be burned down!' At this the terrified family ran out of the school and tried to make for the village, but they were caught up in a flood of retreating French soldiers. Bullets whipped past them as they fled north over the fields, past the French IV Cavalry Corps, IX Corps, and the Imperial Guard, to Stötteritz, and then further north-east to Panitsch on the Parthe, where they were given shelter in the vicarage. They had covered about fifteen kilometres across the war's largest battlefield, but had survived unscathed.

Wenzel Krimer was senior surgeon of a battalion in Jagow's brigade in Kleist's column. He recalled the morning as follows:

The shelling of our line started at about eight o'clock. Our battalion was drawn up in column between two Russian batteries which we were protecting. Opposite us the enemy had set up a whole row of guns with two redoubts in the centre. The fire from at least forty pieces was continuous, but although presumably aimed at our two batteries their range was too great, thanks to the misty weather, and all the cannonballs whistled overhead and landed in the centre ranks. We stood under fire until after ten o'clock without a single ball doing us any damage. Then the mist suddenly lifted, and the enemy's firing opposite us stopped for a moment. We thought that the French must have forgotten all about us, or were about to withdraw; but we were soon to realise just how much they had our welfare at heart. They had realised their previous error and had realigned their guns.

I had dismounted and, wrapped in my broad cloak, was standing at the back of the column beside Captain von Pogwisch. I had just made a remark (that the French battery's regular firing was like a Turkish drum accompaniment to a Hungarian dance) and had taken up the position for such a dance. 'Just be patient,' said Pogwisch, 'They will soon teach us how to dance. There's a growling bear taking a very careful look at us down his black muzzle.'

I laughed, and had just straddled my legs apart, as in that game where children imitate a bird's wings beating, when a shell came over from ahead of us, exploded instantly, smashed an officer and a sergeant in the chest and head, and broke the legs of twelve men in the column. I fell backwards to the ground, convinced that I had been hit. Von Pogwisch grabbed me by the arm and tried to help me up. First I felt my legs, and on finding them undamaged, tried to stand up, but felt something preventing this behind me, through the cloak. On closer inspection it transpired that a shell fragment had whizzed between my legs and, because its velocity was already much reduced, had got caught in the cloak, pulled me to the ground, and struck into the earth behind me.

This was no longer a joke. My companion surgeons had run away. I had plenty to do and ought to have carried out twelve amputations straight away, but I had to limit myself to preventing the wounded men from bleeding to death and having them carried to the rear. I was still hard at work when a second shell came over, carried off the whole upper part of the adjutant's body and decapitated three men. Then it rolled as far as the Silesian Jägers drawn up behind us and caused considerable casualties there. The enemy were now aiming at us much more accurately. Their cannonballs made their way with terrible effect through our column. In under an hour we lost nearly 200 men and five officers killed or wounded. Most of the wounds were severe. Clearly we could not move from our position without endangering the battery we were protecting, but it became equally clear that if we stayed much longer in the same position the entire battalion would be wiped out. The soldiers were gnashing their teeth in rage at not being allowed to attack the enemy and were angrily demanding permission to advance.

Eventually, Major von Ziegler reported to the brigade commander our unpleasant situation and our desire to attack, and received the reply that we could not leave our position until another battalion joined us in the line. If he then liked to try to storm the enemy redoubt facing us, he could do so, but on his own responsibility. The men shouted for joy and there was no holding them now. That redoubt, with its twelve guns, had damaged us terribly and the soldiers were in a savage temper about it. But to storm the redoubt was a risky undertaking.

At last a battalion arrived and with a wild cheer and lowered bayonets our brave men set off to storm the redoubt.

'Children!' shouted Major von Ziegler as we advanced through a fearful hail of fire which knocked down whole files, 'You must wipe the stains of Kulm[19] from your colours! Any man who retreats a single step before we have captured the battery is a cur!' 'Forwards! Forwards!' they all cried, running into the assault. Soon we were under the artillery fire; a column of enemy infantry advanced against us but was rapidly knocked to the ground with butt and bayonet. We reached the redoubt and three attempts were made to storm it but in vain, such was the hail of fire from every side. Then the men just stormed straight over the ramparts. Their fury knew no bounds;

---

[19] Although Kulm was a crushing Allied victory, some of the *Landwehr* battalions had not performed well.

a dreadful slaughter ensued inside, the gunners were cut down by their guns and these were either spiked or thrown off their carriages. All this was the work of ten minutes. The punishment squad particularly distinguished itself in this action.

Clearly we could not hold out for long in the redoubt without reinforcements, but they must surely come because we had pierced the enemy line and it was in the general interest to exploit the chance. Before reinforcements came up two columns of enemy infantry advanced to recapture the redoubt. Twice they were repulsed after heavy fighting. We held on to that which we had taken at such heavy cost. Two other battalions had broken through the enemy line at almost the same time as we had. The right-hand one had pushed back the enemy's flank resting on the Pleisse; our corps made a general advance.

Back in the manor of Markkleeberg, Major Volny led the 1st Battalion Kaunitz in a counter-attack. The fighting was furious. The gatehouse formed an excellent defensive position and, despite their numerical superiority, Aylmard's men could not make headway and their losses mounted. In his report on the combat, Volny wrote: 'At about midday, all the officers except myself were wounded and most of the men were dead or wounded.' They held on despite this and, at about one o'clock, Aylmard pulled his men back towards the Kellerberg. Apparently, Poniatowski saw that there was no serious threat from this quarter and needed Augereau's men to defend the Kellerberg against the Prussian attack from the south. Polish troops were moved down into Markkleeberg to reinforce Augereau's men, while the remaining Austrians were left in possession of Markkleeberg manor house for the rest of the battle.

Markkleeberg, the second phase: the advance of Kleist's 4th Column

The task of Kleist's mixed Russo-Prussian column was to advance north from Cröbern through Crostewitz to take Markkleeberg and Wachau and to occupy the heights between these two villages. The Prussian Colonel von Löbell was sent against Markkleeberg with the 2nd Battalion, 6th Reserve Infantry Regiment, and the 2nd Battalion, 11th Reserve Infantry Regiment. On his right flank was the Russian division of General Helfreich with its four weak regiments each of about 400 men. Further to the right the Lubny Hussars maintained contact with von Klüx's brigade south of Wachau. Following behind this advanced force was the 12th Brigade of Prinz August von Preussen and Major General Lewaschoff's Russian Kürassier brigade.

Despite heavy French artillery fire from the heights of the Kellerberg just west of Markkleeberg, the two Prussian battalions forced their way into the village, threw out Poniatowski's troops, and occupied the track to the sheep farm at Auenhain, which lay in a slight depression. It was 9:30. A bitter combat now developed between the Poles and the Prussians in Markkleeberg, the struggle for possession of which went on all day; sometimes it was in Polish hands, sometimes the Prussians held it, until the latter finally secured a foothold in the southern half of the village from which the Poles were unable to evict them. The French IV Cavalry Corps sought to cut up the Prussians but were taken in flank by Lewaschoff's brigade of Duka's 3rd Kürassier Division and scattered. Two French battalions were thrown into confusion.

To the right of Markkleeberg, Helfreich's weak division advanced as far north as the heights by the Weinteich pond and the Hasenholz wood, where they were forced to halt. Heavy French artillery fire made it impossible for them to stay in this exposed position and they gradually inched their way westwards towards Markkleeberg. This, of course, widened the gap between them and Prinz Eugen's column to their right. In order not to present the enemy with an inviting gap in the Allied line, Kleist despatched Prinz August's 12th Prussian Brigade behind Helfreich's division and onto his right flank. Prinz August attempted to drive north on Dösen with *Oberst* von Schwichow's four battalions (1st Battalion, 2nd Silesian Infantry Regiment, 1st Battalion, 11th Reserve Infantry Regiment, and the 10th *Landwehr* Infantry Regiment) but the much superior II French Corps, supported by Oudinot's Young Guards, forced him back to the line of the road between Markkleeberg and Wachau, where he stood for the rest of the day. The 14th Polish Kürassiers and the Krakus had joined in the pursuit of Kleist's men and Helfreich's division as they fell back, but they were charged and pushed back in turn by the Lubny Hussars and Lewaschoff's Kürassiers.

In this sector of the southern front 33,000 of Napoleon's men had – not surprisingly – staved off the assaults of about 20,000 Allies. The result was a foregone conclusion and the attackers had paid a heavy price for both their temerity and their tactical ineptitude. One wonders how the Duke of Wellington would have managed the Allied troops in this situation. Had Napoleon chosen to counter-attack in force here, the Allies would surely have been scattered.

Wachau: the 3rd Column of Prinz Eugen von Württemberg (II Corps)

It was still dark when Prinz Eugen von Württemberg, in Göhren, ordered his 3rd Column to advance on Wachau. The Russians stumbled into position north of Güldengossa in the dark and deployed a battery of twenty-four guns to their front, which opened an effective fire on the French, both in the village and on the Galgenberg to its east. This barrage was at once answered by a massive French battery of over 100 guns arranged along the heights from Wachau to Liebertwolkwitz. Victor's II Corps had spent the night in Markkleeberg and Wachau, but between eight and nine o'clock on the morning of the 16th he evacuated Wachau and withdrew to the heights north of the village, where Napoleon had concentrated this battery.

Shortly after the bombardment began, twenty-four more Russian guns joined those already deployed, but even their combined fire could not equal that of the French. Even so, despite the hail of projectiles Colonel von Reibnitz led three Russian battalions (of the Minsk and Tobolsk regiments) and three Prussian battalions in a determined assault on Wachau. It was 9:30 am, and Kleist's column had just stormed into Markkleeberg for the first time, while Gortschakoff's 2nd Column had just arrived before Liebertwolkwitz. The three Allied monarchs had meanwhile arrived on the Wachtberg, about 700 metres south of Güldengossa and just east of the Wachau-Göhren road, just after nine o'clock, where they joined Barclay de Tolly.

A Russian officer recorded in his diary how the French guns tore into von Reibnitz's advancing Russian and Prussian battalions:

> Thunder roared, the ground quaked, sparks and flames shot through the air, splinters ripped into us; smoke and flames, blood and death were all around us. In a few minutes seventeen Russian and five Prussian guns lay smashed on the ground. Colonel von Reibnitz, who had led the first assault on Wachau, was carried back, badly wounded. The triumphant enemy pressed hard on the heels of the few survivors of his brigade who followed behind him. Our main line stood in the face of this shock as if turned to stone.

'I said this would happen!' said Prinz Eugen.

'That won't help us now!', interrupted General Prince Schachafskoi, commander of the 3rd Division. 'We are all being killed; the artillery is withdrawing already.'

'Everyone stand fast!' shouted Prinz Eugen. 'Not a man who can still stand will leave his place!' Adjutants and orderlies rushed away to relay the order and to bring back those units which had begun to retreat.

Of his twenty-four twelve-pounders, Eugen had soon lost twenty-three dismounted. But the contest was not all one-sided. By eleven o'clock eleven of the II French Cavalry Corps' thirty-two guns had also been dismounted, while in Bordesoulle's 1st Heavy Cavalry Division, I Cavalry Corps, Colonels Rollaud and de Lacroix, twenty-two officers and 181 men were killed or wounded between nine and eleven o' clock, while the Saxon Kürassier Regiment lost over 200 all ranks.[20]

A second assault was now mounted by the Prussians. Von Klüx's 9th Prussian Brigade pushed forward to within 400 metres of Wachau and occupied the tiny alder wood just to its south-east, but were unable to get into the village itself. However, the Füsilier Battalion, 1st East Prussian Infantry Regiment, and the 1st Battalion, 6th Reserve Infantry Regiment, managed to force their way in, but were swiftly ejected by the superior garrison. The

---

[20] Zelle, p.403, attributes these losses to 'Berckheim's cuirassier brigade'. Berckheim commanded the 1st Light Cavalry Division in this corps.

greater part of these two battalions gradually found its way to a shallow depression just south of the village, where they were sheltered from the French artillery fire. Here they were joined by the two battalions of the 7th Silesian *Landwehr* Infantry Regiment and by two Russian infantry regiments which had advanced from the Auenhain sheep farm to form up on von Klüx's left.

Scarcely had these latter arrived when this composite force mounted a third assault on Wachau between ten and eleven o'clock. The Russians stormed right through the village and out onto the heights to the north, where, however, they were ripped to pieces by close-range French artillery fire. The French then retook both the heights and the village, and the Allies had then to prevent them from advancing south out of Wachau.

Prussian casualties mounted rapidly. The 1st Battalion, 18th Reserve Infantry Regiment, was reduced from 600 men to just eight NCOs and sixty-eight men, all of whom were wounded, while the 7th Silesian *Landwehr* Infantry Regiment shrank from 1,800 men to 160.

The French made repeated attempts to recapture the alder wood held by von Klüx's brigade, the officers leading the way with their shakos on the points of their swords to inspire their men. When this tactic failed, they resorted to beating the men forward with their swords. The Prussian sharp-shooters' answer to these tactics was to let the French advance to within 200 paces, shoot down the easily identifiable officers, and then drive the leaderless men back with their well-aimed fire.

The situation of the Russians on von Klüx's right, in the open fields in front of the Galgenberg, was much worse. Lacking any cover at all, they suffered very heavy losses from artillery fire. Schachafskoi, who commanded here, reported to Prinz Eugen that his men were being destroyed. The prince rode slowly along the line. At each battalion, his question 'How many men have you lost?' would be answered with a silent gesture to the lines of dead lying where they had fallen. Already, seventeen of the twenty-three operational Russian guns in this sector had been disabled and lay wrecked on the ground. Württemberg did nothing to alleviate the situation, however, and the losses of the 3rd and 4th Russian divisions mounted steadily throughout the morning. That the prince – young and inexperienced though he was – lacked sufficient initiative to move his divisions out of the French line of fire, or to at least have them lay down, beggars belief. It was Borodino all over again (where Prinz Eugen had commanded the 4th Infantry Division); the Russian commanders had learned nothing and continued to squander their men to absolutely no avail, as the final casualties of this excessively bloody affair would demonstrate.

One Russian observer has left us this somewhat romantic pen-picture of our young hero this day: 'We saw him, the tall youth, the embodiment of hope, blind and deaf to the dangers, death and terrors around him; with his slim pale face framed by his dark brown locks riding like an angel of death through the ranks.' However, not even the prince was immune to the attentions of the French barrage. While a colonel of artillery was reporting that his guns were almost all out of action and that enemy cavalry was advancing; a French cannonball went through the neck of the prince's horse and wounded the colonel in the stomach. Both men were thrown to the ground, and the colonel shouted to the prince: 'You see we're not in Abraham's lap here!'

Despite their monstrous losses, the Russians held fast in front of the Galgenberg and the Prussians hung on in the alder wood at Wachau, but in the face of such overwhelming French artillery fire there was no question of any Allied advance in this sector. The Russian colonels Feodoroff, Stepanoff and Boristoff were all killed, as were the commander of the 7th Silesian *Landwehr* Infantry Regiment, Major Kickebusch, and all his officers, before finally – far too late – a little common-sense prevailed upon our pale-faced hero and he pulled what was left of his column back south onto Güldengossa. The battlefield he left behind was reminiscent of that of Lützen almost a hundred years before, where the positions of the steady Swedish regiments could be clearly distinguished by the tidy rows of their dead.

Colonel Marbot, of the 23*e* Chasseurs à Cheval, could have taught many of the senior commanders present on both sides a lesson in the economy of human life. He related the following as, in Markranstadt on 19 October, he tallied up the losses of his regiment:

I used the time to inform myself of the losses of my squadrons over the last three days; I was shocked at what I found. The list totalled 169 men, of which sixty were dead including two captains, three lieutenants and eleven NCOs. As we had a strength of 700 on the 16th, this was a large percentage. Most of the wounded had gunshot wounds which boded ill for their recovery. Perhaps our losses would have been twice as great if I had not taken every opportunity to keep my regiment out of artillery fire. I must explain this.

There are situations and occasions in which even the most humane commander of a large formation of troops must expose his men to fire even though they are not directly involved in the battle. It is sometimes the case, however, that when this is not so, ie when the terrain offers cover, that it is not used and thus needless casualties occur. With cavalry, this will be able to be done without risk as, due to their speed of movement, they can rapidly be where they are needed when the moment arrives.

For large masses of cavalry on extended battlefields it should almost always be possible to do this, but it is often ignored.

I witnessed this on the 16th October. General Sebastiani stood with his three cavalry divisions between Wachau and Liebertwolkwitz and had indicated to each one the position that they were to occupy. Exelmans' division was posted in slightly hilly terrain with plenty of hollows. The enemy cavalry was so far off, that there was no danger of them surprising us. I thus used the hollows in my section of terrain to shield my squadrons from the enemy artillery fire. Due to this tactic, I did not lose a man for some considerable time whereas the other regiments had fairly heavy losses. One might have expected that this measure would have earned the praise of the divisional commander but not a bit of it! General Exelmans rode up and ordered me, despite all the protests of my brigade commander, to advance 100 paces, as each regiment must have its share of danger.

I obeyed, of course, and in a short period lost a captain and some twenty men killed and wounded. This completely needless loss enraged me considerably, and ever after this, throughout the rest of the war, I always made it my first duty to preserve the lives of my men as much as possible. The losses of my regiment were always noticeably lower than those of our other regiments, and it gave me much satisfaction to see that my tactic gained much respect and imitation not only among my equals, but also from the corps commander, in contrast to General Exelmans.

***

Shortly after eleven o'clock, Napoleon, being now convinced that the Allies before his southern front were really as weak as they initially seemed, decided to go over to the offensive. Augereau's IX Corps had moved south from Sommerfeld and entered the line of battle at Dösen. I Cavalry Corps came forward to face Wachau, as did the 3rd and 4th Divisions of the Young Guard. The 1st and 2nd Divisions of the Young Guard advanced to north of Liebertwolkwitz and II Cavalry Corps moved up to Klein-Pössna on the eastern flank.

Their tasks were outlined as follows:

'Macdonald's II Corps is to assault the Allied right wing at the Kolmberg and Seyffertshain.

'Murat, with 8–10,000 cavalry, is to break the Allied line between Wachau and Meusdorf.

'Kellermann's IV Cavalry Corps and part of Victor's II Corps are to attack Kleist's Prussians between Wachau and Markkleeberg and to retake the latter place.'

Between one and two o'clock Victor's II Corps bore down on Wachau with the 2nd Division of the Old Guard in support. The weaker Allies in this sector had no alternative but to fall back south past the sheep pens at Auenhain, which were stormed and occupied by Victor's corps at two o'clock. At the same time, Macdonald's XI Corps pushed Klenau's column back and Mortier's II Corps of the Old Guard assaulted the Universitätsholz south of Gross-Pössna at the junction between Ziethen's Prussian brigade of Klenau's 1st Column and Gortschakoff's 2nd Column.

In the Wachau sector things stagnated for about an hour. This is not to say that there was no fighting; the exchange of artillery fire here continued unabated as before. The Auenhain sheep pens were held by General Dubreton's 4th Division, against whom the shattered remnants of Eugen von Württemberg's corps had no chance of success, with most of their artillery dismounted and confronted with the crushing power of the great 100-gun battery at Wachau.

At three o'clock Napoleon ordered Murat's great cavalry force to move against the thin Allied centre and the French artillery battery fell silent as the cavalry obscured their field of fire. This force was so powerful (I and V Cavalry Corps and the cavalry of the Imperial Guard – some 8–10,000 men in all) that they penetrated past Güldengossa, forcing everything out of their way. But the charge was made at too fast a pace too soon, and the horses – already in poor condition even before the battle – were soon blown and could not be pushed any further. Nor had any French infantry or artillery units been sent with them to consolidate their gains. It was a foretaste of Waterloo. When the Allied cavalry counter-attacked the isolated Frenchmen were consequently dispersed and driven back to their own lines. A great opportunity had been missed, but as Murat's exhausted cavalry left the field their artillery at once began to play on the pursuing Allied regiments, who were repulsed in their turn.

On the eastern half of the battlefield, Mortier's men were thrown out of the Universitätsholz by the Austrians and Prussians under Klenau at about four o'clock.

Prince Gortschakoff's 2nd Column

The aim of the 2nd Column was, in co-operation with Klenau's 1st Column on its right, to take Liebertwolkwitz, the left wing bastion of the French line, which was held by Lauriston's V Corps of 13,500 men. Gortschakoff was to assault from the south, while Klenau was to make a right hook and come in from the east.

Whilst waiting for Klenau's 27,000 men to advance from Gross-Pössna though Seifertshain and get into position so that a simultaneous attack could be mounted on the target, Gortschakoff (who could clearly hear the musketry and artillery fire from Markkleeberg and Wachau) advanced independently towards Liebertwolkwitz with his 9,000 men and opened fire on it with his artillery. The Russian infantry and the 10th Prussian Brigade of General Pirch meanwhile waited patiently in line throughout the morning as their artillery deployed and engaged the enemy. Count Pahlen's 5,400-strong cavalry made an abortive assault on the Galgenberg and then also retired behind their artillery to await a more favourable opportunity.

It was at about this time that Schwarzenberg began to send his Austrians back to the main scene of the fighting. His Adjutant, Major Ritter von Böhm, noted in his diary that the decision was made at eleven o'clock. He also states that von Langenau was still with him and remained convinced that his plan would work.

Meanwhile, the Czar had already taken the decision to bring forward the cavalry of the Russian Imperial Guard from Rötha to Cröbern and the low ridge around the Wachtberg. Duka's 3rd Russian Kürassier Division and Rajewski's Grenadier Corps were sent forward to the sheep farm at Auenhain behind what was left of Prinz Eugen's corps. The infantry of the Russo-Prussian guard were ordered forward from Rötha to Magdeborn. Common-sense was at last beginning to prevail among the Allied commanders, and not a moment too soon.

***

At 9:00 am Napoleon had joined Murat on the Galgenberg (Gallows Hill), an insignificant pimple on the landscape between Wachau and Liebertwolkwitz. This position is today marked by an uninspiring square block monument. A few moments sufficed for the Emperor to take in the weak enemy columns advancing over the wide plain towards him and to realise what had to be done to thwart the Allies' plan. Augereau's IX Corps at Zuckelhausen was moved west to Dösen, as was Letort's 2nd Brigade of the 3rd Cavalry Division of the Guard, to support Poniatowski in his struggle against Kleist. Oudinot's two divisions of the Young Guard were transferred west from behind Liebertwolkwitz to north of Wachau to join Victor's II Corps. Friant's division and the cavalry of the Old Guard took post on the heights just south of the sheep farm at Meusdorf behind the centre of the French position. Curial's 2nd Division of the Old Guard was brought forward to behind Lauriston's V Corps west of Liebertwolkwitz, while I and V Cavalry Corps came up to the centre of the line, just north of the Galgenberg.

By 11:00 am the inadequate Allied assaults from the south had lost their momentum and ground to a halt. Although they hung on grimly to their positions, the French counter-attacks steadily increased in ferocity and strength. At Markkleeberg Kleist was now hammered not only by Poniatowski but also by Semelle's division of Augereau's IX Corps. West of the village Sokolnicki's IV Cavalry Corps repeatedly charged Prinz August's brigade and Helfreich's Russian division, but were beaten off by Prussian artillery and *Schützen* from their position in a sunken road and by counter-charges by Lewaschoff's Russian Kürassier brigade and the Lubny Hussars. The Russian cavalry careered on to attack the French infantry, which was advancing behind their cavalry, and caught them unawares. Many of the infantry lost fingers and hands as they sought to protect themselves from the Kürassiers swords by holding their muskets over their heads.

Letort's Guards cavalry (Grenadiers à Cheval and the Lancers of Berg) and Berckheim's 1st Light Cavalry Division, I Cavalry Corps, now entered the struggle and overpowered the Russian cavalry which sought to oppose them. The French advance on Auenhain was unstoppable, and the Allies had to retire south-west into Crostewitz and Cröbern with their backs against the Gösel stream. The Russian and Prussian infantry on the plain quickly formed square in the face of this threat, but for some it was a vain effort. The 1st Battalion of the Krementschug was ridden down and utterly destroyed; 300 corpses marked its last stand.

One of Rajewski's grenadier divisions now came up from Göhren on Kleist's right wing, and the latter attempted another assault on the heights between Markkleeberg and Wachau with his last reserve, the 12th Prussian Brigade. Together with Helfreich's Russians and Löbell's troops which had been forced to abandon Markkleeberg, they stormed up the slopes again. A murderous hail of musket and artillery fire from the French and Polish defenders cut through their ranks; almost at the crest of the ridge the Russo-Prussians gave way to the inevitable and tumbled back down, much reduced in numbers. Only on the west flank could they achieve local success, where Löbell's two battalions – supported by the newly arrived Füsilier Battalion of the 2nd Silesian Infantry Regiment – forced their way into Markkleeberg and took possession of its central and southern parts. Despite the Poles' best efforts they held on here for the rest of the action.

At about midday the Saxon Kürassier brigade of Latour-Maubourg's I Cavalry Corps was transferred from east of Wachau to the west, from where they witnessed (with no small pleasure) the defeat of Letort's Dragoons of the Imperial Guard. This friction between the allies had been generated by the sustained brutality and licentiousness of the French regiment towards the unfortunate local Saxon population, and there had been several fights between the regiments in bivouac. To the eternal credit of the Saxon Kürassiers, they remained faithful to Napoleon and followed him back to France, where he dismissed them with a letter of commendation for their fidelity and service.

The Saxons were now ordered forward to support Berckheim's light cavalry brigade. They moved off at a trot westwards in the direction of Dösen, and just north of Markkleeberg they came across about twenty unlimbered French artillery pieces, in a line facing south, abandoned by their crews and teams and without any escort. The Saxons then came under fire from Polish-held Dösen, probably because in their white coats, yellow facings and black breastplates they had been mistaken for Austrians.

When Kleist's column was forced back by Augereau and Victor, this left Prinz Eugen's 3rd Column before Wachau in an exposed and isolated position. If the Russians could do anything well, it was to die. The great French battery on the Galgenberg heights had been further reinforced by General Drouot, and its volleys of shot and shell now ripped great swathes of death and destruction through the ranks of the Russians so needlessly and stupidly sacrificed by their commanders. But they did not flinch or flee; they stood their ground and were swept uselessly away.

Behind the Galgenberg battery the regiments of the French I Cavalry Corps formed up, waiting for the right opportunity to attack. By this point its commander, Latour-Maubourg, had lost his leg to a cannonball and General Doumerc had taken over. Latour-Maubourg's indomitable spirit may be shown by the fact that he rebuked his weeping valet with: 'Why are you crying you imbecile? You have one less boot to polish!'

Captain Dionysios Charles Parquin, a French cavalry officer, later recalled an incident involving Marshal Oudinot in this sector of the battlefield:

General Lauriston's men defended Wachau bravely; it was taken and then retaken by General Latour-Maubourg's cavalry. That general had lost a leg at about midday with a cannonball. At the same time, General Cöhorn lost both legs to a ball which went straight through the belly of his horse.

Generals Vial and Rochambeau were killed today; the latter had fought with General Lafayette in America.

The cavalry of the Guard stood in order of battle in the centre of the army. I can still see before me General Drouot, on foot, directing the fire of a battery of 100 guns of the Guard with great energy.

As the Emperor had noticed that the right wing, consisting of 19,000 men of the Young Guard under Marshal Oudinot, was in danger, he sent General Letort with 800 cavalry to support him. They consisted of 200 men each of the Chasseurs, Lancers, Dragoons and Grenadiers à Cheval, all of the Old Guard.

The Duc de Reggio [Marshal Oudinot] had already changed his formation from line into squares. I was in the force which the Emperor had sent; we reached the right wing by a flank march, at the trot, in column of platoons. When we arrived, we formed line in the space between two squares.

An attack made on us by Austrian cavalry failed completely and, in fact, gave us a great victory. Due to the position that we had taken up on the field, all escape routes were cut off for the Latour Dragoon Regiment. Their only possible salvation lay in breaking through our line in order to get back to their own.

Marshal Oudinot suddenly rode out of a square and into our line and shouted: 'About turn, riders! There comes an attack!'

In truth, the Latour Dragoons were bearing down on us in a cloud of dust;[21] we faced them like an iron wall and 190–200 fell into our hands.

At this moment, I saw Marshal Oudinot in the middle of the melee, trying unsuccessfully to draw his sword. I saw the danger of his predicament and lost no time in placing myself in front of him with my sabre in my hand. At this critical moment, his excellency drew his pistol and I had the good fortune to save him. The Duc de Reggio was able to reach the safety of one of his squares again.

That evening, I was taken to the marshal's bivouac by his son who was a captain in our regiment. The marshal embraced me, thanked me and shared his modest supper with me. We washed it down with a bottle of wine and a glass of brandy.

***

At 1:30 pm Bordesoulle's 1st Heavy Cavalry Division (2,500 men) deployed for attack. This consisted of the French cuirassier brigades of Bessières and Sopranski and the Saxon brigade of General Lessing, although this latter now had only the *Garde du Corps* since the von Zastrow Kürassiers had been sent off to act against Markkleeberg. Lessing and Sopranski were to assault the Russian batteries to their front, while Bessières' brigade was to follow up in rear as reserve.

---

[21] This cannot be correct; it had been raining hard for days.

The sodden ground and numerous small ditches and watercourses slowed the progress of the charge and canister fire from the target batteries ripped many a rider from his saddle as the regiments clattered southwards on Güldengossa. Part of the Russian artillery limbered up and withdrew before the cuirassiers could catch them, and Russian cavalry joined the melee around the remaining guns. A desperate struggle now took place for possession of the immobilised cannon, until the much-reduced Saxons were eventually victorious. However, when they tried to bring off their prizes this was found to be impossible due to the lack of horses. A Russian cavalry counter-attack then swept down on them and they were forced to race back to their own lines, taking with them only one ammunition waggon and some artillery team horses.

During this combat two Russian dragoons were in the act of overpowering the commander of the Saxon Garde du Corps, Colonel von Berge, when he was rescued by Sergeant Dutzschky, who cut one of them down; the other fled. A little later Dutzschky also rescued *Leutnant* Trützschler of the Garde du Corps from as many as five Russian troopers.

Meanwhile, Sopranski's three regiments had advanced to the left of the Saxons, towards Liebertwolkwitz, where they took a battery of twenty-six Russian guns about a kilometres north of Güldengossa. Their further progress was barred by the defiant squares of Schachoffskoi's division. Bessières' brigade, in the second line, charged straight against the north side of Güldengossa, where they were confronted by the eighteen squadrons of the Russian Imperial Guard cavalry under General Schewitsch, who was killed almost instantly, while General Dawidoff and the other Russian commanders were wounded. The Russian charge consequently ground to a halt in confusion, then fell back south towards Göhren.

It was at about this time that a shell exploded under the horse of Count Pajol, the commander of V Cavalry Corps, breaking his left arm and several ribs and throwing him twenty-five feet into the air. Miraculously, he survived.

Bordesoulle's cuirassiers swept on in pursuit of the Russians over the open, pond-dotted meadows, dangerously close to the Wachtberg, where the Allied monarchs and their retinues stood. Prinz Schwarzenberg – who by this time had taken up his proper place at the centre of affairs – had to request his regal allies to retire. The thin Allied line was about to be pierced. If Napoleon threw infantry after his victorious cavalry, the battle would be won. But the Emperor was no longer watching the progress on his southern front at Wachau; he had left to join Marmont in the north at Möckern.

Just at this critical moment, General Duka's Küirassier Division arrived at Güldengossa. Prinz Eugen led one of the regiments against the front of Bessières' brigade, Duka led the other two into the enemy's flank. Orloff-Dennisoff now joined in with the Cossacks of the Russian Imperial Guard and a battery of Russian artillery was deployed behind a pond to play on the French cavalry. A little to the east of Güldengossa, Count Pahlen's attention was drawn to the turmoil around the Wachtberg and he sent the Neumark Dragoons to investigate. When its commander saw Bessières' cuirassiers thundering down on the Allied commanders' hillock, he ordered his regiment and the Silesian Ulans to charge them in flank. This attack was successful, and Bessières' regiments were driven back in confusion onto Drouot's battery.

Schwarzenberg's Adjutant, Major Böhm, had also been active. He gathered together about 300 Russian Guards cavalry and the skirmishers of the Neumark Dragoons and led them in a charge into the flank of Bordesoulle's cuirassiers as they milled around the captured twenty-six gun battery, causing them to stagger back. At the same time, Schwarzenberg mounted his English thoroughbred mare Favorita, set himself at the head of the Cossacks of the Russian Imperial Guard together with Radetzky, and charged the Frenchmen frontally. Bordesoulle's men wavered under these two assaults, then suddenly broke and fled, abandoning twenty of the captured Russian guns. The crisis was over. That the Allied commander-in-chief, his chief of staff and one of his adjutants were involved in a cavalry melee (in which Radetzky was wounded) indicates just how critical the situation must have been.

Murat had not thought to form a reserve for this massed charge. Some French accounts consequently accuse him of having acted treacherously here, but this is most unlikely.

Zelle has another version of events at this point. According to him, the charge of the Neumark Dragoons and that of the Cossacks of the Guard were repulsed, and it was the Silesian Kürassiers who saved the day, and were reduced to a mere two squadrons during the action: 'Pahlen had also sent the Silesian Kürassiers to support the other two Prussian regiments but they were not needed and remained behind to cover the withdrawal of Klüx's brigade and Schachoffskoi's division which had been formed in square to receive the cuirassiers.' Average strength in each of these two formations was now down to about 100 men.

It was at about this time – 2:00 pm – that the first of Nostitz's Kürassier regiments came north out of Cröbern after having crossed the Pleisse. This was the point at which Prinz August's Prussian brigade and Helfreich's Russians were being pressed back on Crostewitz and Cröbern and Letort's and Sokolnicki's horse were overpowering Lewaschoff's Kürassiers in front of the latter village. The first of Nostitz's Austrian cavalry regiments to reach the endangered section of the southern front from the Elster-Pleisse swamps was the Sommariva Kürassiers. They went into action at once, south of Markkleeberg, against Berckheim's light cavalry brigade, which broke and fled – closely followed by the Austrians – north-eastwards towards Dösen and Probstheida. The Saxons who had been sent to help Berckheim's brigade were swept along with them.

A Saxon officer who took part in this action recalled the event as follows:

When we reached Berckheim, his men were mixed up with the enemy in individual squadrons, so that there were Austrian units to the north of the French Chevaulégers. We Saxons had only just come up when Berckheim rallied his men to face the ever-increasing enemy pressure. But they could not stand even though General Berckheim – bareheaded, as his hat had been knocked off – threw himself into the thick of the melee. He was also swept back in the flood of fugitives who streamed through and around us. Despite this chaos, we stood fast and hacked away at the Austrians. Shortly before they charged us, the Austrians had shouted to us to come over to them; we ignored them. However, we were overpowered and broken. The chase now went on at speed, friend and foe all mixed up together, racing over the plain.

The mad ride continued from the ponds at Dösen as far as Meusdorf. Here we came upon a French square which fired at the Austrians, which stopped them. At this, the mob of fleeing riders pulled up, turned back and counter-charged the enemy, capturing about eighty of them who had ventured too far ahead.

According to Seyfert, the Grenadiers à Cheval of the Imperial Guard were overthrown after a long and bitter melee. As they fled the field the Austrian Kürassiers went after them and crashed into the left flank of Oudinot's Young Guard, throwing them into some confusion. The Guard quickly recovered and fired a volley into the Austrian cavalry, driving them off.

In the meantime, the other two regiments of Nostitz's cavalry division had deployed north of Cröbern; they took up their retreating comrades, who reformed behind them. The day saw no further French cavalry attacks in this sector. According to Zelle (p.415) Austrian Kürassier losses in this action were: Albert Regiment, 128; Franz Regiment, 75; Kronprinz Regiment, 19; Lothringen Regiment, 192; and Sommariva Regiment, 352. Apparently, this episode took place between Wachau and Meusdorf, in the vicinity of Napoleon. The Emperor, as a matter of precaution, rode a few hundred paces to the rear into the midst of the Old Guard, which rapidly formed a protective square around him.

***

Some idea of how badly the Russians and Prussians in the Güldengossa sector suffered between 2:30 and 3:30 this day can be gathered from the memoirs of a Russian adjutant:

> Now all hell was really let loose. It seemed impossible that there could be any space between the bullets and balls which rained onto us. I just thought: 'Now, with God, forwards! I'll get crucified and it's the quintessence of my *kantschu* [whip] for my fine Kalmuck grey!' Now I rode like the wind along the line almost to the extreme right wing. At this point an entire artillery park was about to ride off. 'Halt! Halt!' I shouted and had almost caught up with them when a cannonball suddenly hit my fine grey in the belly and threw us both to the ground.
>
> For some time I lay unconscious under my horse; when I came to, I had a dreadful suspicion that my legs were gone. I lay there in my desperate plight. Cannon rattled past me with their crews running behind. I lost sight of them. Bullets and balls ripped through the air and smashed into the ground

around me, as if God had unleashed all the furies of hell. Finally two gunners came by and helped me, God bless them! They pulled me out from
under my horse and I was able to see that my legs were intact. I staggered to
my feet and hobbled off behind the gunners; I had to get back to my unit
and find another mount. Suddenly the thunder of the artillery stopped.
From the direction of the front came a dull, deep rumbling noise, like the
rattling of a thousand heavy chains. It was the sound of hooves and weapons.
I turned towards the source and saw the entire might of the cuirassiers and
dragoons of the 14th in full career against a dismounted adjutant, armed
only with his broken sabre and a *kantschu*! Luckily, Güldengossa was only a
few metres off to the left and I did not fail to take advantage of its cover. By
good fortune I found a friend there who organised another horse for me
and I was soon able to rejoin the Prinz von Württemberg.

A Prussian officer in von Klüx's brigade at Wachau, *Leutnant* Freiherr von
Firks, who was wounded in the leg during a cavalry charge, has also left us his
account of the day:

> A *Schützen* carried me back out of the firing line. Behind the brigade were
> many wounded, walking back or being carried back. Suddenly we heard a
> murderous artillery barrage from the direction of Wachau and my assistant
> dropped me and ran off. I fell onto a dead gunner. Soon after, several
> French dragoons, who were ahead of their column, passed by but took no
> notice of me. Three hundred paces behind followed a column of French
> dragoons, cuirassiers and grenadiers, coming on at a trot. It had a frontage
> of one regiment and was at least ten regiments deep. I was lucky enough to
> be able to grab the hay rack on the back of a passing Russian ammunition
> waggon which carried me away from the enemy column, over the mill dam
> of Güldengossa to the Wachtberg, where I found my horse, which I was able
> to mount.

The attack of Maison's division and Lauriston's V Corps on Güldengossa

The assault of Bessières' and Bordesoulle's cavalry brigades on Prinz Eugen
von Württemberg's infantry north-west of Güldengossa was supported by a
simultaneous attack by Lauriston's V Corps against Gortschakoff to the
north-east, just after three o'clock. On this flank it was Maison's division
which sought to break the fragile Allied line. Maison was one of Napoleon's
bravest and most capable generals; if anyone could crack this nut, it was he.
    Colonel von Jagow's three Prussian battalions, which formed the garrison
of Güldengossa and of the manor house, were pushed back from its northern
outskirts to about the centre of the village, but at about four o'clock – just in
the nick of time – Allied reinforcements arrived. These consisted of the first
battalions of the Russo-Prussian guards, who had come up from Magdeborn
in the south and stopped the French advance. West of Güldengossa, the two

The three Allied monarchs: King Friedrich Wilhelm III of Prussia (left), Kaiser Franz I of Austria (centre) and Czar Alexander I of Russia (right). The figure to the right of the Czar would seem to be *Feldmarschall* Schwarzenberg.

Napoleon, dictating orders to Marshal Berthier, in the midst of his staff.

The Inner Grimma Gate on 14 October; French wounded from Liebertwolkwitz enter the city.

The Young Guard take on Russian hussars at Leipzig.

Above: Fighting during the battle of Möckern, 16 October.
Below left: Marshal Michel Ney commanded the Northern Front during the battle of Leipzig.
Below right: Marshal Macdonald commanded XI Corps at Leipzig.

Above left: *Feldmarschall* Prince Carl von Schwarzenberg, Allied supreme commander. He wears the Order of the Golden Fleece, the Grand Cross of the Order of Maria Theresia and the Order of Leopold.

Above right: General von Langenau, Schwarzenberg's Quartermaster General. Originally in Saxon service, he made a very successful career in the Imperial Austrian Army.

Below left: Kaiser Franz I of Austria. Despite twenty years of defeats at the hands of the French, Austria's dogged persistence finally tipped the scales against Napoleon in 1813.

Below right: *Feldmarschall* Gebhard Blücher, pictured after the battle, wearing the Grand Star of the Iron Cross.

Above left: General Ziethen's Prussians took Zuckelhausen on 18 October.
Above right: King Friedrich Wilhelm III of Prussia.

Below left: Ludwig Freiherr von Wolzogen, here in Prussian uniform, was involved in several crucial decisions during the battle. He eventually became General of Infantry in Prussian service and was the author of a valuable set of memoirs.
Below right: Grand Prince Constantine, the Czesarawitsch, brother of Czar Alexander I of Russia.

Above left: General of Cavalry Count Wittgenstein. He wears the cross of the Order of Saint George 1st Class.
Above right: Jean-Baptiste Jules Bernadotte, the Crown Prince of Sweden.
Below: Leipzig, 16 October. Yorck's troops in action at Gross-Wiederitzsch.

Leipzig, 18 October. The Austrians storm Holzhausen.

Leipzig, 18 October. The Austrians storm Macdonald's headquarters in Holzhausen.

Leipzig, 18 October. The struggle for Probstheida.

Right: Quandt's tobacco mill; site of Napoleon's headquarters on 18 October, and that of the three monarchs the next day.

Below : Leipzig, 19 October. The flight of the French across the Fleischerplatz.

Leipzig, 19 October. The storm of the Outer Grimma Gate.

Leipzig, 19 October. The demolition of the Elster bridge.

Right: French prisoners of war in Leipzig.

Below: A view of the Halle Gate after the battle.

The Prussian Landwehr celebrate victory on 19 October.

Below left: One of the Apel stones marking the site of the Allied position prior to the storm of Schönefeld on 18 October. Stones marking Allied positions have pointed tops and are evenly numbered in Dr Apel's scheme; they also bear a 'V' on the top for *Verbundeten* (Allies). Stones marking French positions have odd numbers, round tops and bear an 'N' for Napoleon.

Below right: The Dölitz manor gatehouse, taken from the eastern side. The several cannon balls embedded in the wall are highlighted by black paint.

Aerial photograph of the Markkleeberg manor house taken in 1938. The view is from the south and the moat has been filled in. The church may be mostly original but it was certainly damaged in 1813. The manor house itself was demolished after 1947. This picture was kindly provided by Mr Wolfgang Gerlach, president of the historical society dedicated to preserving the gatehouse.

The monument to the Battle of the Nations in the Marienbrunn suburb of Leipzig.

Left: The Russian memorial church. The Russians lost more than 22,000 men at Leipzig.

Right: The Austrian memorial to Graf Bubna at Paunsdorf church.

Prussian Guards regiments and the Garde-Jägers advanced up the road towards Wachau (now the Bornaische Strasse) to a point level with the Auenhain sheep farm. The Russian Leib-Grenadiers, both battalions of the Finland Guards Regiment and some other units advanced to the east of the village at the double. This effective reinforcement caused the French to evacuate Güldengossa, but the dark masses of their reserves on the heights to the north made any further Allied progress impossible.

Maison in person led a second assault on the eastern side of the village but this was repelled by the Russians there, who had now been joined by some *Landwehr* and Jäger regiments. Maison received two bayonet wounds and owed his escape to the speed of his horse. His 16th Division fell back on Liebertwolkwitz in confusion. General Mandeville, one of his brigade commanders, was killed. The Russians followed up at once, but could get no further forward than the ridge before being thrown back in their turn. The crisis in this sector was over, however, and Güldengossa remained in Allied hands. Napoleon's attempt to smash through the Allied front had been frustrated, and Austrian help was about to arrive to the west at Crostewitz, where the hard-pressed Kleist was still hanging on.

Markkleeberg: the arrival of the Austrian reserves

It was now four o'clock and the infantry of Hessen-Homburg's Austrian Reserve Corps, with Bianchi's division in the lead, had left Gautsch and struggled south through the brush and swamps to cross the Pleisse at Grossdeuben (now Debitzbeuden). As the bridge here was broken, *Feldmarschall-Leutnant* Bianchi had to cross the swollen river by a ford pointed out to him by a local resident. This caused considerable delay. They then pushed on northwards to cross the Gösel stream into Cröbern (the stream and village no longer exist), which was filled with Kleist's Prussian infantry and Russian artillery trains. Weissenwolf's division, following behind Bianchi's, had to cope with the same problems and difficulties.

It required Herculean efforts on the part of Bianchi and his staff to force a way through the clutter of cannon, limbers, ammunition waggons, infantry and wounded which choked the narrow lanes. Once through, the battalions and regiments had to reform before the advance could continue. This all took time, and time was in very short supply, as Victor's II Corps and the Young Guard had already taken the Auenhain sheep farm. Letort's dragoons and Sokolnicki's Polish lancers were pushing Kleist's brigades back against Crostewitz, and Prinz August's brigade, Helfreich's division and Lewaschoff's kürassiers south on Cröbern and the swampy Gösel stream. The Allied left wing was in serious trouble, although Kleist's men still hung on grimly at Markkleeberg.

As soon as he was able to, Bianchi went into action. He formed two columns of attack. Graf Haugwitz, with the Hessen-Homburg infantry regiment, reinforced by the Regiment Simbschen, was sent north-east on

Wachau, whilst Bianchi himself led the four battalions of the Regiments Colloredo-Mansfeld and Hiller (with one Battalion Esterhazy as reserve) north-west against Markkleeberg. Haugwitz's column soon neared the French-held Auenhain sheep farm which, with its quadrangle of buildings, stood like a bastion before the Allied line. Its garrison, formed from Dubreton's 4th Division of Victor's corps, had loopholed the walls to improve the defences. Rajewski had already tried to take the place, but despite the bravery of his grenadiers he had been thrown back.

As the Austrians came up, Dubreton's men fired into their left flank. The Austrian commander at once changed direction and charged the farm but was rapidly beaten off. It was not until Weissenwolf's division of the Austrian Reserve finally scrambled through Cröbern that a combined Allied assault achieved success.

Weissenwolf recorded the action in his battle report as follows:

I had the first battalions which came through Cröbern advance [against Auenhain] in *Sturmschritt* [at the charge]. At about five o'clock Colonel Dressery with the 1st Battalion Simbschen, supported by my battalions Call, Fischer, and Portner, made a second charge on Auenhain.

The Simbschen battalion swung to the right to bayonet charge the French drawn up behind the farm. Grenadier Battalion Call, supported by the artillery, advanced straight at the sheep farm despite the enemy canister fire and took it.

Dressery overthrew the French infantry behind the farm and drove them back over the meadows but a counter-attack by their cavalry forced him to form square quickly and to retire.

Meanwhile, the Austrian grenadiers broke into the sheep farm, cut down or captured the garrison and recovered a colour which had been taken from the Russians. They held the buildings through the night despite the fact that a French shell exploded an ammunition waggon inside the courtyard and killed many of the garrison, which now consisted of the grenadier battalions Fischer and Portner; the Simbschen battalion was in support.

During this deadly struggle, Bianchi led the second assault column in person against Markkleeberg. This force consisted of Regiments Colloredo-Mansfeld and Hiller (four battalions) with one battalion of Regiment Esterhazy in reserve. He was soon involved in a serious fight with Semelle's division of Augereau's corps for possession of the place. In this struggle, Bianchi was supported by General Fürstenwärther's brigade of Weissenwolf's division, which came up on his right flank and made for the Weinteiche ponds. Finally, the Austrians forced the enemy out of Markkleeberg completely and advanced northwards up the road towards Dölitz.

The crisis of the day on the Allied left flank was now over as well, despite the fact that Napoleon had thrown the Young Guard divisions of Decouz and Dumoustier, as well as Brayer's 8th and Ricard's 11th Division of Souham's III Corps, into the fight. Souham's corps had been pulled south from Wiederitzsch (which lies north of Leipzig) at about twelve o'clock on Napoleon's express command, despite Marshal Marmont's protests, and represented a serious loss of manpower to the latter in his struggle with the Army of Silesia.

'Better late than never' was certainly the most appropriate way to characterise the appearance of the prodigal Austrian Reserve Corps on the hard-pressed Allied left wing late in the afternoon of this dramatic day. Bianchi's energetic thrust through Markkleeberg broke the will of the French to dispute the field any further.

As evening fell and the fighting died away, the Allied line from Markkleeberg to Auenhain sheep farm was held by the divisions of Bianchi and Weissenwolf. Between Auenhain and Cröbern lay Nostitz's cavalry division and Rajewski's Russian Grenadier Division. Kleist's II Prussian Corps had pulled back to the south of the Gösel stream, behind Cröbern, together with Helfreich's Russian division. To the right of Auenhain was the Prussian Guard, and a strong Russian battery had been set up between Auenhain and Güldengossa. Von Klüx's brigade and the remnants of Prinz Eugen's squandered Russian corps (now reduced to a quarter of its original strength) lay in the shallow valley through which the Cröbern–Güldegossa track ran. The Russian Guard were close to the south of Güldengossa. Count Pahlen's cavalry had set up their bivouac north of Störmthal and Prince Gortschakoff's I Russian corps had set up camp in the northern end of the Oberholz wood.

All the villages in which the day's fighting had taken place were in flames, and they were surrounded by a sea of campfires. Güldengossa in particular had been in the thick of the fighting for most of the day and was the scene of much bitter street fighting. An officer of the 12th Prussian brigade who visited the place on the 17th recorded that:

> The scenes both in Gossa and here were shocking even for a hardened soldier. In all the streets there lay the corpses of the enemy and of our side, stacked up one upon another. The manor of the village – completely ruined – was full of the badly wounded. It was especially gruesome by the surgeons' operating rooms, where heaps of smashed and mangled human limbs lay for all to see.

Cröbern was in no better shape. Such buildings as had survived the artillery barrage and subsequent fires were destroyed by the soldiery in search of food, wood, and plunder. Most of the inhabitants had followed the advice of the Prinz von Hessen-Homburg and had sought refuge in Gross-Städteln, a village to the west beyond the Pleisse. One of those who stayed behind, a man named Krell, was grabbed by the Austrians and taken to the Auenhain sheep farm, where he was forced to carry ammunition to the guns, as many of the gun crews had been shot. That night he was tied to the wheel of a gun to stop him slipping away. He witnessed the destruction of several Austrian ammunition waggons, which were a prime target for the French guns. Apparently it was not until towards evening that the Austrians thought to pull the surviving waggons back into the cover of the sunken track leading to Cröbern.

Crostewitz suffered the same fate as Cröbern. After the day's combat ended the manor was turned into a hospital for about 600 wounded, of whom 170 died. They were buried behind the barn.

Wachau too, the hotly disputed centre of the French line, was in a similar state. The villagers had fled to Gross-Städteln before the battle – all except one unfortunate invalid, who was found dead after the fighting was over. The worst plunderers were the members of the Imperial Guard.

All the horrors of war were visited on those hapless villagers who remained in the vicinity of the fighting. Austrian, Prussian and Russian foraging parties descended on Störmthal and stripped the place of everything edible, everything of value, and everything which would burn. The Allies replicated here the destruction and desolation which the French had so recently visited on the unfortunate inhabitants of Leipzig. Even the entire village windmill vanished, to feed the bivouac fires. The villagers had hidden their most precious possessions in the church, but this did not save them for a minute; everything disappeared. The villagers of Störmthal lost twenty horses, fifty cows and 500 sheep during the night, and the manor lost forty beef cattle, twenty horses, 1,500 sheep. Fifteen hundred *Klafter* (cords) of wood were stolen from the local brewery and many mature trees in the manor park were cut down. The manor itself was put to use as a hospital; patients who died there were simply thrown out of the windows to make room for other unfortunates. The sheep farm was also converted into a makeshift hospital for 400 Russians.

There were so many wounded that no-one bothered about the dead. Seventy to eighty Russians were buried in a mass grave in the Spaliergarten and a Russian colonel was buried in the cemetery with full military honours. After the battle, gangs of co-opted locals went around the battlefield burying the dead where they lay to try to prevent outbreaks of disease. Even in 1814 there were the remains of dead horses all over the area and unburied corpses were found months after the battle in the scrub around the Weinteiche ponds.

The Kolmberg, the right wing of the Allied southern flank

Whilst the Allies fought a co-ordinated battle on the left wing of the southern front, their right wing – the 1st Column under the Austrian *General der Kavallerie* Graf Klenau – was separated from Prince Gortschakoff's right flank by about an hour's march, and fought in isolation around the Kolmberg on the extreme Allied right wing.

On the 15th Klenau's infantry had come up and his troops now occupied positions at Gross-Pössna, Threna and Pomssen. At 5:30 on the morning of the 16th he received his orders from Schwarzenberg's headquarters. He had two targets to take: Liebertwolkwitz and the Kolmberg, which lies about four kilometres east of the village. As soon as the opening shots of the combat on the Allied left wing were heard, *Feldmarschall-Leutnant* Mohr's division was to assault and take Liebertwolkwitz and General Paumgarten's 1st Brigade of this division was then to advance a further six kilometres north against Holzhausen, supported by Splenyi or Schaeffer as necessary.

The reasoning behind this overly-ambitious thrust into open country can only have been so that contact could be made with the Army of Silesia, which *might* have been in this area at this point. The chances of survival for Paumgarten's small force, in the face of the corps of Macdonald and Sebastiani at Zuckelhausen to his front and the main body of Napoleon's army on his left flank, were negligible.

Of Hohenlohe-Bartenstein's division, General Splenyi's 2nd Brigade was to hold the Universitätsholtz wood and Gross-Pössna village and General Schaeffer's 1st Brigade was to come up to Threna. *Feldmarschall-Leutnant* Mayer's Division was to advance to Köhra, two kilometres east of Threna, and General von Ziethen's 11th Prussian Brigade was to stay in Belgershain (two kilometres to the south of, and between, Threna and Köhra) 'to keep contact with Wittgenstein's wing'. Whoever wrote this line had badly misread the map and had no local knowledge.

Count Wittgenstein had stressed to Klenau that his primary target was to be the capture of Liebertwolkwitz and that he would be supported from the heights of Wachau when that place was taken. He also warned Klenau to guard his right flank, as the enemy forces at Holzhausen had been strengthened. Klenau thus advanced and deployed his corps on the low heights between Gross-Pössna and Fuchshain. It was nine o'clock before he achieved this, by which time Prinz Eugen von Württemberg's troops had been in combat for an hour.

Klenau's assault on Liebertwolkwitz began at ten o'clock, but he himself led the larger part of his command against the Kolmberg (also known as the Schwedenschanze, 'the Swedish Redoubt'), an isolated hill four kilometres east of the village, which dominated the countryside and could be seen from miles away. At this point the hill was unoccupied and Klenau placed two battalions of Regiment Kerpen (from Heldensfeld's division) on it, supported by twelve guns.

Shortly after nine o'clock Russian General von Toll (from the Czar's suite) arrived at Klenau's location, atop the Kolmberg, to assess the situation. Toll related that he received a chilly reception from Klenau, who exchanged scarcely a word with him. His queries were answered by Klenau's chief of staff, Baron Rothkirch.

Just before eleven o'clock Marshal Macdonald's XI Corps (four divisions) and General Sebastiani's II Cavalry Corps (fifty-two squadrons), marching south from Taucha, arrived at Baalsdorf and Holzhausen. Seeing the dark masses of 19,000 infantry and 6,000 cavalry approaching, and noting that the small Austrian outpost on the hill was about four kilometres from the nearest support at Gross-Pössna, von Toll remarked to Klenau: 'Your second line is too far back.' Klenau snapped back: 'It will be a long day; I will still need my reserves.' Von Toll tried again, urging that the Austrian troops at Fuchsenhain be brought forward, and this suggestion was supported by Rothkirch, but to no avail. Klenau refused to move a man. When, eventually, Schaeffer's brigade was ordered onto the Kolmberg some time after eleven o'clock it was already too late.

As soon as he arrived on the field, Macdonald realised the tactical importance of the Kolmberg and sent the 35*e* Division of General Gerard to Klein-Pössna (two kilometres north of Seifertshain) and Ledru's 31*e* Division to Seifertshain itself. The divisions of Charpentier and Marchand were directed onto the Kolmberg. With drums beating, Colonel Charras' 22*e Légère* of Charpentier's 36*e* Division (4,000 men) brushed the Austrian skirmishers aside and made for the peak of the hill. The two Austrian battalions had no chance; their supporting battery gave one last discharge of canister then limbered up and rushed off towards Seifertshain. Only eight guns escaped, the other four being captured by the French.

At last – and too late – Klenau was galvanised into action. Hohenlohe-Bartenstein's division was called forward from Seifertshain and Klenau set himself at the head of the leading battalion, that of Regiment Josef Colloredo. Von Toll's adjutant recalled the moment:

> We got to within fifty feet of the French line but then the battalion turned back. Allied cavalry, including four squadrons of the Silesian Hussars and Ulans, which Ziethen had brought up from Gross-Pössna, charged up the hill, retook three of the four lost guns and pushed the advancing French back up to the summit of the Kolmberg. But the cavalry alone could not maintain their position and had to retreat.

The confusion in the Austrian ranks was at this moment so great that Klenau himself was in danger of being captured when his horse was shot from under him. He was saved by a charge of the Hohenzollern and Oreilly Chevaulégers, which then covered the Austrian withdrawal.

It was now shortly past midday, and by dint of much applied stupidity Klenau had managed to deliver the dominant geographical feature on the Allied right flank into the enemy's hands and to waste the lives of several hundred of his men. Napoleon placed such value on this tactical victory that he sent a courier to report it to the king of Saxony in Leipzig and ordered that all the church bells in the city be rung. (Note that it was Napoleon and not the king of Saxony who ordered this.) In a somewhat premature move, messengers rode through the Grimmaische Strasse in the city waving white cloths and crying that the Austrians had been defeated.

Macdonald, meanwhile, wasted no time in occupying the Kolmberg with adequate infantry (the four battalions of General von Stockhorn's Baden brigade of Marchand's 39th Division) and artillery, and throwing up redoubts to increase the hill's defensive value.

In his memoirs, Macdonald describes capture of the Kolmberg very briefly:

> On the 16th October we attacked the Allies with more enthusiasm than sense. One of my divisions took a feature called the Schwedenschanze with the bayonet. I had to hold it. My cavalry came up at the right time and performed very well, but the Carabiniers did very badly. I saw with my own

eyes, ten sabre-lengths away, how one enemy squadron overthrew them. At the end of the conflict both of the fighting parties remained much in their original positions.

However, the extremely literate and imaginative Colonel Marbot of the 23*e* Chasseurs à Cheval (of Wathier's 10th Light Cavalry Brigade, General Baron Exelman's 4th Light Cavalry Division, Sebastiani's II Cavalry Corps) claims that Macdonald had occupied the Kolmberg on the *15th*, as is related in this passage of his memoirs:

> During the night of the 15th–16th October, Marshal Macdonald withdrew all the troops from the Kolmberg back into Liebertwolkwitz. Only I was ordered to stay forward until dawn to hold the hill against any enemy attack. This was no pleasant task as I had to go right up to the foot of the hill and was an hour from any support. The night was clear and the starlight plainly showed us the top of the hill.
>
> As I waited with my regiment for the dawn, an event occurred which – but for an evil stroke of fate – would have saved the Emperor and France and would have made me famous for ever. It was about half an hour before dawn when suddenly three riders appeared on the hilltop. We could clearly see their silhouettes and in the silence of the night we could hear every word they said. They spoke French. One was a Russian, the other two seemed to be Prussians. The former seemed to be in command of the other two for he ordered one of them: 'Ride to their majesties and report that all is clear here; in a few minutes it will be light enough to get a good view.' The officer to whom this was addressed asked if it would not be better to await the arrival of the Life Guards, whereupon the commander said: 'What for? Do as I say; it is clear that there is nothing to fear here!'
>
> We scarcely dared to breathe as we listened to this. After a short time about twenty riders arrived on the hill; one of them dismounted. Although I had not previously thought of the possibility of making a good catch, I had posted two squadrons with orders to await my signal with a handkerchief, at which they were to ride right and left around the Kolmberg and to capture those on top of the hill. I was just about to give the signal when one of my men dropped his sabre in the excitement of the moment, whipped up his carbine and fired a shot into the group on the hill, killing a Prussian major.
>
> In a flash the whole group vanished and although we chased after them, they had such a start on us that the pursuit was useless. I returned to my post absolutely furious.
>
> Later, I heard from my friend, *Oberst* Stosch of the Guards of the Grand Duke of [Hessen-] Darmstadt, that the Czar of Russia and the King of Prussia had slipped through my fingers!

The only truth to be found in this engaging but fanciful tale is that Colonel Marbot and the 23*e* Chasseurs à Cheval were indeed on the Kolmberg – but not on the night of the 15th/16th, because at that point Sebastiani's II Cavalry Corps had only just reached Plaussig near Taucha, about fourteen kilometres away to the north. Marbot's regiment may have been on the Kolmberg during the night of the 17th/18th, when Macdonald had pulled his troops back to a line between Liebertwolkwitz, Holzhausen and Zwei-naundorf, but on the 17th the hill was still occupied by French artillery and Baden infantry. Neither the Czar nor the king of Prussia were ever on the Kolmberg during the entire battle. This episode underlines why Marbot's account of events is generally regarded as a 'ripping yarn' rather than reliable source material. General Pelet has also been credited with a vivid imagination and a highly developed sense of the dramatic with regard to the exploits of the 22e *Légère* and Napoleon at the Kolmberg.

***

The Hessian brigade of Marchand's 39th Division, XI Corps, comprising the 1st Battalion Garde-Füsiliere, 1st and 2nd Battalions Leib-Garde, and 1st and 2nd Battalions Leib-Regiment – a total, on the morning of the 16th, of 66 officers, 166 NCOs, 32 drummers, 148 sharpshooters, and 1,153 men – was involved in the fighting around the Kolmberg. The brigade commander was Prinz Emil von Hessen-Darmstadt, and his report on the day's action reads as follows:

> At nine o'clock a terrific artillery bombardment began and lasted about an hour to our front and to our right. Later it spread, to be all around us. XI Corps was on the left wing.
>
> We followed General Charpentier's division out of Holzhausen; the two other divisions of the corps were deployed in two lines to our left. Sebastiani's cavalry corps was in support of this wing.
>
> It seems that the Allies had attacked. The thunder of the guns was terrible, the fighting hard, but the enemy was repulsed and his post on the Kohlenberg [Kolmberg], or the Swedish Redoubt, was taken by Charpentier's division with the bayonet. The cavalry charged and brought in some prisoners.
>
> Our division now occupied the Kohlenberg and Charpentier's moved into a wood to our right front. The position of the enemy extended from Fuchsenhain on the hill to Gross-Pössna [the Prince calls it 'Gross-Pössa']; both places were strongly occupied and Gross-Pössna had a lot of artillery. XI Corps was not strong enough to take this position so the cannonade was continued until darkness. Our divisions spent the night where they had been during the day. The burning village of Fuchsenhain was held by enemy light troops.
>
> The enemy had also been pushed back from Liebertwolkwitz, that lay off to our right front and seemed to have been the centre of the fighting, but there was no sign that a decision had been reached at any point. As darkness fell, there were flashes of cannon fire to be seen all around us. The battle was not over; this was merely a pause.
>
> On the 17th October, although we were so close to the enemy that we could shoot into one-another's bivouacs, everything remained quiet. Only

the occasional cannon shot rang out to tell us that no armistice had been agreed.

***

Sebastiani's II Cavalry Corps advanced on Macdonald's left wing against Klein-Pössna in three columns. The right-hand column was charged by the Austrian Hohenzollern and Oreilly Chevaulégers, and these were shortly joined by the seven Prussian cavalry squadrons of Ziethen's brigade and the Austrian hussar regiments Erzherzog Ferdinand and Palatine. The clash took place between the northern end of Seifertshain and the Pössgraben stream. Initially the Allies had the upper hand, but the balance swung against them as Sebastiani brought more and more of his regiments into the fight. The Prussians had a considerable proportion of *Landwehr* with them and these regiments acquitted themselves well, but the pressure of Sebastiani's squadrons was too great and the Allied cavalry broke and fell back onto Hohenlohe's division, which was momentarily thrown into confusion as the victorious French squadrons swirled past their right flank.

A French eyewitness to part of this fight was Colonel Saint-Chamans, commander of the 7*e* Chasseurs à Cheval, which was in Exelmans' 4th Light Cavalry Division of Sebastiani's II Cavalry Corps:

We arrived in Leipzig on the evening of the 15th October, a Thursday. Everything suggested that the decisive confrontation of the campaign was about to be fought and that the battle, when it happened, would be terrible. On the 16th, at dawn, our division rode forward to relieve some squadrons of guard cavalry placed at the outposts. My regiment was to the fore and we took over from the Guard Chasseurs. We were placed opposite a regiment of Austrian hussars, separated from us by a small stream.[22] They didn't seem to want to cross the stream and challenge us and we were content to keep the status quo. So we established ourselves and settled down to watch one another, waiting for the order to come so that we could get at one another's throats.

General Boyer, an old friend of mine and now a cavalry general, was established with his brigade in a little village quite near to our own camp. He asked me over to share with him a pâté and a few bottles of white wine. A pâté! I hadn't seen one of those for the last three months. It was eight in the morning, I was dying of hunger. I went. The pâté was shared out between twelve of us, but just as we were about to bite, a terrible and fierce bombardment began; we rushed to our horses and it looked like we would have to fight on empty stomachs, something repulsive to any Frenchman but something which was happening a lot in our army.

I arrived and had my regiment mount and form up for action, the Austrian hussars having done the same. The bombardment seemed particularly

---

[22] The Pössgraben, between Klein-Pössna and the Kolmberg, on the French left wing. The hussars were from Klenau's corps.

fierce on our right, but we forced ourselves to concentrate on matters to our front. To kill some time, we sent out some skirmishers to exchange shots with the Austrians. We were quite weak on this particular part of the battlefield and the Austrians knew this. They brought up a battalion of infantry, which opened up a galling fire on us, quickly followed by a battery of artillery, which was still worse. They shot so well that every missile found a target – I lost so many men and was powerless to fight back, something which hurt a great deal. Things got still worse and disorder began to appear in our ranks; horses were hit, others shied away or reared up in fear and a number of men dismounted in order to help wounded comrades to the rear. Nevertheless, the men were showing courage and were standing up to their ordeal; still, I felt it necessary to show a good example to them and rode up and down in front of the regiment shouting encouraging words.

As I was doing this, I suddenly felt myself lifted out of my saddle and I came crashing to the ground. I lost consciousness.

A cannonball had grazed me, hit my leather pouch-bandolier and driven it into my chest, without, fortunately, hitting me full on. But it caused me immense pain and would continue to do so for many years yet. In fact, I still feel it now.

When I came to, I found that they were carrying me in a cloak to the nearest village, that same village in which, two hours previously, I had almost feasted on the pâté. My mouth felt horrible and I spat into my hand; I was horrified to see that I had spat blood. I felt that my death was now certain, I was in agony and was sure that it was all going to be over in a matter of hours.

I had the regimental surgeon with me and he was accompanied by another gentleman of the same learned profession (from the 23rd or 24th Chasseurs); despite their assurances, I could see that they were troubled. Finally, after a thorough examination, they decided that I had a massive contusion and that they would have to bleed me. I thought that they were wasting their time and I told them so; I would be dead in a few moments.

The village was in danger of being stormed by the enemy, the firing was getting closer and our troops were being pushed back. They decided that it would be better to get me to Leipzig itself, about six miles away. They loaded me onto a stretcher covered with straw and, as I screamed my agonies, carried me off. I was racked with pain which attacked me from the base of my spine to my neck.

We made slow progress and, just as we entered a large village three miles from Leipzig, we saw a host of wounded who told us that the road to Leipzig had been cut by a swarm of Cossacks. I was set down in a still-occupied house. I began to vomit clots of blackish blood and I felt so bad that I begged those who had carried me to put an end to my sufferings. Luckily, they refused to do this.

Towards evening we were told that the road had been reopened and that we could press on to Leipzig. The enemy had been pushed back and his cavalry had been forced to withdraw. I therefore arrived in the city at around eight or nine in the evening and I was taken straight to some quarters prepared in advance. I was still in agony and convinced that my ribs must all have been broken. I once witnessed, at the battle of Ocana in Spain, one of my friends suffering from a similar kind of wound; he had spent two or three days in agony before his eventual death.

I did not sleep that night; I was kept awake by the pain and by the fever, although I was very weak from loss of blood. I worried about the pain and I was terrified that if the French army was forced to withdraw I would be abandoned as I was in no fit state to be transported. What would become of me? The 17th and 18th went by and the agony continued. The pain was not going away and even such a simple thing as a wash down with eau-de-cologne was unbearable pain.

Seifertshain

At this critical moment, the hard-pressed Allies were joined by the Prussian Reserve Cavalry brigades of Röder (Colonel von Wrangel according to Seyfert) and Mytius (eight squadrons of *Landwehr* and the East Prussian and Brandenburg Kürassiers), which arrived at Seifertshain from the Niederholz wood. Wrangel charged at once with the East Prussian Kürassiers and achieved initial success, but the regiment was then outflanked on both wings and thrown back. Both Prussian Kürassier regiments now went into the attack together in line, to such good effect that Sebastiani pulled his force back behind the Pössgraben brook.

A French battery in Klein-Pössna now turned its attention onto the Prussian cavalry and began to shell them, when suddenly, to the surprise of everyone on both sides, *Hetman* Platoff appeared out of his concealed position behind the Hegeholz wood east of Seifertshain with twelve Cossack *pulks* drawn up in line, threatening the French flank. Macdonald halted – he had been outdone! Instead of turning the Allied right flank at Seifertshain and rolling up their weakened line as the Emperor had intended, his own left flank was in danger of being turned.

His position on the heights south-west of Fuchshain having been saved from being assaulted, Klenau, having had quite a shock, was ready to pull in his horns completely; to evacuate Seifertshain, and to consolidate at Fuchshain. His chief of staff, Rothkirch, agreed with him, but von Toll was adamant that the post in Seifertshain had to be held. There followed a violent discussion on the matter, but in the end von Toll had his way. The village was occupied by the 1st Battalion of the Regiment Zach (under Major Hähling) with another battalion of the same regiment in support directly to the rear. All its entrances were blocked with farm carts and barricades, and the walls were loopholed. The 3rd Battalion Zach and the Regiment Josef Colloredo were deployed along the Königsbach stream close to the village, and Austrian artillery was brought forward onto the Rippersberg hill from the heights at Fuchshain, to dominate the approaches.

Macdonald had remained inactive since taking the Kolmberg at about one o'clock, with only his artillery in action against the Allies, but shortly after four o'clock – when Napoleon launched all his forces against the much-weakened Allied line – had ordered his troops to join in the general assault. Gerard's division, with Sebastiani's cavalry in support, had advanced from Klein-Pössna on Seifertshain and penetrated into the village, while Macdonald had led Ledru's division from the Kolmberg against its right flank. The Austrian garrison was forced out after a heroic and bloody defence, but the 2nd and 3rd Battalions Zach had counter-attacked and retaken it. To ensure that it would be held, General von Ziethen then sent two Prussian battalions, two squadrons of hussars and a horse artillery battery from Gross-Pössna northwards to Seifertshain's southern perimeter.

At five o'clock Macdonald assaulted Seifertshain again, but Klenau threw in his reserves. The division of Hohenlohe-Bartenstein flooded forward on both sides of the village and General von Schäffer led the Regiment Josef Colloredo at the charge; this was when Platoff's Cossacks attacked the French left flank. Macdonald's offensive faltered and then wilted, falling back to the Kolmberg and Klein-Pössna. The danger to the Allied right flank was over.

Strangely enough, Gerard's 35th Division did not lose a single officer in the course of the day's fighting.

***

The daughter of the vicar of Seifertshain has left us an eyewitness account of the battle for the village in her *Was wir Erlebten im Oktober 1813* ('What we Experienced in October 1813'):

A terrible cannon salvo, which made the earth shake, announced the start of the battle. In half an hour, a cannonade was raging which exceeded anything we had ever heard.

The view from the church tower showed us that the entire area towards Leipzig was covered with soldiers. The roads as far as we could see were black with marching troops, guns, ammunition waggons, pouring in endless streams towards the battlefield.

An Austrian officer warned us that we should prepare to flee at all costs. Quickly we packed our small bundles and left the houses. The ever-increasing din of the barrage roared through the rooms and rattled the glass in the windows, making the fearful inhabitants grab a few treasured possessions and flee their homes.

Here, in front of the open manor gate, the last few villagers had come together. The danger seemed to come closer by the minute. The unceasing thunder of the cannonade of 350 guns, ripped by the occasional explosion of mortar [sic] shells; the roar of thousands of voices shouting '*Avances!*' from this side and '*Drauf! Drauf!*' from the other, forced the little group of villagers of Seifertshain to the east, to the protective woods. What had become of the peaceful little village! At one end was the dull throb of drums; from the other the shrill calls of cavalry trumpets. The village street had been transformed into an army camp. Some advanced, others retreated. Several empty ammunition waggons, carts full of wounded, sutleresses with barrels of brandy forced their way through the throng. Shot and shell screamed through the air above them. Large dogs ran barking and howling with fear about the village.

The poor village publican, who was sick with typhus, was pushed along on a wheelbarrow with his weeping family about him. The little band of refugees fought their way through the Reserve Corps which had formed up behind the village. After half an hour they reached the vicarage in Albrechtshausen where they were greeted with cries of joy.

But even in this remote hamlet, the din of battle could still clearly be heard. At four o'clock several regiments of Cossacks, with *Hetman* Count Platoff at their head, arrived. He was a fine man with a noble face, penetrating black eyes, and a bearskin cloak. He ate little and carefully studied a map which was spread out before him.

Suddenly an adjutant galloped up on a gasping horse and gave the prince a report. On reading it, he at once ordered all his men to mount up and ride off as it was a report that the Allied right wing was in danger of being outflanked at Klein-Pössna.

The sun had now set; it still lit the church tower in Seifertshain. Suddenly, a column of flames spurted up. It spread quickly. A young girl from the village, horrified by the scene, burst into tears. A Prussian soldier asked her why she was crying; she pointed at the burning village. 'Yes, your fate is hard,' he said, 'but mine is harder. Today I have seen my three brothers die without being able to ease their last moments. I, the last son of my parents, who should be their support, have also been made a cripple today.' And he showed her the stump of his right arm.

Night fell over the blood-drenched battlefield upon which half a million men now lay themselves to rest after the day's work. The horizon was ringed by thousands of campfires which twinkled like stars. The flames of eight to ten burning villages formed one single sea of fires in which windmills and church towers rose up like torches.

At two in the morning, the Allied cannon opened up again due to fears of a French raid but they soon fell silent again. To the north, tricolour flares rose into the air, announcing the arrival of a new army formation, as was proved next day.

On 17th October, a Sunday, a message came in from Seifertshain that two large farms there had been burned down but the vicarage was still standing, if full of officers and soldiers. In Albrechtshain, the level of military activity increased considerably; many Cossacks rode through.

The refugees from Seifertshain, terrified by the wild shouts of the Cossacks, fled again from Albrechtshain; through gardens, over hedges and ditches into the nearby wood. Finally, at four o'clock, they reached the manor house of Brandis [about six kilometres south-east of Taucha], utterly exhausted. But even here they found no peace; in the early hours of the 18th October, more refugees from Beucha arrived in the village. They had left their homes on the urgent advice of Count Platoff, whose headquarters were in Beucha on Sunday.

Quickly they packed a number of carts with bedding and clothes, sacks of flour, apples and geese and, led by the chamberlain of Bünau, they filed out of the hamlet escorted by a Cossack whom Platoff had given them. From the heights of the village of Polenz the refugees had a last view of the plain of Leipzig where today, the 18th October, that great battle would be fought which would bring a crushing defeat for the Emperor Napoleon and his army.

The great plain, more than four hours' march across, was so covered with gun smoke that it resembled a rolling sea of fog which was continually rent by the fiery tongues of the batteries. Here and there, a sharp eye could pick out the red roofs of the abandoned homesteads rising out of the black smoke; also, like arms raised in supplication, numerous towers, burning mills and buildings. From time to time great spouts of flame shot up through the sea of smoke from exploding powder waggons. All this was accompanied by the roaring, rolling thunder of the discharges of over 3,000 cannon.

The refugees reached Grimma [about twenty-two kilometres east of Leipzig]; here, the inhabitants crowded around them and bombarded them with questions. At last, after days of fear and deprivation, the unfortunates found refuge in the houses of friends and relatives. They stayed there until 30th October, constantly worried about the fate of their homes and those who had remained behind.

Vater, the vicar of Seifertshain, had stayed on for some hours after the departure of his children and the other villagers on the 16th, but at two o'clock he also had to leave when the French on the Kolmberg made another attempt to take the village. He, too, later described his experiences:

At four o'clock, the French advanced again on Seifertshain, bombarded it with countless shells and stormed and took it despite the desperate resistance of the Austrian Regiment Zach.

The Austrians had blocked all the entrances to the village; all the trees in the surrounding fields had been cut down and used as barricades. The streets were blocked with carts, ploughs and other implements. A gun had been set up in the gate of the vicarage and four other guns had been placed by the inn at the bridge. But all of this was in vain. The French advanced not only from the Kolmberg but also from Klein-Pössna and broke into the village. The Austrians were pushed back halfway to Fuchshain. Then the reserve corps of Count Platoff came up from Albrechtshain; the Austrians counter-attacked and, after a bloody fight, retook Seifertshain.

Night put an end to the fighting. The flames from the burning village lit up the bodies of the dead and wounded which littered the village and the surrounding area. The inn at once became a hospital; so many amputations were performed there, that it took days of scrubbing to remove the blood from the floor.

The vicarage was also full of soldiers – mostly officers. Despite all their exertions during the battle of the day, they still had the energy to rifle through everything in the place. They read all the letters and papers in the writing desk.

One of them had written 'PAX VOBISCUM' on the wall clock in pencil. Another officer had been looking for a place to sleep in the living room; as all the spaces were taken up by the wounded and the dying, he sat down at the pianoforte and played until one of the wounded died and he could take his place on the straw.

On 17 October – a day of rest in the battle – Colonel Sommer of the Regiment Zach moved into the vicarage. On Monday morning he approached Vater as he returned to the village and suggested to him that he take the chance of a lull in the action to remove anything of value from the vicarage that he possibly could. The young officers helped Vater's maid to pack the items that were to go, even helping her to take down the curtains. The most valuable items had already been packed into the church, where everyone had thought they would be safe. However, on Saturday, a Russian general who wanted to observe the fighting on the Kolmberg had ordered that the church be broken open. The church remained open after he left, and several sutleresses picked through it thoroughly. Vater left with his remaining possessions and Colonel Sommer's best wishes, having been convinced that it would be extremely dangerous to stay there when the combat recommenced.

Liebertwolkwitz

Klenau had been given two tasks: to outflank the French east wing and to co-operate with Gortschakoff's 2nd Column in an assault on Liebertwolkwitz. For this task he allotted Paumgarten's brigade (Paumgarten having already fought in this vicinity on the 14th) and the Regiment Erzherzog Karl Nr 3 from Heldensfeld's division. It was the latter which would first take Liebertwolkwitz at ten o'clock. The force amounted to five infantry battalions, four squadrons of cavalry and fourteen guns, and was commanded by *Feldmarschall-Leutnant* Mohr. The village was held by part of Lauriston's corps.

Despite stiff resistance, Mohr succeeded in taking most of the village, the Austrians pushing as far as the church in a fierce house-to-house fight amidst the burnt-out ruins. This success was short-lived, however. French reinforcements from Charpentier's 36th Division (the 14*e Légère*) were poured in and the Austrians were ejected. It was eleven o'clock. Marshal Mortier, with two divisions of the Young Guard, had also now arrived to the north of Liebertwolkwitz, and Marshal Macdonald had meanwhile taken the Kolmberg. Together, the two marshals were ready to crush Klenau, and to avoid being overwhelmed Mohr pulled back to the Niederholz wood between Liebertwolkwitz and Gross-Pössna.

During the afternoon, when Napoleon was preparing to smash through the tattered Allied line before Güldengossa, orders were sent to Macdonald and Mortier to join in the general assault. Lauriston formed two columns, of which one was directed against Güldengossa while the other was sent against Gortschakoff at the Universitätsholz wood. At two o'clock Mortier's two Young Guard divisions (Barrois and Roguet) moved off from Liebertwolkwitz eastwards against Mohr in the Niederholz wood, while Charpentier's division of Macdonald's corps advanced southwards from the Kolmberg, also against the Niederholz.

General Mohr's 13th and 16th Grenzers holding the wood fought hard against both onslaughts and held firm until General Splenyi was seriously wounded in the abdomen and Mohr was put out of action by a bullet. Pressure from the French battery on the Kolmberg also increased, and more and more of the Niederholz passed into French hands.

It was now four o'clock. Mortier's column pushed forward on Gross-Pössna, which was defended by General Abele's Austrian brigade and parts of Ziethen's 11th Prussian Brigade. Try as they might, the French could not break out of the Niederholz or into Gross-Pössna; as evening came on they were still locked in combat with the Grenzers defending the wood.

A sergeant major of the 150*e Ligne* (General Harlet's 2nd Brigade, 19th Division, Lauriston's V Corps) has left us his account of the day's fighting in this sector. He was a village school teacher from the Hunsrück mountains who had been conscripted early in 1813. His division was advancing down the Leipzig–Grimma road and his battalion must have been engaged in the storming of Gross-Pössna, as Störmthal was not assaulted by the French and only Maison's 16th Division stormed Güldengossa:

When day broke, we could see nothing but the sky and soldiers. We moved into line opposite the Austrians. The Emperor Napoleon stood on a slight hill to our left front with a telescope in his hand. All at once came the command '*Aux armes!*' At this moment all the batteries to our front opened up; balls fell like hail and whistled past us. The first or second took the leg off a soldier and smashed our field kettle complete with the meat in it. The Emperor came past us on his grey, about fifty paces away and at such a gallop as I have never seen a horse travel. The cannonballs ploughed into the ground to the left and right in front of him and behind him so that the earth was thrown over his head. He held his reins in his right hand and with his left he clutched his hat to his head. At every minute we expected him to be hit but he galloped on through it all.

We moved about 200 paces to the left and the 155*e* occupied our old position. We stood in square in a dreadful hail of shot. Within fifteen minutes the battalion had at least 100 men killed and wounded. The brigade commander rode up and ordered our commandant to move us away as he had not seen that we were directly under a battery. We now moved down into a meadow in a valley. Before us was a hill; behind us a stream. Shells came over the hill. My Voltigeur Heinen, who hailed from Bonn, had an apple; he cut it in two and gave me half, saying: 'Here my dear Sergeant Major, let's eat this together – who knows if we'll be here tonight.' The apple was not eaten when a cannonball came down the valley and took off the heads of five Voltigeurs in the third rank on the left wing, including that of my good Heinen. As I was standing behind him, I was so covered with his blood and brains that I could scarcely see. I had the bodies taken to the rear and went down to the stream to wash and to clean up my uniform as best I could. A howitzer shell landed in the stream not two paces from me and I was soaked with water. The *Souslieutenant* who stood with me on the left wing moved off to the right wing – to the Lieutenant – and said to him: 'There'll be another coming this way!' My principle, however, was: 'Stay where you are put.' He had scarcely moved to the right wing when a cannonball smashed his ankle. Minutes later, the Lieutenant lost a leg.

The drummers sat behind the front on their drums. A cannonball went through both skins of a drum; the drummer, who had been sitting astride it, went head over heels up in the air but was otherwise unhurt. At last came the command: '*Voltigeurs en avant!*' And now we advanced joyfully over the hill and onto the open fields where we were greeted with a discharge of canister because the Captain had not ordered us to deploy. Another shot went over us. I thought of the old saying: 'You can hear it whistle but you don't know where it came from or where it's going to.'

It was very hectic all afternoon. We stormed forward and pushed the enemy back. As I had just reversed my ramrod and inserted it into the muzzle to ram down the charge, a canister ball hit it and bent it so badly that I could no longer use it. I picked up an Austrian one and used that. Soon a musket ball smashed the stock of my musket so I was forced to find another weapon on the field – which was no problem.

That was a hot day! When you heard and saw the thunder of the artillery, the rattle of musketry, the bursting of the shells, the charges and butchery of the cavalry, you would believe that not a man could survive.

Now it was near evening. We were supposed to capture a village to our right which was held by the Austrians. After a hard fight we succeeded but our divisional commander, General Rochambeau, who had ordered the assault, was fatally wounded during the struggle.

As we burst out of the other side of the village we saw the Austrians drawn up in heavy masses; their musketry and canister rained down on us so that we had to turn back. We took the place and lost it again. On our last withdrawal I was hit in the foot by a spent ball. We made camp but had nothing to eat this evening, neither had we all day, but we hadn't thought about it.

The action at Lindenau

The Leipzig suburb of Lindenau assumed a special significance in this battle. In 1813 it was a separate village, walled on its western side but open towards the city, standing at the end of a long dam or embankment on the main road from Leipzig towards the west (now the B87 and B7 combination). This was Napoleon's major line of communication back through Weissenfels,

Naumburg and Weimar to his great depot at Erfurt, and on to Mainz and France itself. The embankment was punctuated by four bridges, which carried the road through a two-and-a-half kilometre wide region of swamps, brush, and meandering, swollen streams and rivers (the Luppe, the Elster and the Pleisse) that lay between it and Leipzig. Unfortunately, the area has long since been drained and built over and the rivers canalised, so that it is unrecognisable today.

Extending for several kilometres to either side of Lindenau, this waterlogged terrain presented a considerable obstacle and rendered any attempt to outflank the village extremely difficult. The road was therefore Napoleon's *only* escape route if he should be defeated, and was thus a potential bottleneck through which the defeated French army would have to burst if it wanted to escape. Were the Allies to seal this bottleneck with an adequate force, Napoleon and his whole army would be trapped on the east bank of the Pleisse. He would then have no choice but to either surrender or make a desperate attempt to fight his way out northwards through the Army of Silesia, across countryside which his locust-like army had already stripped bare.

As we shall see, for some reason the Allies did not choose to block the bottleneck, although Schwarzenberg's original plan had proposed that not only Gyulai's III Corps but also the Army of Silesia should be involved in an assault on Lindenau from the west. This, however, would have been a total waste of Blücher's force and would have allowed Napoleon to use Marmont's corps and the divisions of Delmas and Dombrowski against the Army of Bohemia in the south. The wider tactical picture on 16 October was that the only Allied troops across Napoleon's potential escape route were Ignaz Gyulai's III (Austrian) Corps and General von Thielmann's *Streifkorps* at Markranstädt. Dr Zelle credits Gyulai with 20,000 men in his III Corps alone and castigates the Austrian for being too feeble a commander to take the ripe plum of Lindenau with its handful of heroic defenders. In actual fact, Gyulai's corps nominally consisted of the following troops on the 16th:

Feldmarschall-Leutnant Graf Crenneville
– *Generalmajor* Hächt: Grenz Infantry Regiment Warasdiener-Kreuzer Nr 5 (one battalion, 889 men); Grenz Infantry Regiment Warasdiener-St Georger Nr 6 (one battalion, 1,016 men); Chevauléger Lancer Regiment Klenau Nr 5 (seven squadrons, 915 men); Chevauléger Lancer Regiment Rosenberg Nr 6 (six squadrons, 804 men).

Feldmarschall-Leutnant Graf Murray
– *Generalmajor* Graf Salins: Infantry Regiment Erzherzog Ludwig Nr 8 (three battalions, 2,890 men); Infantry Regiment Würzburg Nr 23 (two battalions, 1,846 men).
– *Generalmajor* Weigel: Infantry Regiment Mariassy Nr 37 (two battalions, 1,296 men); Infantry Regiment Ignaz Gyulai Nr 60 (two battalions, 1,652 men).

Feldmarschall-Leutnant Prinz Philipp von Hessen-Homburg
– *Generalmajor* Baron Csollich: Infantry Regiment Kottulinsky Nr 41 (three battalions, 2,293 men); Infantry Regiment Kaiser Nr 1 (two battalions, 1,606 men).
– *Generalmajor* Grimmer: Infantry Regiment Kollowrath Nr 36 (two battalions, 1,746 men); Infantry Regiment Frehlich Nr 28 (two battalions, 1,969 men).

However, of this total of twenty battalions of infantry (17,203 men) and thirteen squadrons of cavalry (1,719 men), along with one three-pounder horse artillery battery and four six-pounder 'Brigade' foot batteries, Gyulai had – on the 14th – been ordered to detach one Würzburg battalion, one Erzherzog Ludwig battalion and half a six-pounder battery to garrison Weissenfels, and to send Graf Salins with two Erzherzog Ludwig battalions, a squadron of Rosenberg lancers and two guns to Naumburg, to guard the Saale crossing there. In addition a squadron of the Rosenberg Lancers had been detached to Schwarzenberg's headquarters. The strength of Gyulai's corps at Lindenau on the 16th was thus in reality only fifteen weak battalions, eleven squadrons and five batteries, or about 13,370 men.

It had been Schwarzenberg's original intention to make a serious attempt to assault Leipzig through Lindenau, not only with the III (Austrian) Corps but also with Blücher's Army of Silesia. However, after wrestling with the various possible permutations he decided to use Blücher's army on the east bank of the Pleisse (against Napoleon's main body) instead, which was undoubtedly the safer – and much more sensible – decision.

Also operating with Gyulai were the following smaller contingents:

The *Streifkorps* of Russian Lieutenant-General von Thielmann
– The Brigade of Lieutenant-Colonel Freiherr von Gasser: Chevauléger Regiment Hohenzollern Nr 2 (two squadrons, 210 men); Chevauléger Regiment Klenau Nr 5 (one squadron, 140 men); Hussar Regiment Kienmayer Nr8 (one squadron, 100 men).
– The Brigade of *Generalmajor* Prinz Biron von Kurland: Silesian Hussar Regiment Nr 2 (two-and-a-half squadrons, 200 men); 2nd Silesian National Cavalry Regiment (two squadrons, 250 men); Neumark Dragoon Regiment (*Freiwillige-Jäger* Squadron).
– The Don Cossack Brigade of Colonel Count Orloff-Denissoff: The Gorin II and Jagodin II *pulks* (600 men in all).
– Artillery: two Austrian HA howitzers, two Cossack HA guns (unicorns).
Totals: eight and a half squadrons and two *pulks* (1,500 men) and four guns.

The *Streifkorps* of Austrian Colonel Count Mensdorf-Pouilly
– Hussar Regiment Erzherzog Ferdinand Nr 3 (two squadrons, 260 men); Hussar Regiment Hessen-Homburg Nr 4 (one squadron, 130 men); the Don Cossack Gorin I and Illowaiski X *pulks* (400 men).
Totals: three squadrons and two *pulks* (790 men).

The total force operating against Lindenau was thus about 15,600 men.

It was not only the extremely strong nature of the Lindenau position which resulted in Gyulai's limited achievements there on the 16th; his orders quite specifically excluded the option of making a serious assault.

On the 13th, Gyulai had received a letter in Weissenfels from Schwarzenberg, who was then in Altenburg. It stated that '*dass, nachdem General Yorck gegen Leipzig einen Angriff unternehme, General Graf Wittgenstein in der Früh (am 14. Oktober) eine forzirte Rekognoszirung veranlasse, es unerlaesslich sey, dass auch Sie, durch vorpussierte leichte Truppen in der Frühe sowohl auf der Strasse von Lützen, als auch auf der von Pegau, eine gleiche forzirte Rekognoszirung vornehme.*' ('. . . as General Yorck is going to attack Leipzig [and] General Graf Wittgenstein will undertake a reconnaissance in strength early tomorrow (14th October), it is essential that you also make a reconnaissance in strength with light troops both on the road to Lützen and on that to Pegau.') This meant a twin probe, north-east towards Lützen (up the B87) and south-east towards Pegau (on the B176, now partially eaten away by lignite excavation).

On the 14th, therefore, Crenneville's 1st Light Division (under Gyulai's personal command) advanced through Lützen and on towards Leipzig, with light French patrols falling back before them to Lindenau. Csollich's brigade was left at Röcken, west of Lützen; Mensdorf's *Streifkorps* went to Döhlen (between Lützen and Markranstadt); and Hessen-Homburg's division went to Muschwitz, in the direction of Pegau.

Next day, the 15th, Gyulai's III Corps was to concentrate at Lützen with the two *Streifkorps* off to the north-east, keeping contact with General Saint-Priest's Russian Corps of the Army of Silesia and part of Liechtenstein's division, and making contact to the east with the advanced guard of Meerveldt's II (Austrian) Corps. Gyulai's orders for the 16th read:

Das III A.K. des Grafen Gyulai versammelt sich früh praezis 6 Uhr, mit der leichten Division des Fürsten Liechtenstein und dem General Thielmann, bei Markrannstadt. Wahrscheinlich nimmt die kolonne des General Saint Priest von der Blücherischen Armée denselben Weg, und vereinigt sich zu selben Zwecke mit der dritten Armée-Abteilung. Auf ein oder die andere Weise bricht der General Graf Gyulai früh um sieben Uhr von Markranstadt auf, greift den Feind an, den er vor sich hat, und rückt auf Leipzig.

Die Hauptbestimmung dieser Kolonne ist, die Kommunikazion zwischen der Hauptarmee und der des General Blücher zu erhalten und durch ihren Angriff ihrer Seits auf Leipzig den der übrigen Kolonnen zu erleichtern, Sie hat daher, von Lindenau aus, sobald als thunlich, rechts zu detachiren, um den Angriff der Meerveldtschen Kolonne auf Konnewitz zu erleichtern.

Im Falle die Kolonne des Grafen Gyulai mit grosser Uebermacht gedrückt würde, geht ihr Rückzug auf Mölsen, und von da nach Zeitz.

(The III Army Corps of Graf Gyulai will concentrate at precisely six o'clock tomorrow morning, together with the light division of Prince Liechtenstein and General Thielmann, at Marktranstadt. Probably the column of General Saint-Priest of Blücher's army will come the same way and will join up with the III Army Corps. One way or the other, General Graf

Gyulai will leave Markranstadt at seven o'clock, will attack the enemy to his front and will advance on Leipzig.

The main task of this column is to maintain communications between the main army and that of General Blücher and – by means of its attack on Leipzig – to ease the task of the other corps. As soon as possible, therefore, you are to detach troops to the right from Lindenau, to support the assault of Meerveldt's column on Konnewitz.

In the event that the column of Graf Gyulai is attacked with overwhelming force, they will withdraw on Mölsen and from there to Zeitz [ie, to the south].)

It is clear from this order that Gyulai had two functions: to provide the connecting link between the two armies; and to provide support for Meerveldt. His 'advance on Leipzig' was to be merely a feint, and it had been anticipated that he might well be forced to withdraw. There is no mention at all of his being required to take Lindenau.

On the night of the 15th/16th the Austrian *Rittmeister* Baron Marschall had come to Gyulai's headquarters from Blücher's (where he acted as liaison officer) to explain the Prussian plan for the following day's operations. Blücher had no confidence in an assault on Lindenau, as it would be pointless even if it succeeded. In a note he explained that the terrain at Lindenau was so difficult that any planned attempt to take the place must fail. Thielmann confirmed Blücher's opinion and added that it would be impossible to hold Lindenau if they took it, and impossible to assault Leipzig from it, as the approaches led over four bridges on a long causeway. There was no feasible outflanking route. The enemy could therefore 'hold Lindenau with one brigade against a whole army'. There would consequently be no co-operation from Saint-Priest for any assault on Lindenau.

The French garrison in Lindenau at the start of the action was part of Margaron's 39th division (the garrison of Leipzig) and included the 2nd Battalion 96*e Ligne*, 2nd Battalion 103*e Ligne*, 1st Battalion 132*e Ligne*, and the 1st Battalion, 3rd Baden Line Infantry Regiment. Also present was General Baron Quinette's 2*e* Brigade, 4*e* Heavy Cavalry Division of Arrighi's III Cavalry Corps, which consisted of one squadron each from the 13*e* Cuirassiers and the 16*e*, 17*e*, 21*e*, 26*e* and 27*e* Dragoons, and half a battery of horse artillery. At the start of the Allied attack the French defenders amounted to about 3,500 men and sixteen guns: Their commander was initially General Arrighi, but he handed this responsibility to General Bertrand when the latter came up with his 7,000-strong IV Corps from Leipzig to support Margaron.

The French position had been reinforced by the construction of three earthworks on the 15th, built using local labour. One of these was directly behind and to the north of the village on the road west to Merseburg; another was west of the village on the road to Markranstadt near the pond; and the third was to the south, near to Plagwitz, 200 metres from the windmill.

Despite all these factors, Gyulai considered it his duty to make a convincing show in front of Lindenau, and made his dispositions accordingly. His forces were divided into three columns and a reserve, as follows:

1st Column, Prinz von Hessen-Homburg: Warasdiener Grenz Infantry Regiment (one battalion), Jägers (1st or 2nd Battalion, it is not clear which), *Generalmajor* Weigel's brigade (the Regiments Ignaz Gyulai and Mariassy), and thirty Cossacks from Mensdorf's *Streifkorps* as advance guard. Due to the difficult terrain, this column had no artillery allocated to it. Its instructions were to advance from Markranstadt via Ruckmannsdorf, Böhlitz and Ehrenberg, to the left-hand side of Barneck, to Lützsch. From Lützsch they were to launch an assault on Lindenau *if* the 2nd Column had softened it up sufficiently with its artillery.

2nd (Main) Column, Graf Gyulai: Infantry Regiment Frehlich (two battalions), Warasdiener Grenz Infantry Regiment (one battalion), all the cavalry, three Brigade foot-artillery batteries, one twelve-pounder battery, and two howitzers. Its aim was to make a frontal assault on Lindenau by means of an artillery bombardment, to prepare it for an assault by the 1st Column. Its route was from Markranstadt through Schönau.

3rd Column, *Generalmajor* Csollich's Brigade and the rest of Liechtenstein's Light Division (Infantry Regiment Frehlich and a Grenz battalion). Csollich was to advance through Klein-Zschocher and then turn north to assault Lindenau from the right.

Reserve: Infantry Regiment Kollowrath (two battalions) at Schönau.

Due to concern for the safety of the left flank of the 1st Column, Gyulai sent one battalion of the Infantry Regiment Frehlich seven kilometres away to the north-west, to Dölzig, to cover the fords over the Elster and Luppe at Horburg and Maslau.

No immediate assault was mounted once the troops were in position, as there was no sound of any action from the Army of Silesia's front. Finally, there came a report from the observation post on the church tower in Markranstadt that the Army of Bohemia was in action over the Pleisse. The signal to start the advance was then given.

As soon as the enemy saw the 2nd Column approaching, they formed two lines on the heights of Plagwitz before Lindenau and mounted an attack with infantry and cavalry. Gyulai ordered his cavalry forward and, after two charges, the French were forced back to the Plagwitz windmill. The Austrian cavalry was then drawn up (with a refused left wing) at the side of the road, as escort for the artillery, which unlimbered and opened fire on the village. Their infantry formed assault columns to both flanks.

The right-hand column (Csollich) advanced on Klein-Zschocher. After a hard fight, in which the Grenz Infantry Regiment Brooder and the 7th Jägers under *Oberst* Veyder were distinguished, the village was taken. The column then advanced northwards on Plagwitz, which was strongly held and supported by artillery sited on the far side of the Elster. The assault failed, and a strong French cavalry charge caught Veyder's troops as they fell back. The Austrian infantry were surrounded and hard-pressed, but the two Cossack *pulks* charged into the rear of the French cavalry, causing them to scatter and withdraw, enabling the Austrian infantry to withdraw to Klein-Zschocher. The French cavalry suffered heavily from the Austrian twelve-pounders and withdrew to the River Luppe.

***

The 1st Column had meanwhile contacted the enemy before Lützsch, thrown them back, and taken the place. Their further advance – against firm enemy resistance – was through close and difficult terrain and they were subjected to heavy fire by French artillery on the far side of the Kuhburges Wasser stream. Despite this, they pushed on to Lindenau – which by this time had been set ablaze by Austrian artillery fire – and took possession of part of it.

Gyulai now assaulted Lindenau in turn and penetrated the village before he was thrown back with loss. After reforming, he tried again, this time with eight companies of the Infantry Regiment Mariassy and the 2nd Jägers. Once again the assault was initially successful, the Austrians even capturing two guns, but the strong fire of the French artillery beyond the river eventually drove them back and the two guns had to be abandoned.

Bertrand's IV Corps now arrived on the scene and his artillery was at once brought into effective action. It was also at about this time that news arrived that Meerveldt's planned assault through Connewitz had failed. In the meantime Gyulai had sent out patrols to the north to make contact with the Army of Silesia, but as yet these had not reported back.

At about five o'clock there was considerable activity among the French in Lindenau, and shortly afterwards part of IV Corps mounted two assaults against Klein-Zschocher. Csollich's brigade and one battalion of the Infantry Regiment Frehlich, supported by artillery and Cossacks, counter-attacked and drove the French back into Lindenau with heavy loss. Darkness then began to fall, marking the end of the day's fighting.

Gyulai's feint attacks had cost the Austrians over 2,000 killed and wounded. It had been a very expensive exercise and had achieved nothing. The same number of enemy forces could have been held down at Lindenau with a simple demonstration. On the French side, officer casualties comprised: 8*e Légère* six killed and sixteen wounded, 23*e Légère* one killed, 96*e Ligne* eight wounded, 103*e* three killed and ten wounded, and 132*e* one wounded. The Baden Light Battalion was almost completely destroyed. The total French loss is given by Zelle as 'scarcely 800 men; fifteen of his forty-eight guns had been dismounted'.

Austrian dispositions for the night were: one battalion of the Infantry Regiment Frehlich in Klein-Zschocher; Mensdorf's corps formed the outpost line from Klein-Zschocher to Leutzsch; six companies of the Grenz Infantry Regiment St Georger formed the garrison of Leutzsch and Barnek; and a single battery and battalion each of the Regiment Frehlich and the Grenz Infantry Regiment Warasdiener-Kreuzer were in Schönau. All other troops were to the rear in Markranstadt.

General von Toll had this to say about the action here:

The action at Lindenau was least flattering for the Allies. It was in Gyulai's power to take this important village and thus to cut off the enemy's retreat.

However, convinced that the task was too difficult, and being too timid, Gyulai wasted four precious hours with elaborate and needless preparations. And then – as is usually the case – when it was too late, he made his move.

By this time, Ney had sent up Bertrand's corps and Defrance's cavalry division from Eutritzsch.

To add to this, the repeated Austrian assaults were made from the north – from a direction where no success was possible.

After having suffered considerable loss, he then accepted that victory was impossible.

It would seem that when von Toll wrote this, he had no access to Gyulai's orders or to details of the difficulties of the terrain or the extent of the detachments which Gyulai had had to make. In the opinion of von Thielmann, Lindenau was a very hard nut to crack; but it was not Gyulai's job to crack it.

***

The Baden General Graf Wilhelm von Hochberg was present in Leipzig during the battle. He was *Chef* of the 3rd Baden Light Infantry Regiment, the 2nd Battalion of which participated in the defence of Lindenau in the afternoon. He described the action as follows:

On the 16th October I rode out to the Kohlgarten early in the morning and saw the Emperor just leaving. At nine o'clock I heard heavy cannon fire from the direction of Liebertwolkwitz. I visited all the town gates as the Duke of Padua [General Arrighi] had delegated his command of Leipzig to me. I then rode to General Margaron in Lindenau, who had just come under attack. General Bertrand's corps came up in support. The garrison suffered very heavy losses from the concentric fire of the guns which General Gyulai had deployed. The four companies of my regiment which fought there lost 96 killed and 150 wounded; ten officers were among the latter. This was the heaviest loss which a Baden battalion had ever had. At the day's end there were only two officers and about eighty men left fit for duty and none had been captured.

My brother Max came under fire for the first time here today; a cannonball struck his helmet a glancing blow.

On the Steinweg I met Marshal Ney, who assured me that the battle was won. I answered that there was no sight of this yet. In the town they were singing a Te Deum to celebrate the Emperor's victory. I returned to Leipzig and climbed the tower next to the house in which the Duke of Padua was staying, from where I saw the defeat suffered by Marshal Marmont's corps.

***

The Reverend Schlosser, vicar of Gross-Zschocher, four kilometres south of Lindenau, has left us an account of the events of 16 October in his *Erlebnisse eines sächsischen Landpredigers*. His experiences were typical of those of thousands of unfortunate inhabitants of the Leipzig area:

Just to the west of our village there was a camp of about 6,000 Austrians. They were commanded by General Csollich [of Hessen-Homburg's division], a Croat by birth, a tall, good-looking man. These men did not plunder because the general maintained good discipline, but feeding them was very difficult.

We could not give them bread, salt, beer or brandy because we had none ourselves, but there were plenty of vegetables in the fields and we had to supply them with meat. At one time it was thirteen cows in one day including our last one, a prize example that provided for us; we much regretted seeing her being driven off.

The Austrians and French drove one another back and forth; took and lost the village. Countless balls and bullets fell upon it – one man found 200 in his small garden alone – but no fires were started.

A swarm of about twenty to thirty Cossacks had broken into my house the day before, each with an empty bottle which they wanted to have filled with brandy. As we could only give them a little each they became angry, grabbed me, pushed me up against the wall and threatened me with pistols and sabres, shouting furiously. My good wife fell about the dirty neck of the most furious one and my little daughter clung about her knees and wept loudly, crying for mercy. But I would have been done for had not an Austrian NCO come in just in time. He saved my life by explaining the situation to the Cossacks and protecting me.

We could not stay in our house any longer. We left it and went with the teacher and his family to the church, where many villagers had stored their most precious possessions. While we lived here, I received two invitations, one from a general, the other from two officers who said they were old friends from our university days.

I went first to see the general, who was eating. He greeted me with the question: 'Well, Reverend, have you had something good to eat and drink?' 'No, general, I've had nothing at all to eat,' I replied. 'Oh, why not?' 'Considering the great danger threatening the village and the villagers, one's appetite vanishes – even if one *had* anything to eat.' He then asked me to climb up the church tower to spy out the situation of the Allies to the east and to report to him if they advanced.

Having been dismissed by him, I went to the hut of the two officers. I asked them to tell me their names as I did not recognise them. 'Ah, Reverend,' was the answer, 'we weren't at university; we just wanted to talk to you.'

'And what can I do for you?'

'What about a pot of coffee?'

'If I am not mistaken, my wife still has a small bag; if this is so, you may have it.'

'When I next went to see the general after about half an hour, to report that the Allies had advanced for three-quarters of an hour during the last hour, he was very pleased to hear my message.

On the way back, cannonballs suddenly started to fall in the camp so that the earth around me shook. The soldiers, who had just finished cooking, ran to their muskets; the general swung himself onto his horse, drew his sword and set himself at their head. They then set off against the French, who had crept up on the village from Klein-Zschocher, and drove them back to their previous position.

The two officers who had asked for coffee did not get any as the bag which my wife had was snatched from her and it was the only one we had.

The battle of Möckern

This action, perhaps more than any other in the Wars of Liberation of 1813–15, was to prove that the rotten Prussian army of Jena and Auerstädt was truly a thing of the past. The achievements of Yorck's corps in taking this village against bitter resistance cannot be too highly praised. 'MÖCKERN' is truly a battle honour that any army could be proud of. Such a feat of arms could only have been carried out by men of all ranks whose morale was excellent.

In contrast to Schwarzenberg's confused fumblings in the south, Blücher, as commander of the Army of Silesia, had one very clear aim: to close with – and destroy – Napoleon. It was to this end that he had made his bold advance westwards out of Silesia, through the Oberlausitz and down the Elbe to Wartenburg, following von Bülow's defeat of Oudinot's thrust on Berlin at Gross-Beeren on 23 August and his own victory over Macdonald at the Katzbach on 26 August. He had forced the crossing of the Elbe at Wartenburg on 3 October and headed south-west, turning Napoleon's northern flank.

Leaving Tauentzien's IV (Prussian) Corps in the Dessau area to guard the approaches to Berlin, Blücher then swung around the enemy's flank – dragging the unwilling Bernadotte and his Army of the North along with him – in a manoeuvre reminiscent of Napoleon at Ulm in 1805. As the two Allied armies closed in on Leipzig from the north, the Army of Bohemia approached them from the south. The conjunction which Napoleon *had* to prevent was in the process of completion. To prevent it, the Emperor left Dresden on 7 October, intending to destroy Blücher in isolation. Forewarned of this advance, Blücher crossed to the west bank of the Mulde on the 10th, and by the evening of the 12th was on the west bank of the Saale at Halle, whilst Napoleon – with the Imperial Guard – was far to the east at Düben on the Mulde.

At this point the Emperor's forces were scattered about the region in an extremely uncharacteristic manner. Two corps were locked up in Dresden; about a third of the French army was 100 kilometres away to the west in Leipzig; another third was around Wittenberg and Roslau on the Elbe (sixty kilometres to the north of Leipzig); and Napoleon's Guard, VI Corps and Lefebvre-Desnouëttes' cavalry corps were between Wittenberg and Leipzig. This diffusion in the face of the enemy should be compared with Napoleon's deployments in 1805 and 1806.

On 15 October Blücher left Halle, crossed to the east of the Saale and advanced south-east on Schkeuditz and Leipzig. This route was also on the east bank of the Elster and well away from the dead-ends of Lindenau and Connewitz. He commanded 54,500 men but knew that he would get no support from Bernadotte in any combat which he fought on the 16th; the Crown Prince was dragging his feet as slowly as he could. In fact, Bernadotte spent the 15th and the 16th with his 65,000 men at Zörbig (about twenty-two kilometres north of Halle) on the present-day B183, five kilometres west of Autobahn A9, and made no effort whatever to go to Blücher's aid in the fateful struggle which took place only thirty-two kilometres away.

As it was, Blücher had to fight alone with one eye always on his left flank (towards Düben), in which direction he suspected Napoleon's main body to lay and from where any French interference would therefore come. The swampy tract of the Elster protected his right flank.

On the morning of the 16th Blücher sent out his entire cavalry on an armed reconnaissance to establish the strength and whereabouts of the enemy. This told him that the villages of Freiroda and Radefeld (to the north of the new A14), and Stahmeln and Wahren (along the present-day B6 on the east side of the Elster) were occupied by enemy infantry. Further, there were enemy forces off to his left flank (on the B2 towards Wittenberg), at Krostitz and at Düben on the River Mulde. This confirmed that he needed to protect his left flank against a possible thrust from the Wittenberg area. As a result, Langeron's corps was given the task of attacking Freiroda and Radefeld, Yorck was to advance down the B2 on Möckern and Leipzig, and Sacken's corps was placed in reserve behind Langeron, facing towards the supposedly threatened left flank. It is clear that the 'fog of war' had led Blücher to completely misunderstand the enemy's true dispositions. As a result, Yorck's unfortunate corps would suffer very heavily, but would cover itself in immortal glory in winning a brilliant victory which also sealed the outcome of the entire battle.

Blücher's order was simple, and read: '*Das Korps Langeron greift Freiroda an, dann Radefeld. Das Korps Sacken folgt diesem Angriff in Reserve. Das Korps Yorck marschiert gegen Leipzig.*' ('Langeron's corps will attack Freiroda, then Rade-feld. Sacken's corps will follow this assault as reserve. Yorck's corps will march on Leipzig.')

As Yorck's troops marched out of Schkeuditz for Möckern, Blücher stood at the side of the road together with his staff and watched them pass. He took off his cap and spoke Paul Gerhardt's prayer: '*Anfang, Mitte und Ende, Herr Gott, zum besten wende*' ('Beginning, middle and end, Lord God, turn it for the best').

The French forces opposing Blücher on the 16th were commanded by Marshal Ney and consisted of Marmont's VI Corps, Souham's III Corps (which had come down from Dessau), Bertrand's IV Corps, and Arrighi's III Cavalry Corps. Dombrowski's independent division came in from the direction of Düben at about midday and took post on the right wing of the French line at Wiederritzsch, next to Bertrand's corps. The combined strength of these corps totalled about 42,500 men.

Luckily for Blücher, Napoleon had already stepped in – unintentionally – to give him the help denied by Bernadotte, ordering Bertrand's corps off to Lindenau to support Margaron, while the divisions of Brayer and Ricard of Souham's corps and Defrance's cavalry brigade were sent on their trek down to Dölitz and Wachau through the defile of Leipzig. Napoleon's motive in stripping Ney of such a high proportion of his forces was that he needed all the resources he could muster on the southern front to crush the Army of Bohemia, and was convinced that Blücher would attack Leipzig from the west and not from the north. Once again, the chronic shortage of good cavalry for reconnaissance purposes had blinded the Emperor, which seriously affected his decision making. This also resulted in an order being sent to Marmont at seven o'clock that morning telling him to leave his position and entrenchments at Möckern and march south over the Parthe, through Leipzig, to deploy before Liebertwolkwitz.

Marmont was in the act of moving off, and Souham's III Corps had marched to take his place between Wahren and Lindenthal, when the increasing clouds of enemy troops advancing south-east from Schkeuditz caused Ney to countermand Napoleon's order. Ney and his subordinate commanders were now convinced that the entire Army of Silesia was bearing down upon them. Marmont quickly returned to the northern front. However, as he considered his original position to be too long for his three reduced divisions, he occupied the space between Möckern and Eutritzsch instead, about two kilometres to the rear of the first position and facing north instead of north-west. The earthworks which the French had only just built between Wahren and Lindenthal were thus abandoned without a fight, but light troops were sent to occupy the villages of Lindenthal, Breitenfeld, Freiroda and Radefeld. There were now about 34,300 French and allied troops on this sector of the front, 18,600 of them in Marmont's VI Corps, which was supported by the cavalry divisions of Lorge and Fournier.

Langeron was the first to close with the enemy; he drove the French out of Radefeld and advanced eastwards on Breitenfeld. Yorck made for Lindenthal and the small copse before it, the French being pushed out of both after a Prussian battery opened fire on them with canister at close range from the Teichdamm. The Prussian artillery also silenced the French guns in the earthworks next to Lindenthal. The French light troops then withdrew into the main position at Möckern, the movement being covered by General Graf Normann's Württemberg cavalry brigade. Marmont saw at once that Möckern was the key to his position and gave orders for a strong garrison to be put into it. This consisted of the 2e and 4e Naval Infantry Regiments, who were fully aware of the importance of holding their post. The rest of Lagrange's division were posted to the east of the village.

Blücher and his staff watched the French withdrawal to the south with astonishment. They had fully expected the enemy to withdraw to the *north*! After rapidly reviewing the situation it was determined that the Prussians should alter the direction of their assault. Accordingly, Yorck and Langeron made a wheeling movement to the right with Sacken following. Langeron's new target was Wiederitzsch, held by Dombrowski's division, while Yorck made for Möckern. Still concerned for the safety of his flank, Blücher placed the cavalry of Korff and Wasiltschikoff at Breitenfeld. Möckern was held by Lagrange's 21st Division, with the divisions of Compans and Friedrichs extending to his right. Behind this line were the cavalry brigades of Graf Normann and Lorge.

The detachment of the Allied cavalry to their left flank had left a gap in the line between Yorck and Langeron. Yorck's infantry being arranged in two lines consisting, from west to east, of the 1st, 2nd, 7th and 8th Brigades, he ordered his left-hand brigade – the 8th, under General Hünerbein – to move to the left to cover this gap. The 8th Brigade thus took very little part in the storming of Möckern. Yorck's cavalry, under Colonel von Jürgass, had two regiments on the left wing of Hünerbein's brigade and the third behind the centre of Yorck's line.

This portion of the battlefield has been heavily developed and is now scarcely recognisable. In 1813 the village was sited on a slight hill with a steep drop into the Elster close to the western side. The approaches from the north (nowadays Georg-Schumann-Strasse) were commanded by the manor farm buildings and the brewery. On the crossroads in the centre of Möckern (probably the crossing of the Georg-Schumann-Strasse with the Slivogt-Strasse) stood an old, round, stone tower from which the French could command all the streets. The village consisted largely of individual farm buildings crowded along the narrow, crooked streets, and was ideal for defensive purposes. The French artillery were deployed at a brickworks on a hill to the east which had good fields of fire to the north. South of Möckern, the ground rose towards Gohlis. The countryside was open and flat.

It was two o'clock in the afternoon when Yorck's order to assault Möckern reached Major von Hiller, the commander of his advanced guard, and the first Prussian troops to enter the village comprised von Hiller's point, under Major von Klüx. This consisted of three companies of Jägers (two of the Garde and one East Prussian), the Fusilier Battalion, 2nd East Prussian Infantry Regiment, and the 4th Battalion, Silesian *Landwehr*. Hiller followed with his main body, consisting of the Leib-Grenadier Battalion, one battalion each of the 13th and 14th Silesian *Landwehr*, 1st Battalion, Brandenburg Infantry Regiment, the West Prussian Grenadier Battalion, and the 2nd and 12th Reserve Infantry Regiments. His cavalry comprised two squadrons of the 2nd Leib-Husaren, three of the Brandenburg Hussars, the Brandenburg Ulans, the East Prussian National Cavalry Regiment, and the 5th Silesian *Landwehr* Cavalry; and his artillery consisted of the 2nd Horse Artillery and the 12th Foot Artillery. The latter battery deployed to a position midway between Wahren and Möckern and engaged the French artillery to the east of the village and in the village itself.

As Hiller advanced, a company of Austrian Jägers under Lieutenant Gelber from Gyulai's corps at Lindenau, who had found their way through the bush and swamps of the river barrier, appeared on his right flank. They joined in the Prussian assault and were greeted with loud cheers.

Major von Klüx's troops penetrated into the manor farm north of Möckern but could get no further and fell back. When von Klüx reformed his men and tried again his force came under fire not only from the from the front but also from a company across the Elster. A strong French counter-charge then threw the Prussians back again. Nothing daunted, von Klüx gathered his men and made a third assault. This time the Austrian and Prussian Jägers went along the bank of the Elster and engaged the French on the far side, while the East Prussian Fusiliers and the Silesian *Landwehr* (under Major Graf Wedell) recaptured the manor house complex and pushed forward into the village as far as the crossroads, where their thrust ground to a halt. After a violent hand-to-hand combat the Prussians were thrown out yet again and pursued by the Naval Infantry. At this point the Leib-Grenadier Battalion (who had been searching for a ford over the swollen Elster) came up unexpectedly from the river into the French left flank and forced them back into Möckern.

The fourth assault by von Klüx's gallant men was stopped, once again, at the crossroads in the village. Taken in front by canister and in both flanks by heavy musketry, the Prussians could make no further headway and fell back once more. By this time the northern half of Möckern was filled with the dead and wounded of both sides and the fighting surged back and forth over them. The victorious French charged after von Klüx's men and on into the battery lines. In the ensuing melee they took a howitzer.

Now – at last – von Hiller's main body came up. He rallied the tired troops under heavy enemy fire and started the fifth attack on Möckern. Von Klüx's three battalions, reinforced by the *Landwehr* battalions of Rakowski and Thiele and the 12th Reserve Infantry Regiment, forced their way back into and through the village and out the far side. Here, however, they were greeted with close range canister fire from a battery just to the side of the road and fell back into Möckern, which was now in flames, having been set on fire by the French as they withdrew, the latter abandoning their own wounded to their fate in the flames.

Meanwhile, the Brandenburg Infantry Regiment had come around the east side of the village and was advancing straight into Marmont's great battery, which was located athwart the cemetery. However, raked with canister and taken in the left flank by a naval battalion, the Brandenburgers had no option but to seek refuge in Möckern. Losses on both sides were by now extremely heavy, the 2e and 4e Naval Infantry and the 37e *Ligne* being practically destroyed in the fighting here.

It was now clear to von Hiller that he was incapable of taking Möckern alone. He sent a report to General Yorck to this effect, and the 2nd Brigade of Prinz Karl von Mecklenburg-Strelitz was sent up in support. It seems incredible that Yorck had allowed this unequal struggle to drag on for so long. Amazingly, however, the morale of von Hiller's men was still excellent – despite their repeated reverses and heavy casualties. He fired his men on to new efforts with: '*Heute, ihr Brüder, muss das Schicksal Deutschlands entschieden werden!*' ('Today, brothers, the fate of Germany must be decided!') As von Hiller wrote in his report:

> I thus assaulted the village again. Everyone burned with passion to get to grips with the enemy and rushed forward at my cry that Germany's fate must be decided today, striding over the bodies of their fallen comrades with a great cheer.
>
> I was forced to throw in my reserve, the West Prussian Grenadiers but, despite the rage and bravery of my men, it was impossible to silence the fire of the enemy battalions inside the houses. However, I had the pleasure of seeing the advancing enemy grenadiers and sailors of the Imperial Guard[23] turn and run before the courage of my men (mostly *Landwehr*); as they did so, I saw the other brigades of the corps advancing.
>
> At this point, I was wounded. With the blissful knowledge that we would win, I fell unconscious.

At the same time as Hiller was wounded, so was Major Thiele. Rakowski was killed leading his battalion in this charge, as was Graf Wedell, whose dying call to his men was: 'Children, save the Fatherland! God help us!' But even this fifth, superhuman effort was not enough to break the French resistance. Fresh battalions poured into Möckern. The West Prussian Grenadier Battalion, cut off by enemy troops who had come over the Elster, had to hack its way to safety with musket-butt and bayonet, losing most of their officers and many men in the process.

During this action, Yorck had been watching events from alongside the advanced guard's artillery, with the cavalry, right in the thick of it, with bullets whistling all around him. It was soon clear to him that his light guns were having little effect on the French pieces. 'Those fellows will get a surprise!' he shouted, and ordered an adjutant to bring up the heavy artillery. They soon appeared, cheering as they came. Rapidly unlimbering, they were quickly in action in an artillery duel that had few equals. The French projectiles fell among the Prussian cavalry behind the battery and casualties mounted; Yorck ordered them to form in a single rank to minimise losses.

Now – at last – Mecklenburg's brigade came down the main road with bands playing and colours flying. The Prince was at its head. They deployed on the hill east of Möckern. The leading battalion was the 1st Battalion East Prussian Infantry Regiment Nr 1. It charged straight at a battalion of 4*e Artillerie de la Marine* which, together with the 37*e Légère*, had been thrown into the fight. The Prussians closed to within fifty paces before, hit by a salvo from

---

[23] This is a mistake. The *Marins de la Garde* were not present at Möckern.

the front and by flanking fire from Möckern, they suffered such heavy losses that they broke and turned aside to join the advanced guard north of the village. Behind the fusiliers came Colonel Lobenthal with the regiment's two musketeer battalions. The first charged straight at a battalion of *Infanterie de la Marine*, overthrew it, and went on for the guns. French infantry behind the pieces came forward through the gun lines, and in the ensuing melee both Prussian battalions were thrown back.

When Prinz Karl came up to rally his men a cannonball cut down his horse. He mounted another but this too was killed by a cannonball. A third ball badly wounded the prince himself, and command passed to Colonel von Lobenthal, who at once called up a battalion of the 2nd East Prussian Regiment. This battalion, formed in line in a hollow, poured a destructive fire into the French gun crews and caused the infantry beyond to fall back. Von Lobenthal now ordered a charge on the guns, but Marmont thwarted this move by throwing in part of Compan's division. As this threatened his left flank, Lobenthal was forced to fall back and was himself wounded during the withdrawal. All the field officers in his brigade were now either dead or wounded, as were half the men.

Meanwhile, the bloody struggle – and the fire – in Möckern itself raged on. The French garrison had been continually reinforced since the fighting began but their losses had been as terrible as those of the Prussians. The house-to-house fighting was bitter in the extreme and it often happened that one side held the ground floor of a building while the other held the upper storeys. The Prussian units became completely mixed up with one another, and command passed from the generals to the most senior member of each isolated combat group. The Prussian advanced guard had by now lost thirty per cent of its men, and in this sixth attack von Klüx himself was wounded.

Whatever the cost, Yorck was determined to have the village, so that the losses to date should not have been in vain. In one final effort, he ordered in his last intact brigade, that of Steinmetz. As they moved forward, they were joined by the remnants of Prinz Karl's brigade (now commanded by Prinz Wilhelm von Preussen, the king's brother). Behind them rode the Leib-Husaren. Marmont, of course, was as determined to hold the burning village as the Prussians were to take it from him. He called up his reserves, and the great French artillery battery of forty guns by the cemetery redoubled its efforts to destroy the advancing enemy.

Steinmetz advanced up the road as before. Once in the centre of Möckern, however, he sent the battalions of Walther, Seydlitz and the Silesian Grenadiers down a side road to the eastern edge of the village. Here they were greeted by a salvo of canister which sent the leading *Landwehr* battalion reeling back. Major Seydlitz was wounded. However, Major Burghoff's grenadiers coming up behind them were undeterred. Forcing their way through their confused *Landwehr* comrades, they charged the French with the bayonet. Casualties were frighteningly high on both sides. The remaining two battalions of Steinmetz's brigade advanced over the open country to the east of Möckern but were greeted with such heavy fire from the front, and also in their right flank from the village, that they wavered as well. All their mounted officers were wounded and the advance came to a standstill.

When Major Maltzahn saw this happen, he gathered his own two battalions (those of Majors Mumm and Kossecki) and – followed by the East Prussian Grenadiers – stormed forward against the French position. Canister ripped through the Prussian ranks; Steinmetz and Losthin were wounded, Kossecki and Maltzahn were killed. Mumm and all the captains of his battalion were rapidly killed or wounded. Incredibly, despite this havoc and chaos, the Prussian advance continued. Major Leslie – already wounded twice – led his grenadiers on until he was hit again. 'Forward, lads!' were his last words.

The fate of the day hung in the balance. The contesting infantry surged back and forth, in a confused mass, before the French battery at the cemetery. The decisive moment was near.

Yorck rode forward to Major von Sohr, who was behind the Prussian infantry with the Brandenburg Hussars, and shouted to him through the din and the smoke: 'Charge! If the cavalry don't do something now, everything is lost!' Sohr pointed out that his three squadrons alone were incapable of bringing about the desired decision. Yorck sent an adjutant back to the Reserve Cavalry; after ten minutes (they seemed like years) they trotted up. Von Sohr gave the order: 'Trumpeter, sound the trot!' and his regiment moved forward against the advancing French line. The shock of the cavalry threw the startled enemy infantry into confusion, and they were overthrown and cut down. The survivors fled back onto – and through – the battery; six guns fell into Prussian hands.

The Prussian cavalry had thus decided the day. The usually terse and laconic Yorck met the wounded Major von Sohr (holding his sabre in his left hand after having been shot in the right arm) after the action was over. Yorck told him: 'I owe today's victory to you alone and I will never forget you and your regiment.'

Graf Normann rushed up with his Württemberg cavalry brigade to try and restore the situation, but just as he was about to charge into the flank of the Brandenburg Hussars he was himself taken in flank by *Oberst* von Katzeler at the head of the Brandenburg Ulans and the 5th Silesian *Landwehr* Cavalry. The Württembergers were overthrown and driven back into the French infantry behind them, who broke in their turn. The Prussian Hussars cut into them, taking more prisoners and another gun.

The seven Prussian cavalry regiments now thundered along the French line hacking and stabbing at everything in their way. The crisis had passed; the French were crumbling and breaking away to the rear. Just one more push was needed. Yorck therefore called up his last cavalry reserve – the Mecklenburg-Strelitz Hussars – and urged them on into the melee.

***

The Mecklenburg-Strelitz Hussars had, as usual, been given the task of covering their artillery battery. While waiting patiently through the long hours of enemy artillery fire that this entailed, another cavalry regiment had ridden up behind them in full parade dress, with long white plumes in their hats and with drawn sabres. They were the Swedish Mörner Hussars from the advanced guard of the Army of the North, who had come up to see the enemy. The main body of their army, they said, was a day's march behind them. They declined an invitation to join in the battle and rode off again. Shortly after the Swedes had left, Sir Charles Stewart also rode up, resplendent in his red uniform, cocked hat and plume, and mounted on a magnificent horse. He rode quietly past the Mecklenburgers and directly towards the enemy, as if out on a quiet hack in the English countryside. A cannonball which just cleared his head caused him to do a smart turnabout and make off for a safer spot at a speed reminiscent of Ascot race course.

Yorck's order to attack came at about five o'clock, and the regiment moved thankfully forward, just as the wounded Prinz Karl von Mecklenburg was carried past them to the rear. Sickness and the provision of a detachment of 150 men for duty elsewhere meant that regimental strength was down to just 280 sabres. As they rode past General von Yorck, he indicated the enemy infantry line to their commander, *Oberst* von Warburg. 'They've been near to breaking once already. They're steady now, but if they start to waver, charge them!'

Finally, the moment came. As the French infantry fell back, the Mecklenburgers charged. The French infantry formed square but the hussars broke it at once and the slaughter began. A cry of 'Enemy cavalry!' caused the Mecklenburgers to rally outside the square to meet this threat, but *Ordonnanzoffizier* Timm saw a French officer running off with an eagle. He raced after him, cut him down and seized the prize.[24] The rest of the enemy infantry, seeing the eagle taken and Prussian infantry coming up, surrendered. An immediate count of prisoners realised one colonel, two lieutenant-colonels, twenty-one other officers and 384 NCOs and men. In the course of the evening the Mecklenburg-Strelitz Hussars brought in over 500 more captives and a howitzer, complete with team. Of the regiment's own eighteen officers, three were killed and three wounded.

Now Marmont's troops lost heart. Everywhere his infantry squares were bursting apart or dissolving to the rear as Prussian cavalry swirled among them. The diary of the Lithuanian Dragoons described the dramatic scene as follows:

> We had broken through the enemy mass. Regardless of the hail of lead, we had penetrated into the centre of the thickest formation when suddenly the defeated French behind us regained their fighting spirit, picked up the weapons they had just discarded, and fired into us again. The result was a gruesome bloodbath. It was a dreadful scene. We pushed on into the terrified mass; those that were not cut down by our sabres were trampled down by the horses. The unfortunates lay in heaps of 20–30. Certainly, not one of

---

[24] The history of the Mecklenburg Hussars states – wrongly – that the eagle was that of the Sailors of the Guard.

this regiment of Sailors of the Guard[25] would have survived had we not suddenly received a discharge of artillery fire from the left which caused us to fall back. Nevertheless, we had taken most of them and those who escaped left their packs and muskets in our hands so that they could run faster.

A French account of the destruction of the 1*er* Naval Artillery Regiment is taken from the memoirs of Captain Jean-Louis Rieu, a company commander:

We were deployed in line as if for a review, but in two ranks instead of three so as to show a longer front, and this was a bad sign. I can still hear Mutel, who carried the colours, asking whether he shouldn't put the eagle back in its case because its glitter in the sunshine provided the enemy with a target; and the major's reply, at the top of his voice, that on such a day one could never let an imperial eagle shine too much. Very soon the profound calm was succeeded by the din of artillery and musketry fire. Our only battery was smashed in the twinkling of an eye by the enemy's formidable artillery, and as a crowning disaster, an ammunition waggon full of shells and charges caught fire and spewed death on all sides. Our skirmishers were pushed in by superior numbers. In readiness for receiving cavalry we changed from line into mass formation, but the grapeshot merely ploughed deeper gaps in our ranks. However, we stood fast in the hope that reserves would arrive to support us – vain hope!

There we were, suffering increasing damage from the grapeshot, still in line by battalions in mass formation. No orders reached us, we could hear no leader's word of command, and we felt that we had been abandoned on the battlefield. This is explained by the fact that Marshal Marmont and General Compans had been wounded. I am not sure whether General Pelleport had been too, but in any case I didn't see him again. As for my blustering little major, he was nowhere to be seen! I discovered later that he had used a scratch as a pretext for retiring shamefully from the melee, and so had the lieutenant in my company, both of them without saying a word to anyone. If the major in command of the regiment gave no sign of his presence, it is no doubt because he was bewildered by the turmoil. At least he did not run away, and we met up with him again as a prisoner.

Meanwhile the Prussian infantry battalions were approaching so close, thanks to their artillery support and our immobility, that their ranks met ours, so much so that a sergeant-major named Mourgue took them to be French on account of their blue greatcoats, which were like our own. He

---

[25] As has already been pointed out, the *Marins de la Garde* were not present. The unit which was cut down here and lost its eagle to the Mecklenburg-Strelitz Hussars was the 1*er Régiment Artillerie de la Marine* (the heroes of Lützen and Dresden), of which thirty-three officers were killed during the fight. Martinien shows the *Artillerie de la Marine* as being at Wachau on 16 October, but this too is wrong, as is Zelle's attribution (p.430) of the capture of its eagle to the Prussian Lithuanian Dragoons.

went unofficially to one of these battalions to warn them that they were firing into their comrades and was very lucky to escape being captured.

Our position was becoming untenable. Besides the enemy artillery which was killing us at point-blank range, an imposing force of cavalry waited a mere twenty metres away for us to break, when they would spring at us like tigers waiting for their prey. Our companies were becoming more and more disorganised, and very soon the battalions, being crowded together, presented nothing more than unformed heaps, which still fired a few shots and whose officers no longer had any influence unless they stayed there in person and physically held the soldiers back. This could not last very much longer. The instinct for self-preservation, even if prompted by bad motivation in these circumstances, became too strong. The men broke and fled.

The report of *Oberst* von Wahlen-Jürgass, commander of Yorck's cavalry, described the last phase of the action from his perspective:

> At about one o'clock our infantry had finally been able to penetrate into the village and the commander [Yorck] ordered the cavalry to advance and assault the enemy left wing. I carried out this order at once by leading the 1st West Prussian Dragoons and the Neumark LWk Regiment forward at a trot with the Lithuanian Dragoons following in support. The West Prussians hit the enemy [some squadrons of Chasseurs] first, overthrew them and took four limbered cannon, then chased the enemy, together with the rest of the cavalry, back on Gohlis, taking several hundred prisoners and cutting down many more along the way. Then I saw several intact columns of enemy infantry off our left flank. I left the West Prussians in front of Gohlis, where the enemy had reformed. I then gathered in the rest of the brigade which had become disordered in the chase as is usually the case. The Lithuanians were still in compact order. I ordered them to wheel about and to charge the nearest square. This they did and cut them down where they stood as a later inspection of the battlefield showed. The enemy infantry to left and right of this square scattered; those directly behind it fled to the rear in such a dense mob that the cavalry could not force their way in. At last we gave up the chase because of the dark.

Just as the Prussian cavalry charged at Möckern, a beaming Graf Brandenburg rode up to Yorck from Wiederitzsch with the following report: 'The battalions on the left wing have taken all the batteries. The enemy is totally defeated!'

***

Yorck's left wing was made up of the 7th and 8th Brigades of Generals von Horn and von Hünerbein, and had been deployed north-east of Möckern up to the Landsberger road. They were opposed by the divisions of Compans and Friedrichs of Marmont's VI Corps. Towards evening, von Horn's 7th Brigade made a charge against the centre of the enemy position, the Leib-Regiment and the *Landwehr* battalion of Graf Reichenbach in the lead.

Ignoring the canister which ripped through their ranks, they marched inexorably on, cheering as they went. Shouts of 'Long live the king!', 'Forwards! Forwards!' and 'We must win!' rang out as they advanced without firing a shot. The French guns limbered up and galloped off just in time to escape capture, and the Prussians drove on into the battalions to the rear of the empty gun lines. Lorge's cavalry division was thrown against them but could not charge home, and the now unsteady French infantry fell away before the victorious Prussians.

Left of Horn, Hünerbein's 8th Brigade advanced at the same time into the teeth of heavy French artillery fire. Colonel von Borcke, Majors Götze and von Othgraven and many other officers of the brigade were killed early in the advance but their men were unstoppable and pushed on through the din, the screams, the shouted commands and the smoke. Friedrich's 21st Division tried to stop them with their bayonets but, after a short melee, they too broke and fled. The character of the fighting here can be shown by the example of Major von Krosigk. Ahead of his fusiliers, he grasped the right-hand man of the opposing line and felled him with one punch. Krosigk was at once shot and stabbed down. As he died he waved his men on with his sword. 'Leave me, go and win!' were his last words.

Blücher wrote of Major von Krosigk in his report of 20 October to the king: 'Major von Krosigk, a rare patriot, leaves only daughters. His estate, which he has already once abandoned voluntarily to the enemy's depredations, in order to be able to fight for the holy cause, will fall to rich heirs and not to his bereaved and impoverished family.' Krosigk had been arrested by King Jerome's Westfalian gendarmes in 1811 and thrown into prison in Kassel for his pro-Prussian activities. In the autumn of 1812 he had been released but his entire fortune in Westfalia was confiscated. In March 1813 he was one of the first to offer his sword to the resurgent Prussia, for which the French confiscated his estate at Popplitz near Halle in Saxony. He had visited the place shortly before the battle to find it devastated; but the material loss was more than compensated for by the loyalty of his peasants. They had saved whatever they could for him – even his library and his wine cellar – and had kept their rents aside for his return.

General von Horn's report described the struggle on the left as follows:

> The fire of the enemy centre was most murderous; our left seemed to be bogged down and Graf Brandenburg brought me the news that the battle on the right was so finely balanced that we would have to withdraw in face of superior enemy forces if my brigade did not restore the situation. Graf Schwerin, who commanded the 1st Battalion of the Leib-Infanterie-Regiment, had begged me after the victory at Wartenburg, to give his battalion an opportunity to prove its dedication to king and country. At this critical moment I thus pulled the 1st Battalion, Leib-Regiment, out of the second rank and into the first, set myself at its head and led it against the centre of the enemy battery.
>
> All my battalions followed me with such bravery that I shall forever con-

sider it the greatest honour to have commanded them on this critical day. The other two battalions of the Leib-Regiment pushed their way into the front rank; the heavier the canister fire became, the louder became the cheering of my battalions. Not a shot was fired by my entire brigade; the artillery could not keep up with my battalions.

I was now in the rear of the enemy artillery and of the column which attacked Möckern. Graf Reichenbach, who commanded my right wing, threw his battalion at the battery which was bombarding Möckern. The enemy abandoned it. Now my right wing assaulted his infantry, which stood formed in deep masses before Möckern. At this moment, Major von Sohr's 10th *Landwehr* Cavalry Regiment charged into these masses and cut them down. The enemy abandoned all the batteries in the centre.

An enemy cavalry regiment came on as if to charge my infantry. I advanced against them with the Leib-Regiment and they withdrew behind their infantry. Graf Reichenbach's *Landwehr* battalion also beat off an enemy cavalry attack with great courage. The *Landwehr* strove to outdo the Leib-Regiment at every opportunity.

As the advance of my left wing had not been able to keep up with me due to the losses of the 8th Brigade, the enemy right wing, formed in deep masses, threw itself on my left flank. Whenever such a mass approached, I attacked it from three sides with my infantry and drove it back with heavy loss.

Regardless of the fact that these masses defended themselves bitterly, and despite the fact that several of our cavalry charges were beaten off, my infantry pursued them furiously. It was my aim – and that of my officers and men – to destroy the enemy; we didn't bother about the guns we had taken, I can thus not report how many there were.

I have been closely associated with the Leib-Regiment for a long time and am now doubly happy that they have been able to secure this victory for the Fatherland; I will thus be so bold as to ask that this regiment be awarded some honour appropriate to its standing in the eyes of that Fatherland.

***

The French resistance was broken. Marmont's right wing withdrew in good order but his centre and left fled the field in confusion, infantry and cavalry units wildly mixed up together. The morale of Yorck's survivors soared.

Marmont himself had been wounded twice during the fighting, firstly when four French ammunition waggons blew up behind Möckern, and again at the end of the day while leading Friedrich's division against the final Prussian assault. Despite this he remained in command. Now he rode back to the Gerbertor gate in Leipzig and ordered General von Franquemont's 38th Württemberg Division of IV Corps to cover the withdrawal of the routed troops. This 'division' was now only 900 strong, having suffered heavy losses in the battles of Dennewitz and Wartenburg. Its situation at Leipzig closely resembled that at Borodino the previous year, by which time its original three brigades had by then been reduced to three battalions. Franquemont's troops deployed at the bridge over the Rietzschke at Gohlis.

Some of the men from Marmont's left wing withdrew up the Elster; others crossed the swollen river into the Rosenthal on a bridge formed by pushing waggons into the water. Marmont led the remnant of his corps back eastwards over the Parthe to Schönefeld. General Compans had also been wounded in the day's fighting.

Yorck's corps bivouacked on the battlefield and lit no fires due to the proximity of the enemy. To shelter from the biting wind, walls were thrown up using the bodies of the fallen. The Prussians had lost over 7,000 men in this battle, including 172 officers. Marmont had also lost about 7,000, including 2,000 captured, and an eagle and forty-three guns (although Ney's report refers to the loss of 'some thirty' guns). The next day, Sunday the 17th, Yorck ordered a church service for his corps to give thanks for its dramatic, desperately expensive victory.

The Russians at Wiederitzsch

Blücher had not witnessed the epic struggle between Yorck and Marmont; he had spent the day on the left wing of the Army of Silesia with Langeron's and Sacken's Russians. This is perhaps excusable, as he still believed that the enemy main body was liable to appear from that quarter, over Hohenossig. His mistaken concern for his left flank was only reinforced by the total lack of information from the Army of Bohemia on the southern front.

Thus it was that the corps of Langeron and Sacken dallied throughout the 16th, confronted – initially – only by Dombrowski's weak division of some 2,500 men and the divisions of Brayer and Ricard. These latter two divisions marched off south at Napoleon's express command at twelve o'clock but were replaced on the northern front by Delmas' 9th Division, Fournier's 6th Light Cavalry Division and Avice's Cavalry Brigade, who brought French strength here to only 8,500 men.

Dombrowski's men had occupied Wiederitzsch in order to assist the arrival of Delmas' division and the train of III Corps from Düben in the north-east. Blücher consequently ordered Langeron to take this place. The first Russian assault was made by Kapsewitsch's X Corps with Rudsewitsch's cavalry division to his left rear in support. The Poles put up a stout defence but were soon forced out of the village by the stronger Allied force and fell back on Eutritzsch, three kilometres to the south. They were pursued by General Emanuel with the Charkoff and Kiev Dragoons and the Dorpat and Livland Mounted Rifles. General Olsufiev's IX Corps and General Korff's cavalry division then advanced into Wiederitzsch.

However, the Franco-Poles reformed in Eutritzsch and made a determined counter-attack which – briefly – wrested control of Wiederitzsch back from the Russians before another Allied assault, led by the Schlüsselburg Infantry Regiment – which advanced without firing a shot – threw Dombrowski's men out.

At this point a strong enemy column was spotted by Blücher's staff coming down south from Düben. It was Delmas' 9th Division of 5,000 men and the train of III Corps. This vulnerable and isolated division should have been snapped up gratefully by the Army of Silesia, but the 'fog of war' had so clouded Blücher's vision and that of his staff that they interpreted the long column as the first element of Napoleon's long-awaited main body bearing down on their flank, and reacted accordingly. The advance of Kapsewitsch's corps in pursuit of the Poles was called off and Olsufiev's corps was redeployed to the left flank towards Podelwitz (between the present-day B2 and B184 routes) to attack the train.

General Langeron's report of the day reads as follows:

> General Olsufiev at once sent General Udom [9th Division] with the 10th and 38th Jäger Regiments and the sharpshooters of the Regiments Nascheburg, Apscheronskoi and Yakutsk to occupy the wood to our front to prevent the enemy from taking it; but despite this, Delmas captured it.
>
> The French defended the place bitterly in order to win time for their train to withdraw.
>
> The Regiments Riaschsk and Kolywan were sent to support General Udom, and in the ensuing violent struggle the Regiment Riaschsk took the colour of the 125e *Ligne*.[26] The French had to evacuate the wood.

The 2e Provisional *Légère*, the 145e *Ligne* and the 10e Hussars put up a determined resistance here. Zelle (p.426) puts the losses in this action at 2–300 for Delmas and 1,500 for Langeron. Delmas withdrew eastwards through Seehausen to Neutsch on the Parthe. Many of III Corps' waggons also had to abandon the road to try to reach the safety of Leipzig via detours. As they were slow and cumbersome, however, some 100 waggons, six guns[27] and 500 prisoners were taken by General Bukowin and his four Cossack regiments, who had pushed eastwards to the Düben road.

During this combat, Dombrowski had tried to cross the Rietzschke stream to penetrate into the gap between the corps of Yorck and Langeron. The latter countered this threat with General Wasiltschikoff's two infantry regiments and General Bistrom's brigade of Saint-Priest's corps (the 1st and 33rd Jägers), which until then had been in Lindenthal. These forces sufficed to neutralise this threat and the combat at Wiederitzsch stagnated for the rest of this day. Yorck had lost 7,500 men, compared to Langeron's 1,500 out of 12,000 men.

***

Major Ernst Moritz Arndt had spent a busy night in Schkeuditz. As dawn broke on the 16th he was sent on another mission, as he tells us:

> In the grey mist of the morning of the 16th, I mounted my Trakhener stallion and trotted over to General Langeron, who commanded one of

---

[26] This is uncertain, as the 125e was part of the Magdeburg garrison and not in Delmas' division. Zelle also denies it.

[27] Zelle (p.425) denies that any guns were lost.

Blücher's corps. During the night, an officer had come in from Prince Schwarzenberg's headquarters with the important news that the main army was advancing from Altenburg on Leipzig. So, the genial plan of surrounding Napoleon at Leipzig had been exactly executed and the decisive battle could begin.

As I mounted my horse, it was my dearest wish that all the blood that was so soon to drench the old battlefield in the plain around Leipzig would not have to be shed in vain.

I was accompanied by an escort of sixteen Cossacks who quickly scoured the area around us like bloodhounds. As we rode into the village of Freiroda, which had been occupied by the French that morning, I heard the familiar thunder of the Prussian artillery which told us that General von Yorck was already at grips with the enemy.

At this moment, I would gladly have given up my major's epaulettes in favour of commanding my old battery against the enemy. The sound of the cannon came ever closer and the old peasant who was my guide told me that it was closing in on Möckern.

I reported to General Langeron in French. He was a cold, very correct man of very cultivated appearance. After I had finished, he turned to his chief of staff and addressed a few, harsh, words in Russian to him. He told me that I should go to his advanced guard which was commanded by General Saint-Priest, a French émigré, where I would soon find an opportunity to get into the fight.

I trotted over to the Russian advanced guard. General Saint-Priest was a polite French aristocrat of impeccable manners, like so many of them that I had met in the 'nineties. He spoke warmly of the courage of the Prussian heroes, but I quickly sensed that my presence made him extremely uncomfortable. I did not have much time to dwell on this for we made contact with the enemy.

General Dombrowski's Polish division had occupied a village and the Russians were soon involved in a hefty fight with the Poles. It was the bitterest fight I have ever seen in my life and one could soon see the deep hatred that existed between the Russians and the Poles.

The Russian infantry advanced with great courage and determination but the individual soldiers did not understand how to operate on their own in the gardens, streets and farmyards of the village. Thus the Poles, who included many veterans who had just returned from Spain, were able to hold on to the village for a long time despite being in a considerable minority.

The Russian general, who seemed to be a very brave man personally, rode at the head of the assault column and spurred his men on to make a rapid charge. As his general's hat was very distinctive, the Polish tirailleurs all shot at him and his greatcoat was repeatedly shot through – as I could see – without it bothering him in the least.

As I was riding just behind him in my Prussian uniform, which must have also caught the marksmen's eyes, the balls whistled closely past my ears and my cap and greatcoat collar were shot through.

The fight had gone on for almost two hours with very few breaks when the enemy finally evacuated the burning, half-ruined village and we could advance. One of Blücher's ADCs brought General Saint-Priest the order to assemble a battery of thirty-six heavy guns and to bombard Marshal Marmont's corps which was deployed on the heights near Eutritzsch. 'That's your speciality, major,' shouted General Saint-Priest sardonically to me, 'ride over there and tell them how to aim their guns so that Blücher's headquarters will at last be satisfied and will stop complaining to my Czar about me!'

So I galloped back to the Russian reserve battery and relayed the general's order to the general commanding the artillery. The Russian artillery advanced with their fine teams at a sharp trot and I directed the general to a small hill, which seemed to me to be the best spot. And soon there began such a thunder that even my old gunner's ears were deafened by it.

To oppose us, Marshal Marmont had assembled a great battery which poured a hail of round shot at us, most of which – happily – passed over our heads. Next to us, Yorck's artillery was thundering away, and when our thirty-six guns opened up as well, the hellish concert was complete. I had dismounted from my black and was observing the terrific spectacle which unfolded all around us on foot. A Prussian ADC rode up to the Russian cavalry, which was quite close to us, and ordered it to advance.

At the same time, I received an order to reconnoitre the area between Langeron's and Yorck's corps to find in advance suitable sites for massed batteries. Whilst doing this, I came under such heavy fire that I thought I would be blown to shreds at any moment. Miraculously, nothing happened.

So it was that I came up to Yorck's corps which had just been fighting so heroically at Möckern. The Prussian cavalry were just advancing to deliver the decisive blow, and I would have liked to have ridden with them had my duty not dictated otherwise.

It was a wild turmoil; cannon thundered, musket salvoes crashed out, drums beat, trumpets sounded, horses' hooves stamped; all mixed up with all sorts of words of command, and – unfortunately – frequent cries of pain from the poor wounded who lay helpless on the ground and were now crushed by the advancing cavalry.

The fine Mecklenburg-Strelitz Hussars trotted past me first; their sabres held high as they crashed into the enemy; they were followed by the East Prussian National Cavalry Regiment among whom I had so many friends.

When this mass of cavalry had passed, I came up to dear old Horn's brigade, which had distinguished itself in this action as in so many others before. Splendid old Horn was at the head of the famous Leibregiment; he raised his sword on high, gave a loud Hurrah! and the drummers – as many of them as were left, for Horn's brigade had suffered terrible losses – beat the advance. Horn's deep bass voice rang out: 'Any man who fires a shot is a cur! Forward! Long live the king of Prussia!' The whole regiment answered: 'Hurrah, the king of Prussia!' as they advanced into the enemy canister.

The Silesian *Landwehr* battalion of Graf Reichenbach – now with scarcely the strength of a full company – was in reserve. When the *Landwehr* men saw the Leibregiment go in, they in turn shouted: 'Hurrah, the king of Prussia! Forwards, the *Landwehr* must have their share, the line mustn't do this alone!' And they were off, like an unstoppable mountain stream, into the canister of the enemy battery.

These were scenes that inspired each good, Prussian heart, for they showed that, apart from high-sounding words, there was a splendid spirit in our present Prussian troops, be they line or *Landwehr*. May this always be the case, for then the state of the Hohenzollerns will stand firm and respected.

It was fully dark before I was able to find my way to General Yorck and deliver my findings as to potential sites for large batteries around Möckern. At the end of the action, he had set himself at the head of the Deathshead Hussars, drawn his sabre and given the order: 'March – march, long live the king!' The subsequent charge was a complete success.

As I came up, he was just dismounting from his horse which was quivering with the strain of the hard work it had done. He took a large piece of buttered bread and a glass of Schnapps from his groom's canteen, the first refreshment he had had since the morning. He listened to me carefully and then said some friendly words to me, which was seldom the case with him.

***

Wilhelm Ludwig Victor Graf Henkel von Donnersmark, commander of the 1st Cavalry Brigade in Yorck's corps, recalled the closing stages of the fight at Möckern as follows:

It was about five o'clock in the evening when we saw the enemy bringing up a lot of guns onto the heights at the Leipzig side of Möckern, and we did not to wait very long before they started to bombard us with some forty guns. The wounded started to come back in such numbers that at first sight it looked as if complete battalions had been scattered. Now the last brigade, that of *Oberst* Steinmetz, came up, but he too was soon wounded.

This assault was supported by two squadrons of the Brandenburg Hussars under Major von Sohr and the Mecklenburg Hussar Regiment. Our infantry had just thrown the enemy out of the village, when this cavalry went around the back of the place, swooped down on the rear of the battery and captured most of it.

This was the signal for a general advance. The Reserve Cavalry was called up, *Oberst* von Jurgass in the first line with the West Prussian Dragoons and I in the second with the Lithuanians.

I had the honour to have General von Yorck and Prinz Friedrich von Preussen, together with his escort, *Oberst* von Pirch II, riding in front of my line with drawn sabres.

The West Prussians took some guns and threw the enemy cavalry and infantry back into Gohlis. I have rarely experienced such fire as we advanced under, for even the Russians under Langeron, who had previously deployed to our left, were happily firing into us. This error was quickly corrected.

Due to this rapid advance, some battalions of the Sailors of the Guard,[28] in blue greatcoats, were cut off on the road to Schkeuditz. It was beginning to get dark when General von Yorck ordered me to attack.

Here, I must give the greatest credit to the Lithuanian Dragoons, including the Volunteer Jäger squadron, who had performed to the highest standards during the entire campaign under the splendid *Oberst* von Below, for the way in which they carried out the next manoeuvre could not have been done better on the parade ground. I had them turn right about by troops, right wheel in squadrons and charged the battalion in echelon with the 5th Squadron in the lead. We had to jump both the ditches which lined the road; there were enemy Tirailleurs in them but they did not fire a shot. The French were in column and hurrying towards Wiederitzsch; their officers shouted: '*Serrez vos rangs!*' But that did not help at all; we got among them and there followed a great bloodbath, so that when Horn's brigade came up there was not much left of the battalion.

I shouted '*Rendez-vous!*' to a tall officer, but he answered: '*Tuez, bougre!*' and at that instant, the Lithuanians cut him down. One of the French batteries was chased into a pond up to their necks.

That was how the victory was won; but the cost was high – for over half the corps was killed or wounded. We took many guns, an eagle and two colours as well as several thousand prisoners including many gunners.

The end of the day

As darkness fell the sea of campfires around the embattled city of Leipzig again flared up to warm the tired survivors of the day's bloody work. A Hessian soldier on the Kolmberg wrote in his diary:

> It was the worst bivouac that we had experienced on this campaign. The weather was wet and windy. There was no food, no water, no firewood. Broken wheels, musket stocks and saddles were used instead. To cook anything we had to use water from puddles in which lay the blood of men and horses. We sent out a lot of patrols and posted many picquets and half the men had to be under arms at all times.

Napoleon's bivouac was set up on a dried-out pond next to the old brickworks at Meusdorf. The Old Guard formed square around it as usual. He had spent the last hours of daylight on the little hill north of Wachau. In the afternoon, elated by the successes of his troops at Auenhain, Güldengossa and on the Kolmberg, he had ordered the church bells in Leipzig to be rung; now even he had to admit that his optimism was a trifle premature. The

---

[28] This is a repetition of the popular error; the *Marins de la Garde* did *not* fight at Leipzig.

enemy had not broken and fled; he had shot his bolt, and there was no prospect of him being able to renew the battle on the 17th with any hope of success. The battered Allies had been joined by almost 100,000 fresh troops, while he had not been reinforced at all. Only Reynier's VII Corps remained intact as a reserve.

The incoming reports of his corps commanders increased his concern. From Lindenau, Bertrand wrote:

> We have been attacked by a force of Austrians and Russians which is stronger in infantry and artillery than we are. Almost all our ammunition is used up; it is thus essential that we are resupplied before dawn. I shall also need reinforcements as my position is too extended and difficult. The enemy is trying to outflank us on both wings. They have already crossed one arm of the Elster on the left wing. I shall work on the entrenchments tonight in order to strengthen my position. I need reserves because the enemy might break through at points where I do not expect them.

From the east – in Holzhausen – Macdonald reported that he was confronted by 40–50,000 enemy troops and that he expected that his weak and over-extended left wing would be attacked next morning. From the north, Marmont wrote that he would only be able to send in his casualty returns on the 17th as he must regroup his forces. He was opposed by over 60,000 infantry and 12,000 cavalry and they were getting stronger by the hour. Marshal Ney, the overall commander of the northern sector, reported that Marmont's VI Corps had lost over half its strength and that Dombrowski and Bertrand had also suffered badly. If he were to be attacked on the 17th by superior forces, he would have no alternative but to fall back south on Liebertwolkwitz.

Napoleon sent an aide, Colonel Gourgaud, to inspect the corps on the southern front and to report to him personally on their condition. Gourgaud confirmed his worst fears. Victor's II Corps had suffered particularly badly in the fighting at Markkleeberg and Wachau. Everyone was exhausted and very depressed at the way the Allied forces kept increasing in numbers throughout the day. All ammunition parks were very close to empty and prisoners reported that Bennigsen's Reserve Army and the Army of the North were expected to join the Allies during 17 October. Messengers had been sent to Reynier to speed up the march of his VII Corps from Eilenburg south-west to Leipzig.

Poniatowski wrote:

> VIII Corps and Kellermann's cavalry corps have lost a third of their men and many officers. All ammunition stocks have been used up. I have insufficient ammunition. All infantry cartridges have been used; the cartridge pouches and the ammunition waggons are empty. The slightest delay in ammunition resupply could cause us heavy losses as we have not enough to maintain combat for one hour.

The Allied noose was closing rapidly about Napoleon's neck. It had taken eight years and innumerable, needless, defeats but at last the Emperor's opponents had learned how to fight this new style of war. The Trachenberg Plan had worked – despite all Schwarzenberg's blundering on the 16th.

Napoleon slept even less than usual this night; he was increasingly aware of the gravity of his predicament and of the great possibility that he might suffer a serious defeat the next day. He had gambled for high stakes, assuming that, as usual, his enemies would make mistakes and give him the crushing victory that he so urgently needed. Of course, they had made many errors in the battle, but Napoleon had made a few himself. He had tried to wage war in his accustomed style with an army that had lost its edge. Perhaps his greatest mistake was to underestimate the fierce, new fighting spirit which permeated all ranks of the Prussian army. This was not the same decadent force that he had smashed so effortlessly in 1806; this was not the army responsible for the shameful and spiritless capitulations of Erfurt, Hamlin and a dozen other well-stocked fortresses. The commanders and men he faced at Leipzig burned with a desire to avenge these past insults and to rid themselves of French mastery for good. The morale of his own army, by contrast, was at a dangerously low level.

In Leipzig, every house was filled with wounded and refugees. The flood of casualties was so great that the city authorities had to open the municipal corn store, which was rapidly filled with 6,000 wounded. And still the streams of unfortunates poured into the city through the storm and the icy rain; thousands lay – and died – unprotected, untended, hungry and thirsty, on the wet cobblestones in the streets. Some of the more fortunate crept into empty flour barrels that had been removed from the corn store. Starving soldiers combed the city's rubbish heaps for food waste to eat, and the civilian population was no better off. The bakers in Leipzig – those who still had stocks of flour – had been ordered to bake bread only for the French military commissaries; sentries were posted in each bakery to ensure that this rule was obeyed.

One baker's apprentice recorded the events of this terrible night as follows:

> .A lot of bread had been gathered in my master's house in accordance with the instructions; there must have been at least 2,000 six-pound loaves. It had not been collected even though the soldiers, exhausted from the battle, were starving. To guard these supplies there was a picquet of three to four men in each baker's shop. Suddenly, in the middle of the night, we noticed that the bakehouse was full of French soldiers all busy filling their packs, bags etc with bread. They had already taken several hundred loaves. They had got into the house by breaking the shutters to a back room. In that room was the body of a man laid out; next morning, we found that they had stolen the coffin lid and the shroud.

General Graf Wilhelm von Hochberg of Baden recorded the following meeting that night:

That evening I was called to the Duke of Bassano; he was very depressed. He ordered me to arrest the Bavarian General von Raglovich as Bavaria had joined the great alliance against France on 8 October.[29]

I tried to evade this task as I could see that we would soon be in the same situation. I sent a message to General Raglovich telling him that I had an order to arrest him and hoped that I wouldn't meet him.

And so it was. I saw the general again on 20th October in Czar Alexander's headquarters when I was in the same situation that he had been in on the 16th.

***

Zelle (p.420) gives Allied losses on the southern front on 16 October as follows: 'Meerveldt – 4,000; Kleist – 6,000; Eugen – 3,600; the Austrian cavalry – 1,000; Rajewski and Gortschakoff – ca 6,000; Klenau – ca 4,000; the Austrian reserves – ca 2,000. The total was thus about 27,000 without the 2,000 prisoners reported by Poniatowski.' He adds that the real total was never really established. However, even with corps commanders of the calibre of Prinz Eugen von Württemberg on the field, these figures seem to be somewhat overstated. When the prince handed in his casualty list to Barclay that night, the latter at first refused to believe what he read. The prince retorted: 'If Your Excellency refuses to acknowledge the deeds of those still left alive, then perhaps a look at the dead on the battlefield where we fought will convince you!'

French losses on this front are not known with any accuracy. Zelle estimates them at 16,000, apparently extrapolating this total from Martinien's lists of officer casualties. The Poles lost about one third of their strength. When he had been promoted to Marshal of the Empire by Napoleon, Poniatowski had responded with: 'Oh Sire, we are all prepared to die for you.' Now his words were getting uncomfortably close to being transformed into reality.

The total Allied loss at Leipzig on the 16th is estimated by Zelle (p.431) as 38,000 killed and wounded and 2,000 captured. French losses are given as 23,000 killed and wounded, and 2,500 men and sixty guns captured.

After Borodino, these figures represented the heaviest loss of life suffered in a single day since the commencement of the Napoleonic era. Saturday 16 October 1813 held this unenviable record until the First World War.

---

[29] Raglovich commanded the 29th Division, XII Corps, and had received an order calling him home at the end of September as the Austro-Bavarian negotiations progressed. Napoleon had refused to let him go.

Chapter 6

Sunday 17 October

Murat arrived early at imperial headquarters at Meusdorf. He and Napoleon then walked up and down for about half an hour deep in earnest conversation, reviewing the situation and the courses of action still open to them.

Napoleon's options were, indeed, limited: he could either fight or run. To add to his dilemma, two new Allied armies were even now joining the wolf pack which encircled the tired remnants of his army. The wolves had themselves suffered terribly on the 16th, but they were now in such a superior position – in all respects – that they would overpower him in any contest in the near future. There was no possibility of mounting an offensive operation from his present position, with his crippled army almost out of ammunition. Shortly after this meeting, orders were sent out for the French troops to reoccupy the positions at Dösen, Wachau, Liebertwolkwitz and the Kolmberg which they had held the previous day. This was a ruse to deceive the Allies as to the true condition of the *Grande Armée*, they were to believe that Napoleon was fully prepared to renew the contest. It was a bold decision – really the only one the Emperor could make – and it paid off. For if he had tried to withdraw from the southern sector, which his troops had held at such a high cost, it is likely that it would have caused a collapse in morale which could have resulted in his entire army dissolving into a mob of refugees, fleeing into Leipzig to save their own skins.

The numerical balance had swung very much against Napoleon on the 16th, despite the Allies' horrifying losses. On the right wing he had the Guard, II, V, VIII, IX and XI Corps, Lefol's division, and four cavalry corps, totalling some 82,000 men under Murat's command. In the centre was Reynier's VII Corps with 8,000 men, and on the left wing, under Macdonald, were III and VI Corps, Arrighi's III Cavalry Corps, and Dombrowski's Poles, a further 33,000 men in all. Mortier was at Lindenau with 9,000 Guards, Bertrand was at Weissenfels with 10,000 men, and in Leipzig itself Margaron had 3,500 more. Leaving Bertrand out of the equation, 135,000 French troops (including 5,000 belonging to unreliable vassal states) would have to fight against 268,000 Allies on the 18th. Of the latter, 112,000 had not yet been engaged in the battle.

There were also the French garrisons of the German fortresses to be considered. Approximately 130,000 men had been left in Danzig, Dresden, Glogau, Hamburg, Küstrin, Magdeburg, Stettin and Torgau, and if Napoleon was to be defeated now these would almost certainly be lost. 130,000 trained soldiers and their commanders could not be replaced as easily as could muskets, uniforms, waggons, guns and ammunition. Such items were available in large quantities in his arsenal in the fortress at Erfurt, some 135 kilometres away to the west. If he could only reach the depot there with sufficient men he could re-equip his forces and fight his way back to France, and there raise yet another army to restore his fortunes.

The deep respect with which he knew that most of the Allied commanders – particularly Schwarzenberg – regarded him was a psychological advantage which he might yet be able to utilise to his political advantage in parallel with whatever purely tactical measures could be taken to ensure his army's survival. There consequently remained a faint chance of a negotiated armistice or even a (temporary) peace, during which he could disrupt the Allies' unity and rebuild his forces. With his immediate tactical plans decided, Napoleon therefore turned his attention to the possibility of negotiations. The Austrian General von Meerveldt, who had blundered into captivity on the 16th, was called in to see the Emperor shortly after midday. Meerveldt reported the subsequent conversation as follows:

At two o'clock in the afternoon of 17 October Emperor Napoleon called me to him. After he had made some complimentary remarks about our attempt to take his army in flank, he told me that, as a mark of his high regard for me, he was going to release me on my word of honour.

After some questions as to the strength of the Allied armies, he confessed to me that he had not thought them to be so strong; he asked if we had known that he was with the army and I confirmed that we did.

N: 'So, you intended to fight a battle with me?'

M: 'Yes, sire.'

N: 'You are mistaken as to the strength that I have concentrated here; how many men do you think I have?'

M: 'At the most 120,000.'

N: 'I have 200,000. I think I have underestimated your numbers; how many do you have?'

M: 'Over 350,000, sire.'

N: 'Will you attack tomorrow?'

M: 'I do not doubt it, sire. The Allied armies, trusting in their greater numbers, will attack your majesty every day; they hope to bring about a decisive battle and the withdrawal of the French army.'

N: 'Will this war last for ever then? It's time to end it once and for all.'

M: 'Sire, that is the wish of us all and peace lies in your majesty's hands; it depended upon your majesty to make peace at the Congress of Prague.'

N: 'They were not honest with me, they tried to trick me, they set too close a deadline; such an important matter cannot be decided in ten days. Austria missed the opportunity to set herself at Europe's head. I would have done everything that she asked and we would have dictated to the world.'

M: 'I cannot conceal from your majesty that in Austria we are convinced that you would have dictated terms to Austria.'

N: 'But someone has to make the proposals, even if it is Austria! As far as Russia is concerned, she is under England's influence and England does not want peace.'

M: 'I am not at all informed of the intentions of my government, sire.

Everything that I say to your majesty must be regarded as being my own opinions; but I know that the Kaiser, my lord, is totally determined to act in unison with the Allied courts and that he expects this union of purpose to bring about a lasting peace. Your majesty knows that the Allied courts share the wish that peace should be achieved as quickly as possible.'

N: 'Well then, why do they not accept my offer to negotiate? You must see that England does not want peace.'

M: 'Sire, I know with certainty that we await daily an answer to the offer that your majesty has made [to England] and that we think it will be positive.'

N: 'You will see that she will not agree.'

M: 'England needs peace badly herself, sire, but she needs *peace*, not just an armistice. A peace based on terms which ensure that it will last.'

N: 'And what do you think these conditions might be?'

M: 'A balance of forces in Europe that would limit France's dominance.'

N: 'Well then, England should give me my islands back and I will return Hanover to her. I am also ready to give up the annexed *Départements* and the Hanseatic towns.'

M: 'I think, sire, that they will insist on the re-creation of Holland.'

N: 'Oh! It will not be able to exist; no-one will recognise her flag; an isolated Holland would fall under England's influence.'

M: 'I believe, sire, that England's maritime principals are merely a product of the war and will be amended when the war is over; if that is the case, your majesty would have no more need to keep Holland.'

N: 'Well, we shall have to negotiate about this independence, but, with England's attitude, this will not be easy.'

M: 'It would be a generous decision and a great step towards peace.'

N: 'I long for peace; I would make sacrifices – great sacrifices – but there are things that are matters of honour for me, which I could not give up in my situation; for example my protectorate of Germany.'

M: 'Your majesty knows only too well what an obstacle your protectorate of Germany is to the re-establishment of the balance of power in Europe and will thus understand that it cannot be reinforced by a peace. Our alliance with Bavaria and other states of the Confederation of the Rhine, the prospect of including Saxony, will rob your majesty of part of your allies and we believe that the rest will follow when they see the power and successes of our superior strength.'

N: 'Oh! Those who do not want my protection may do as they wish. They will regret it; but my honour forbids me from abandoning the protection of the rest.'

M: 'I remember that your majesty once said to me that it was essential for peace in Europe that France should be separated from the other major European powers by a belt of smaller, independent states. Were your majesty to be prepared to return to this reasonable principle, which your majesty formulated in much more peaceful times, the welfare of Europe would be assured.'

The Emperor gave an answer to this which was not negative. There followed a short silence, then the Emperor said:

N: 'Good, we shall see, but this will not bring peace. How can I negotiate with England who wishes to limit to thirty the number of ships of the line I may build in my harbours? The English themselves know how unacceptable this condition is, that's why they don't mention it, but I know what they want.'

M: 'Sire, I was convinced at the beginning of this conversation that the aim of the Allied powers in this war was the re-establishment of the balance in Europe. England cannot ignore the fact that the extension of the coastline under your majesty's control, stretching from the Adriatic to the North Sea, would allow you to build a fleet two or three times as strong as that which Great Britain would have. And with your majesty's talent and energy, the obvious outcome may easily be calculated. How else will they try to avoid this imbalance other than by limiting the number of ships that may be built in France's harbours; while your majesty would not return to the agreement that you yourself made when you set yourself at the head of the kingdom of Italy, that is to say, to give that country independence again as soon as peace was achieved? I am not aware of anything that your majesty has published that has revoked this undertaking that you laid upon yourself. It would contribute much to calm in Europe; Europe would regard this as a great sacrifice which would be much more preferable to your majesty than trying to limit the number of ships which France would be allowed to build. You would have all the credit for this peace and after you have achieved the highest military fame, this peace would give the you the time to complete all those magnificent projects which you have started in France and to found the happiness of your empire, which would be so dear to you.'

The Emperor admitted that this would be acceptable to him.

N: 'In any case, I would not agree to anything which would lead to the re-establishment of the old order in Italy. This country, unified under a single ruler, would comply with the general system of European politics.'

M: 'Concerning the Duchy of Warsaw, I assume that your majesty would relinquish this?'

N: 'Of course; I offered it but they did not accept it.'

M: 'Then perhaps Spain would be a bone of contention?'

N: 'No; Spain is a dynastic matter.'

M: 'Certainly, sire, but I assume that the warring parties do not all support the same dynasty.'

N: 'I have been forced to evacuate Spain. This question has thus been settled.'

M: 'It seems, then, that peace is possible.'

N: 'Well, send me someone whom I can trust and we will reach agreement. I am always being accused of proposing armistices, so I will propose none, but you have to admit that the general good would only benefit from one. If it is wished, I would be prepared to retire behind the Saale, the Russians and Prussians would fall back behind the Elbe and you would go back into Bohemia. Poor Saxony, that has suffered so much, would be neutral.'

M: 'Due to supplies and forage we would not be able to relinquish Saxony, even if we did not wish to see your majesty back over the Rhine by the autumn due to our superior strength. The Allied armies, I believe, would never agree to your majesty staying on this side of that river if there were to be an armistice.'

N: 'With reference to that, I would first have to lose a battle, that may happen – but it hasn't happened yet.'

If one examines Napoleon's offer of mutual withdrawals, it will be seen just how cunning it was. He was prepared to withdraw behind the River Saale (some thirty kilometres to the west of Leipzig) if the Austrian army would pull back south into Bohemia (over 100 kilometres away) and the Russo-Prussian armies would withdraw eastwards to the east bank of the River Elbe (sixty kilometres to the east of Leipzig). But it is difficult to judge if Napoleon expected anyone to take his proposal seriously. Any half-wit could at once see that it was advantageous only to Napoleon and must be doomed to rejection by the Coalition. It called for the Allies to abandon their stranglehold on their extremely dangerous and cunning enemy, to unravel their carefully integrated armies, to give up large tracts of strategically important territory, to place themselves behind geographical obstacles, and to put themselves once again in the perilous situation of being destroyed in isolation, one by one. All the heavy sacrifices of the past seven years would have been thrown away in exchange for a few minor provinces, which would fall into their hands anyway – together with much, much more – if they could only stick together long enough to see the job through.

Spain, which the French had no hope of controlling anyway, had great relevance to the Leipzig situation. The longer the French had to maintain an army there to oppose the Duke of Wellington's advance into southern France, the fewer resources Napoleon could concentrate against the Allies in Germany.

Following the discussion, Meerveldt was escorted through the front lines and went to Kaiser Franz in Rötha. The Kaiser made it clear at once that he would only discuss Meerveldt's conversation with Napoleon in the presence of his allies. When the Czar and the Prussian king arrived they quickly recognised the implications behind Napoleon's ploy and made it plain that they would not even answer his offer.

This left Napoleon with only two courses of action: to surrender, or to run for Erfurt and then the Rhine. Surrender was obviously out of the question, which only left flight. But what was the best way to achieve this?

It was not until Sunday evening that Napoleon issued new orders to his army, when he finally realised that he had to secure his only available with-drawal route as quickly as possible. This ran through Lützen, Weissenfels and Kösen (the present day B87) to Weimar and Erfurt, of which Weissenfels was already occupied by the enemy (Salins' brigade of Gyulai's corps). To clear this blockage, Bertrand's IV Corps in Lindenau, Guilleminot's 13th Division of Reynier's VII Corps (which had just arrived at Schönefeld and Abtnaundorf) and Quinette's 2nd Cavalry Brigade of Defrance's 4th Heavy Cavalry Division were despatched to Weissenfels. With them went General Baron Rogniat, commander of the Engineers, in order to prepare adequate bridges over the Unstrut and the Saale. His absence from Leipzig over the next two days was to have far-reaching repercussions for the subsequent withdrawal of the army. Bertrand's place in Lindenau was meanwhile taken by Mortier's II Young Guard Corps.

As well as giving consideration to potential river-crossing problems – the Beresina experience had not been lost on him – the Emperor was also mindful of similar factors in his present location. He was fully aware of the Elster-Pleisse-Luppe river complex's value as an obstacle and gave orders for the only remaining route over the rivers to be blocked once the last units of the *Grande Armée* had crossed. This was to be done by preparing the Elster bridge, over which the Ranstädter Steinweg (now the Lützener Strasse) passes, for demolition. Amazingly, however, he gave no orders for additional temporary bridges to be built over these obstacles to facilitate the withdrawal of his army, although he later maintained that he did. And none of his highly-prized kings, princes or marshals seem to have given the problem a moment's thought. It is true that his bridging train was in Torgau fortress, but he still had enough engineering assets to hand to have carried out this task. In any event, no bridges were built, and this was to prove fateful for much of his army on the 19th.

One version of events has it that Colonel Montfort of the engineering staff begged Berthier to issue orders for bridges to be built. Berthier, however, answered that: 'One must know how to carry out the Emperor's orders, but one should not have the temerity to anticipate them.' This illustrates just how far the management of the *Grande Armée* had become a one man affair. If Napoleon did not order it to be done, it would not be done, and not one of his underlings dared to question his decisions or make constructive suggestions. Even the Emperor knew this to be the case. He said: 'Everything in the army rests on me, I must think of everything.' It was therefore Napoleon himself who gave orders on the 17th for the great mass of transport to begin its move through the city and across the river barrier.

***

On the Allied side, it had been expected that the battle would be renewed on the 17th. In the southern sector, the Army of Bohemia was so badly knocked about that its condition dictated no more than defensive action, and Schwarzenberg's orders on the evening of the 16th read: 'The army will remain in the same order of battle which it occupied at the end of today's combat.' However, apart from the re-occupation of their positions, as already outlined, the French made no moves to renew the combat in the south and the day passed peacefully.

In the north, Blücher was not informed of Schwarzenberg's intentions for the 17th. Acting on his own initiative, he considered it to be his duty to exploit Yorck's victory at Möckern to push Marmont further back on Leipzig. During the night Marmont had withdrawn his VI Corps to the east bank of the Parthe, to Schönefeld, but Delmas' division and part of Arrighi's III Cavalry Corps were still on the west bank between Gohlis and Eutritzsch. Blücher therefore decided to take both villages and then to push on south to assault the outer Halle Gate, which was held by the remnants of Dombrowski's division. The assault was to be made by Sacken (on Gohlis) and Langeron (on Eutritzsch); Yorck's battered heroes were to be held in reserve.

The Russian artillery opened up at ten o'clock and its thunder was clearly heard by the Allies in the south. The din alarmed Marshal Ney, who rode over to Gohlis, which was held by the handful of remaining Württembergers. These he replaced by Dombrowski's division, which repulsed Sacken's first attack. Seeing that Gohlis was going to be a problem, Blücher decided to change tactics and to push on against Eutritzsch with Langeron's corps. This time he had more success; the village was only lightly held by Delmas' division, which broke and fled, the Russian cavalry pursuing it in the direction of Schönefeld. Two of Arrighi's cavalry divisions deployed against them, but the Russian hussars overthrew and scattered them after a brief melee; some fell back on Leipzig, while others crossed to the Heiteren Blick (on the present-day B87, towards Taucha) on the east bank of the Parthe. Here they passed Reynier's VII Corps coming down towards Leipzig. Delmas' regiments suffered only one officer casualty in this fight, thus the defence cannot have been at all serious, but he did lose five guns.

Captain von Nostitz, Blücher's ADC, described the event in his diary as follows:

> According to the arrangement made with the main army [Army of Bohemia] the general assault on the French positions was to take place on 17 October. All preparations had been made and Blücher waited impatiently – and in vain – for the agreed signal. The great Battle of the Nations had been postponed to the next day.
>
> Nevertheless, the enemy had advanced some infantry and a battery on the plain and opened up a lively artillery fire.
>
> 'If I were still at the head of my old hussar regiment, I would attack that infantry from the front, go round the flank and take the battery,' said Blücher to General Wasiltschikoff, who was beside him. 'If your excellency will allow, I will try with my hussars,' replied the Russian. Permission was readily granted, the attack was executed by four hussar regiments with great determination, and to Blücher's intense delight – he watched it – the guns were captured together with 500 prisoners.

Graf Henkel von Donnersmark, visiting Blücher's corps, also witnessed this charge:

> The cavalry of our corps, under the active and brave General Wasiltschikoff, who distinguished himself at every occasion, made an excellent attack on

General Arrighi's French cavalry. As the Russian cavalry was forming up to charge, I spotted my friend, a captain of hussars, who was among them. He sat his horse in his usual, competent style, but his face was pale and his expression unusually grim. 'Goodbye, comrade, my servant has the letters that you should send to my family,' he called to me. Then the trumpets sounded, and the Mariupol, Alexandria and White Russian Hussars trotted off.

I could not resist the temptation to go with them, as I had nothing to do for the moment. Our cavalry went on at a cracking pace and the officers, who had burned with envy when they heard how Yorck's cavalry had distinguished itself the previous day, kept shouting '*Paschol, paschol!*' ['Go, go!'] to their men.

The enemy regiments did not stand the shock, but turned and fled towards Leipzig with us on their heels like a thunderstorm. Now and again there were minor clashes during this chase, and in one of them my captain had come up against a Westfalian officer – a clever fencer – who had stabbed him straight through the heart so that he fell dead from his horse.

We found his corpse on our ride back; the sabre was still in his chest. The blade was so badly bent, that it required great strength to pull it out. When I examined the hilt of the weapon more closely, I found that it bore the crest of a well-known Hessian aristocratic family.

In this attack on General Arrighi's cavalry, we came almost up to the suburbs of Leipzig. We took a lot of prisoners, and I captured a French squadron commander and took his sabre. Our losses were not inconsiderable, for on the way back we took fire from a French infantry column. At this point my prisoner, whose horse I was leading by the bridle, was killed by a French ball. In his holsters I found several letters and diaries that were addressed to his wife, who lived in a castle in Savoy. Later, in Naumburg, I handed these in to the post office together with the letters of my dead friend.

The captured horse was big but in poor condition, so I exchanged it with a Russian field officer for a strong Cossack horse; now I owned three such Don Cossack mounts. They are excellent for use on campaigns where there are lots of hardships, but they do have some beauty defects.

While General Wasiltschikoff's cavalry were mounting their bold attack – one of the best that I ever saw Russian cavalry make – the infantry of Sacken's corps was not idle. The general had advanced on the right wing and soon clashed with Dombrowski's Polish division [at Gohlis].

Honour should be given to whomsoever earns it, even if it is the enemy, and in this case I must admit that the Poles repeatedly beat off the Russian assaults even though heavily outnumbered. Finally, they had to fall back, but they marched off in good order and took up another position closer to Leipzig. When the Poles and Russians clashed in this campaign, they always did so violently, asking for, and giving, no quarter, so deep was the hatred between these two nations that are at once so similar and so dissimilar.

General von Blücher wanted to exploit the morning's successes with his whole army and made preparations to cross the Parthe and to attack Leipzig, when suddenly an order came in from Allied headquarters directing us to stop all further hostilities for the day. The old boy cursed and shouted and made harsh remarks about certain people in positions of high command, but there was nothing for it but to obey. The advance was abandoned and the troops bivouacked where they were.

General von Zeschau, commander of the 24th Saxon Division of VII Corps, wrote in his diary:

We marched through Heiteren Blick towards Leipzig and saw enemy columns advancing against us from all sides. A lively clash flared up between the opposing outposts on the Parthe. Suddenly, the French that we could see at Schönefeld ran off; their train soldiers cut the traces of their waggons and rode off on the horses.

The Saxon division had piled arms and was resting. This flight of the French filled me with foreboding. I thus had the assembly beaten and addressed the men roughly as follows: 'Comrades, this example which you have just seen will have no effect on you. We fight today for our king. Every true Saxon has cause to gather all his strength to fulfil his duty. Are you ready to do this?' I was answered by a loud 'Yes!' I then raised three cheers for the king; the men all joined in. Their morale was good.

In the midst of the fleeing French troops, Reynier ordered the Saxon division to deploy in two lines facing south-west across the road towards Schönefeld. No French stragglers were allowed through. As there were no further attacks by Blücher, Reynier advanced on Schönefeld to support Marmont.

Oberkanonier Böhme of Captain Dietrich's Saxon foot artillery battery recorded the event as follows:

We reached Taucha at six o'clock in the morning of 17 October and halted on a field of potatoes near the windmill and enjoyed our last breakfast before the battle. It consisted of potatoes roasted in the campfires. At eight o'clock we moved off again. At Heiteren Blick we halted and deployed into line of battle. After we had double loaded our guns with ball and canister and trained them on Schönefeld, a mass of Frenchmen came running towards us from that place. We did not know what to make of this and believed that the French were abandoning us. But soon the event was explained and we calmed down again. We did not fire a shot all day. This same day, we were issued with a loaf, worth about eight Grosschen, which was supposed to be shared out between twelve gunners and twenty-two train soldiers. We were in a cabbage field and stilled our hunger with cabbage leaves; there was nothing else. It rained all day so that we were all soaked through. Lieutenant Voss of the infantry came to visit me and told me that he was going to visit his family in Leipzig. He asked me if I would like him to go to my parents. I was delighted with his offer, asked him to give them all my best wishes and to tell them that I was here and would be fighting in the forthcoming battle.

He came back next morning bringing me greetings from my parents and some food. With the help of my comrades it was all gone in no time. From here we moved to Paunsdorf where we took post by a windmill.

The rest of the day was uneventful; towards evening, the divisions of Zeschau and Durutte moved a little to the south-east to Paunsdorf. Guilleminot's 14th Division had already left to join Bertrand's corps at Lindenau.

During these events, Sacken's Russians had taken Gohlis at the second attempt despite the brave defence of Dombrowski's Poles, whose flank had been exposed by the flight of Delmas' division. The Poles withdrew in good order to the Pfaffendorf outwork and then into the Rosengarten area between the Pleisse and the Elster.

Blücher was now in possession of the north bank of the Parthe close up to the town and had aimed to cross to the southern bank to assault Leipzig from that side before evening; this was before the order from Schwarzenberg arrived postponing the assault until the next day. In the southern sector, General Graf Colloredo's I (Austrian) Corps of some 17,000 men had arrived – in an exhausted condition – at Magdeborn, from Chemnitz and Borna. Bennigsen's Reserve Army had also come in from the siege of Dresden, and on the afternoon of the 17th his patrols made contact with elements of the Army of Bohemia at Naunhof and Fuchshain, some five kilometres east of Liebertwolkwitz.

Coming up from Bohemia with Bennigsen's army was Austrian General Bubna's 2nd Light Division, but at Nossen, thirty-four kilometres west of Dresden, Bubna parted company with the Russians and went off on his own towards Hubertusberg and Wurzen, twenty-three kilometres east of Leipzig, on the east bank of the River Mulde. On 16 October Bubna was at Döbeln, some fifty-five kilometres south-east of Leipzig (where Route B169 crosses the Mulde), when he heard the distant thunder of the great battle around the city. He at once headed for the tell-tale sounds and reached Hubertusberg after a march of fourteen hours; his rearmost battalion arriving at one o'clock on the morning of the 17th. They hurried on to Wurzen, where Bubna dropped off a detachment to hold the crossing. A flying bridge was improvised to ferry the infantry across while the cavalry swam the river. At dusk on the 17th Bubna's leading elements reached Machern (about five kilometres east of Taucha on Route B6) and Gerichshain. Here, strong enemy columns closed in on him from his front and right flank. At this critical point he also received a report that a thousand French troops were closing in on Wurzen.

With the enemy threatening him from three sides, and with no knowledge of the outcome of the fighting round Leipzig, Bubna's plight was unenviable. Happily for him, his cavalry patrols met with some of Platoff's Cossacks between Beucha and Zweenfurth, about five kilometres south-east of Taucha. He had at last made contact with the extreme right wing of the Army of Bohemia.

He now received a despatch from Bennigsen, from Fuchshain to his south, ordering him to place his division between Seifertshain and Paunsdorf to the north. The next morning he was to be at Klein-Pössna, two kilometres north of Seifertshain. The threatening enemy columns had meanwhile melted away in the dark.

***

The strenuous efforts of Bennigsen, Bubna and Colloredo to reach and participate in this critical battle contrasted crassly with the studied lethargy and inactivity of Bernadotte, Crown Prince of Sweden. This dubious ally had accompanied Blücher as far as Halle on the Saale, some twenty kilometres north-west of Leipzig, but had then let him fight alone at Möckern on the 16th, holding the Army of the North inactive the whole day at Landsberg, just east of Halle. Despite the fact that the din of the battle was clearly audible Bernadotte did not lift a finger to help.

Sir Charles Stewart (the British military representative in Bernadotte's headquarters) was beside himself with rage. During the morning of the 16th, he wrote to the Crown Prince saying that honour and duty commanded that they take part in the great struggle going on just to the south. He further alluded to the commitments that the prince had entered into in order to receive the considerable subsidies which Britain was paying him. The eyes of the British nation were upon him; if the French were beaten, the British people would not understand his indifference to taking part in the great victory. There was no reaction.

Sir Charles was more pointed in a second letter, written in the evening the same day:

> Your Royal Highness, I return from General Blücher's battlefield. I dare to beg Your Royal Highness to break camp this instant and to move to Taucha. There is not a second to be lost. I speak now as a soldier and Your Royal Highness would only regret it if you did not march at once.
>
> I have the Honour to be Your Majesty's most humble servant.
> C Stewart.

Not surprisingly, Bernadotte took offence at the contents of the letter with its thinly veiled criticism of his talents as a commander and as a gentleman. Stung into partial action, he did move the Army of the North to Breitenfeld, four kilometres to the north of Möckern (now just south of Autobahn A4), on the 17th, but that was as close to danger as he was prepared to go. He knew that Gyulai's corps was at Lindenau, blocking Napoleon's withdrawal to the west, and he feared that the Emperor might consequently break out to the north. Rather than stand directly in his path and risk the possibility of being crushed by the imperial Fury as he rushed out of Leipzig, Bernadotte therefore considered it safer to take up a position off to one side.

On the morning of the 18th Blücher went to Breitenfeld to confer with Bernadotte, and the following decisions were made:

1. Blücher gave the Crown Prince a corps of 30,000 men from the Army of Silesia. This corps would be under Bernadotte's command and would assault

the enemy from Taucha. With the rest of his army, Blucher would maintain his position before Leipzig and would try to take the city.

2. If Napoleon was to turn on the Armies of the North and of Silesia, they would combine to resist him until the Army of Bohemia came to their aid.

This meant that, in order to get the reluctant hero to take any effective part in the struggle at all, Blücher had given him the greater part of his own army, the rump of the Army of Silesia left under Blücher's command numbering only 12,000 men.

Following this meeting, the Crown Prince summoned Sir Charles Stewart, who has left us the following account of their conversation:

> When I entered the Crown Prince's room he was surrounded by his generals and I was not a little surprised to see him approach me with an expression of scarcely-controlled rage on his face. He led me into a window niche and spoke very quietly to me so that the others could not hear us. 'How, General Stewart, what right do you have to write to me ? Have you forgotten that I am the Crown Prince of Sweden and one of the greatest army commanders of our time? If you were to be in my position, what would you think if someone wrote to you as you have to me? You are not accredited to me as a minister. You are only here through my friendship and you have caused me much displeasure.'
>
> I answered him in a respectful tone: It was possible that my ardour had taken me too far; but – in the light of the manner in which I understood my duties – I could not regret what I had done. It was true that I was not formally a British minister to the Swedish court, but I was responsible for all Britain's military interests in northern Europe, that Britain was paying the Swedish army, and that my reports as to the manner in which this army carried out its responsibilities must have great influence on the relationships between the two courts. I was not capable of such vanity as to compare my military views with those of so a great a commander, but that it did not take much intelligence to see that HRH had actually been forced into taking his last actions, that his previous orders had plainly been in contradiction to the Combination System and against the agreed dispositions of the Allied armies and that now was not the moment for diplomatic reserve.

***

The troops of the Army of the North inflicted much damage to the villages around Breitenfeld. The whole area between that place and Podelwitz (the site of the battle of 1631) was covered with troops. They plundered the villages and took all the cattle, and horses and men were requisitioned to remove the wounded from the battlefield of Möckern. The men returned, but the horses were never seen again. As usual, anything that would burn was taken to feed the countless campfires; in some cases whole houses vanished. Even the presence of the Prussian General von Borstell in the schoolhouse in Podelwitz proved to be no deterrent to the looters. The men were not violent, but conditions forced them to take whatever food they could find, as the army's own logistics system had completely failed. In Breitenfeld alone, where Bernadotte's headquarters were, the soldiers took eighteen horses, fifty bullocks and all the pigs and poultry. The courageous mistress of the manor ran after the departing looters with a maid, pushed over a Cossack and took back the last string of six cows to the safety of the farmyard.

Passing through Taucha the same day, the Saxon 24th Division of General von Zeschau behaved just as badly as other troops. Shortly after Reynier's VII Corps left the town, the first Cossacks of the Army of the North entered it, early in the afternoon. These were soon followed by the main body. They swarmed over the landscape and captured the French outposts in the area, then camped outside the town gates throughout the night and demanded to be supplied with wood, oats, hay, straw, food and – above all – spirits in large quantities.

General Graf Wilhelm von Hochberg of Baden remembered the day as follows:

> On the 17th I was supposed to relieve the Württemberg General von Franquemont at the Halle Gate and General Dombrowski in the Löhrischen-Garten. As it was not yet daylight, I met the former in the house where he was staying, next to the gate where he and his officers were laying on the floor. In the dark I trod on one of the officers which caused an uproar. It was the Prinz von Hohenlohe. Only after much shouting could I make General von Franquemont understand why I was there.
>
> I then went to General Dombrowski, whom I found in the Löhrischen-Garten, wrapped in a bearskin. The combat had already begun and a cannonball smashed into a stone figure and the fragments whizzed past our ears. Dombrowski fell on my shoulders, so happy was he to be relieved of his post with his 600 Poles.
>
> At the outer Halle Gate, which was shut, there was a terrible scene. Many wounded, with smashed and amputated legs, were trying to climb over it in order to get into the town. Major von Holzing [3rd Baden Light Infantry Regiment] made a sortie with fifty men during which he cut down a Russian officer and brought me his sash, which I still have. We lost a lot of men; *Leutnant* von Khuon was wounded in the neck. The town was heavily bombarded and caught fire in several places.
>
> I was called frequently to the Duke of Padua, who did not leave his quarters. From the tower next to his house I could see how the enemy ring around Leipzig was being drawn ever tighter.

Writing on the 18th, *Generalmajor* von Schäffer reported of von Holzing's sortie that: 'At this critical moment, Major von Holzing took command; the Russians were trying to break down the gate. He gathered the men, had the gate opened and led his men in a bayonet charge. This surprised the enemy and they were thrown back past Gohlis.'

***

Within Leipzig itself Sunday was another day of fear and rumour for the inhabitants and refugees. From the activities of the French it had become clear to all that the victory celebrations ordered the previous day had been somewhat premature. Shortly after nine o'clock the town was awakened by the thunder of artillery from the direction of the Halle Gate. Projectiles fell inside the city and damaged houses in the Fleischergasse, the Nikolaistrasse and on the Brühl. The city streets presented a terrible sight, crowded with dead and dying soldiers expiring untended in their own blood. The conduct of the French towards their wounded comrades was indescribably heartless. However, the city council was threatened with the full fury of Napoleon's rage by the French authorities – and particularly by Maret, the Duc de Bassano – if they did not at once make available the necessary hospital facilities for the wounded. All the public buildings except the Nikolai church were already filled with casualties, but no-one thought of holding a church service anyway. Even the nine waggons which rumbled backwards and forwards through the streets between the makeshift hospitals and the cemeteries from five o'clock in the morning until well after dark were not enough to remove all the corpses.

To make matters worse, the town had been totally cut off from its food suppliers in the surrounding countryside. On the 16th the appearance of the last bread waggon to get through sparked a food riot as everyone fought to get one of the precious loaves at whatever price, a struggle in which the strongest and most brutal came off best. Every household in Leipzig was forced to hand over without delay whatever was demanded of them by the soldiery, be it food, drink, tools, clothing, money, bedclothes or beds.

The garrison of the city was already making provision to resist an assault. Every able citizen was forced to work on its entrenchments and other fortifications. Houses in appropriate locations were commandeered, the walls loopholed and garrisons put in them for the coming battle. The Württembergers occupied the outer Halle Gate and its adjacent houses, loopholed the walls and built an earthen wall across the gate. Cannon were set up in the gardens outside the walls to command the north bank of the Parthe.

But while the mood of the French soldiery was depressed and nervous, that of most of the German contingents of the garrison was bordering on the festive. The company of Badeners at the gate by the orphanage were offering to sell their muskets and openly saying that they would not resist the Allies.

As night fell, the nervous Leipzigers could tell from the surrounding campfires that the defending troops had fallen back much closer to the city than they had been the day before.

Chapter 7

Monday 18 October

The battle for Leipzig

Monday was to see the commencement of the French army's retreat. The irony of the date was not lost on some, who noted that the retreat from Moscow had begun exactly one year ago.

On the morning of 18 October, von Gneisenau wrote to his wife:

> I write to you on the morning of a battle, the like of which has scarcely been seen in the history of the world. We have surrounded the French emperor. This battle will decide the fate of Europe. The day before yesterday, Blücher's army won a fine victory at Möckern. We were opposed by the best French corps – that of Marshal Marmont – as well as IV and VII Corps, part of the French Guard and a Polish corps. The fight was long and hard, it cost a lot of blood but we threw the enemy out of his positions. Our plans were ably complemented by the bravery of the troops. We were formed up in battalion masses, the enemy guns wrought great havoc in them. Our *Landwehr* battalions were splendid. If a cannonball killed 10–15 men, they shouted 'Long live the king!' and closed towards the centre over the corpses.

Baron von Odeleben records that Napoleon's day began very early.

> Napoleon drove to Reudnitz, where he got out at Marshal Ney's house, who was deeply asleep with all his staff in the Emperor's old headquarters. He stayed there until about five o'clock [in the morning], then drove around the city and on to Lindenau to General Bertrand. He viewed the bridge and the area where Bertrand had been attacked two days ago. He also ordered General Bertrand to march for Weissenfels. Sometimes in his coach, sometimes on horseback, he then returned through the suburbs to Stötteritz by the same route.
>
> It was eight o'clock. The Guard had arrived at Stötteritz. The Emperor ate breakfast in one of the farms there. The increasing thunder of cannon from all sides soon woke up the entire headquarters. The uninterrupted fire of heavy guns could be heard from Markkleeberg, Dölitz and Liebertwolkwitz. The Swedish Redoubt [ie, the Kolmberg] had been evacuated by the French during the night and the king of Naples had taken post before Probstheida with the corps of Marshals Victor and Augereau. Right at the beginning of the combat, he sent to Napoleon requesting reinforcements because of the greatly superior forces ranged against him.
>
> The Allies wanted to force the crossings of the Pleisse simultaneously at Dölitz, Lösnig and Connewitz. Napoleon rode over to the area and stopped at the tobacco mill. Here, he began and ended this great day that was to strip

the laurels which Lady Luck had until then woven around his brows. A battered, half-destroyed windmill stood before him as a threatening, evil omen of how fickle luck could be.

One of Leipzig's suburbs was afire. The shells fell in the city, even onto the house in which the king was staying on the market square. Schönefeld, Stötteritz, Dölitz and Liebertwolkwitz were in flames. The mist and the smoke almost concealed the area from view, but the mist cleared and the day was fine. Although the French were tired, hungry and ragged from the previous marches and privations, they fought with great valour, at least in the area around Napoleon. Surrounded on all sides, they suffered the disadvantage of having superior artillery against them. Though there were some thousands of stragglers in the city there was no sign of a general flight.

Prince Poniatowski had the most difficult task, but he mastered it completely and justified the high trust which Napoleon had placed in him. His small infantry corps – down to 5,000 men now and to 2,700 by the end of the day – did its utmost. Fifteen officers of Poniatowski's staff were killed or wounded at Leipzig. This courage, from a nation which could scarcely expect the restoration of their country by Napoleon in the present circumstances, was all the more remarkable for this.

The Emperor spent over an hour on the right wing of the battle. Now he hurried to the front ranks of his army at Probstheida, partly to see the situation with his own eyes, and partly to encourage his men. He arrived at the moment when the Allies advanced from Zuckelhausen and Holzhausen in great strength and seized part of Probstheida.

Horses, wounded, and all supernumeraries streamed in crowds to the rear. Napoleon flew into the front ranks; filled the gaps with the reserves of the Old Guard and soon returned to his battered windmill, where he spent the rest of the day.

The brave king of Naples held off all attacks and stormed the village of Probstheida, which was the target of the assaults.

Whilst on the 16th the advantages of the terrain had lain with the French, today the Allies occupied many of the low, but dominant hills from where they poured their concentric artillery fire into the French army. The enemy artillery demonstrated their terrible strength. In a short time, over a dozen damaged cannon were sent to the rear past the spot where Napoleon stood, and thousands of wounded went back into the city. After six or seven hours of heavy firing, the French began to run out of ammunition. Perhaps for the first time in his martial career, the Emperor ordered them to conserve their stocks!

During the course of the morning, an adjutant of General Reynier had brought news of the defection of part of the Saxon artillery and cavalry. At three o'clock he received confirmation that the infantry too had left the French ranks.

Up to now, Napoleon had maintained an air of greatest calm and equanimity. He walked up and down with a mostly cool, reflective and introverted air. This latest news did not alter his demeanour, although a certain displeasure showed on his face. He rode up to the king of Naples, who had beaten off another fierce assault, spoke with him for a while, sent him some artillery support to Dösen then returned to the windmill where he had a fire lit.

It was dusk already but the fire burned well into the night.

Finally, exhaustion seemed to overcome both sides. The right wing at Connewitz and Dölitz had held its position since morning, but from Stötteritz to Schönefeld much terrain had been lost.

It was dark. The artillery fell silent; only the occasional musket shot rang out. The earth and the sky both twinkled with countless fires. Napoleon had already given Prince Berthier permission to order the retreat and Berthier was, as usual, dictating orders in his brief manner to some adjutants at a small fire. Deep silence reigned round about. The artillery generals Sorbier and Dulauloy were saying that a renewal of the fight would certainly be possible if they had 30–40,000 fresh troops and some hundreds of ammunition waggons, but...

They had brought the Emperor a wooden footstool on which he soon fell asleep, exhausted by the strain of the last few days, his hands lightly folded in his lap. At this moment he was just the same as any other mortal carrying the burdens of misfortune. The generals stood, silent and gloomy, around the fire, and the retreating troops trudged past a short distance away.

After about a quarter of an hour, the Emperor awoke and threw a great, wide-eyed stare around about him. He seemed to ask: 'Am I awake or is this a dream?' He quickly gathered himself and gave the order to an officer to go to the king of Saxony and tell him that he could not visit him today.

As this unfortunate soul [the king of Saxony] was now in such a hopeless situation, Napoleon sent him a messenger to tell him that he might make his own decision to make the best peace that he could with his enemies; Napoleon's only concern was that the king should ensure that the French wounded were cared for. At the same time, the Emperor allowed the few remaining Saxon troops, including the Leibgarde battalion that had been serving with the Imperial Guard, to return to the king. This took place on 19th October.

The feelings that raged within such a man when the entire structure of his fame and fortune was crashing down about him can scarcely be appreciated by lesser mortals. Napoleon had experienced such critical moments before, in Egypt and in Russia. Moments of defeat which only his unshatterable belief in his skill and his fate allowed him to overcome.

The desire to arise from the ashes of a disaster to the amazement of the world had lent wings to his new schemes in the past. In earlier years he had been able to lay the blame for all his defeats at the door of overpowering external factors.

But now, the Imperator had been so soundly defeated for the first time in his life, before the gaze of all of educated Europe, that it would be more difficult than ever for him to silence the criticism of that nation whose homes were now to be threatened by the victorious armies. To put it briefly, he had lost an incomparable battle. He would now draw his enemies on to the sacred soil of France, which had not been invaded since he came to power, and this at a time when the exhausted nation could scarcely be expected to bring forth the strength, the men and the materials needed for its defence.

Even if he found positive expressions to describe the events, at the end of the day he could not disguise the damage that had been done.

The Emperor stayed by the campfire until after eight o'clock. At first, his quarters were to be set up in Thonberg, but as all buildings in the area were filled with wounded, there was no room for him. He rode to the Rossplatz and took rooms in the Hôtel de Prusse. How poetic that he was to stay here when he had just been forced to flee from the state of the same name.

Napoleon was busy until far into the night with the Duke of Bassano, Caulaincourt and Berthier. Caution dictated that everything should be ready so that we could leave at once and the horses had been ready since two o'clock. The coaches and the main body of the headquarters were already in Lindenau.

Napoleon did not leave Leipzig until eleven o'clock on the 19th October. He could be seen, sometimes busy, sometimes in his dressing gown, at the window. The march of the French troops through the city went on without interruption. At half past eight we heard firing from the direction of the [outer] Grimma Gate. At nine o'clock Napoleon mounted his horse and rode through the [inner] Grimma Gate to the king's house. He dismounted. The king received him with the usual etiquette and led him up to his room where the queen was. The retinue stayed in the outer room.

On the square were some Saxon and Baden troops. The conversation between the monarchs lasted over a quarter of an hour, in which Napoleon doubtless expressed his desire to be able to support him more effectively. They then parted and the king accompanied the Emperor to the stairs as court etiquette required.

From the moment when the Emperor mounted his horse finally to leave Leipzig, he was very obviously deeply depressed. Rapt in thought – or perhaps thinking of absolutely nothing – he rode diagonally across the square towards the Ranstädter Gate, and as this was completely blocked with the monstrous queue of troops and waggons, he rode around the inside of the city, past the two blocked gates and the Thomas church to the Peterstor Gate. Here, the Emperor orientated himself briefly and rode back to his quarters on the Rossplatz, or – more correctly – along the avenue to the area of the Bürgerschule.

The attack had become most violent on this side and balls flew into the town. The suburbs were occupied with French troops. The corps of Poniatowski and Lauriston formed the rearguard and should have defended the suburbs from house to house in accordance with their orders. Napoleon initially wanted to burn down the suburbs, but he then abandoned the idea, and this crime would not have helped him. He now turned back, rode past the Peterstor Gate and around the town to the Ranstädter Steinweg. Due to the massive crowds of troops, it was almost impossible for the Emperor to make headway; he and his retinue had to squeeze through the crush one by one.

Ammunition waggons, sutlers, gendarmes and cannon, cows and sheep, women, grenadiers and coaches, the healthy, the wounded and the dying – all were so crushed together in a great mass that it was scarcely possible to move forward far less to think of any organised resistance.

If the enemy were to break through here, then no-one would have escaped because the entrance to the outer Ranstädter Gate, through which all had to pass, was so narrow that apart from one waggon, only a couple of pedestrians could pass. True, a bridge had been built over the Elster in the so-called Richters Garden, but this was so badly constructed that it collapsed after a short while. This worsened the predicament of those left behind. Perhaps it was the cause of Prince Poniatowski throwing himself into the Elster in order to avoid capture.

Napoleon followed the great stream of fugitives on the great road to Lindenau. Here he halted and tasked various officers with informing the confused mass of men where they were to go in order to find their corps again. These points had been set up to both sides of the roads to Weissenfels and Merseburg.

After having reinstated some order here, the Emperor went into the mill at Lindenau and went upstairs. The cannon fire in the city grew more and more intense; one could hear the whistling of the cannonballs and the rattle of musketry. Suddenly the artillery fire stopped. It was about eleven o'clock. Shortly after this, the headquarters moved off to Markranstadt.

***

Colonel Griois (commanding the foot artillery of the Imperial Guard) had fought on 16 October in the great battery on the southern front on the Galgenberg, between Wachau and Liebertwolkwitz. On the 17th his guns had been pulled back to the centre of the French position. In his memoirs he records his own account of events on Monday the 18th, the decisive day of the conflict:

On 18 October at three o'clock in the morning, an orderly officer brought me an order to set off with my artillery for the town [Leipzig]. I made the necessary preparations and we set off. But all roads were completely blocked ... with troops of all arms moving in the same direction. I could get on only very slowly and had to stop every quarter of an hour to allow my long column to close up again.

Happily, there was clear moonlight for without it there would have been chaos.

The start of our march had been marked by a series of explosions and a great fire as all the waggons and caissons which could no longer be moved due to lack of horses were being burned with their contents. This spectacle caused a deep depression in me for it reminded me of our retreat from Moscow. It was a bad omen.

A lively cannonade began and between seven and eight o'clock an orderly officer joined me during one of our frequent halts, which caused such delays on the road. He told me that the Emperor had ordered me to take one of my batteries to the position now occupied by the divisions of the Old Guard. The other three were to continue their march. I accompanied that battery which was to rejoin the Guard; we turned off to the left and soon arrived with my eight guns of the 5e *Compagnie* at a windmill in the centre of the Old Guard's position.

The Emperor was there surrounded by his staff. Before him was the battalion of the grenadiers of the guard which the king of Saxony had sent to the Emperor. It was composed of fine strong men, dressed in white[30] and very smart. These were the only Saxons who had remained loyal that day, and after the battle the Emperor had sent them back to the service of the king. It is embarrassing to say that these same grenadiers would fire from the ramparts of Leipzig onto the same troops with whom they had fought on the previous day.

I reported to the Emperor who told me to park my battery in his bivouac and to be ready to move off when the order came.

The fire was very lively to our left where there were two batteries of the horse artillery of the Guard. A young train soldier rode across to us from them mounted on a wounded horse. He told me that the commander of these batteries, *Chef de Escadron* Georges de Lemud, had lost a lot of men and horses and needed replacements urgently. I told the soldier that I had only the bare minimum of both with me and could spare him none. I advised him to ride over to the grand park of the artillery of the guard which was a little way to the rear, under the walls of Leipzig; they would issue him with replacements. 'I know that,' he replied, 'but I am wounded by a ball on the foot and I don't think I have the strength to ride that far.'

I looked down and saw that his leg was shattered, with blood pouring from the wound. I cannot tell you what a deep effect his simple heroism had on me. I told him to go into Leipzig and have his wound dressed and I sent one of my men to escort him there.

Such admirable devotion to duty, such quiet courage; they belonged to the times of chivalry, yet they were here; in a young man, a conscript. How many other of our young men were motivated by these same honourable concepts? A few days later I rode past a stretcher on a caisson; it was my young soldier, as pale as death and very weak. I rode off and found Surgeon-Major Boileau and asked him to look at the wounded man; Boileau ampu-

---

[30] This is difficult to understand. The Saxon Leib-Grenadier-Garde wore red tunics.

tated the shattered leg. I then lost contact with the young fellow but I fear that he succumbed to his wound.

Meanwhile, the firing was getting very lively in front of the Emperor's position. He could see that the horse batteries were suffering badly and could not hold on much longer. He asked me to replace them with my battery which I did. De Lemud's command had lost a lot of men and horses and withdrew to replenish its ammunition.

I advanced and set up my eight guns to the left of the village of Connewitz on our extreme right wing and opened up a lively fire.

The battle surged back and forth; the Poles under Poniatowski held the village and to my left were Mortier's Young Guard. We advanced when our troops did and changed front as necessary to engage the best targets. As the enemy infantry were getting uncomfortably close and causing casualties among my gunners, I asked General Drouot, who was commanding in this sector this day, to send me some infantry protection. He sent up the battalion of Velites de Florence, who were part of the Guard, and they soon taught the enemy to have some respect.

Towards evening it became clear that the battle was going against us. I saw Marshal Poniatowski; he looked depressed, as if he knew what fate would befall him next day.

Night fell and the firing died down along the front. An orderly officer of the Emperor arrived and told me to retire with my battery to the walls of Leipzig; we moved off. When we reached the town I found my other three batteries waiting for me there. They had been employed at other points on the battlefield. We settled down on the glacis amid the throng of men, horses and equipment which were concentrated there.

I had had nothing to eat all day except a frugal breakfast and was overwhelmingly tired. I fell asleep in the warmth of the campfire despite the noise and clatter of the troops who kept coming and going.

A few moments later, an orderly officer arrived from the Emperor; he ordered me to set off at once with my artillery, to pass through the city and to go on to Lindenau. He added, as he accompanied me, that the Emperor and his suite were already on the move and that the Emperor would be staying in a house in the suburbs.

We moved off into Leipzig, preceded by the orderly officer, and crossed the town without any great difficulties. We finally arrived at Lindenau and went into bivouac with other units of the Guard.

***

In contrast to the preceding days, the 18th dawned fine with bright sunshine. As we have seen, Napoleon had driven to Marshal Ney's headquarters at Reudnitz in the early hours and then gone out at five o'clock to Lindenau, where he had ordered General Bertrand to set off for Weissenfels. Mortier's Young Guard corps replaced the departing troops. He then drove back to Stötteritz, just two kilometres north of Probstheida, where he abandoned his carriage, mounted a horse, and carried out an inspection of his army's new dispositions. He set up his headquarters by Quandt's tobacco mill, now a short walk to the north-west of the gigantic memorial to the battle, and stayed there for most of the day. As usual, the Old Guard (the divisions of Curial and Friant) was deployed around him.

The emperor's forces now totalled somewhere between 130,000 and 160,000 men (sources differ considerably), deployed as follows:

At Lindenau – Marshal Mortier with his two divisions of the Young Guard.

North of Leipzig – south of Gohlis and with the Pleisse at their backs were Dombrowski's redoubtable Poles and the city garrison under Margaron. They extended to the outer Halle Gate and the Pfaffendorf outwork. In front of the infantry was Lorge's 5th Light Cavalry Division of Arrighi's III Cavalry Corps.

The left wing under Marshal Ney – Marmont's VI Corps was at Schönefeld (about three kilometres east of Margaron's command and separated from him by the River Parthe), while von Zeschau's Saxon division of Reynier's VII Corps was at Paunsdorf. Durutte's division of VII Corps was in reserve at Sellershausen.

The centre under Marshal Macdonald – XI Corps was in Zuckelhausen, Holzhausen and on the Steinbergen hill just west of Holzhausen. Behind them was Sebastiani's II Cavalry Corps. To the west of these was Lauriston's V Corps between Probstheida and Stötteritz, with units forward at Zwei-naundorf and Mölkau. General Walther's guards cavalry division was to the south of this sector, just west of Zuckelhausen, and Nansouty was to the north-west at Stötteritz with the rest of the cavalry of the guard.

The right wing under Marshal Murat – This held a line in the south from the Pleisse eastwards to Probstheida. Victor's II Corps was at Probstheida with Augereau's IX Corps to his west, with forward elements in Dösen and Dölitz.

As before, Poniatowski's VIII Corps held Connewitz and Dölitz with Semelle's 52nd Division of IX Corps in the water meadows east of the Pleisse opposite Connewitz and Lefol's division in Connewitz itself. To the north, behind Poniatowski, was Decouz's division of the Young Guard and Keller-mann's IV Cavalry Corps, which was reinforced by Krukowiecki's 18th Light Cavalry Brigade from Dombrowski's division. Just west of Probstheida was V Cavalry Corps, now commanded by General Milhaud in place of Pajol, who had been wounded on the 16th.

The Reserve was composed of I Cavalry Corps (commanded today by General Doumerc) between Stötteritz and Strassenhäusern, and the Old Guard around the hamlet of Thonberg, with Napoleon's headquarters at the tobacco mill to the south of the Old Guard.

The two most vulnerable points in the French perimeter were in the north-east (along the road from Taucha into the left wing) and in the south-east, where the road from Grimma pointed like a dagger towards the heart of Leipzig through the right wing. A distinct strength of the French position, however, was its interior lines of communication, the advantages of which were fully exploited by Napoleon.

The Allied plan

Schwarzenberg had divided the Allied armies into six assault columns, each with the simple task of attacking to its front until victory was achieved. Lederer's division of II Corps, however, was restricted to continuing its operations opposite Dölitz and Connewitz, which were of little more than nuisance value. In contrast to the 16th, the Allied formations were much more concentrated and coherent.

The Army of Bohemia (confronting the French right wing under Murat) was divided into two assault columns. The 1st (Austrian) Column under the Erbprinz Friedrich von Hessen-Homburg, numbering some 40,000 men, consisted of the corps of Colloredo and Meerveldt, now commanded by Liechtenstein, and extended from west of the Pleisse eastwards to just west of Probstheida. Its forming up place has since fallen victim to opencast mining, which extends north as far as the line just before Markkleeberg-Wachau. East of them was the 2nd Column under Barclay de Tolly, consisting of 50,000 men of the corps of Gortschakoff, Eugen von Württemberg, Kleist's Prussians and the Russo-Prussian Guards. It was aimed at Probstheida.

The 3rd Column consisted of General Bennigsen's Army of the Reserve and was opposed to Macdonald's centre. It included Klenau's IV (Austrian) Corps, which was part of the Army of Bohemia and confronted Zuckel-hausen. Stroganoff's division was aimed at Holzhausen, and Dokturoff's corps at Zweinaundorf. On his right wing were Bubna's 2nd Light Division, aimed at Paunsdorf, and Platoff's Cossacks holding contact with the Army of the North.

The 4th Column was made up of the Army of the North and the Russian corps of Langeron and Saint-Priest (some 80,000 men), opposing the French left wing from Paunsdorf to the Parthe.

The 5th Column under Blücher consisted of Yorck's battered heroes and Sacken's Russian corps (only about 25,000 men in all). This was to the north of Leipzig, between the Parthe and the Pleisse, confronting Dombrowski's Poles.

The 6th Column was Gyulai's III (Austrian) Corps, with Liechtenstein's division and the *Streifkorps* of Thielmann and Mensdorff under its command. They were west of the Elster at Klein-Zschocher and had the task of attacking the road out of Lindenau. Zelle estimates Gyulai to have had 18,000 men on the 18th (p.439), but this is impossibly high, as he had started on the 16th with only 15,600, had lost over 2,000 that day (also according to Zelle), and had not been reinforced since. In reality Gyulai had about 13,400 men on the morning of the 18th and had to transfer one brigade of these to the 1st Column, so that he probably had only about 10,000 men in all.

Total Allied strength on the battlefield on the 18th was – according to Zelle (p.436) – 268,000 men (which must be reduced to about 264,000 to allow for his overestimation of Gyulai's corps), to oppose the 135,000 available to Napoleon. Other estimates state that the ratio was about 295,000 men to 160,000. Obviously this is a very controversial topic, but in any event, the

Allied figure was a fantastic achievement for Schwarzenberg and the Allied monarchs – and Sir Charles Stewart – and one of which even Napoleon would have been proud. 'March separately, fight united.'

Even with this numerical superiority, however, Allied battle management was still somewhat timid; there were no white-hot combats such as had taken place at Möckern and Wachau two days before. Instead, there was a series of 'crumbling assaults' such as were undertaken by Montgomery's 8th Army at the Battle of El Alamein in 1942, when his initial frontal assault failed.

Incredible as it may seem, Bernadotte was still dragging his feet. After having been given command on the 17th of most of Blücher's army as a sop to tempt him to join in the battle at all, he had the temerity to then send an aide to the Prussian commander proposing that their two armies should change places! His exact motivation may only be guessed at – treachery springs to mind – but Napoleon would have destroyed them both if Blücher had agreed and the two armies had attempted to cross-march under his nose. The chaos would have been incredible. The whole suggestion was a re-run of the muddled Allied strategic thinking seen in the Netherlands campaign of 1793. The sanity of any commander who could even consider such a useless, needless, dangerous operation at such a time and in such a situation must be questioned. At any rate, Blücher bluntly refused to entertain the idea and instructed von Bülow, in secret, that he was to engage the enemy on the 18th whether or not he received orders to do so from his dubious temporary commander.

The course of the ensuing battle is best followed by examining the individual fortunes of the various Allied columns.

The 1st Column

This column was on a start line from Gross-Städteln to Crostewitz and was the closest column to the enemy lines. To ensure a co-ordinated Allied assault, it had been ordered to wait in its starting position until the 2nd Column had come up to Liebertwolkwitz and Störmthal and the 3rd from Seifertshain and Fuchshain. However, when it became clear that the French had already withdrawn their main forces to the line Connewitz–Probstheida, Hessen-Homburg decided to ignore this instruction and advanced his column on its own, so that it was already in action around Dölitz and Dösen, alone, at eight o'clock, when the 2nd Column had only just set off from its start line. So much for co-ordination and discipline.

The column's advanced guard consisted of Hardegg's division of Colloredo's I Corps, followed by a first line made up of Bianchi's division of the Reserve, the brigades of Haugwitz and Mecsery, and Wimpffen's division of Colloredo's corps; and a second line comprising Weissenwolf's grenadier division, Greth's division of Colloredo's corps, and Nostitz's cavalry division. Lederer's division was on the left wing, in the meadows west of the Pleisse south of Connewitz. Incredible as it must seem in view of the heavy casualties pointlessly suffered there on the 16th, his orders were to persist in trying to break through the Connewitz defile. When they advanced over the battle-field of the 16th, the sights which confronted them made even the hardest veterans shudder as the gun wheels rolled over the corpses which covered the ground.

Hardegg's division advanced west of Wachau on Dösen, while the divisions of Weissenwolf, Bianchi, Lederer and Nostitz moved on Dölitz, up the axis of today's Bornaische Strasse. Wimpffen and Greth advanced past the empty, smouldering ruins of Wachau and on to the sheep pens at Meusdorf, where the weak French outpost was swiftly ejected. A rapid and strong French counter-attack nearly retook the complex and the situation was only stabilised with the help of Pirch's 10th Prussian Brigade of Kleist's II Corps. Part of the 7th Prussian Reserve Infantry Regiment under Captain Schüler and the 1st Battalion of the Austrian Infantry Regiment de Vaux Nr 25 of Wimpffen's division made a determined bayonet charge which threw the French back with heavy loss.

At this point, Hardegg had taken Dösen to the west with a determined charge by two squadrons of the Hessen-Homburg Hussars under Lieutenant-Colonel Simony and a squadron of the Riesch Dragoons under *Rittmeister* Stietka. The village was then occupied by two battalions of the Deutsch-Banater Grenz Infantry Regiment. They did not hold their prize for long, however. Decouz's division of the Young Guard advanced on Dölitz and threw the unsupported Grenzers out, the Allied second line being still too far back to intervene.

Now the brigades of Haugwitz and Mecsery came up. Haugwitz advanced to the east of Dölitz and assaulted the copse there. The advance was made through difficult, close terrain and in the face of heavy fire from Semelle's 52nd Division of Augereau's corps; despite this, Haugwitz's 2nd Brigade of Bianchi's division took the copse.

The Allies made no further headway in this sector, although the fighting was heavy. Augereau's men succeeded in retaking Dösen and at two o'clock pushed on into the wood by the village. This was held by the 1st Battalion of the Austrian Infantry Regiment Reuss-Greiz Nr 18, of Mecsery's 2nd Brigade of Alois Liechtenstein's division, and they were pushed out. The 1st Battalion was now joined by the 2nd and by the Infantry Regiment Hessen-Homburg and an unidentified battalion of Grenzers, and together they recaptured the wood.

The loss of the village caused a flurry of concern in the headquarters of the Army of Bohemia and at about midday couriers were sent off to recall Gyulai from Lindenau, and Duka's 3rd Russian Kürassier Division from the Reserve, to stiffen the front at Dösen. The effect of this nervous reaction was to give the *Grande Armée* absolutely unimpeded access to their escape route to Weissenfels. Not only that, but Gyulai spent the rest of the day in pointless marching, rather like the French III Corps on the 16th and D'Erlon's corps at Quatre Bras in 1815.

Just after midday a brigade of Greth's division came up between Dölitz and

Dösen, as did the rest of Haugwitz's brigade and part of the advanced guard. Together they took not only Dösen but also the heights which run from north of the village eastwards to the Monarchenhügel. The fight now stagnated in this sector.

***

At the start of the day's work, the brigades of Beck and Quallenberg of Bianchi's corps had advanced up the Borna road to what was left of Markkleeberg. Finding no enemy troops here, they pushed on northwards to Dölitz, where they bumped into the Polish forward post, which was promptly ejected. The Austrians then pushed on towards Lössnig, where they took the first few houses. This advance was effectively supported by a battalion of the Infantry Regiment Wenzel Colloredo of Lederer's division from beyond the Pleisse. Part of Lederer's artillery (four howitzers and some cannon) had been manhandled over to the river bank and were able to bombard the enemy's west flank during this advance.

These initial Austrian successes caused Napoleon to send a division of the Young Guard under Oudinot from Probstheida to Lössnig to throw them out. Rothembourg's brigade of Curial's 2nd Division of the Old Guard (Poles, Italians, Westfalians and Saxons) and the Chevau-légers of Berg followed. With Oudinot in the centre, Augereau's division to his right and Poniatowski to his left, the French pushed Hessen-Homburg's forces back and retook Dösen and Dölitz. To stabilise the line, Weissenwolf's reserve division was quickly pulled forward from Markkleeberg. Weissenwolf led Call's grenadier battalion in a charge against Dölitz. They mounted the barriers that had been erected in the streets and threw out the Polish lancers of Kellermann's[31] IV (Polish) Cavalry Corps. The Prince of Hessen-Homburg was wounded in this action, and, according to Seyfert, Graf Nostitz took command in his place. Zelle, however, maintains that it was Colloredo who assumed command, which is more likely. Graf Nostitz was wounded by a musket ball during the afternoon, but this did not deter the tough old soldier from staying in command of his own unit for the rest of the day and throughout the 19th.

The Austrian grenadier battalion had lost heavily in this combat and fell back through Dölitz again, while the grenadier battalions of Fischer and Portner doubled up to support their comrades. In heavy combat the village was then taken back and was successfully held against all further French assaults. Wurmb's brigade of Greth's division now came up beside Dölitz, its Infantry Regiment Czartoryski Nr 9 occupying the gardens while Infantry Regiment de Ligne Nr 30 remained south in reserve. Men of Lederer's division (Infantry Regiments Kaunitz Nr 20 and Wenzel Colloredo Nr 56) still held the manor of Dölitz during this action and crossed into the village to support the grenadiers.

---

[31] Sokolnicki was actually in command on the 18th.

The Austrians made several thrusts at Lössnig from Dölitz in the course of the afternoon. Beck's brigade forced its way into Lössnig several times, but on each occasion Poniatowski's Poles and Decouz's Young Guard threw them out again. It was not until *Feldzeugmeister* Graf Colloredo himself led two regiments of Greth's division in an assault that the village finally changed hands.

The Austrians then pushed on against Connewitz but were repeatedly frustrated by a combination of Semelle's division, Lefol's weak division, Poniatowski's Poles (whose strength fell from 5,000 to 2,700 between 15–19 October) and Rothembourg's brigade of the Old Guard, which included the Saxon Garde-Grenadiere. In the evening the Chevau-légers of Berg were surprised in Connewitz and scattered.

Quite early in the day, Lederer abandoned the useless attempts to force the Connewitz crossing and concentrated on supporting his comrades at Dölitz from across the Pleisse. With a few guns that he had managed to drag through the brush and swamps he bombarded the Polish-held manor house of Lössnig. The ground floor of the building was filled with wounded but the Poles used the upper storeys to snipe at Lederer's men. Lederer engaged the house with a howitzer, the third shell setting it on fire. The blaze spread rapidly, and the Poles had to evacuate the wounded and abandon the place, which burnt out completely. The Polish generals Kaminiecki, Sierakowski and Tolinski were all wounded during the fighting here.

As on previous days, the Poles had continued their looting of the villages they occupied. One wealthy citizen of Leipzig who had a house in Dölitz described the fate it suffered:

> It is horrifying to see what has been done out there. Whole rows of my choice books, which I had not been able to remove to Leipzig, have been burned. Someone lit a fire in the panelled parlour of the garden pavilion which went out of control and would have burned the entire structure down, had not the gardener been able to put it out in time. This all happened under the eyes of the colonel whose men were living in my house. He and the arsonists are not French but Poles.
>
> They would not let my trusted gardener anywhere in the house except in the cellar. They are keeping 150 horses in my garden – or what used to be my garden and is now a place of devastation.
>
> My house was tolerably treated by the officers. Apart from these 'guests' – to whom I can give nothing – there are between forty and sixty men quartered in my wife's house. Yesterday I paid, just for these men, 618 Thalers for September.

***

Johann Jakob Röhrig was a Company Sergeant-Major of Voltigeurs in the French infantry at Leipzig. He was a native of the old German provinces on the left bank of the Rhine annexed by France. He seems to have been somewhere in the path of the Allied 1st Column on the 18th:

On the 17th October there was no fighting, just the occasional musket shot from the outposts. There was no chance of finding anything to eat.

Before dawn on the 18th, we took post a fair way to the rear, on some heights to the right of Leipzig; we were the reserve. We lay around in our bivouac and could see nothing but the sky and soldiers – we overlooked a great stretch of the battlefield – when up rode a fine mass of cavalry with high feather plumes. We were, of course, glad of the support. They were several squadrons of Gardes d'Honneur; young, rich lads who had paid to arm and equip themselves, all in the best style.

The stepson of Captain Kaufmann Kopp, of Koblenz, was with them. He came to our bivouac to visit his stepfather. When the latter told him that they would have done better to have stayed at home, the lad answered: 'We have been so well drilled, that we can take on the best Hungarian hussars!'

The captain laughed and pointed down onto the plain and said: 'Just ride down there, you'll find your man!'

We watched them go; no sooner were they on the plain than they charged, probably at a battery. Suddenly, a swarm of Austrian or Russian cavalry came out from behind the corner of a wood and took them in flank. There was a dreadful carnage. Many of them now came back; one had lost his shako, another his sabre, a third his horse. Some bore terrible sabre wounds.

So they rode back to the Rhine. We at least saw nothing more of them, except one in Erfurt who had only one boot.

So we stayed on these heights for a little while and watched the battlefield, at least as much as the clouds of smoke would permit. Then suddenly came the command: 'Take up arms, forwards!' We went into the line of battle, we Voltigeurs in the skirmishing line. Despite our best efforts, we had to fall back. The half-circle that our army occupied around Leipzig shrank more and more together; the shot and shell crossed in the middle of it. The hares ran around exhausted and didn't know where to go.

Now I saw a shell land in a powder waggon, just as a gunner was standing there with his pouch and was about to fill it with cartridges to fill the trail chest. The waggon flew up into the air together with the crew and the horses. I don't know what happened to them except that the gunner suffered nothing more than having a face as black as a raven.

We fought, as I said, very bravely all day, but we had to fall back and we gradually got quite close to Leipzig, on the right-hand side. If I am not mistaken, it was called Gossa. After hard fighting, we had to withdraw before the greater Austrian numbers and leave the village in their hands.

Murat, the king of Naples, rode up with his 'Tral dal Tera' and shouted: '*Mes enfants, il ne faut pas quitter ce village la, autrement nous sommes perdus.*' ['Children, you can't abandon the village or we are lost.'] We stormed forward again, supported with heavy canister fire, and retook the place.

On the far side of the village, we settled down behind the clay walls which surrounded the gardens and cut loopholes in them with our bayonets. I was standing together with several Voltigeurs, firing at the Austrians and not taking much notice of anything else, when suddenly we heard a great cheer, and looked around to see that we were now cut off from our regiment by an Austrian counter-attack.

What were we to do now? I really did not want to go into Austrian captivity. I saw a door which led from the courtyard into a cellar, so I slipped inside without the enemy noticing and hunched down in a corner. Whilst I was sitting there, thinking of this and that, I heard one shell after another exploding outside. I could also hear the Austrians in the courtyard plainly speaking German. So, I could not leave my hiding place, even though I expected a visit from a shell because the doors faced our battery position. Also, an Austrian might enter the cellar.

Finally, the German voices faded away and I heard: '*En avant, avancer!*' I was also aware of a loud crackling noise. I went to the door; a large clump of burning straw fell from the roof. I could not stay here any longer as the roof had been set on fire by a shell. I had scarcely got to the gate of the courtyard, when the roof fell off.

But now I was out of the frying pan and into the fire, because I was between two fires. The Austrians were in front of me and my comrades were behind me. What should I do? There was not much time to think. So I took my musket and ran towards my comrades, who were pushing the Austrians back again. Whilst doing this, I had one ball through my shako and three into my pack; the last one went through to my shirt.

It was a miracle that I was still alive, but my guardian angel was still with me.

I had scarcely reached my regiment, when a shell burst nearby and a piece of it bounced off a wall and hit me in the right side so hard that I was winded.

The Austrians advanced again and we had to fall back and leave them the village. Now the Emperor in person led forward some companies of the Young Guard and off we went again with an '*En avant, vive l'Empereur!*' to beat the enemy, and we recaptured the village, but at the cost of a lot of lives.

Here, I saw the Emperor under a hail of enemy canister. His face was pale and as cold as marble. Only occasionally did an expression of rage cross his face. He saw that all was lost. We were only fighting for our withdrawal. We held the village. It became dark; the fighting died away. But what a wailing and lamentation there was in this place! All the houses were full of wounded from the fighting of the 16th, and those who could not walk were lost, because the village was burning and they had to burn with it...

Now my side began to swell and to be very painful; the captain advised me to go to the field ambulance which was close by... When I got there, the surgeon gave me some barley flour and water to drink, and I had to put on some cold compresses.

On the way I had a bit of luck in that I found two French crowns on a dead captain. Unfortunately, I couldn't eat them, however hungry I was.

There were many amputations being carried out. Then they didn't make as much of a fuss about it as the doctors do nowadays. Then, they didn't much care if the patient lived or died. I watched as an officer of cuirassiers had his leg taken off above the knee. He sat on a bench on which his damaged leg was laid; his other foot was on the floor. He watched the operation carefully without a grimace.

The operation went as follows. Above the chosen point of amputation, the limb was tightly bound with a cloth to stem the loss of blood. The flesh was cut through to the bone, the flesh at once pulled back, and the bone sawn through. The arteries were then pulled forward with a pair of pincers and tied off, or cauterised with a hot iron. The flesh was then pulled forward and a piece of cloth soaked in flour and water or goulard was laid over the stump and tied in place.

This was all the work of a few minutes. The surgeon said that I was in no danger and could return to my unit. It was dark; as I looked for my regiment, I came upon a fire with some grenadiers of the Old Guard around it. There were some potatoes roasting in the embers and my mouth watered at the sight. I was as hungry as a shark. We had been at Leipzig for five days and had only eaten on two of them.

I got into conversation with one of the old Moustaches, who had so many service chevrons on his upper sleeve that he must have served for twenty years. Gradually, I turned the conversation to the potatoes and said that he would do me a great favour if he would give me some. But he said that he couldn't do that as they were not his own but belonged to his section. Then I remembered the two crowns in my pocket. I showed them to him – they say that gold blinds the world – and it worked. I gave him the crowns and he gave me eight or ten small potatoes. Who could be happier than I was? Unfortunately, there was no bread or salt.

Finally, I found my regiment. There was no food to be had; the men were forbidden to go into Leipzig, and the ruined village was empty. All that could be found were some raw mangolds, cabbage stalks and apples.

A small brandy cost 2, 3 or 4 Grosschen and that was bad.

I still cannot understand that such a clever commander as the Emperor could let us starve. It would have been a very different life in the army if sufficient food had been available. And yet, no-one who has not experienced it can have any idea of the enthusiasm which burst forth among the half-starved, exhausted soldiers when the Emperor was there in person.

If all were demoralised and he appeared, his presence was like an electric shock. All shouted; '*Vive l'Empereur!*' and everyone charged blindly into the fire.

The 2nd Column at Probstheida

Most of the inhabitants of Probstheida had fled the village on 13 October when the French troops flooded over the surrounding plain like hordes of locusts, eating everything that could be eaten and burning anything that would burn. The son of the village teacher (Sander) has left us an account of their flight:

Early on Wednesday 13th October we too were driven out of our home to escape the threats of the hungry soldiers on the search for food. They thought nothing of using force to get their way.

My father was the treasurer of the Wachau Schoolmasters' Widows and Orphans Fund and was holding quite a large sum of money. We buried half of it in the churchyard and the other half under the baptismal font in the church.

The heavy, iron-bound church door would have defied all the efforts of the plunderers and we took the three heavy keys to the door with us and set off for Holzhausen. Here, to our astonishment, we found the inhabitants still busy, baling up the tobacco they had just harvested.

We continued through heavy rainstorms, trudging between bodies of troops, dodging marching columns until we reached Klein-Pössna where the schoolteacher Wind gave us shelter for the night.

On the morning of 14th October we climbed the tower of Klein-Pössna church in order to see what was happening in our abandoned home village. At ten o'clock a cannon shot rang out from the area of Liebertwolkwitz and then a column of flames rose up from the village. Soon a heavy cannonade began which made the church tower tremble.

Fear drove us out of Klein-Pössna too; we walked to Wolfshain and stayed here through the 16th October, horrified by the din of the battle close by.

Towards evening, we saw a fire's glow from the direction of Probstheida. Late that night we learned from a straggler that a campfire by a thatched barn in that village had set light to the structure. As this barn was very close to the school and the church, we were very worried. We thus set off before dawn on the 17th October, a Sunday, and went to Beucha village. From the churchyard on a hill there we looked over to Probstheida.

Our worst fears were painfully realised. A mighty column of smoke and flames billowed up from our church tower. All our possessions, which we had hidden in the church, had gone up in smoke. My father buried the now-useless keys to the church door in the churchyard in Beucha.

***

The Czar, King Friedrich Wilhelm and Schwarzenberg accompanied the 2nd Column from early in the morning, Kaiser Franz joining them at two o'clock on that celebrated pimple, 'The Monarchs' Hill', now a wooded knoll to the west side of the Prager Strasse, opposite the junction with the Schiller-strasse.

This column consisted of Kleist's II (Prussian) Corps and the following Russian formations: Gortschakoff's I and Württemberg's II Corps, Rajewski's VIII Grenadier Corps, the Kürassier Divisions of Duka, Depreradowitsch and Kretoff, the light cavalry, and Count Pahlen's cavalry. Its reserve consisted of the Russo-Prussian Guards. The column's start line stretched from the Auenhain sheep pens in the west to the road just south of Liebertwolkwitz in the east. The formations were ranged along it from west to east as follows:

First line – Kleist's II Corps, Gortschakoff's I Corps.
Second line – Tchoglokoff's 2nd Grenadier Division, Württemberg's II Corps.
Third line – Count Duka's 3rd Kürassier Division, Pisareff's 1st Grenadier Division.
Fourth line – Russian Light Cavalry Division, Kretoff's 2nd Kürassier Division.
Fifth line – Count Pahlen's cavalry on the right (the left wing being left empty).

Behind them were the Guards and Prereradowitsch's 1st Russian Kürassier Division. Thanks to his unimaginative tactical expertise and the generosity with which he handled his men's lives, Württemberg's II 'Corps' now totalled no more than 1,800 men.

Even before the advance began at eight o'clock, the Allied troops could hear firing off to their left front, where the impetuous Hessen-Homburg was already fighting around Dölitz and Dösen.

The 2nd Column's initial aim was to take Liebertwolkwitz with Gortschakoff's corps. It was only lightly held and was easily taken. Kleist's target was Wachau, but the enemy had evacuated the place, so they pushed on for the Meusdorf sheep pens, where they could see white-coated Austrians under Wimpffen and Greth of Hessen-Homburg's 1st Column engaged with the enemy. The Austrians had already taken and lost this complex once but it was presently held by two French battalions and two cavalry squadrons. Now Wimpffen's men and the 7th Prussian Reserve Infantry Regiment (Pirch's 10th Brigade) took it back again.

By this time, the Allied 3rd Column had captured Holzhausen, two kilometres off to the north-east, and the way was clear for the united columns to push on for Probstheida. At two o'clock, the 2nd Column was about 1,000 paces from the French lines at Probstheida, on a line which today stretches west from Zuckelhausen to the old Dösen Heilanstalt (hospital); this is at about the junction of Chemnitzer Strasse and Gorbitzer Strasse.

The deployment of the 2nd Column was as before except that Pahlen's cavalry had moved to the west side, behind the 2nd Russian Grenadier Division. The Russo-Prussian Guards were just south of Monarchs' Hill with Depreradowitsch's Kürassiers behind them. As on the 16th, this reserve was not engaged during the day, and it was the first to fifth lines which did all the fighting. Their assaults were to prove fragmentary and unco-ordinated, and thus wasteful and ineffective.

Probstheida was held by Victor's II Corps and was the key to the French defence, being at the juncture between Napoleon's centre and right wing. The village was linear in plan and lay on an east-west axis to the east of the road. It was double-walled and had only a few entrances. There is nothing of it to be seen today. The flat, open lands around it gave the defenders (Vial's 6th Division) good fields of view and fire and provided the attackers with no cover. It had been reinforced, and Napoleon had massed strong batteries of Young Guard artillery, gun-to-gun, to either side, to crush frontal assaults and to frustrate outflanking attempts.

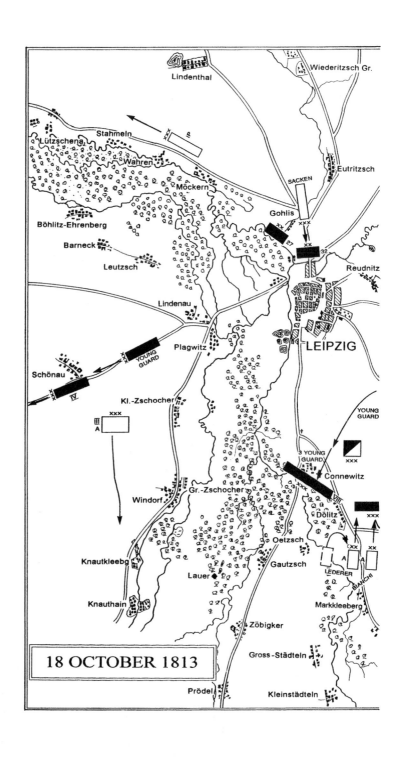

18 OCTOBER 1813

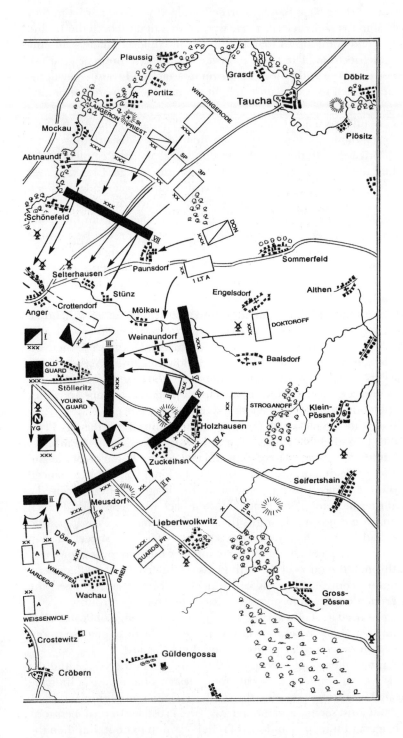

After studying the village Barclay correctly judged it as too hard a nut for the 2nd Column to crack on its own. He wanted to wait until both the 1st and 3rd Columns had come up so that a joint assault could be made – an eminently sensible decision. The Czar, however, would have none of it; at two o'clock he ordered the 2nd Column to begin its attack on Probstheida alone, and so it did – much to Napoleon's delight. So much for co-ordination and common-sense.

The first assault was made by the brigades of Pirch and Prinz August with the heroic remnants of Eugen von Württemberg's Russians in reserve. Pirch's 10th Brigade, with the 9th Silesian *Landwehr* Infantry Regiment in the lead, reached the outer wall unhindered; it was unoccupied. Climbing over it, they found themselves in a ring of gardens about fifty paces wide, between the outer and inner walls. The inner walls were heavily manned and the Prussians found themselves in a killing pen. Shot to pieces from the front, they could receive no effective assistance from their comrades beyond the outer wall, who could not see – only guess at – what was going on within the village. The ancient walls were also found to be made of timber and clay, so that the Allies' artillery projectiles went straight through them leaving only a very small hole.

Some Prussian skirmishers eventually found a door in the inner wall, broke it open, and fanned out into the core of the village. From here they were able to shoot the defenders on the inner wall in the back and soon drove them off into the wide central street. Other Prussians followed and they succeeded in driving the garrison out of Probstheida and back to the French second line to the north. However, a strong counter-attack was launched at once and, after a hard and bloody struggle, Pirch's men were thrown out.

While the 10th Brigade was fighting its way into Probstheida, Prinz August's 12th Brigade had attacked its east side. Despite destructive artillery fire, the 11th Reserve Infantry Regiment and the Fusilier Battalion of the 2nd Silesian Infantry Regiment, under Lieutenant-Colonel von Funk, advanced right up to the narrow eastern perimeter of the village, but here received a salvo of canister at point-blank range and fell back with heavy loss. French cavalry then bore down on the right flank of the retreating Prussians, who fortunately had time to form battalion squares before the shock. Russian Kürassiers charged up to help the Prussian infantry but were overthrown and fled right through the ranks of the 11th Prussian Reserve Infantry Regiment. With admirable control, the Prussians quickly reformed and stopped the pursuing French cavalry, thus giving the Russians time to regroup.

Prinz August tried a second assault against the eastern edge of Probstheida with the same battalions as before. Placing himself at the head of these troops – with their own officers at his side – he led them forward.

Vial's men had meanwhile occupied all the houses in the village and the well-placed French artillery wrought great destruction as the advancing troops pushed on through the din, the smoke and the rain of shot and shell. Incredible as it must seem – and indeed was – the Prussians nevertheless took half the village and fifteen abandoned French cannon to boot. But then the fire from the massed Young Guard artillery ripped into them again. Rochambeau's 19th Division of Lauriston's V Corps was in reserve between Probstheida and Stötteritz. It now advanced, relieved the tired remnants of Vial's division and drove down into Probstheida. Much of the village was now ablaze and the opponents fought in and through the burning houses. Despite the best efforts of the outnumbered Prussians, the 12th Brigade was again forced out.

But Kleist was not yet done. Even as the exhausted 12th Brigade still fought in the village, Pirch's 10th Brigade advanced against the south face of Probstheida and General von Ziethen's 11th Brigade arrived from Zuckel-hausen. The latter had been detached on 16 October and had fought alongside Klenau's Austrians in the east, on the heights of Gross-Pössna. Today it had formed the extreme left of Bennigsen's 3rd Column, and after participating in the capture of Zuckelhausen had been sent to Kleist's corps to help in the desperate struggle for Probstheida.

The first troops of the 11th Brigade to join the battle here were the Fusilier Battalion of the 1st Silesian Infantry Regiment and the 2nd and 3rd Batta-lions of the 10th Reserve Infantry Regiment. They advanced to the eastern end of the burning hamlet, but as they tried to get in the spent 12th Brigade was being forced out, blocking their way. Both Prussian brigades fell into confusion and had to retreat towards Zuckelhausen. By now, the eastern and southern sides of Probstheida were lined with thick rows of dark blue clad corpses.

A member of the 12th Brigade remembered the bloody fighting for Probstheida in his memoirs:

The 18th of October was more murderous for our regiment than the 16th. We were to be in reserve this day; the brigades of Pirch and Klüx were to carry out the assault. Prinz August von Preussen addressed us as follows: 'Comrades, we are in reserve today. But if we should go into action, just remember that the French that we are fighting are the same that we defeated at Gross-Beeren, at Dennewitz, on the Katzbach, at Kulm and at Nollendorf. You, like me, would far rather lose your lives than lose the honour of the name of Prussia.'

Until two o'clock it went as planned, then came the order: 'The 12th Brigade will take Probstheida, the centre of the enemy position, by storm.'

Probstheida was occupied by 8,000 elite troops who were well entrenched behind garden walls and in houses, and behind them were the Guard.

We moved up via Meusdorf and the brickworks against Probstheida. The first thing that hit our skirmishers – of which I was one – was an artillery crossfire. It didn't take long for us to be scattered. We reformed and threw ourselves into a sunken road up against the loopholed garden wall of the village. We waited until the French had fired a full volley at our main body, jumped out of the road and rushed forward to take half the village. The surprised French fell back before us, abandoning a battery of ten guns in the centre of the village. We were about to seize the prize, when there came a shout: 'French cavalry has come around the village and is taking us in rear!' We had to abandon the guns to take cover in the houses. The French cavalry did not appear, for the Russians had made a counter-charge and driven them off.

This was a serious error for us, because the French recovered from their surprise, manned their battery and sent a salvo of canister against us. We wanted to retake the battery, but the French had brought up reinforcements and now advanced against us in superior strength. We were lucky to get out of the village alive. We raced through the gardens and climbed over the high garden wall. The French were so close behind us that they caught some of us as we were straddling the wall.

Outside the walls, we huddled against them between the loopholes, waited until the French had fired a volley through them, and then fled back to our lines.

We had lost a lot of men and took no further part in the action. Our regiment entered the campaign with 2,500 men. After the battle of Leipzig we had 300 men fit for duty. Eighteen officers had been killed.

The king of Prussia was very gracious to us when we marched past him in Leipzig. One of our bravest officers in the storm of Probstheida was a seventeen-year-old son of a country gentlemen. Not less remarkable was our battalion's drum major, an Israelite, not twenty years old. In the storming of Probstheida, he slung his drum on his back, picked up a musket and pouch from a dead man and was one of the first into the village.

It was at this point that Eugen von Württemberg's 'corps' came up the road from Meusdorf and took post between the 10th and 12th Brigades. The princes Schachowskoi and August von Preussen placed themselves at the head of their men and led them back into the smoke and the din of the battle in the fiercely burning village.

The courage and ferocity shown by both sides in the battle for Probstheida was truly unique, as were the losses they suffered. General Vial was killed there, as were many other French generals and staff officers. His division had the highest number of casualties, but Rochambeau's also suffered terribly. Victor was in the thick of things too, giving orders, motivating his commanders, reorganising shattered battalions. On the Allied side, Pirch's 9th Silesian *Landwehr* Infantry Regiment lost over half its strength, and the gallant Russians of Wurttemberg's corps lost a further 600 men in the final attack.

***

On his little knoll by the tobacco mill, about a kilometre north-west of the blazing village, Napoleon watched the conflict round Probstheida closely. He knew how vital it was that the village be held but was increasingly concerned at the swelling stream of casualties limping or being carried off to the rear. To make matters worse, the artillery ammunition supplies were now perilously low.

Through the smoke of the cannon, the musketry and the burning villages, the Emperor could make out the heavy masses of the Allied reserves south of the Monarch's Hill. The time had come; Napoleon sent orders for Friant's division of the Old Guard to move forward from Thonberg. When they came up, he set himself at their head and led them forward, heedless of the danger, the shot and the shell. From close behind Probstheida, as evening fell, Napoleon personally directed the French defence, and, despite all their efforts and sacrifices, the Allies were thrown out of the blazing ruin for the last time. An attempt by the Old Guard to advance south, however, was stopped by the Allied artillery on the low hill about 500 metres away. Generals Baillot, Montgenet and Rochambeau were all killed during the fighting here, while French regiments which especially distinguished themselves were the 2*e*, 4*e* and 18*e Ligne* and the 11*e Légère*. Even Prinz August von Preussen wrote most flatteringly of the enemy's valour in the battle of 18 October.

Lack of effective Allied co-ordination, aggravated by their external lines of communication, had allowed Napoleon to reinforce this vital front unhindered by any serious threat from the north.

***

Another of Colonel Marcellin de Marbot's ripping yarns concerns the fight for Probstheida:

> Despite the terrible cannon-fire and the constantly renewed, violent enemy assaults, our troops held their positions along the whole line. Between Probstheida and Stötteritz Marshal Macdonald and General Sebastiani had also beaten off all attacks by the Austrians under Klenau and the Russians under Dokturoff, when suddenly, over 20,000[32] Cossacks and Baschkirs swarmed down on them. The Baschkirs attacked Sebastiani's cavalry corps.
>
> In a flash, these barbarians surrounded our squadrons uttering terrible shrieks and firing clouds of arrows at us. These were irregular troops and not very effective as they are not trained to operate in close formations; it was only their great numbers which made them dangerous. Their arrows did not do us much harm as most of them were fired up into the air to fall into our midst.
>
> One of my NCOs was victim of a more serious arrow wound. The arrow entered his chest and penetrated through him to come out of his back. The brave fellow broke off the point with both hands and pulled the shaft out of his chest. A few moments later, he dropped dead.
>
> Not long after this, I was hit in the thigh with an arrow four feet long, which penetrated about an inch into my leg. The surgeon soon pulled it out and I kept it as a souvenir, but I lost it some time later...
>
> When night fell, the troops of both armies were roughly in the same positions as they had occupied at the start of the battle. My regiment, and indeed the whole of Sebastiani's corps, drove in their picket stakes to tether their horses in the same places that they had used on the previous three days. Most of the battalions also used their old bivouac sites. So this battle,

[32] Dokturoff actually had just 800 Cossacks and Baschkirs.

which our enemies celebrated as such a great victory, was in fact a drawn match, because despite our inferior numbers, and despite all the shameful treachery in our ranks, we had fought against almost all the nations of Europe and had not lost one inch of ground.

***

Maximilian von Thielen, on the staff of the Army of Bohemia, has left us this fascinating illustration of the varied level of inter-Allied co-operation during the struggle for Probstheida:

It was about four o'clock in the afternoon. The enemy was holding out with unparalleled stubbornness and several times tried to fight his way out of the village with infantry and artillery. For us to have stormed the place in these circumstances would certainly have cost many lives. In order to save the bloodshed, Prinz Schwarzenberg forbade any further attacks on the village and gave orders that the enemy were to be pinned down by increased artillery fire, but every Austrian artillery battery was already in action, so Graf Radetzky ordered me to find some guns and bring them up.

I rode back and hurried to the first artillery unit I saw. It was a Russian battery; General Arakcheev was standing there with the last heavy battery of the Russian Guards, surrounded by a crowd of dismounted gunners. Regardless of the fact that he was under orders from Prinz Schwarzenberg to bring up artillery, he flatly refused to do so unless it was on the orders of the Czar. Only on the insistence of the battery commander, who did not want to stand idly by and watch the battle while his comrades might be earning awards, did I receive any support, and after a brief exchange, Arakcheev shouted his '*Paschol!*' ['Go!'] to the commander.

We went off at a trot and a gallop up hill and down dale, and when I had conducted him to a spot which I had previously selected on the high ground from whence I had come, I waited for the results of the first shots then hurried back to the hill where the monarchs and the Prince were watching the struggle. I reported to Radetzky, who took me to Schwarzenberg and said: 'Here is Thielen, back again.' The field marshal slapped me on the back and said: 'Thank you, my dear Thielen! I shall not forget you.'

With the arrival of the battery the enemy's attempts to break out of the village came to a stop, but the cannon-fire continued on both sides until nightfall. On the 19th we found forty gun barrels buried in Probstheida; the carriages had been burned on watch fires during the night.

***

The scenes which confronted returning villagers days after the battle were recorded by the teacher Sander's son:

On Thursday 21st October, we at last returned, with an escort of Austrian soldiers, to Probstheida. There was almost nothing left of the village. The whole south side, the church and the vicarage were just smouldering heaps of ruins.

Not only the doors and window frames were missing from the school but also the steps and the floorboards. Prussian soldiers were busy gathering up the wounded and loading them onto farm carts to take them into Leipzig. Everywhere there lay thousands of dead and the returning peasants had to bury them. Big pits were dug in the village and in the surrounding fields, each designed to hold 40–50 dead. This dreary labour went on until the feast of St Martin on 11th November when the last of the fallen was buried.

Everything that had been in the church had been destroyed. The family tutor of the Probstheida vicar, Ebermann, had managed to save the parish registers from the flames at the last minute; a French Lieutenant, Saint-Gris, had helped him do it.

We found the money that we had hidden in the church; due to the fierce heat of the fire, it had turned yellow.

The 3rd Column at Zuckelhausen, Holzhausen and Paunsdorf

The leading elements of Bennigsen's Reserve Army of Poland arrived at their appointed place on the battlefield at Fuchshain, about five kilometres east of Liebertwolkwitz, as evening fell on 17 October. This column's start line ran from just north of Gross-Pössna north-north-east to Klein-Pössna. Apart from Bennigsen's own army, the column consisted of Graf Bubna's 2nd Light (Austrian) Division, Graf Klenau's IV (Austrian) Corps, Ziethen's 11th (Prussian) Brigade, Count Pahlen's cavalry division, and Count Platoff's Don Cossack Corps, all from the Army of Bohemia. All of the attached forces (except Bubna's division) had fought against Macdonald on the 16th.

Bennigsen's task was to assault Napoleon's eastern front, to which end he had over 60,000 men under his command. He had direct contact with Barclay de Tolly's 2nd Column to his left, but his right flank hung in the air because that vain, dilatory military genius – the Crown Prince of Sweden – was still at Taucha on the Parthe and would not deign to advance to his allotted position (the area between Paunsdorf and Abtnaundorf on the Parthe) until four o'clock on the afternoon of the 18th. Bennigsen was thus forced to extend his right, which diluted the concentration of the forces in his real sector of responsibility and left him thinly spread over a front of six kilometres.

During the night of 17–18 October, Bennigsen issued the following order to his commanders:

> The advanced guard of the Army of Poland under General Stroganoff, supported by the cavalry of General Kreutz and part of Klenau's corps, will assault the Kolmberg at eight o'clock in the morning from the eastern side. The main body of Klenau's corps, however, will assault the Kolmberg from the front and from the western side. At the same time, Klenau will also take the Niederholz wood.[33]

---

[33] About 500 metres south of the Kolmberg.

Twenty-four Russian twelve-pounder guns will bombard the Kolmberg from Seifertshain. The 12th Russian Infantry Division under Prince Chowanskoi will support this assault and, at the moment of success, will push forward on the road to Holzhausen. Repninskoi's cavalry brigade will form a second line behind the advanced guard and will join in the battle if needed. The 12th and 26th Infantry Divisions under General Dokturoff will make a concealed flank march behind the ridge at Fuchshain and the wood at Seifertshain and will make a surprise attack on the French-occupied village of Klein-Pössna. Graf Bubna, with the 2nd Austrian Light Division, will cross the Beucha; Graf Platoff will cross the Parthe at Zweenfurth. Both generals will fall on the flank and rear of the French at Hirschfeld and will take command of the main road from Wurzen to Leipzig.

The French garrison on the Kolmberg on Sunday 17 October was a battery of twelve-pounders and General Marchand's 39th Division of Baden and Hessen-Darmstadt infantry of XI Corps. Marshal Macdonald spent the day there and stayed until late that night. From the summit they could clearly see the deployment of the considerable Allied forces before them.

On the morning of the 18th Bennigsen's troops were arranged for the day's action, from left to right, as follows: Ziethen's 11th Brigade and Klenau's corps aimed at the Kolmberg; Dokturoff's corps with the cavalry of General Tschaplitz and the 12th, 13th and 26th Infantry Divisions (under Generals Prince Chawanskoi, Lindfors and Paskiewitsch respectively) aimed at Holzhausen; and Bubna's division, with Platoff's Cossacks on the extreme right, swung out to make a wide right hook towards Paunsdorf through Engelsdorf and Sommerfeld.

The Czar was present in this sector in the morning. As he rode past the 2nd West Prussian Infantry Regiment he called out to them: '*Heute ist der Tag, dass wir sie aus Moskau jagten, Kinder haltet euch brav, es wird gut gehen!*' ('Today is the day we threw them out of Moscow, Boys, just do your duty and everything will be alright!') It was the anniversary of the battle of Tarutino.

The column's advance had to await the arrival of Bubna's Austrians at their start point at Klein-Pössna, but as soon as he had this confirmed Bennigsen set his army in motion. To its great surprise, Klenau's corps found that the most dominant feature in the area – the Kolmberg – had been abandoned by the French an hour beforehand. Klenau rode to the summit and saw the enemy reforming for the defence of Zuckelhausen and Holzhausen, about three kilometres to the north-west. He left some artillery and Infantry Regiment Koburg Nr 22 on the hill and set off with the rest of his command for Liebertwolkwitz, which was still occupied by light French forces. These were ejected by General Abele of Heldenfeld's division and Infantry Regiment Alois Liechtenstein Nr 12 and were driven back north to Zuckelhausen. Paumgarten's brigade joined in this advance and resumed the position it had occupied on the 14th, north of the Kolmberg. Ziethen's Prussians also advanced on Zuckelhausen after having passed through Liebertwolkwitz.

At this point Bennigsen could hear the heavy roll of the guns off to his left, but to his right all was silent. Concerned that Napoleon – for whom he had great respect – could well thrust into this apparent gap in the Allied line, he sent orders for Dokturoff to extend his troops to the north towards Baalsdorf.

By ten o'clock Ziethen's Prussians and Hohenlohe-Bartenstein's Austrian division were in front of Zuckelhausen, Lindfors' division was east of Holzhausen, and Chowanskoi and Paskiewitsch were between Holzhausen and Baalsdorf. Bubna was between Engelsdorf and Sommerfeld and Platoff was north of the latter. Strangely enough, however, it was two o'clock in the afternoon before the assault began.

Marchand's 39th Division had deployed for the defence of Zuckelhausen with ten companies in line to the south-east, two companies in the village itself, and two battalions in rear as a reserve. Unlike most of the villages on the battlefield, the layout of Zuckelhausen and Holzhausen have changed remarkably little over the years. Gerard's 35th Division was 600 metres to the north on the Steinberg hill, where the Stötteritzer Strasse and the Mölkauer Strasse now cross. Charpentier's 36th Division was defending Holzhausen. Sebastiani's II Cavalry Corps were north of the Steinberg, and Walther's Guard's Cavalry Division was to the south, behind Zuckelhausen.

Zuckelhausen

Ziethen's Prussians attacked this village from the south whilst General Abele's Austrian brigade assaulted it from the east. After a hard fight, the Germans of the 39th Division (Badeners and Hessians) were thrown out between twelve and one o'clock. Unlike the French in Holzhausen – who later fled in a confused mass – these men withdrew in good order onto the Steinberg. Later they went back to Stötteritz together with Gerard's division. The Hessian Leib-Regiment lost two officers and ninety-one men; the Leib-Garde about the same; the 1st Battalion of the Light Infantry lost about thirty per cent of its strength and the Badeners lost about 200 men.

After this, Klenau's Austrians moved towards the Steinberg, while Ziethen's 11th Brigade was ordered to march off to the south-west to rejoin the Army of Bohemia at the Monarchenhügel. In view of the over-extension of Bennigsen's line, and the continuing absence of the Army of the North on his right flank, this would seem to have been a rather foolhardy – if selfless – decision.

Prinz Emil von Hessen-Darmstadt's brigade was part of Marchand's 39th Division, XI Corps. His report of the action here reads as follows:

> At four o'clock in the morning of the 18th October came the order that we were to move off to Holzhausen in one hour's time. Charpentier's division moved off behind us and the cavalry covered the retreat. The divisions were drawn up before Holzhausen; our division was allocated to the defence of Zuckelhausen. The front of the village was covered by the 1st Battalion, Garde-Füsiliere, 1st Battalion Leib-Garde and the Baden Regiment Grossherzog. The 2nd Battalion Leib-Garde covered the right flank of the place,

the Baden Regiment von Stockhorn linked us up to Holzhausen, and the Leib-Regiment was in reserve on the hill to our rear to safeguard our retreat. All the artillery of the division was concentrated into one battery before Zuckelhausen and the hill to our right front was occupied by the French.

Before these dispositions could be completed, all the troops in the first line were attacked; soon there was intense fighting going on all around us. The French to our right (mostly cavalry) pulled back in a fighting withdrawal, using their skirmishers and their artillery. The division in front of Holzhausen soon followed them, but in a less orderly fashion, despite the fact that our artillery was very active in supporting their defence.

The whole enemy line now advanced towards us, and while Zuckelhausen was bombarded with artillery of a much heavier calibre than our field pieces could offer in return, strong enemy skirmishing detachments of infantry and cavalry moved forward between Holzhausen and our position and sought to link up with other such detachments which were pursuing the French who were retreating in disorder from Holzhausen. But a hail of musketry from our village soon checked them and secured the withdrawal of our artillery through the village, which was now exposed by the fact that both our flanks were open.

The infantry fell in behind them and, after clearing the village, formed into divisions of closed columns and marched up the hill – with a rare air of cool order, despite heavy enemy artillery fire and the fact that the head of the column was now under fire from the enemy skirmishers – towards the Leib-Regiment.

This regiment had already charged the Austrian skirmishing line once and had thus taken up the French troops retreating from Holzhausen. The 1st Battalion, Leib-Garde, also deployed one of its companies *en debandade* to the right so that they could work together with the sharpshooters of the 1st Battalion, Garde-Füsiliere, in keeping the enemy away from our flank.

The corps thus continued its withdrawal to Stötteritz under continually rising pressure from the enemy, who was becoming increasingly bold. Here, the Prince of Neufchatel, coming from the centre of the army, ordered a halt and thus, literally, stopped what could have been a complete flight of the French troops on this flank.

Emboldened by the morale-boosting presence of the Emperor, this corps rapidly reformed its units and ranks. The artillery was redeployed and took up the fight with the enemy again and were reinforced with new guns.

All, both French and non-French, have seen and recognised the fact that only our German division of XI Corps retained its morale and good order; obeyed its orders; did not break ranks, and remained unshaken in the face of the dissolution of the French and the Italians. All behaved very well; I could not pick out one battalion for any special praise.

The first half of the day was over, and with it, the progress of the enemy on our wing. I detached the 1st Battalion, Garde-Füsiliere, in skirmishing order to cover the guns and formed the other battalions in line of battle to the right of the Badeners, with their backs to Stötteritz. The position was not good. Shot and shell rained down on us from all sides and, even though most of them missed us, I became very aware that we could be exposed to very heavy losses.

The regimental history of the Garde-Füsiliere, deployed to protect the guns, contains the following passage:

Meanwhile, the Emperor appeared to the right of Stötteritz with part of the Old Guard; he had Murat make a cavalry charge against the advancing enemy with a division of Cuirassiers and they did in fact push the enemy back a little. But soon, the enemy skirmishers – Russians this time – flooded back towards us and attacked the artillery of Marchand's division. At about four o'clock, we received orders to counter-attack them together with the 8e Hussars, with whom we had operated in 1809. The Hussars went first, the Garde-Füsiliere followed with lowered muskets at the double. As the Hussars charged, the Russians threw themselves flat on the ground and let them flood over them. They were not harmed either by the horses, which shied away from treading on them, or by the Hussars' sabres, which were too short to reach them. Then they jumped up and fired into the backs of the Hussars. But when we came up they ran off, all except about twenty that we captured.

We now deployed into open columns of divisions [half battalions] under heavy artillery and musketry fire, and sent out our sharpshooters under *Leutnants* von Dressel and Luck. In a short time we had lost so many men that we were ordered to fall back to Stötteritz. This was carried out in good order. *Leutnant* von Dressel was wounded in the head, but it did not seem to be too bad; but as he was going back to the first aid post he collapsed and died.

Another example of the spirit of the regiment this day was the cool conduct of Sergeant Nahrgang of Captain Lyncker II's 3rd Company, who had often been distinguished in earlier campaigns. Whenever a ball cut down a file of his company, he placed himself in front of the gap and ordered: 'Quiet! Close files!'

Füsilier Adam, of Captain Fresenius' 2nd Company, had been ordered to give his musket to a sharpshooter and to take the marksman's defective one in return; he answered the officer: 'If you order me to do this, I have to obey, but my musket and I are inseparable. If it is to go forwards, permit me to escort it.' His wish was granted; he went forward into the skirmishing line and did very well.

Prinz Emil's report continues:

As the corps was exposed to this extraordinary fire to absolutely no purpose, I ordered the battalions to take cover in the deep ditches which were before their lines. The 1st Battalion of the Leib-Garde thus joined the Leib-Regiment in one of the ditches and the 2nd Battalion of the Leib-Garde moved into a protective hollow together with the Baden infantry. This was most advantageous, as the ground that we had been standing on was ploughed up in all directions by shot and shell.

As the French six-pounder balls are slightly larger than ours, there were

very soon four of our six-pounder guns which were jammed and had to be
sent to the rear. These were soon followed by two more pieces for the same
reason. Our artillery fired 855 shots this day.

The enemy artillery fire continued until dark at the same intensity. The
dead and wounded mounted even in the ditches. One ball cut the heads off
Captain von Schwarzenau and my Adjutant, *Leutnant* Graf Erbach, at my
side, and tore off Captain von Rosenberg's left arm.

When darkness fell, the fighting stopped. We bivouacked on our positions
and passed a quiet night.

That evening, we received orders to send all vehicles back through
Leipzig and over the bridge onto the road to Lützen. Only one ammunition
waggon was to be retained with the serviceable guns, and only one infantry
ammunition waggon for all the infantry battalions. I gave command of the
two cannon that had been repaired, and the two vehicles that were to stay
with the corps, to *Leutnant* Scholl (Captain Müller and *Leutnant* Kuhlmann
had been wounded) and sent all other vehicles to the rear.

The approximate loss of today's action is 35 killed, 181 wounded, one
captured and 162 missing.

Holzhausen

After a preliminary artillery bombardment by Klenau's guns, General de
Best, of Heldensfeld's division, assailed Holzhausen from the south with
Regiments Württemberg Nr 38 and Kerpen Nr 49. They fought their way into
the open centre of the village but were pushed out by the reinforcements
which Charpentier threw in. Lindfors' Russians now came up from Klein-
Pössna and the divisions of Chowanskoi and Paskiewitsch advanced on the
north side of Holzhausen. This massive concentration of power was too
much for Charpentier's men, and between one and two o'clock they broke
and fled back onto Gerard's reserve on the Steinberg. Klenau sent his cavalry
after them, consisting of Chevaulégers regiments Kaiser Nr 1, Hohenzollern
Nr 2, O'Reilly Nr 3 and the Palatine Hussars Nr 12. The French were by now
in such disarray that the cavalry took several guns. Holzhausen, meanwhile,
was ablaze.

Bennigsen's divisions of Chowanskoi and Paskiewitsch and Klenau's Austrians pursued the fleeing enemy westwards towards Stötteritz, leaving the
French on the Steinberg to be dealt with by Lindfors. The latter was ordered
to advance through Holzhausen to join his comrades, but the intense heat
and collapsing buildings rendered this impossible. A broad gap now yawned
in the Allied line; Bennigsen seemed to have forgotten his former caution
and took no action to close it. Sebastiani therefore seized the moment and
set his II Cavalry Corps in motion. Fortunately Chowanskoi saw the threat in
time and rapidly formed squares, so that Sebastiani's cavalry could achieve
nothing and were repulsed. The Regiments Narwa and Smolensk especially
distinguished themselves in this action.

Count Pahlen's cavalry division (from Barclay's Russians of the Army of Bohemia) and Kreutz's Russian cavalry now mounted a counter-charge from Zuckelhausen northwards against the Steinberg. Walther's cavalry division was overpowered and fell back on Stötteritz. The Grodno and Sumy Hussars passed around the hill and followed them. It seemed that a decisive moment was at hand for the Allies in this sector until Count Pahlen – leading his men from well in front – had his horse shot from under him and was himself wounded (as was Sebastiani). The impetus of the chase then abruptly petered out. Even so, Macdonald abandoned the Steinberg and joined in the general withdrawal to Stötteritz. Austrian and Russian artillery were at once put onto the Steinberg, from where they hammered the retreating French.

As well as Sebastiani the French generals Bessières, d'Augeranville, du Coeotlosquet, Ledru and Sopranski were also wounded in the fighting here, and I Cavalry Corps suffered more casualties than it had on the 16th. Officer losses on the 16th were ninety-six, but on the 18th amounted to 110. Sebastiani's II Cavalry Corps lost fifty-seven officers on the 16th and sixty on the 18th.

Of the thirty-two houses in Holzhausen twenty-one were destroyed, as was the church. The latter was not rebuilt until 1818 and the work could only be started thanks to a gift of 600 Thaler from King Friedrich August and a grant of a further 400 from the British support fund. It received new bells in 1820, the smaller of which was cast from a gun left on the battlefield. It bore the following inscription:

From the metal of one of those guns
which brought certain death to thousands
And also once destroyed this church,
The wise hands of the craftsman
Converted me to a noble instrument
And now I hang here as a sign of peace.

Typhus broke out following the battle and, as in many places in the Leipzig area, much of the population died. For years afterwards Holzhausen was a ghost town. The owner of the local inn alone buried in his garden the corpses of forty-five people who had died in his house.

The intensity of the fighting here may be judged by the fact that the inhabitants retrieved 3,600 cannonballs from the immediate vicinity of the village. These were taken into Leipzig, where the army bought them for one Grosschen a piece.

Paunsdorf

While the struggles for Zuckelhausen and Holzhausen were going on, Bubna's division and Platoff's twelve Cossack *pulks* were making their wide right hook five kilometres to the north.

Bubna's men at Brandis had been roused at three o'clock that morning.

Their first target was to take Klein-Pössna, and after setting off they were confronted with the swollen River Parthe west of Beucha. There was no bridge, so it had to be waded. Getting the guns across took much time and effort, while the artillery vehicles had to turn back and cross at Borsdorf some four kilometres to the north. When Bubna eventually reached Klein-Pössna at eight o'clock it was to find that the French had evacuated the place. He thus pushed on through Hirschfeld and Engelsdorf towards Paunsdorf. At Engelsdorf he surprised Macdonald's artillery train, which fled in great confusion back onto Reynier's VII Corps at Stüntz and Paunsdorf.

Reynier had two divisions – Baron Durutte's 32nd and von Zeschau's Saxon 24th – Count Guilleminot's 13th Division being now at Lindenau. On the morning of the 18th the Saxons, who had bivouacked at Paunsdorf overnight, marched north to the Heiteren Blick outwork to join Reynier and Durutte's division. Reynier had received instructions to send the Saxons off to Torgau fortress, as their reliability was beginning to be questioned in the light of increasing numbers of defections amongst Napoleon's German contingents. Consequently between seven and eight o'clock Reynier ordered von Zeschau to set off for Torgau. He then rode north to Nautsch on the eastern bank of the Parthe, where the church of St Thekla stands on a slight hill. From the church tower he could make out Platoff's Cossacks on the main road before Taucha on the Parthe, blocking the way to Torgau. Reynier therefore recalled Von Zeschau and ordered him to take his division back to Paunsdorf and deploy it across the road to Wurzen (now Route B6).

As the Saxons marched off again at ten o'clock, Platoff's Cossacks came down from Taucha. At the same time, the Russian Dorpat and Lifland Mounted Rifle Regiments (from General Emanuel's 2nd Mounted Rifle Division of Langeron's Corps of the Army of Silesia) crossed the Parthe at Mockau and advanced on the Heiteren Blick, about three kilometres to the north-east of Paunsdorf on the Leipzig–Taucha road (now the B87). To delay them, von Zeschau left a detachment consisting of Colonel von Lindenau's 26th Light Cavalry Brigade (four squadrons each of the Prinz Clemens Chevaulégers and the Hussars), von Sahr's light infantry battalion (presently commanded by Major von Selmnitz) and Birnbaum's horse artillery battery as a flank guard.

Uniting their forces, the Russians attacked Lindenau's two regiments (a little over 500 strong), who had formed front to oppose them, and threw them back behind the ammunition waggons of the Saxon Light Battalion. Though they reformed, it was clear to the Saxons that they could not protect the battery, which was therefore sent off to Paunsdorf with an escort of Chevaulégers. There followed a short conference among the cavalry brigade's officers, after which they split into two groups, consisting of Colonel Lindenau and Majors von Feilitsch and Hintze on the one side, and the rest of the officers on the other. The latter group went back to the brigade and ordered the men to sheathe their sabres. The two regiments then rode back towards the enemy, but when a short distance from them they halted and gave a 'Hurrah!' The Saxon officers then rode forward and declared that they wished to go over to the Russians. This was greeted with great jubilation, and the two regiments were sent off to join Yorck's corps over at Möckern. They took no further part in the battle. Lindenau and his two companions, meanwhile, rode back to Paunsdorf.

The Light Battalion was now alone, on an open plain, with massively superior enemy forces deploying around it: Bernadotte's Army of the North was at last beginning to materialise close by, having reached Plaussig on the Parthe. The chances of the isolated battalion reaching the French lines across four kilometres of open ground under such circumstances were nil, and after a brief discussion Major von Selmnitz capitulated to the Russians on condition that his men would not be disarmed. This was agreed, and Cossacks escorted the battalion to Seegeritz on the Parthe. It was now eleven o'clock. At Seegeritz, Bernadotte himself appeared and congratulated them on their decision. He said: 'I know that you have had no bread for six days. There are potatoes here, cook them! If you wish to join us in the fight against the enemy, I grant you three hours rest, then take up your arms!' However, the battalion declined to fight against its ex-comrades and was sent to a Swedish depot at Freiroda, north of Lindenthal, where it was issued with grain which was at once milled and baked into bread. On 20 October the battalion rejoined its division in Leipzig.

Professor Steffens, present at Blücher's headquarters, has left this account of the arrival of the two Saxon cavalry regiments there on the 18th:[34]

> This day presented us with a surprising spectacle. A force of strange cavalry came towards us over the plain in good order. Blücher was undoubtedly informed of their approach. They were Saxon cavalry, who had deserted the enemy and were coming over to us. They had an air of something strange and wonderful about them and the events that we saw unfolding before us. The riders halted before us; quiet, determined yet sad. Their commander rode forward towards ours, who awaited him with dignity. The Saxon officer said that they had long awaited this opportunity to end their unnatural alliance, which had forced them to fight against their own people. Only now was this possible. But he pleaded for understanding; they did not wish to fight in this battle. Their unhappy king was in Leipzig.
>
> Blücher spoke briefly to them in a friendly manner; granted their wish and directed them to a spot behind the lines. As they rode off, I watched them for a time with inner sympathy; I could imagine how they felt in their depressing situation.

***

The main body of the Saxon division was meanwhile involved in the violent struggle for Paunsdorf. Colonel von Brause's brigade was on the Taucha road, just west of Paunsdorf, with two companies of the Infantry Regiment von Lecoq in the village itself, together with a French battalion from

---

[34] Seyfert, p.192.

Durutte's division. General von Ryssel's brigade had taken post by the windmill at Stüntz,[35] about 800 metres to the south-west. North-west of the Franco-Saxons, towards Schönefeld, was Durutte's division, and then Delmas' division of Souham's III Corps. Behind Delmas, partially in Schönefeld itself, was Marmont's VI Corps, up against the Parthe, with his cavalry in rear.

The three brigades of Bubna's Light Division (Niepperg, Wieland and Zechmeister) advanced athwart the road and was taken under fire by the three batteries of Saxon artillery (two horse batteries and a twelve-pounder battery) which were sited between Paunsdorf and Stüntz. After a ninety-minute artillery duel, General Zechmeister led his 6th Austrian Jäger battalion against the blazing village and threw out its garrison. However, wind blowing the flames and smoke into the faces of the Austrians aided a Franco-Saxon counter-attack, which retook some of the village and forced the Austrians to withdraw. The Liechtenstein Hussars moved forward to take up the Jägers, but the enemy did not advance out of Paunsdorf.

Zechmeister next led the Jägers and the Peterwardeiner Grenzers at the village, whilst Reynier sent in part of Durutte's division to reinforce the hard-pressed garrison. The fight in the burning village raged back and forth. Finally, Bubna committed Neipperg's brigade (the 5th Jägers and Hussar Regiment Kaiser Nr 1) and Wieland's brigade (Infantry Regiments Erzherzog Rainer Nr 11 and Würzburg Nr 7 and the Blankenstein Hussars Nr 6) to the fight. After a hard struggle, the Franco-Saxon garrison was ejected for the last time. In the artillery duel which had accompanied the action, most of the Austrian gun crews and teams were killed or wounded. Of the sixty-six houses which had stood in Paunsdorf on 14 October, half were totally destroyed in the course of the battle and the other half damaged, twenty of them badly.

Bubna's achievement in taking and holding Paunsdorf with his single division, opposed by two enemy divisions, cannot be underestimated.

It was now two o'clock, and the leading troops of the much-needed Army of the North (the Prussian divisions of Borstell and Prinz Ludwig von Hessen-Homburg of von Bülow's III Corps) now came up on Bubna's right and joined in the fight.

The actions of the Army of the North

Early on the morning of the 18th, Blücher rode over to the headquarters of the Crown Prince of Sweden and demanded that Bernadotte cross the Parthe at once. Bernadotte declared that this would be far too dangerous unless Blücher gave him command of the corps of Langeron and Saint-Priest in addition to that of von Bülow. To his eternal credit, Blücher agreed; but he had had enough of the cowardice and chicanery of this vain upstart. He

---

[35] This mill was still standing in 1913.

resolved to stay in Bernadotte's headquarters for as long as possible. If his dubious ally should make the slightest attempt to remove himself or any part of the army under his command from the battlefield, Blücher was determined to depose him and take command himself.

It was now seven o'clock and the vain Gascon was still posing and procrastinating even as the thunder of the cannon could be heard from the south. Blücher's patience snapped. *'Donnerwetter!'* he roared in the Crown Prince's face, then mounted his horse and galloped furiously off to his own headquarters. At last, Bernadotte must have become aware of the universal contempt in which he was held by those around him. Mindful also of Sir Charles Stewart's open threat regarding his financial rewards, he was sufficiently stung to give the order for his troops to move off – in the direction of the battle. However, the snail-like pace of his advance was such as to ensure that his army would not arrive at the scene of the action until four in the afternoon. As the columns of Barclay and Bennigsen did not join battle until two o'clock, this enabled Napoleon to transfer his forces to the most threatened sectors during the morning. In fact, so fragmented and unco-ordinated was the command situation on the Allied side that a German wit came up with the following joke: *'Wer hat bei Leipzig befehligt? Gott der Vater allein!'* ('Who commanded at Leipzig? God the Father alone!')

Following the transfer of von Bülow's corps to his command, the Crown Prince of Sweden had issued the following order to his corps commanders:

> General von Bülow will set off at once with the III (Prussian) Corps for Taucha. There he will force the crossing of the Parthe and take up a position on the far side. He will send patrols out towards Wurzen and will take up contact with General von Bennigsen's corps. While General von Bülow is forcing the river, the Russian corps of General von Wintzingerode will march on Taucha and follow Bülow's movement. General von Wintzinger-ode will send cavalry patrols towards Eilenburg and Wurzen in order to secure Bülow's left flank.

General von Bülow received this order in Güntheritz to the north of Leipzig – where he had spent the night – at nine o'clock in the morning. He set off through Hohenheida, Seehausen and Cradefeld to Taucha. Wintzingerode's Russian cavalry had occupied Taucha early that morning so his crossing was secure, but it is confusing that Bernadotte's order gives the impression that Wintzingerode should be following the Prussians. Hessen-Homburg's 3rd Prussian Division (together with von Bülow) crossed the Parthe at Grassdorf, just north of Taucha, while those of Borstell and Krafft crossed in Taucha itself. However, the latter two divisions were delayed as the crossing was difficult, and von Bülow hurried on with just one division towards the sounds of battle. By two o'clock he had deployed north of Paunsdorf. He described the mood of the moment thus:

> The massive cannonade at Leipzig could be clearly heard at Taucha and seemed to come ever nearer. The infantry and cavalry started to trot, even

though everybody was very tired. The burning desire to get to grips with the enemy gave them wings. Many of the soldiers called for bread; others made signs that they were thirsty. The villagers of Cradefeld vied with one another to slake the soldiers' thirst as much as possible, in that they set water butts at the roadside. The soldiers said to them: 'Pray for us that we win, otherwise you're all lost!'

The arrival of the Prussians swung the balance of power in the Allies' favour in the Paunsdorf sector. Von Bülow took over command and Bubna withdrew his battered brigades along the road towards Wurzen as the Prussian horse artillery batteries deployed and began to bombard Durutte's division. This conventional artillery was supported by Captain Bogue's newly-formed rocket artillery battery of the Royal Artillery, which operated with the Army of the North. (The modern descendant of Bogue's Rocket Battery is the only British unit to carry the battle honour 'Leipzig'.)

General Stewart was with Bogue at the Heiteren Blick in the thick of the enemy fire, directing the rockets as the battle raged. His ADC, Lieutenant John Jones, recorded the following details concerning the troop's activities here:

> At the commencement of the action on the morning of the 18th, Captain Bogue addressed himself to General Wintzingerode, commanding the advance of the Crown Prince, expressing his desire to see the enemy, and requesting permission to engage. The General, much struck with the gallantry and spirit of the address, granted as a guard a squadron of dragoons, and requested Captain Bogue to follow his own plans and judgement.
>
> Captain Bogue lost no time in advancing to the attack of the village of Paunsdorf, then in possession of five of the enemy's battalions, upon whom he opened, in advance of the whole army, a most destructive fire. This was returned by musketry, and for some time a very hot combat ensued, when the enemy, unable to withstand the well-directed fire of Captain Bogue's brigade, fell into confusion and began to retreat. Captain Bogue, seizing the moment, charged at the head of the squadron of cavalry, and the enemy, terrified at his approach, turned round, and taking off their caps, gave three huzzas, and every man, to the number of between two and three thousand, surrendered to the Rocket Brigade, which, I believe, did not exceed 200 men.
>
> The intelligence of this success being communicated to the Crown Prince, he sent his thanks to Captain Bogue for such eminent services, requesting at the same time that he would continue his exertions: and the brigade proceeded in consequence to the attack of (I believe) the village of Sommerfeld[36] still further in advance. Sir C. Stewart accompanied the brigade and I was of the party. The situation taken up on the flank of the village was exposed to the most heavy fire, both of cannonballs and grapeshot from the

---

[36] In actual fact Sellerhausen.

enemy's line, and from the riflemen in the village. A ball from the latter soon deprived us of the exertions of poor Bogue; it entered below the eye and passing through the head, caused instantaneous death.[37]

The Congreve rockets made a very deep impression on Wenzel Krimer, who witnessed them in action:

In front of us was just such a devilish rocket battery. Each time a rocket was fired and went hissing and shooting forth into an enemy column and exploded, one saw whole files hurled down. The scorched and battered bodies lay in great piles where they fell. At first the French did not seem familiar with this new weapon of death and stood up against it; but when they saw what fearful destruction it wrought and in what a ghastly manner the victims died, even if only a drop of fuel came too near, there was no holding them. Whenever they saw a rocket coming, whole columns ran away and abandoned everything.

***

After some softening up of the enemy by their artillery, the Prussian infantry made ready to advance. In the north, Major von Müllenheim and Captain von der Schulenburg led the 2nd Battalion, 3rd East Prussian Infantry Regiment, and the 1st and 2nd Battalions, 4th Reserve Infantry Regiment, against Paunsdorf, while on their left the 6th Austrian Jäger Battalion launched their third assault. The Franco-Saxon garrison fled and regrouped behind Durutte's division. The Allies pushed on behind them. The effects of Bogue's rockets on the enemy were dramatic. Though they were often erratic they spread terror amongst Reynier's men, who soon broke and fled back south-west to Stünz and Sellerhausen.

Hessen-Homburg's division came up to the west of Paunsdorf, near the road, while the divisions of Borstell and Krafft arrived and formed to his right and rear. Wintzingerode's corps meanwhile advanced to fill the gap between Borstell's right wing and the Russians of Langeron's corps, which was fighting at Schönefeld on the Parthe. The Allied ring was drawing closer. As the first French line at Schönefeld collapsed, Marshal Ney rapidly organised another, which stretched from Schönefeld through Sellerhausen to Stüntz.

Having taken Paunsdorf, von Bülow aimed to advance further south-west through Stüntz and Sellerhausen. He called up all available artillery to prepare the way and gradually concentrated seventy-six guns in the angle of the

---

[37] Bogue lies buried alongside the south-west wall of Taucha cemetery, next to General von Mannteuffel, where his friends later erected a shrine in his honour. In 1814 Bernadotte sent the Swedish Order of the Sword, IV Class, and a gift of 10,000 Thalers to Bogue's widow. In 1820, as king of Sweden, he also sent silver medals of the same order to Sergeants Michael Taylor and Robert Chalkely, Corporals Edward Marks and William Wareham, and Bombardier John Guy, who had also fought at Leipzig. The reverse of each medal bore: 'FOER TAPPERHET I FAELT' (for bravery in the field).

roads to Taucha and Wurzen. Their first target was Sellerhausen, which was
very soon in flames. Bogue's rocket battery came up to support the bombardment but placed itself so badly in the way of its Allies' guns that some of
these had to suspend their fire. Even before the British could set off their first
rockets, the French made a quick sortie out of Sellerhausen in the lull,
attacked the advanced rocket battery, and killed Bogue and some others of
the crew. Luckily, the Prussian infantry then hurried up to protect the
artillery, Major von Polczinski and two battalions of the 4th Prussian Reserve
Infantry Regiment charging the enemy with such determination that they
fled back into Sellerhausen with the Prussians hot on their heels, and were
thrown out of it. However, south of Sellerhausen were large forces of French
infantry and cavalry, and the Prussians could make no further headway. A
French counter-attack then drove Polczinski and his men out of the village.
The Prussians reformed at Paunsdorf while the artillery of the Russian
Colonel Dietrichs and the Prussian Captain von Glasenapp stopped the
pursuing French Cuirassiers and infantry in their tracks. Polczinski's battalions lost so heavily in this action that they had to be taken out of the line
for the rest of the day.

Hessen-Homburg's 3rd Division was now deployed south of Paunsdorf, in
contact with Bubna's light division to its left. Von Borstell's division was west
of the village, between the Taucha and Wurzen roads. To his right, the
Russians of Wintzingerode (Woronzow's advanced guard) extended to the
north of Schönefeld and the Parthe. The belated Army of the North was at
last beginning to appear in strength, and its ranks thickened ever more as it
deployed north of Paunsdorf.

It was between four and five o'clock that von Bülow noticed an enemy
advance beginning from Stötteritz, aimed north-east towards Mölkau.
Napoleon had launched Nansouty and his Guards cavalry together with
twenty guns (but, strangely, no infantry support) against Dokturoff's Russians
in Unter-Zweinaundorf. This thrust was – predictably – beaten off by the
Russian infantry, and the French cavalry withdrew into Stötteritz.

Seeing that the area south of Sellerhausen, Stüntz and Mölkau was thus
free of the enemy, Bernadotte ordered von Bülow to take the first two of
these villages, which were garrisoned by the divisions of Delmas and Durutte.
Hessen-Homburg's 3rd Division moved on Stüntz as evening fell. The East
Prussian battalions of Müllenheim and Friccius led the way. Müllenheim's
men took the place with little trouble, their work made easier by the Austro-
Russian capture of Mölkau to the south-east and the support of an Austrian
Jäger battalion.

Taking Sellerhausen was more difficult. It had a strong and determined
garrison and the initial Prussian assault – made by Major von Gleissenberg's
Fusilier Battalion of the 3rd East Prussian Infantry Regiment and the 2nd
East Prussian Grenadier Battalion – was too weak to succeed. Only when four
more battalions of Colonel von Krafft's 6th Division under Major von Reckow
joined in on the right was the village taken. Here, too, the Austrians provided
a helping hand, in the form of the Peterwardeiner Grenzers and the

Liechtenstein Hussars. It was completely dark by the time the village finally fell at six o'clock, when night put an end to the fighting. Gleissenberg's men then occupied the ruins of Sellerhausen, while Müllenheim took post in Stüntz. The divisions of Delmas and Durutte withdrew south-west to a new line at the junction of the Taucha and Wurzen roads. General Delmas himself had been mortally wounded in the fighting, and his division had suffered about fifty per cent casualties. General Maran was also wounded, while Marshal Ney had four horses shot from under him. A contemporary observed that: 'The steadiness, the coolness, the energy, the cold-bloodedness of this part of the French army are beyond all praise. Martial virtues never shone so brightly, never were such heroic deeds followed by such misfortune.'

***

Despite its great superiority in this north-eastern sector of the battlefield, and even allowing for its delayed arrival, the Army of the North had achieved relatively little. Only von Bülow's corps had been involved in the fighting. Wintzingerode's Russians were kept in the second line and only their artillery had been in action. The Crown Prince's precious Swedes were well out of harm's way by the church of St Thekla in the north, while throughout the day Bernadotte had acted as a brake on the impetuous Prussians, who were burning to avenge years of national humiliation at the hands of the French. As the Crown Prince said to von Bülow at Paunsdorf that morning: '*General, Sie werden meinem Befehle pünktlich gehorchen. Ich weiss, dass Sie und die Herren Preussen in einem Punkte mir nicht gern folgen, nämlich bei dem Verbot vorwärts zu gehen!*' ('General, you will obey my orders promptly. I know that you and your Prussians don't like to follow me in one respect, namely in being forbidden to advance!')

Under these circumstances, von Bülow's actions here deserve even greater respect. As he had said to Blücher the previous evening: '*Wo es das Wohl meines Vaterlandes und Europas gilt, werde ich nicht fehlen!*' ('If it concerns the interests of my Fatherland and Europe I will not be found lacking!') He certainly stood by his words at Paunsdorf on 18 October, as a man and as a general.

Only now did Bernadotte at last appear in the front line. His contribution to the day's action was to order inaction, as he forbade any pursuit of the defeated enemy.

The 4th Column: Langeron's Corps at Schönefeld

Langeron and Saint-Priest had been placed under Bernadotte's command by Blücher with the proviso that Bernadotte would only exercise that command when he appeared on the battlefield; until that point, they remained Blücher's. In the prince's absence, Blücher ordered both corps to cross from Wiederitzsch to the left bank of the Parthe between Mockau and Plaussig and to advance south to engage the enemy's VI Corps, which was drawn up between Schönefeld and Paunsdorf. All bridges over the river had been destroyed and the ground was sodden from the rain which had fallen during the previous few days.

Blücher joined Langeron's corps as it was crossing the river at eleven o'clock. Langeron's corps would be the right wing in this action, Saint-Priest's the left. The French had occupied Mockau but they were thrown out by General Rudsewitsch's Advanced Guard (7th, 12th, 22nd, 30th and 48th Jägers, Infantry Regiments Schlüsselburg and Olonetz and part of General Emanuel's dragoon brigade). An inhabitant of Mockau later described how 'the shouting and screaming of the soldiers, the roar and rattle of the cannon and musketry, the bursting shells, the whimpering and cries for help of the wounded and those buried in the collapsed buildings were hideous. The smoke and dust so darkened our world that no-one knew what time of day it was.'

After this the attack on Schönefeld commenced. One of Blücher's ADCs (Nostitz) described the early part of the day as viewed from his headquarters:

> The ground rose a little on this side of the river and from these heights we could see an amazing spectacle. On a long ridge in the distance we could see the *Grande Armée* advancing. It was the mighty host of the man who had reigned and terrorised this continent for so many years, advancing to do battle. The procession was interminable; as regiments appeared in the east so their comrades before them vanished into the west. It was as if an entire nation was on the move. The scenes of the migration of the German tribes into present-day Germany must have been like this. The mighty spectacle gripped us all. We sat and watched it in silence for a long time.
>
> It was here that *Oberst* von Müffling gave this grim contest the name by which it is now known: 'The Great Battle of the Nations'. We stayed here on the plain for some hours. All around us we could hear the din of combat; far off lay Leipzig; here, in the eye of the storm, it was tranquil. The hours passed by unnoticed. The reports of various actions which were brought in kept us in great tension. Until now I had not been exposed to the dangers of a battle. Now Blücher turned to me – all his other adjutants had already been sent off on missions: 'Find General Langeron,' he said, 'and give him the order to storm Schönefeld village. He can expect no help from other troops, but the enemy must be thrown out!'
>
> I hurried off. Langeron had been battling for possession of Schönefeld for some time already and it had changed hands several times. The flames from the place were my beacon. I found the general in the first houses of the village. He was a serious man of stern, commanding appearance. The enemy had just retaken most of the village. The Russian were fighting stubbornly in the flames just before us. I relayed my order; he replied in an annoyed fashion: 'My troops have been fighting for hours; they are tired, exhausted and much reduced in numbers. Without support I will not be able to evict the enemy.'

Schönefeld was held by Marmont's battered VI Corps and behind them were part of Souham's III Corps.

A member of the French garrison of Schönefeld, Erckman-Chatrian of the 6e *Légère* (III Corps), later recollected his own experiences during the day's fighting:

By two o'clock in the afternoon half of our officers were dead or wounded. Major Gemeau was wounded, Colonel Lorain had been killed. All along the river we saw nothing but heaps of dead and wounded who had tried to escape the carnage. Some struggled up on one knee to fire a final shot or to make a last thrust with the bayonet.

Strings of corpses floated down the River Parthe. You saw the face of one, the back of another; of others, just the feet. They followed one another like wooden rafts. No-one paid them any attention – as if one of us might join them at any moment! The Russians formed up in two columns. They came on into the valley with their muskets in their arms, in splendid order, and assaulted us twice with great bravery. The gunfire kept getting heavier. Wherever you looked there was nothing but the enemy, who surrounded us more and more. If we threw back one column, a new one appeared and we had to start all over again. At about three o'clock the Russians launched their third attack. Our officers gave their orders for the defence. We fought from house to house; in every lane. The walls came crashing down from the artillery fire. The roofs fell in. There was no more shouting as there had been at the start of the battle. Each fought with cold, stark rage. The officers had picked up the muskets of the fallen and taken their pouches. They bit off the cartridges like common soldiers. After the houses we defended the gardens and the churchyard. There were more dead on the ground than under it. Those who were killed dropped without a sound. The remnants took cover behind a wall, a rubbish heap, a tombstone. Every inch of ground cost a man's life.

It was dark when Marshal Ney brought up reinforcements – the rest of the divisions of Brayer and Ricard. The remnants of our regiment gathered together again and threw the Russians back over the old bridge; by now all the handrails had been destroyed. On the bridge were posted six twelve-pounders and the artillery duel with the enemy went on until seven o'clock. The gunfire lit up the bridge like lightning; in these flashes we could see clumps of dead men and horses swirling slowly in the current and being swept under the structure.

At 7:30, as some cavalry came up on our left-hand side, we were at last ordered to withdraw. There were now only 2–3,000 men and the six guns in Schönefeld. We marched back to the Kohlgärten without being pursued and went on to bivouac in Reudnitz.

Both Marmont and Souham were wounded here, but they had forced Saint-Priest to fall back, as his artillery had run out of ammunition. The French reinforcements, which had arrived at four o'clock, numbered 7,000 men with forty guns.

Bernadotte had seen this critical development and – in a rare moment of positive action – had sent up sixty of Wintzingerode's guns and twenty

Swedish pieces under Colonel Cardell. These were formed into one battery stretching from the Taucha road to Schönefeld. Schönefeld was then assaulted again; by Olsufiev on the north side and by Kapsewitsch, Saint-Priest and Rudsewitsch from the south and east. General Brayer launched a counter-attack but was driven off, and Souham's III Corps was pushed back to the windmill on the Rohrteich pond, where it stayed until nine o'clock that night, when it fell back south to Reudnitz. The corps had lost 117 officers and about 5,000 men this day and had only two generals left on the field.

To the left of Souham's corps another French force had advanced from Volkmarsdorf to the Taucha road, where Wintzingerode's cavalry, under Generals Orurk and Manteuffel, charged it and forced it to withdraw with the loss of four guns. It was in this action that General von Manteuffel was killed by a musket ball.

In the late afternoon General Woronzoff's corps held the position on the Taucha road, but there was no further activity in this sector. The Swedes arrived on the field and formed up behind the Russians and Prussians between the St Thekla church and Heiteren Blick, but did not come into action. By nightfall the French left wing had been forced back to the outer suburbs of Leipzig, thanks to the heroic efforts of Langeron's men. Allied losses in these actions to the north of the city were: Langeron, 3,710; Wintzingerode, 390; Blücher, 733; and the Swedes, 37.

Most of Schönefeld was burnt to the ground, including the church and the manor, much of the damage being caused by the British Rocket Brigade. About a thousand sheep, pigs and cattle perished in the flames.

***

The vicar of Plaussig remembered the events of this terrible day in the Schönefeld sector as follows:

> All the villagers had fled from the village onto the meadows by the Parthe and had set up camp there as well as they could. Only I, my wife and three children and our maid, who was sick with typhus, were left in Plaussig because the Allies were already drawn up in battle order. The terror that we went through that morning was indescribable. All my family were shrieking in fear: 'Father! Where can we go that will be safe?' The only thing I could suggest was that we flee into the garden behind the barn, if that didn't work I just had no idea what we should do except to hide in the sacristy of the church, which was fireproof. If that didn't work I was at a loss. We had no bread so we gnawed raw potatoes as we ran out into the garden. I was carrying two children and my wife was clutching our eleven-week-old infant. Help came soon, however; the Crown Prince of Sweden sent a trumpeter to us to tell me that the immediate danger of Plaussig being bombarded seemed to be past, as the enemy on the other bank of the Parthe at Portitz had come over to the Allies, so the river crossing would not be opposed. But now new dangers threatened us. Prussian engineers arrived and threw bridges over the Parthe. All the trees on my meadow down at the river bank

were felled in order to provide a covering for the waggons that they had pushed into the Parthe. Then they took all the doors from the village to lay over the tree-trunks, even the great door of the manor which took thirty Swedes to lift it. After this was finished the Allied army came up and crossed the river. Between the church and the vicarage came a column of cavalry; infantry marched at the double through my garden and courtyard. The ground shook so much that the two clocks which my friend had wrapped in waxcloth and sacking and buried there were later found with broken springs and chains. All the rooms of my house were filled with students from Breslau, Halle and Frankfurt on the Oder; they belonged to a *Freikorps* and were plundering my library. They had no shame. I made it plain to them that they, supposed friends of knowledge, were robbing a vicar of his means of livelihood. 'Haven't you heard,' they shouted back, 'in war you don't ask for justice and honesty, for discipline and retribution? For this insolence you will be paid back!' Then they went up into the attic where the parish archives were kept, ripped up books and records and used them to wrap up the things that they had just stolen.

The night of the 17th–18th October General Graf Manteuffel spent in the chapel at Seegeritz from where he could oversee the battlefield with a telescope which he set up on the table. Next morning he issued his orders from here. He left the chapel at eight o'clock in the morning. A few hours later he was carried, half dead, to Taucha. A cannonball had brushed him and caused such shock to his internal organs that a fever broke out and he died that same day. His widow set up a monument to him in Taucha cemetery.

The battle began at nine o'clock. The gunfire was so heavy that the earth shook. The windows rattled so hard that we thought that they would smash. All around us were Russian soldiers shouting and running to and fro. There was scarcely any room for us to stand. In the south and south-west, wherever we looked, we saw burning villages. The flames from Schönefeld were blown towards us by the strong winds. It was evening before the Russians went away, but on the 19th October others came looking for food. We had been told that the Russians loved children; trusting to this, my wife hid some baby clothes under our eleven-week-old infant in his basket-work crib. As soon as the Russians came in, they rushed to the crib, threw the baby out onto the floor and took the clothes. For love of the child, my wife snatched them back and I ran off with them. The soldiers were so furious that one of them struck her in the belly with the butt of his musket so hard that she died a premature death a few years later.

***

Dr Seyfert, the vicar of Taucha, has also left us an account of events on 18 October:

At nine o'clock the Crown Prince of Sweden arrived; his army marched through the village the whole morning and went on to Grassdorf, Cradefeld,

Seegeritz and Plaussig. Their columns were as wide as the road. The villagers stood in their doorways and cheered them on. We had never seen such a parade before. The infantry (mostly Prussian Jägers and *Landwehr*) did not march as is usual when going into action but trotted beside the cavalry horses, which were also trotting, so keen were they to get at the enemy. The closer they got to the gunfire, the faster they ran.

During the fighting in Paunsdorf (in which the manor and some forty houses were burned down) many of the inhabitants went into the old castle there. Two senior officers came in; they had a list containing the names of fourteen villages, including Taucha, which were to be set alight if the Army of the North were to be forced to withdraw. One of the officers said that the threat of such a withdrawal was very great. You can understand the terror which gripped everyone in the area. But this terror did not last long. As the French under their famous generals were fighting desperately to escape, it was quite likely that they would succeed in pushing their foes back, as it is certain that Napoleon did not intend to withdraw through Leipzig or he would have built more bridges over the Pleisse and the Elster.

The night of the 18th–19th October was the worst for Taucha. First, the headquarters of a Russian prince were to be set up in the village. Two officers with an escort came in. One of them, who spoke German, ordered bread to be brought for the prisoners of war that they were escorting. When we asked him if the Allies had won, he said, 'Of course! Or we wouldn't be here!' After they left, the mortally wounded General von Manteuffel was brought in. Finally, at ten o'clock, a Cossack officer arrived who said that he was the ADC to the general. He brought his horse into the room and shouted for food and drink. We had prepared a meal for General Manteuffel but we had to give it to this mad officer. But because we couldn't give him his favourite drink (vodka) he raged on worse than before. If a Cossack officer was so coarse and unmannerly, we all had good cause to fear for much worse from his men.

This fear was soon to be realised! There was suddenly a riot in the village streets. Cossacks stormed into the houses and tried to tear off the doors and windows. Sometimes there were more than twenty of them in a house and they roared in their rough, terrifying, bass voices, 'Brud! Schnapps!' They rampaged all over the houses, broke open all possible containers and took everything that they could lay their hands on, towels, shirts, stockings, underwear, clothing.

Our teacher was lucky enough not to be bothered with such looters. The front of the schoolhouse was covered in Latin words and letters and the Russians thought that it was a sacred place. They all crossed themselves as they passed it and none dared to enter it.

It was clear that we all prayed for dawn to come and put an end to this night of terror. At last the cocks crowed – for the last time! They had thus betrayed their presence! The Cossacks rushed to find them and took every one.

On the 19th October many Russian ammunition waggons passed through

Taucha, as did many other vehicles under Cossack escort which went north to Eilenburg.

At twelve o'clock the Prussian Lieutenant-Colonel Graf von Lottum arrived and began to prepare the manor as a hospital for Prussian troops. An officer of Ulans, Ewald Baron von Kleist von Kurland, brought in the body of his cousin, a *Kornett* in an Ulan regiment, who had been shot near Pauns-dorf, and had him buried in the cemetery.

Captain Bogue, of the British Rocket Battery, was brought in and buried with military honours. Early on the 19th, General von Manteuffel was brought in. He died next day and was buried on the 21st with military honours. At five o'clock in the evening Sir Charles Stewart (a British Lieutenant-General, brother of the British statesman Lord Castlereagh, who played a role in the partition of Saxony at the Congress of Vienna) came in with four coaches. After having a meal, all, including the general, wrote until three o'clock in the morning and despatched couriers. Without doubt, the reports of the great victory at Leipzig were written here and sent off to London.

The 5th Column: the corps of Sacken and Yorck at the Halle Gate in Leipzig

Following the battle of Möckern on 16 October, Yorck's battered corps was in no fit state to indulge in another serious fight. Blücher had given Langeron's corps to the Crown Prince of Sweden, which left only Sacken's corps available for use on the northern side of the city. This was drawn up at the junction of roads between Eutritzsch and Gohlis, while Yorck's corps was on the road north of Möckern. Opposing Sacken, between Gohlis and Pfaffendorf, were Dombrowski's redoubtable Poles, now reduced to about 1,500 men. Sacken's first assault here was made by General Newerowski with the regiments Odessa, Simbirsk, Tarnopol and Wilna and the 49th and 50th Jägers. In support was Colonel Rachmanoff with the regiments Kamtschatka and Ochotsk and the 5th Jägers.

When Major Gorgaud, one of Napoleon's orderly officers accompanying Dombrowski, saw the Russians forming up in such numbers he galloped off and reported the precarious situation of the Poles and the threat the Russians represented to the only route out of the Allied trap. Napoleon immediately despatched Pachtod's division of the Young Guard, 6,000 strong, through the city, and these arrived at eleven o'clock, before Sacken's assault struck home. The opposing forces on the northern front were now balanced, enabling us to appreciate the great advantage of the French interior lines.

An officer of Sacken's staff recorded the events which followed:

The Russians fought with admirable courage but the first assault failed. The French are extremely clever at defensive combat in houses and gardens and this skill was demonstrated again here today. In vain the Russian officers exposed themselves to the enemy fire which cut down so many of them. The advance ground to a halt and we could not force our way into Pfaffendorf.

From the Rosenthal and from the Halle suburb came heavy French artillery fire. General von Sacken was most annoyed that we could not take Pfaffendorf; repeatedly he led the assaults himself, straight into fire that seemed to come from the mouth of hell itself.

The enemy – particularly the Poles – mounted heavy counter assaults and we were in danger of losing Gohlis. At this critical moment, Sacken sent for help to Yorck. Just as a battalion of the Young Guard was advancing out of the Rosenthal, across the Pleisse and into Gohlis, the Prussian Leib-Regiment and the East Prussian Fusilier Battalion came doubling down from Möckern, took them in flank and stabilised the front. Sacken was now able to mount another assault on Pfaffendorf. The Russians broke into the place but were greeted by such a hail of fire from the defenders of the village and from the flanking positions that they were thrown out again.

After the battle of Bautzen, the village of Pfaffendorf had been converted into a huge field hospital. As the fighting raged anew on the 18th numerous fires broke out in the area and almost all the unfortunate sick and wounded died in the flames. An eyewitness in the town described the harrowing scene:

It was terrible to see how these unfortunates tried to save themselves. Many Russian soldiers repeatedly braved the flames to go into the burning buildings and rescue at least their own wounded. Some of these noble fellows were themselves overcome by the smoke and fell victim to the fires.

Some of the wounded, often wearing only a smoke-blackened shirt, their suppurating wounds undressed, limped or crawled out of the blazing buildings to save themselves. I took one young Polish officer, who had lost his nose, one eye and his left cheek, but who still clung on to life, on my saddle to our ambulance. On the way there, I was given an order to go to another location so I handed him over to the care of a lightly wounded Russian. They had scarcely gone two paces when a ball from a French battery in the Rosenthal cut them both down.

This burning French hospital in Pfaffendorf was the most horrific thing I have ever seen.

Despite all the din of battle, the screams of the unfortunates in Pfaffendorf could be heard clearly by those living in the Gerbergasse behind the French position. After this fire, the Russians made no further attempts to storm Pfaffendorf. The Poles held their position before the gates of Leipzig, while the gatehouse itself and the houses to either side were held by Badeners, who fought with the same bravery and firmness as the Poles. The road in front of the gate had been blocked with an earth rampart pierced for four guns, which poured a hail of canister at the Russians. They fired so fast that an inhabitant of Leipzig recounted how he saw the gunners running down the river bank to soak their mops in the Parthe to cool down the barrels.

Another eyewitness of events was the young theology teacher to the family of a merchant, Förster, who lived in the Gerbergasse:

The French General Rochambeau was carried into our house wounded. He had been hit in the stomach on 16th October at Liebertwolkwitz. His son, a colonel and ADC to Murat, two doctors, servants and some Gendarmes came too. On Monday the 18th October at ten o'clock, the Allied assault on Leipzig began. A terrible cannonade thundered about us from an eighteen-gun battery which had been set up in the Löhrschen Gardens. Allied shot, shell and canister rained down into Leipzig. The projectiles smashed into our roof and soon the courtyard was full of broken tiles. The family fled to take refuge in the small cellar. The general's staff walked calmly about in the courtyard and brought us canister balls which had rolled from the roof. It was a miracle that no fire broke out as a shell had landed in the hayloft over the stables but had failed to detonate. Another had landed on the third floor, in front of my room, and a third had smashed through the great gable of the storehouse and had exploded in a bale of 20,000 corks which were now scattered all over the floor.

The artillery fire was heaviest at noon. When darkness fell, we could see from the attic burning villages all around. At exactly four o'clock the church tower in Schönefeld collapsed. At one o'clock in the morning of 19th October, I was awakened; General Rochambeau had just died. His son wished his body to be buried in our small garden behind the storehouse so that he could later collect it and take it to France after the end of the war.

Förster advised him against this; he feared that the enemy would dig him up to search for valuables. Colonel Rochambeau advised Förster to save himself and his family in the city of Leipzig as this suburb would almost certainly be stormed. However, it would not have been possible for us to have forced our way through the dreadful crush of soldiers and guns in the Gerbergasse had it not been for Colonel Rochambeau and his Gendarmes as they took his dead father into the city in a light, basket-topped *chaise*. The merchant Förster, his wife, four children, the maid and I went in the middle of the Gendarmes and with great difficulty we finally succeeded in fighting our way through the crush and into the inner Grimma Gate.

A family was cowering in a room in another house in northern Leipzig when a shell burst in the chamber and ripped an arm off one of the children. The mother shrieked and wept. The child said: 'Mummy dear, don't cry; I'll grow another one, won't I Daddy?' It then died.

The 6th Column: Gyulai at Lindenau

After the losses it had suffered on the 16th, Gyulai's III Corps south of Gross-Zschocher – less all its earlier detachments and Crenneville's division, which was at Cröbern, way down to the south-east of the battlefield on the east bank of the Pleisse – was left with only about 10,000 men. However, several historians have credited him with 15,000 and have consequently criticised him heavily for his failure to bottle Napoleon up in Lindenau. Nevertheless, Gyulai can still be justifiably accused of complacency, and of allowing himself to be caught with his guard down, as events will show.

At ten o'clock, General Belair of Bertrand's corps had burst southwards out of Plagwitz (next to Lindenau) with the 13*e Ligne* and the Württemberg cavalry to assault the Austrian forward outpost in Klein-Zschocher. Belair's task was to open the *Grande Armée*'s escape route to the fortress depot at Erfurt. The Austrian garrison of Klein-Zschocher, consisting of most of the 1st Jäger Battalion under *Oberst* Lütz, allowed itself to be surprised, pushed eastwards against the Elster and captured, as there were no bridges in the area over which they could escape.

Alarmed by the sounds of this combat two kilometres to the north, Gyulai sent the 3rd Battalion, Infantry Regiment Kottulinsky, under *Oberstleutnant* Arbter, from Gross-Zschocher to reinforce the isolated Jägers, but this unit too was broken, Arbter being mortally wounded and 300 of his men taken prisoner. At this early stage in the conflict, therefore, Gyulai had already deservedly lost eighteen officers and 696 men through his lack of attention.

Now the 2nd Battalion, Infantry Regiment Kaiser, under Major Broda, was fed into the contest from Gross-Zschocher as General Belair, encouraged by his early successes, pushed on southwards. This time however, the Austrians had a battery of artillery in support and Belair was smartly repulsed. Gross-Zschocher was now held by part of Czollich's brigade and a battalion of Infantry Regiment Kaunitz from II (Austrian) Corps.

The advance of Bertrand's IV Corps westwards out of Lindenau cut off part of Gyulai's reduced corps, a detachment of the 2nd Jäger Battalion and a detachment of the Chevauléger-Regiment Kaiser having been north of the Weissenfels road. These were forced to cross the River Luppe and the Rosenthal swamps and joined up with the Yorck's corps of the Army of Silesia at Möckern.

To hold Gyulai in check to the south of the Weissenfels road, Quinette's Dragoon Brigade, reinforced by Italian and Württemberg cavalry regiments, took up post west of Plagwitz whilst Bertrand's IV Corps marched off to head the withdrawal. Their place was taken by Mortier's II Corps of the Young Guard.

Zimmermann's history of the Hessian Garde Chevaulégers Regiment has this to say about the day's combat here:

The regiment was in General von Wolff's 29th Light Cavalry Brigade in Bertrand's IV Corps. On the 14th October IV Corps took post at Lindenau and was not involved in the fighting of the 16th. On the 18th October, Bertrand was given the task of securing the withdrawal route of the *Grande Armée* through Markranstadt to Lützen. Wolff's brigade was to act as escort to two batteries of horse artillery and was reinforced by two Württemberg cavalry regiments.

The four regiments only amounted to 700 sabres, however, 150 of whom belonged to the Hessian Garde Chevaulégers. The two batteries and the cavalry brigade advanced to Plagwitz, south of Lindenau, and engaged an Austrian battery which they soon silenced. The cavalry charged and captured some Austrian Jägers. The route to Lützen was secured.

That night, IV Corps withdrew to Weissenfels and next day they formed the vanguard of the retreating French army. On 28th October, the Hessian cavalry – now 100 strong – reached Hanau.

Leutnant Karl Christian von Martens, who commanded a company of Württemberg infantry, has left us his account of these events:

The 18th October. The day of the great decision had arrived. But this time, the sun of Austerlitz did not shine for the Conqueror of the World! We had spent a bad night in the avenues of Leipzig. At times we were digging trenches, at others we were leaning against trees with a sharp north wind whipping rain into our faces. Without food, without firewood, without straw to lie on; very few of us got any sleep that night.

We were not to take part in the great battle this day. General Bertrand received orders to march for Weissenfels, to clear the plain of Lützen of any enemy, and to secure the crossing of the Saale with his corps, of which we were part and which had about 15,000 men.

At six in the morning, we left our site behind the Gerbertor and had great difficulty working our way through the mass of all sorts of train vehicles to the banks of the Elster. But the enemy had built us golden bridges. Two French infantry divisions and French cavalry followed our column. The march to Lindenau along the narrow dam and over the many bridges over the many arms of the Pleisse and Elster went only very slowly. Many wounded left Leipzig and joined us and they were a pitiful sight, just like that which I had seen the previous year after the battle of Borodino in Russia. The sabre cuts on the heads of these unfortunates were bound up with sackcloth; they carried their helmets on their arms and their faces and clothing were black and stiff with dried blood.

We had a clash with Gyulai here, who had occupied Lindenau and Plagwitz with detachments of his corps. The enemy was thrown back on Zschocher and we were able to continue our withdrawal unhindered through Lützen towards Markranstädt. Gyulai lost a Jäger battalion of 700 men and eighteen guns, and retreated towards Naumburg in order to reach the defile of Kösen before the French. There were 6,000 Austrians of all arms to our left flank, and this threat forced us to move only in squares under cover of our cavalry. At Markranstädt there were some delays due to the train waggons; the enemy used the opportunity to bombard us a little but no damage was done although seven waggons were lost. To cover the train we were sent to act as rearguard together with three regiments of French dragoons. We reached Lützen at about midnight and cooked what we could find on the same field that we had used before the ambush [of Lützow's *Freikorps*] of the 17th June. In the light of the fire, I could see the monument to the great king of Sweden. Since we were last here, someone had cut down the three poplar trees that used to stand around the stone.

***

Although Zelle (p.443) alleges that Mortier 'easily beat off all assaults by the Austrians who were twice as strong as they were', we now know that there were no Austrian assaults against Lindenau on 18 October. Schwarzenberg had ordered Gyulai to adopt a passive posture here and had no plans to try to block the French escape route. In addition Mortier's corps was at least as strong as Gyulai's much reduced force. Gyulai therefore withdrew the main body of his III Corps to the south to cross the Pleisse and join the Army of Bohemia, leaving only Moritz Liechtenstein's Light Division and the *Streif-korps* of Mensdorff and Thielmann to observe the French withdrawal on the west bank of the Elster.

Towards evening Gyulai received the following message from Schwarzenberg:

> The enemy is being squeezed from all sides and will probably fall back on Naumburg. Your Excellency will use all your energies to try to get there before him to occupy the position at Kösen. The bridge there must be defended to the last. The entire Austrian cavalry and Meerveldt's corps will concentrate tomorrow at seven o'clock in the morning at Pegau in order to march to Naumburg which Your Excellency alone can lead them to. If you come under too much enemy pressure you have no alternative but to fall back on Zeitz. If you are assaulted in this place by the Emperor with overpowering force, you must cause the enemy (who is making a desperate attempt to escape) as much damage as possible. At all events, you must ensure that you do not suffer a defeat yourself. And if the way for the retreat – for the French – is opened, you have only to keep the cavalry close on his heels.

It can therefore be seen that Schwarzenberg had absolutely no intention of trying to bottle Napoleon up in Leipzig, a decision with which the Allied monarchs must have agreed. Gyulai was instructed not to risk his command but to make the capture of the Kösen bridge his top priority. This bridge across the River Saale (nowadays on Route B87) lay on Napoleon's most direct route to salvation at Erfurt. On 21 October Gyulai won the race and held the bridge against all Bertrand's efforts.

Schwarzenberg has often been reproached for allowing Napoleon to escape from his self-made trap at Leipzig. In later years, he answered such criticism with the observation that: 'We did not have sufficient troops to hold all possible exits in strength. Anyway, it is not always advisable to drive an enemy, who is still strong, to desperate measures.'

As the French IV Corps hurried westwards from Leipzig, *Feldmarschall-Leutnant* Murray, commanding the small Austrian force at Weissenfels on the Saale, felt himself too weak to stop them. He thus sent a courier to General Salms in Naumburg that the French were approaching, destroyed the bridge, and withdrew south-east towards Zeitz.

The defection of the 24th Saxon Division

The average strength of the Saxon 24th Division's units at Leipzig on 18 October was about thirty-five per cent of what it had been on 1 August. Modern military thinking is that the average combat unit or formation becomes ineffective when its strength drops below fifty per cent. In addition they had received no regular rations for weeks, no accommodation in the cold, wet weather, and had been required to undertake extreme marches both by day and by night. Their horses had received no oats and had thus become weaker by the day. On 15 October the hussars had to abandon twenty-seven horses which were simply too weak to continue.

The senior officers of the Saxon division had discussed going over to the enemy on the morning of the 18th. When the defection of the light cavalry and the light battalion became known at one o'clock, the brigade commanders and others told the divisional commander, General von Zeschau, that he must send an officer to the king to obtain instructions on how the rest of his troops were to conduct themselves. Von Zeschau sent a staff officer – Captain von Nostitz – to Leipzig to inform the king of the defections and to tell him that von Zeschau feared that the infantry might follow suit. After von Nostitz left, the two brigade commanders, von Ryssel and von Brause, agreed that they should go over without delay. Other officers suggested that the division should march into Leipzig and form a protective guard around the king, who was by now openly seen as Napoleon's prisoner rather than his ally. However, one glance at the chaos of troops, waggon trains, guns, wounded and stragglers which milled around between them and the city caused this idea to be dropped at once. Permission for the move would have been required from Marshal Ney anyway, and he was most unlikely to have given it, as he blamed the Saxons – unjustly, but in the strongest terms – for the loss of the battle of Dennewitz on 6 September.

The whole contingent was enraged that Ney had sought to blame them for this defeat. They had fought bravely, suffered 2,000 casualties, and withdrawn in good order, covering the withdrawal while French units had fled in complete confusion. Ney had nevertheless reported to Napoleon: 'All foreign units show the worst morale. So it is with the Saxon army. It is not to be doubted that these troops will turn their weapons on us at the first possible opportunity.'

Reynier, who had commanded the Saxons at Dennewitz, protested most energetically at Ney's false report and on 9 October, at Torgau, Napoleon had spoken to them in a reconciliatory tone at a parade in which many of the division's officers and men were presented with the cross of the Legion of Honour. But while the French units cried out their usual '*Vive l'Empereur!*', the Saxons had remained silent.

On 16 October General Reynier wrote to King Friedrich August of Saxony from Düben – with Napoleon's approval – saying that he would prevent the Saxon troops from marching off to Torgau if that was what the king desired. The king could not bring himself to make a decision, so events took their tragic course. Now, on 18 October, the senior officers of the Saxon division again awaited an answer from the king, which arrived just after two o'clock.

The note which von Zeschau gave to von Nostitz has never been found, but whatever questions it contained, the king's answer to them read like a response from the oracle at Delphi. It read:

> *Herr Generalleutnant von Zeschau! Ich habe stets Vertrauen in meine Truppen gesetzt und tue es in dem gegenwärtigen Augenblicke mehr als jemals. Die Anhänglichkeit an meine Person können mir solche nur durch Erfüllung ihrer Pflichten beweisen, und ich bin von Ihnen gewärtig, dass Sie alles anwenden werden, um selbige dazu anzu-halten. Hiermit bitte ich Gott, dass er Sie in seinen heiligen Schutz nehme.*
> *Leipzig, den 18. Oktober 1813*
> *Friedrich August*

(Herr *Generalleutnant* von Zeschau! I have always had confidence in my troops and have now at the present time more than ever. Dedication to myself can only be proven by fulfilling one's duty and I am assured by you that you will do everything to ensure that this happens. I ask God to protect you.)

Von Zeschau read the note to his brigade commanders and staff and said that he would follow the king's orders. Colonel von Brause admitted that he could not do otherwise. General von Ryssel was more direct; he said that there was now a conflict between their duty to the king and their duty to their fatherland.

The Saxon officers knew that the campaign was lost and suspected that Napoleon would ruthlessly sacrifice the German troops to save his French regiments, as he had done at the Beresina the previous year. They were convinced that they would best serve their country by going over to the Allies at once, thus saving as much of the Saxon army as possible. This would also help to lessen the reparations which the Allies would surely demand from Saxony for having stayed at Napoleon's side for so long, and would reduce the opportunity of the French to do even more damage to the Saxon infrastructure than they had already. The French custom of living off the land and making a war pay for itself had reduced Saxony to ruins and star-vation.

In the early afternoon General von Ryssel sent for Lieutenant-Colonel Raabe, the commander of the divisional artillery. When he arrived, von Ryssel disclosed to him the decision of the infantry to go over to the enemy. Raabe replied that without the king's permission this would be impossible. Von Ryssel told him about the king's mysterious reply to their query and gave him a choice: either come over with the infantry or stay with the French. The latter would mean the loss of his guns and would expose his men to the wrath of their ex-allies.

The crisis facing the Saxons after the loss of Paunsdorf just before three o'clock was serious; the tactical situation now dictated that they act quickly. Von Bülow's Prussians were advancing steadily from the north and Bennig-sen's Russians and Austrians from the east. Due to the old rivalry between

Prussia and Saxony, it would be too risky to go to von Bülow's corps as the Saxon advance would certainly be interpreted as an attack. Von Ryssel thus aimed to go over to Bennigsen's army.

Raabe decided to join the infantry in their desperate plan and gathered his batteries (nineteen serviceable guns) north of Sellerhausen. General Reynier saw the move and ordered Raabe's twelve-pounder battery to withdraw to Sellerhausen in view of the enemy advance. Raabe was now forced to act; either he obeyed Reynier's order and lost control of half of his guns, or he had to go over to the Allies *now.* Grasping the nettle, he ordered his guns to move off – initially at a walk, then at a trot – in the direction of Zweinaundorf. Seeing this, von Ryssel ordered his brigade to follow them. Von Zeschau galloped over, halted the infantry, and told von Ryssel not to move without his express command. He then rode off to Reynier, and von Ryssel at once resumed his march at the double. Reynier, meanwhile, tried to catch the disappearing Saxon artillery but was forced to abandon the attempt.

Von Zeschau now reappeared alongside the Saxon infantry brigade, removed von Ryssel from command, and replaced him with Major von Holleufer (of the Liebgrenadiergarde, but presently commanding the Prinz Anton battalion). He ordered von Ryssel to report to Reynier and explain himself; von Ryssel refused, set his spurs to his horse and galloped off towards the enemy, waving at his units with a white kerchief to follow him. The French cavalry which was deployed behind the Saxons initially interpreted this move as a heroic attack and greeted it with a loud chorus of '*Vive l'Empereur!*'

Meanwhile, Durutte's troops had broken under the Allied attack and fled back in confusion on Sellerhausen, taking part of the Saxon Prinz Anton battalion with them and abandoning three guns. Russian cavalry (Pahlen's brigade of Wintzingerode's corps, consisting of the Riga Dragoons and Isum Hussars) chased after Durutte's broken division, now mixed up with the Saxon infantry, and surrounded and captured the Prinz Friedrich battalion. As soon as Durutte's division had rallied, Reynier's chief of staff, Baron Gressot, had galloped across to it and ordered the artillery to fire on the remaining Saxons.

A Saxon gunner recorded his personal experience of the Saxon division's final hours in French service and its defection thus:

Shot and shell were raining down on us. A ball ripped the head off the man next to me. It rolled along the ground still with the shako on. We stood in this fire, which went on with only minor interruptions, until two o'clock, after which it lessened slightly. Many of us were by this time dead or dying. By this time several French generals and many Saxon field officers had arrived by our battery. They seemed to be arguing and talking about three o'clock. As they dispersed our officers told us the following. There was going to be a 'hot' half-hour soon which would go off well if only we kept our courage. It came. Enemy firing against us had stopped. We were ordered to limber up the gun, to turn it around and to move off as fast as we could, towards the enemy. We had run some thousands of paces and were out of breath when several regiments of Cossacks came riding towards us, cheering. They rode through our ranks to protect us from any attacks from the French; it was then that we realised that we had gone over to the enemy. The French poured a hail of fire at us. We ran on to Engelsdorf where we stopped and gathered our breath. The Russians and Austrians brought us brandy and were very friendly towards us. In Engelsdorf was a sheep farm with a lot of sheep. That night most of them were slaughtered by us. There was also a lot of fruit, but unfortunately no bread, which was the thing we were missing most.

Von Ryssel and his troops were taken up north-east of Zweinaundorf, initially by the Cossack *pulk* of Andrejanoff III and then by all the Cossack and militia regiments of General Stroganoff's division, and were taken to Engelsdorf. Here, Raabe agreed to form a four-gun horse artillery battery which was used in Stroganoff's division. The rest of the Saxons – at von Ryssel's request – were not sent into action against their old allies.

General von Zeschau led those Saxon troops which remained with the French back to Sellerhausen. The units were the infantry regiments Prinz Anton, four officers and eighty-eight men; Prinz Friedrich, three officers and 101 men; von Niesemeuschel, seven officers and 279 men; and von Anger, five officers and 176 men. From Sellerhausen they soon afterwards returned to the Grimma Gate in Leipzig, picking up a detachment of Sappers (two officers and thirty-five men) at Crottendorf on the way. That evening they were joined by two detached companies of the Grenadier Battalion von Anger. In addition General von Lessing, commander of the Saxon Kürassier brigade, expressly refused to go over to the Allies, saying to his men that they should not abandon Napoleon in this critical moment.

The number of Saxons who changed sides on the 18th totalled about 3,000 all ranks, the gap in the French line caused by their defection being filled by the 1*er* and 2*e* Chasseurs à Pied of General Christiani's 2*e* Brigade and the Grenadiers à Cheval of the Old Guard. However, Grabowski (on p.129 of his memoirs) alleges that the entire Saxon army went over to the Allies (as does Napoleon in his own memoirs) and adds that the Bavarians did as well; but no Bavarian regiments even fought at Leipzig. He also alleges that the Saxon artillery was at once brought into action against the troops of Macdonald and Reynier and caused them to retreat, whereas no Saxon artillery came into action against the French on the 18th.

Though the defection of the Saxons was a clear act of treachery the motivation of those who ordered it may, perhaps, be sympathised with in the light of Friedrich August's incomprehensible response to their request for orders. Many French writers have blamed the loss of the entire battle on this event, but this would seem to be an exaggeration given the overall situation at the time at which it occurred.

The ubiquitous Colonel Marcellin de Marbot of the 23*e* Chasseurs à Cheval wrote the following regarding the defection of the Saxons:

The Crown Prince of Sweden, Bernadotte, had as yet not joined in the battle. It has been said, that it was only in response to urgent requests from Blücher – even threats – that he finally agreed to cross the Parthe with his Swedes and with the Russian corps placed under his command, upstream of Mockau, at a spot where the Saxon Hussars and Lancers stood. As these men saw the Cossacks of the Crown Prince's army advancing on them, they moved forward as if to attack them, then suddenly swerved to one side and went over to the enemy, forgetting that their old king was still in the midst of Napoleon's army.

Bernadotte led his army on the left bank of the Parthe against Sellershausen, which was occupied by troops from Reynier's corps. These were mostly from the contingents of the Confederation of the Rhine, and as the general [Reynier] had witnessed the defection of the Saxon cavalry, he expected nothing better from the infantry and placed them under the supervision of French cavalry. Marshal Ney, however, whose trust was not so shaken, ordered the Saxons to support a French regiment which was holding Paunsdorf. They were on their way there when, misled by their perfidious commander, General Ryssel, they broke into a run towards the enemy lines.

Some of our officers, who could not believe in such treachery, admired their bold attack, and General Gressot, Reynier's chief of staff, rode after them to rein in their foolhardy courage. All he found was their hostility.

The defection of such a considerable mass of troops ripped a great hole in our line and, what is worse, infected all the other German units in our ranks with the same virus. Soon we saw the Württemberg cavalry following the Saxons' example.

The Crown Prince of Sweden not only took the faithless defectors into his army, he demanded that their artillery should at once take part in the battle.[38] As if this were not enough, this ex-Marshal of France, in order to be able to mow down even more of his ex-comrades, requested from the English emissary the use of the Congreve rocket battery which was attached to his army.

As soon as the Saxon battery had been placed alongside the Russian guns, their commander put the finishing touch to his treachery by shouting to the Russians: 'Now the French can taste the rest of my shot themselves!' and opened fire with a mighty salvo from all his guns. He subjected us to a hail of projectiles which cost my regiment thirty men including the veteran Captain Bertin, whose head was ripped off by a cannonball.

Thus it was, that Bernadotte, a Frenchman, whose French blood had brought him a crown, stabbed us in the back.

***

The veteran Captain Coignet, Napoleon's Baggage Master, witnessed the defection of the Saxon division at first-hand, and recorded it in passing in his Eighth Notebook:

---

[38] Napoleon makes the same false claim in his memoirs.

The next day, the 18th October, early in the morning, the Allied army again took the initiative. From where I was, I saw the French divisions fall into line on the battlefield. The whole battle front was before me. The heavy columns of the Austrians came out of the woods and marched upon our army. Seeing a strong division of Saxons marching upon the enemy with twelve pieces of cannon, I ordered all my men to eat their soup and hold themselves ready to start. I galloped over towards the line, following the centre of this division; but they turned their backs upon the enemy and sent a volley of shot upon us. I was so well mounted that I was able to get back to my post, which I ought not to have left. By the time I got back, I had recovered my presence of mind, and I said to the grooms: 'Mount at once to return to Leipzig.' Two minutes after, an ADC galloped up and said: 'Start at once, Captain. Go across the river; it is the Emperor's order. Follow the boulevards and the great causeway.'

I started off, putting the head groom at the head of my *equipages*. As we came near the boulevard, I came across a gun drawn by four horses and two soldiers. 'What are you doing there?' I cried to them. They answered me in Italian: 'They [the gunners] are dead.' 'Take your place there in front of my waggons. I will save you. Now go on, gallop, take the lead!' I felt very proud to have this gun to open the way. Once on the first boulevard, I gave orders not to allow the train to become separated; but here a great danger awaited us. When we reached the second boulevard, I went to get a light from a bivouac fire on the lower side of the promenade, and had scarcely lighted my pipe when a shell burst near me. My horse reared. I did not lose my balance, but the balls went through my waggons. A terrible wind was blowing. I could not keep my hat on my head. I took it off and threw it into the nearest waggon. Drawing my sabre and riding along the train, I shouted: 'Grooms, keep your postilions in place; the first who dismounts, blow out his brains. Have your pistols ready, and I will split the head of the first man who moves. A man must know how to die at his post if need be. The waggons must be saved!'

Two of my grooms were struck; the grape shot cut two buttons off the coat of one of them and tore the coat of the other, and I received ten cannonballs in my waggons. But only one of my horses was wounded, and I found myself entirely out of danger when we came to the opening of the canal which runs along the promenade and receives the waters of the marshes on the right side of the city. Here was a small stone bridge and we had to cross it in order to reach the great causeway which ends at the long bridge. I saw in front of me a brigade of artillery which was just going over the small bridge. I galloped up and found a colonel of artillery who was taking his guns over. I went up to him. 'Colonel, in the name of the Emperor give me your protection and let me follow you. Here are the Emperor's waggons, the treasure and the maps of the army. I have orders to take them over the river.'

'Yes, my brave fellow, as soon as we have crossed, be ready, and I will leave you twenty men to help you over the river.'

'Here,' said I, 'is a gun which had been abandoned. I hand it over to you, ready harnessed.'

'Go and fetch it here,' he said to the two gunners, 'I will take it along with me.'

I then galloped back to my train. 'We are all right,' I said to the grooms, 'we shall be able to cross. Get ready to move.' I took my stand beside the little bridge and my waggons came up. I said to the gunners, 'Go back to your pieces,' and I thanked those good men heartily.

When we came to the main road, I found no artillery there; it had all gone galloping off to fall into position. But I met the ambulances of the army, commanded by a colonel of the Emperor's staff, who occupied the middle of the road. My head groom said to him: 'Colonel, be so good as to let us have part of the road.' 'I take no orders from you,' said the colonel. 'I will inform the officer in command.' replied the groom. 'Let him come to me. I will wait for him.' The groom came and told me; I galloped off. When I reached the colonel, I asked him to give me half of the road. 'Just as you did for the artillery,' said I; 'you can easily move to the right and we will go by at the double.'

'I take no orders from you.'

'Is this your final answer, colonel?'

'Yes.'

'Well, in the name of the Emperor, move to the right or I shall hustle you off.' I pushed him along with the breast of my horse, repeating: 'Move to the right, I tell you.' He took hold of his sword. 'If you draw your sword, I'll knock your head in!' He called some gendarmes to his aid, but they said: 'Settle it with the Emperor's Baggage Master yourself; it is no concern of ours.'

The colonel still hesitated. Turning towards his ambulance, I had it moved aside. As I passed the colonel, he said to me: 'I shall report your conduct to the Emperor.'

'Make your report. I shall wait for you and go in after you; I give you my word for that.'

I crossed the long bridge; on the left of it was a mill and between that and the bridge there was a ford where the whole army could cross without any danger. But this river is walled in and very deep; the banks are perpendicular. I mounted the plateau with my seventeen vehicles, and took up a position under cover of a battery. When night came on, the armies were in the same position as at the commencement of the battle, our troops having valiantly repulsed the attacks of four united armies. But our ammunition had become exhausted. Our guns had fired off, during the day, 95,000 rounds, and we had only about 16,000 left. It was impossible to hold the battlefield much longer and we had to resign ourselves to retreat.

The next episode of this anecdote took place that evening, in the imperial bivouac west of Lindenau:

At eight in the evening the Emperor left his bivouac to go down into the city, and established himself in the inn, the Hôtel de Prusse, where he spent the night dictating orders. I waited for him, but he did not come till the next day; however, Count Monthion was despatched to give orders to the artillery and the troops. He [Monthion] sent for me. 'Well, how about your waggons? How did you get on with that job?' 'Very well, general; all the household establishment of the Emperor is safe, as well as the treasure and the maps of the army. Nothing was left behind; but I have had ten balls through my waggons and two grooms slightly wounded.' And I related my adventure on the causeway with the colonel. He told me that he should report it to the Emperor. 'Do not disturb yourself,' he added, 'I will see the Emperor tomorrow morning. Let him [the colonel] show himself; he should have been on the battlefield, picking up our wounded, who were left in the hands of the enemy. He will get his desserts from the Emperor. You were at your post and he was not.' 'But, general, I was pretty rough with him. I threatened to break his skull. If he had been my equal in rank, I should have sabred him; but I was certainly wrong to be so disrespectful to him.'

'Never mind, I will attend to it all. You will not be punished. You were under the authority of the Emperor, and not his.' One may imagine how relieved I was.

The defection of the Württemberg cavalry

Since having been misused by Arrighi (on Napoleon's instructions) to attack Lützow's Prussian *Freikorps* at Kitzen on 17 July – in the middle of the armistice – Graf Normann, commander of the 25th Light Cavalry Brigade, had been in deep disfavour with his king, Friedrich I. On 17 October Normann had gone to General von Franquemont, commander of the 38th Württemberg division, IV Corps, to discuss what he should do if the French were to be defeated. Franquemont showed him a secret instruction from the king which said that in this case, the Württemberg contingent was not to cross the Rhine with the French but was to return to Württemberg. Franquemont also imparted anew the king's great displeasure at Normann's conduct at Kitzen.

Normann returned to his brigade a very confused man. Already two officers and thirty men of his brigade (Prussians by birth who had entered Württemberg's service after the collapse of Prussia in 1806) had deserted to the Allies between 9–14 October. It was common knowledge that Bavaria had abandoned the French cause, and Normann's officers were already openly discussing the fact that General Franquemont had instructions to leave the French if things went badly with them.

Early on the 18th, Marshal Marmont rode up to Normann and said, in a loud tone that all the officers could hear: 'If the enemy do not attack, we shall leave Leipzig at twelve midday.' But at three o'clock in the morning, the Allies had begun to prepare their concentric attack and by ten o'clock it was in full swing.

Normann had to think quickly. If the French were beaten here today, his command would certainly be sacrificed in the subsequent retreat. His king would thus lose the last formed troops that he had. If he went over to the

Allies, he would be following the spirit of the king's order that Franquemont had shown him. Also, he doubtless hoped to be restored to royal pleasure by saving his two regiments. His officers surrounded him and begged him to take them over to the Allies, where their hearts had already been for months.

Without further hesitation, he formed his brigade into column and trotted over to the Cossacks, at the very same time that the Saxon light cavalry brigade went over.

That night, Normann wrote a report to his king:

> Your Majesty, I must most humbly report, that this morning, I found myself in a situation in which it was clear that the brigade would be pointlessly sacrificed. VI Corps had been completely scattered on the 16th and we only saved ourselves by our flight. Today, it was assaulted by superior forces and I was cut off with the brigade. The victorious Allied forces advanced on all sides and I was able to save the brigade only by going over to them.
>
> I was at once taken to the two Allied monarchs[39] and received permission to remain, armed, in the Allied rear until conditions permit us to return to the Fatherland, or until Your Majesty decides what to do with the brigade.
>
> The tide of events did not allow me to make contact with General Franquemont; I had to make a decision quickly and alone, and took this opportunity to save 600 brave men for the Fatherland.
>
> In the battle of the 16th, five guns were dismounted and I was forced to abandon them in Leipzig. The present state of the brigade is 556 horses and one cannon, with ammunition waggons and good teams.
>
> In bivouac, $1\frac{1}{2}$ hours from Leipzig, 18th October 1813.

King Friedrich, however, was not a man of generous or forgiving spirit. He ordered Graf Normann and *Oberstleutnant* von Moltke (commanding officer of the Jägerregiment zu Pferde König) to be arrested as soon as they re-entered his kingdom, and had both cavalry regiments disbanded; all their officers and men were to lose all their Württemberg medals and awards, but were subsequently used to raise the Jägerregiments Nr 4 Prinz Adam and Nr 5. The two regimental commanders were cashiered. Luckily for Normann and Moltke they were warned of their impending fate in time and escaped. Moltke eventually became a *Feldmarschall-Leutnant* in Austrian service, but the Kaiser found no employment for Normann, the villain of Kitzen. Only after the death of King Friedrich on 30 October 1816 was Normann permitted to return to his Fatherland, though he was banned from entering Stuttgart. He eventually died of typhus on 15 November 1822 in Missolonghi, fighting for Greek independence.

***

Württemberger Sergeant Benedikt Peter of the Jägerregiment zu Pferde König recorded the following account of his unit's participation in the events of 18 October:

---

[39] Only the Czar and King Friedrich Wilhelm were present.

Since the clashes at the beginning of October, the squadrons of von Moltke and Einsiedel had been combined into one. Von Normann's brigade now moved off through Düben, Köthen, Halle to Delitzsch where, on 13th October, they bumped into enemy troops near Radefeld. Under *Oberstleutnant* von Moltke, our squadron and one of the Leibregiment were pushed forward. We received heavy artillery fire. In a short interval, the *Leibschwadron* was on the right wing, our squadron under *Oberstleutnant* von Moltke of the Königsjägers (where I was in front of the 1st Troop) was on the left. Sergeant Böhm was in front of his troop of the *Leibschwadron*.

Suddenly, his squadron commander turned his horse around and called on his men to go over to the enemy with him; the French were finished. It was just at the point that most of the men were about to follow him, when Sergeant Böhm saved the situation. He turned his horse around, drew one of his pistols, and said: 'I'll shoot anyone who rides out!'

His officers had had time to arrest their commander, but not one of them moved; they just sat there like lumps of clay. I never heard that Sergeant Böhm received the slightest praise for what he had done.

When we fought against the French in 1814, we Württembergers were always keen to get at them, and we Jägers were always in the advanced guard. But what would happen to discipline if, when the brigade was under fire, just anyone could say: 'Now we're going over to the enemy'? The soldier is sworn to obey his king and his colours.

After this captain of the Leib-Chevaulégers, two other officers went over to the Allies during the artillery fire, naturally both foreigners! For because King Friedrich wanted to have a strong aristocracy in his land, he took on anybody from north Germany who had a 'von' in front of his name. The fellow would certainly be made an officer – only rarely without extra allowances. There were plenty of officers with field experience in Württemberg, and every Württemberg soldier would gladly have obeyed them. If these foreigners then messed the men about too much, they should have been thrown out of the country.

One of these heroes took over a squadron of the Leib-Chevaulégers whose commander had gone over to the enemy at Radefeld, only to do the same himself two days later at Delitzsch when the Cossacks gave the rearguard a hard time. His squadron then gave the Cossacks a drubbing. A day later, an *Oberleutnant* of our squadron was out on patrol; he found a ford and rode through it to desert to the enemy, abandoning his troop.

That's how things were with us as the great Battle of the Nations was fought at Leipzig.

It was at about ten o'clock on the 18th October, and it was all quiet where we were but as if all hell had broken loose on the right wing, when all the officers of the brigade were gathered together as if to be given the daily passwords from the general. The brigade was in column of troops, both regiments side by side, and all were dismounted. I was leaning on my sabre, watching the officers and thinking: 'Something big is going on here!'

Then our corps commander, Marshal Marmont, rode up and asked: 'Well

Count, how are you, what does it look like?' Normann answered: 'It doesn't look good, the right wing is already retiring in disorder.' The marshal replied: 'Order will soon be restored. We must now get down to business – have them mount up!'

We mounted up and moved off to attack. Normann ordered the three pieces that we still had from our horse artillery battery, and all the led horses, to join the brigade, and I assumed that we were to form the left flank guard of our corps. But we marched straight ahead, through a valley, with the road from Leipzig to Taucha on the heights to out right-hand side. There on the right, on a hill by the road, was a fine farm complex called the Helleblick [Gasthof zum Heiteren Blick] where the Russians had set up a large battery. The entire heights were crowned with guns and black with Cossacks as well. I spoke to my troop, I wanted to prepare them in case we were going to charge and take these guns. At all events, there should be no hesitation; we would have to take the first salvo, but we must not allow the gunners to load and fire again. Only speed and determination would bring us victory. If we turned back at the first salvo, we would certainly get the second one and the whole regiment would be lost. If, however, we pushed on after the first salvo, victory and fame would be ours.

As I spoke to my men, about fifty guns opened up a telling fire on us. The gallop was at once sounded and we were off, but no sabres had yet been drawn. Graf Normann was a fair way ahead of the brigade; now he pulled out a white cloth and at the same time a fanfare was sounded. Within five minutes, we were in the enemy's ranks.

As we breasted the heights, we came upon masses of cavalry. Austrian, Russian, Cossack. They all greeted us with open arms, and I must admit that I felt very uneasy. I believed that they all thought we were cowards, and that hurts a soldier who was worth something better.

Finally, we came to *Hetman* Blado [Platoff], who was sitting on a bench. Graf Normann rode up to him and saluted. Platoff got up and he was very tall. I thought he was going to touch the sky. An unfortunate ADC of Marshal Marmont's had ridden over with us. He had been sent by the marshal to stop what he thought was going to be a brave suicidal attack into all the guns and cavalry, and now he stood, dumbfounded, in the middle of the enemy army! He dismounted and stood there, one hand on his sabre, the other on his forehead, awaiting his fate.

Blado sent an ADC to him to demand his sabre. This the honourable man refused to surrender; he had been lured into this situation by trickery; he did not wish to be untrue to his emperor or to his fatherland. They should either kill him or send him back to his own troops. The *Hetman* went up to him, patted him on the shoulder and said in a friendly manner: 'I shall send you back over the line – I'll have you back again before this evening!' He gave him three Cossacks as an escort and the worthy fellow was sent back through the outposts.

As the defection of our brigade was not generally known among the Allies, we were given an escort of Baschkirs. We got on well with these children of nature. One of the officers demonstrated their archery skills; he set up one of their sugar loaf-shaped felt caps twenty paces away and fired arrows at it. In eight or ten shots he hit it only once, but the arrow was so slow that it only went through one side of the cap. So we showed them what we could do with pistols; with the third shot I put two holes through his hat. Everybody laughed; and so we passed the whole day with children's games.

Our brigade now marched behind the Austro-Russian army. At Jena, General Colloredo reviewed us, then went into a house with all the officers and offered to take the brigade into Austrian service on good pay. The brigade would remain a Free Corps, would receive a recruitment bounty and remount allowance, but would have to cover all other expenses. Our officers refused the offer, but gave their words of honour not to fight until orders from our king arrived. The brigade was then ordered to return home.

Regarding the manner in which the French had generally treated their allies of the Confederation of the Rhine, General Antoine van Dedem van der Gelder, a Dutchman, had the following comments to make:

> The French were to complain loudly when their allies deserted them during the famous days of Leipzig, but I venture to ask them whether they would tolerate humiliations and bad treatment from allies more powerful than themselves, and whether they would not turn against men who devastated their country, burning and plundering everything, beating and raping without any redress being made and oblivious to every complaint. Well! That is what the Saxons and other Germans had been suffering for years. In Dresden I saw a detachment of the Queen's Dragoons arrive in the square. The French officer sent them away in a brutal manner, treating them as German animals and good-for-nothings. I went and reported the matter to Count de Monthion, who replied: 'Well, what do you want, General? Let them sort out their own affairs.' And that is how every complaint by a foreigner was treated. The French soldier is a good comrade; but among the generals there are a few who are puffed up with the pride the Romans had, considering themselves superior to every other nation. Furthermore, they always regard a foreigner as inferior in everything and made to be dominated by them.

Bennigsen's eastern sector, late afternoon

Thanks to the arrival of von Bülow's III Corps before Paunsdorf, Bennigsen was able to concentrate his forces more densely in the Paunsdorf–Zweinaundorf sector. Bubna's division was drawn south to the right wing of the Russians of Dokturoff's corps, just east of Mölkau. Up to this moment Dokturoff had been held in check by the cavalry of Sebastiani, Walther and, later, Nansouty with the Cavalry Corps of the Imperial Guard. Now, however, with the progress of the Army of the North to his right, Bennigsen saw that the moment had come for him to take Zweinaundorf and Mölkau.

Baalsdorf was the first village in this sector to fall, being taken by Dokturoff. Zelle (p.452) says that: 'Baalsdorf was defended by the 6*e* and 112*e Ligne* of Henin's 1st Brigade of Gerard's 35th Division; the 2nd (Italian) Brigade of General Zucchi was apparently not engaged here. Gerard was wounded; General Aubry was killed.' However, Six records that General Aubry de la Boucharderie, commander of the artillery of Macdonald's XI Corps, was wounded and taken prisoner, not killed. He was the only general Aubry present, but Martinien does not confirm that he was wounded.

Bennigsen's assault on Ober- and Unter-Zweinaundorf began at about five o'clock (though Zelle maintains, on p.452, that the village fell at three o'clock). Stroganoff assaulted Unter-Zweinaundorf and Klenau moved on Ober-Zweinaundorf. Bubna's Austrians meanwhile attacked Mölkau (which was held by Lauriston) from the north in a wide, swinging hook movement. Bubna soon took Mölkau, but the struggle between Stroganoff and the French garrison of Unter-Zweinaundorf got nowhere until Paskiewitsch's 26th Division joined in. The French cavalry charged repeatedly and over-threw their Russian opponents twice, but then Gleboff's brigade of Chowanskoi's 12th Division took the copse by the manor which allowed the Russians to bring forward two batteries of twelve-pounders and deploy them by the windmill. The fire of these twenty-four guns ripped into the brave defenders of the blazing village and they were forced to fall back west to Stötteritz. To the south, Klenau had taken Ober-Zweinaundorf at four o'clock without too much trouble. Napoleon's eastern and northern fronts were beginning to cave in.

Klenau now sent the regiments Zach and Josef Colloredo to assault Stöt-teritz. If he could take this village, the very heart of Napoleon's position would be pierced. But the Emperor had taken the appropriate action and formed a massive artillery battery on the threatened point. As the Austrians advanced they were met with a storm of shot and shell and were forced back into Ober-Zweinaundorf. A strong French column then drove against the burning village, but their efforts to retake the place failed in the face of determined resistance from the Regiment Zach. Darkness put an end to the fighting.

***

The sun had set when General von Langenau, Schwarzenberg's Quarter-master General, told Maximilian von Thielen and two companions to sit and take down orders for that night and the next day:

Storm lanterns were brought, but scarcely had the first one been lit, and we had not yet settled down to write, when a cannonball came over and landed in a tree a dozen metres to our right. Langenau did not allow himself to be disturbed, and shouted 'Write!' and began dictating. Another shot came over and then two more without hitting any of us, although they were probably aimed at us. As the light did not vanish, the firing stopped, and for a short time we went on writing without hindrance. You can well imagine that the three of us were not in the best of spirits, since we need only to have gone a few paces down the hill to have got out of the enemy's line of fire. But not one of us made a move; the general went on dictating, and we continued writing.

The incident was not mentioned immediately afterwards – not until, during the pursuit, General Langenau and five of us, including the two other officers who had been taking his dictation that night, spent the night in a room in Schmalkalden. We were lying on straw, when at about midnight a report came in which required an order to be issued by the prince. Langenau dictated this, and while the orderly officer took it to Schwarzenberg for signature and we awaited his return, we talked of this and that. I reminded the general of the occasion of the evening of the 18th and asked him why he had not just gone a little way down the hill to find a safer place since he must have realised how dangerous our situation was.

The general laughed and said in a bantering tone, 'Tell me now, you Austrians, if I had retreated a little way with you, you would have thought the Saxon had no courage, wouldn't you?' 'Well, yes,' I said. 'We too realised that the general would have thought the same of us, so we said nothing either!'

***

The Baden General Wilhelm Graf Hochberg's terse recollection of the events of this dramatic day reads as follows:

> At nine o'clock on the morning of 18th October a heavy bombardment began. The Duke of Padua did not leave his quarters all day; indeed, he wanted me to stay with him, but in view of my duties, I refused to do this. He called me to him several times during the night and was extremely worried. In short, I could not comprehend his conduct.
>
> As the Austrians had withdrawn from Lindenau, the withdrawal of the French army began and I sent back my carriage, all the baggage and the artillery to Weissenfels during the night.

Marcellin de Marbot's memoirs give us a general idea of the state of the French army's morale as the likelihood of retreat became a reality:

> Napoleon had no alternative but to order a withdrawal. This would be extremely difficult considering the terrain we held. It consisted of meadows, wet ditches and three small rivers with many small defiles which we now had to cross under the eyes of the enemy. And it was clear that the enemy would exploit our problems at every opportunity.
>
> Of course, all these obstacles could have been overcome, had the ditches, minor streams and particularly the Pleisse, the Parthe and – especially – the Elster, which received many tributaries around the town, been provided in good time with an adequate number of wide bridges. The material to build these essential bridges was available in abundance in Leipzig and its suburbs and surrounding villages. And there had been plenty of time and plenty of

labour available to build them since we had taken up position at Leipzig. Even on the 17th much could have been done.

Despite this, astoundingly, absolutely nothing had been done in this direction. In a convergence of unfortunate circumstances and irresponsible negligence and omissions by the responsible authorities, no attention had been given to this eminently important aspect.

Nothing can conceal this monstrous fact. Among all the documents that have been preserved for us on this famous battle there is not one, in fact *not a single one* that could serve as proof that any provision had been made for a retreat if this had been needed.

None of the officers that survived the catastrophe, no historian or any other writer that has described this gigantic battle, has been able to prove that the commanders of this army ordered such preparations, or even thought about the building of such crossing points or of the preservation of existing bridges.

In fact, it is only General Pelet – a great admirer of Napoleon – who, some fifteen years after the battle, wrote that the Commissary General Odier (also Commissary of the Imperial Guard) repeatedly assured him during the morning planning conference (he does not say which day) that he was present when Napoleon ordered a general of the general staff to consider the building of bridges and gave him the responsibility for this task.

General Pelet does not mention the name of the general concerned, but it would be very interesting and important to learn who it was.

In other places, Napoleon's secretary, M[onsieur] Fain, wrote in his memoirs that the Emperor had ordered the building of new crossing points in order to ease the crossing of these wide swamps.

I do not know how history will judge the truth of these late claims, but even if we accept their veracity, there are some historians who think that Napoleon should not have placed this vital task in the hands of just a single officer of the general staff, but should have ordered the chief of the general staff to require that all corps commanders ensure that adequate crossing points were built in their sectors in case a retreat should become necessary.

But these are criticisms that are easily said and are not placed at the right doorsteps. They do not alter the fact that no-one bothered about the matter. The real cause of this omission is attributable to a situation that was then known only to a few insiders. It was as follows.

The chief of the general staff was Marshal Prince Berthier, who had not left the Emperor's side since the famous campaign in Italy in 1796. He was a very talented man, industrious and reliable in his work, but who – despite this – often had to suffer under Napoleon's outbursts of rage. He had developed such a fear of the Emperor's moods that he finally decided that he would allow it to become a completely one-way relationship. He would never take an initiative, never ask a question, merely execute the written orders which were passed to him.

This system, which maintained the relationship between master and servant, was most harmful to the well-being of the army, for regardless of the genius and industry of the Emperor, it was just impossible for him to see and to attend to everything. His massive workload dictated that certain things would be forgotten and not attended to.

In accordance with this state of affairs, Marshal Berthier had developed a stereotyped answer to the repeated requests from the various corps commanders to order the construction of supplementary bridges that he received in the last few days: 'The Emperor has not yet ordered anything to be done.'

It was notorious that you could not move him from this standpoint. And so, when the Emperor gave the order for the withdrawal to the Saale on the road through Weissenfels on the night of the 18th–19th, only the few existing crossings over the many watercourses were available.

Due to the enormous losses which our enemies had suffered, they did not dare to attack us and were already in the act of withdrawing themselves, when they observed that our trains were withdrawing through Lindenau on the road to Weissenfels and concluded that the Emperor was preparing for the retreat of his army. This at once altered their decision and they made dispositions to exploit our movement to the full.[40]

Whilst the troops moved out through Lindenau, Marshals Ney and Marmont and General Reynier were defending the Halle and Rosenthal suburbs. The corps of Lauriston, Macdonald and Poniatowski followed one another into the city and occupied the loopholed walls. Everything had been so prepared that the stiff resistance of our rearguard would allow the army to withdraw in good order.[41]

Nonetheless, Napoleon, who wished to spare the city the horrors of street fighting, allowed the magistrate to send messengers to the Allied monarchs asking for an armistice of a few hours to permit the orderly evacuation of the town. This humanitarian proposal was rejected and the Allies thought nothing of exposing a flourishing German city to destruction.

In their indignation over this, several of our generals suggested to the Emperor that, to secure our withdrawal, our troops should be withdrawn into the town centre and that all the suburbs – except for Lindenau – should be set afire to hold up the enemy.

I am of the opinion that our decision to withdraw without a fight gave us the right to use any means at our disposal for our defence and that the fire would certainly have been very effective and we should have used it. Napoleon could not bring himself to do it, and this exaggerated generosity cost him his crown, for in the fight which now took place we lost almost as many men as in the three-day battle.

Indeed, the consequences were even more damaging due to the dissolution of the army which resulted, without which we would have reached France as a still considerable force.

---

[40] There is no evidence that the Allies were considering a withdrawal at this time; quite the contrary.
[41] As we will see further on, this was far from the truth.

The resistance which the weak remnants of the retreating army put up against the enemy for three months is proof enough of what could have been done if all of those who survived the battle had been able to cross the Rhine with their weapons and in their parent formations. It is likely that France would have repelled the invaders.

***

Jean-Toussaint Arrighi, Duke of Padua, was commandant of Leipzig. At three o'clock on the morning of 19 October he summoned the town council together and informed them that Napoleon had ruled that they were to nominate a delegation to go to Allied headquarters and negotiate an armistice for three days. 'If the armistice is agreed to, then Leipzig will suffer no more harm; if it is not, we will defend ourselves and hang on for as long as possible. As long as one stone stands on another, the city will only be taken by storm!'

The delegates selected were the Council Steward Müller and Tax Inspector Wichmann. Müller and a French trumpeter were sent off to find Blücher, while Wichmann went to seek out Schwarzenberg. Müller found Blücher and Sacken between Eutritzsch and Mockau to the north of Leipzig and delivered his message. Blücher saw straight through it as a device to win time for Napoleon. He ordered the assault to be pressed home but did give orders that there was to be no looting.

Wichmann reached Schwarzenberg on the slight hill by Quandt's tobacco mill. His account of the night's events makes interesting reading:

It must have been about 8:30 at night when I entered the council chamber. The council were waiting for me to give me a letter for Prince Schwarzenberg which was still being written. I hesitated as the job seemed to be very urgent – that I should ride at once onto the battlefield, find the Allied monarchs and beg them to protect Leipzig. That would be dangerous. The mayor said that he hoped – and knew in advance – that I would do the right thing for my fellow citizens. I had to say yes as the danger for the city was great and the catastrophe was rushing down on us very fast. A lively horse was waiting for me and I had a foot messenger to escort me. No-one else wanted to come with me. As I came out into the square, the Emperor and King Friedrich August were in the upper bay window of the Thomas house. In the Peterstrasse an officer of the suite of the Duc de Padoue caught up with me and handed me a pass signed by the Emperor to allow me to pass through the sentries. At the outer Peterstor Gate was Marshal Augereau with his staff. I gave him the pass, told him what my task was and asked for a trumpeter and a German-speaking gendarme, which were at once provided. On the *chaussée* along the Flossholz [going south, towards Connewitz] were infantry and cavalry deployed in order of battle, about 3,000 men. Just over the *chaussée* ditch, towards the small pond, was a cavalry regiment and next to it a battery of five or six guns firing slowly but continuously towards Strassenhäuser.

At the end of the Schiessgraben musket balls began to whistle past. A few paces further on my horse became so wild that it was impossible to go on. I rode back to Marshal Augereau and asked him for another mount. He at once had one brought up with a velvet saddle cloth. This new horse was much better and despite all the bullets whistling past us, we soon reached the avenue which leads to the Brandvorwerk farm. Here I gave the hussar trumpeter a white flag and told him to ride ahead. The gendarme followed him and I was about fifty paces behind him.

Suddenly, my horse reared up and tried to turn back. I saw blood pouring from its foreleg. I took the gendarme's horse. The trumpeter rode along the totally deserted *chaussée* and I followed. At the stone cross before Connewitz was an Austrian outpost. A Jäger officer took me to the nearest field officer. A captain of the general staff arrived and I gave him the letter and demanded to be taken to Prince Schwarzenberg as quickly as possible.

The staff officer said: 'He's probably at Dösen with the two emperors.' I asked him to take me to the nearest general. He first had me blindfolded by an officer of hussars; the trumpeter was also blindfolded. Now we rode fast across country; a hussar *Wachtmeister* led my horse. I could see a lot as the blindfold was loose. Soon we met *Feldmarschall-Leutnant* Cray. He greeted me well and said that Czar Alexander had expected a messenger yesterday.

I don't know where we were but there was heavy combat going on nearby as the balls whistled over our heads. We moved away. An orderly officer now came up to take me to the Czar. After some time my escort changed, then we halted. I heard Prussian being spoken. My escort told me to remove my blindfold, which I did. Nearby I saw the outline of a Dutch windmill and crowds of Austrian, Prussian and Russian officers. *Oberst* von Ryssel (of king Friedrich August's staff) came past.

'Here they come, put your blindfold back on!' said a Prussian staff officer. We rode forward.

'You come from Leipzig?'

'Yes, sire.'

'Are you a Saxon?'

'Yes, sire.'

'A Leipziger?'

'Yes, sire.'

'Very well. Take off the blindfold.'

King Friedrich Wilhelm of Prussia was only about two paces away.

'Are the French still strong in Leipzig?'

'Since yesterday they have been in full retreat, sire, their forces in Leipzig are insignificant.'

'Where is the Emperor?'

'When I left he was still in Leipzig, sire.'

'Where is your king?'

'In Leipzig, sire, eagerly awaiting the moment when he can throw himself into the arms of the Allies.'

'Leipzig has nothing to fear from my soldiers,' said the Prussian king.

The Czar and his suite rode up. The Czar spoke with Prince Schwarzenberg. *Oberst* von Ryssel stood before him. The Czar then turned to me and spoke to me for about a quarter of an hour. Among much else, this is the gist of the discussion.

'You are the messenger from Leipzig?'

'Yes, sire. I didn't know that the Allied monarchs would be here; I was told to give my message to Prince Schwarzenberg and to beg for the generosity of the victors.'

'I have it,' said Schwarzenberg.

The Austrian Kaiser arrived. 'Are there many troops in Leipzig?' he asked.

'Sire, they are in full retreat since yesterday,' I responded.

'Are they, then, Saxon troops that still defend the city?' asked the Kaiser.

'Not at all, sire; the Saxon troops are in the market square with ordered arms and await the arrival of your majesty's brave troops so that they may join them in the fight against the common enemy,' I replied.

'That is not true!' retorted the Kaiser. 'Even this morning, they have fought against us with bitterness!'

'I would not dare to contradict your majesty,' I replied, 'but your majesty may have my head if there is a single Saxon soldier still fighting against you.'

'And the king?'

'Convinced of his errors, sire, he will bless the moment when, freed of his dependence, he may throw himself into the arms of the liberators of Europe.'

'That is a lie! It isn't true!' snapped the Kaiser. 'Your king has not changed his mind. He brought this misfortune upon your land! He has broken his promises, and with his stupidity has extended the horrors of this war! Your entire mission seems suspicious!' And – turning on von Ryssel – 'As does yours!'

The Kaiser then turned to Schwarzenberg: 'Explain to him what I just said; that king Friedrich August made a bad decision and that in his stupidity he is the cause of all this suffering which is plaguing Saxony. It's not *my* fault that Saxony is at its last gasp! Tell him that I have greeted as brothers all Saxons who have joined us; but I can only regard as an enemy someone who has behaved as his king has! If the French in Leipzig are weak, let him have his troops take command and open up the gates to end this battle and slaughter!'

The Czar then said: 'Tell your king, and tell your city, that I and the two other sovereigns do not wish to prolong their misery. We want only the happiness of the people.'

'Don't say a word!' whispered a Prussian officer in my ear, 'or our men will be in Leipzig before you are!'

The Czar then said: 'General Ostermann will go with you; ride with God!'

Chapter 8

Tuesday 19 October

Major Carl Friccius of the Königsberg *Landwehr* battalion wrote a description of the environs of Leipzig in 1813, and his clear account is the best one that we have:

> The closest villages could be seen as the outworks, the suburbs as the main walls and the old town as the keep of the castle. If the defence were to be organised in relation to these features, with specific commanders and corps allocated to each sector and their efforts agreed and co-ordinated, the capture of the town would have probably taken several days and the withdrawal could have been carried out without heavy loss.[42]
>
> Traditionally, the area of the peripheral villages Reudnitz, Volkmarsdorf, Strassenhäuser, Krottendorf and Anger was the kitchen garden of the town and was known as the Kohlgärten [the cabbage gardens]. As this area progressively became built up, it became divided into various localities which received the names given above.
>
> The town itself consisted of the old town and the suburbs and formed an irregular square which, at the time of the battle, was defended by a wall, a wide, mostly-dry ditch and the stout old city wall. The old town was divided into the Peters quarter, the Ranstädter quarter, the Halle quarter and the Grimma quarter. The major streets in the old city were also named after these quarters. Entry into the old town was through four gates, also named after these quarters and which, at the time of the battle, still had their towers. The Peterstor Gate was in the south, the Grimma Gate was to the east, the Halle Gate was to the north and the Ranstädter Gate was to the west.
>
> Access to these gates was only possible over arched stone bridges. Apart from these gates, there were other, smaller access points for pedestrians. The Halle postern was close to the Halle gate, the Barfüsserpförtschen [Barefoot Postern] was between the Ranstädter and the Peterstor Gates, the Thomas Postern was also between these gates and the Zuchthauspförtschen [Prison Postern] was between the Grimma and Halle Gates.
>
> On the west side of the old town were great gardens including the Reichels, Reichenbachs, Richters and Rudolfs. These were enclosed by the several arms of the Pleisse, the Elster and other streams and by broad, low-

---

[42] Napoleon had obviously devoted as little attention to the possible defence of Leipzig as he had to the preparation of adequate bridges over which to withdraw. Berthier probably stonewalled any suggestions regarding the defence as completely as he had on the subject of bridges. However one looks at it, the actual defence was a very ad hoc affair and the defenders lacked any conviction that they would succeed.

lying meadows. The suburbs to the northern and eastern sides of the old city were known, like the gates and the main streets, by the names of the old town quarters; Grimma, Halle, Ranstädter and Peters. Open places and broad walks [esplanades], planted and lined with trees, separated the old town from the suburbs. These have now been extended by the pulling down of the old town walls, the filling in of the moat and the levelling of the outer walls.

The suburbs were enclosed by light, thin walls made of clay, brick or sometimes planks, which had their own gates and posterns which were named after the inner gates: the Outer Grimma, the Outer Halle, the Outer Ranstädter and the Outer Peterstor Gates.

Apart from these entrances, the suburbs had others such as the Rosenthaler, the Hinter [often called the Schönefelder Schlag], the Windmühlen [Windmill] and the Sand [now called the Friedrichs] Gates.

A Kohlgartentor is often mentioned but this is merely another, older, name for the Outer Grimma Gate. It really ought to be known as the Dresden Gate as the Spitaltor should be called the Grimma Gate. Between the Outer Grimma Gate and the Hintertor, and not far from the latter, was a light wooden gate which was a private entrance for the owner of the Milchinsel and was usually kept shut.

The outer gates were strongly barricaded from the inside with chevaux-de-fris, tree trunks and other obstacles which was really a waste of time because close to the gates were weak walls which could easily be broken through. Loopholes had been made in these walls.

Exact details of the final French attempts to defend the city on the 19th are one of the least well-known aspects of the entire battle of Leipzig. Accounts of the fighting largely gloss over the morning of the last day. Maps exist showing the outer town walls being manned by the corps of Souham, Marmont, Macdonald and Poniatowski, and accounts of the storming of Leipzig lead one to believe that all these corps were involved in an orchestrated and stubborn defence, a street-by-street fight to the death. Had this really been the case the Allies would have suffered tens of thousands of casualties and the struggle would have gone on for days. But the fighting on the 19th was over in a couple of hours. No doubt the aforementioned corps were in the city on the morning of the 19th – many of them were caught there when the Elster bridge was destroyed – and it is very likely that they were in the suburbs attributed in the maps. It is also highly probable that parts of these formations even became involved in the morning's fighting, willy nilly, as the Allies poured into and through the town. But the fighting had the character more of a panic-stricken mob, fleeing to save their skins, than an organised military operation.

In fact, the final defence of the city was delegated by Napoleon, through Arrighi, to General Graf Wilhelm von Hochberg of Baden and a handful of men. Von Hochberg later recalled the dramatic day thus:

The 19th October dawned and with it the decision in this great drama. At four o'clock the army began to move off and we heard artillery fire which came ever closer. Waggons, stragglers, wounded, officers' horses, parts of the headquarters... The Duke of Padua [Arrighi] hurried off. Soon the Guard followed but a double row of waggons and artillery vehicles on the Promenade, which links the city with the suburbs, caused much confusion and delay.

At eight o'clock the Emperor arrived with the King of Naples and both dismounted at the king of Saxony's house; we could see the latter in animated conversation with the Emperor in the upstairs bay window. After this, the Emperor rode across the market place to the Ranstädter Gate; but, as this was so blocked with waggons and horses that no one could get through, he left the town by the small postern on the Promenade. As he crossed the square, where part of our troops and the Saxon Guard were drawn up, I decided to withdraw out of his way unless he force me to promise to defend the town to the last. I do not need to detail what fate awaited Leipzig if I were to attempt this.

I did not wish to be involved in the certain destruction of our remaining troops and a German city in order to spare the French some casualties. The troops that were available to me for the defence of the town consisted of two battalions of Badeners and an Italian battalion as well as 1,200 Saxons,[43] but these latter were destined for the protection of their monarch.

When, early on the 19th, VIII and XI Corps and the remnants of VII Corps occupied the suburbs of Leipzig, I recalled all but a few of the outposts of the garrison (that I left in the gardens of the Pleisse and Elster) and redistributed them to the main gates, the posterns and some other entrances and adjoining buildings.

The Halle Gate was given a guard of 100 men; the so-called Hintertor, the Grimma Gate, the Peterstor Gate and the Ranstädter Gate received fifty men each. The Italian battalion went into the theatre, other troops were posted in the Pleissenburg and other suitable buildings. All other minor entrances were barricaded and the rest of the brigade was drawn up in the market square.

Thus the weak garrison was deployed for the defence; without a single gun, a redoubt, a street barricade or trench, they were totally dependent on their muskets and bayonets. They had no orders for a withdrawal route or where to go to make a last stand.

I brought these matters to the attention of the Duke of Padua and suggested that the Pleissenburg, by virtue of its position and strong construction, might be a suitable place for a prolonged defence. He answered that the place was filled from top to bottom with 10–12,000 wounded.

The irresponsibility of the entire French army command was demonstrated not only by their faulty preparations for the defence of the town, but also in the total lack of any provisions for a speedy and easy withdrawal. No

[43] Napoleon had carefully arranged matters so that the French corps were able to get out of Leipzig early in the evacuation, and had formed the army's rearguard mainly out of 'expendable' foreigners – Germans, Italians, and his faithful Poles.

extra bridges had been constructed over the arms of the Pleisse and the Elster and no causeways had been built through the swamps through which they flowed. Everything – infantry, cavalry, artillery and countless trains – fought with and through one another on the single way to the only bridge over the Elster – and this was not defended by a bridgehead.

Chaos, hold-ups and confusion happened all the time.

As soon as the Emperor had left Leipzig, I went to the Duke of Padua and requested my orders. At the same time, I reminded him that he ought really to inspect the arrangements that I had made and leave his room at last. He replied that I should rejoin the troops in the market square and he would join me there shortly. I waited there a long time. As the situation worsened, and I repeatedly sent messengers to find him to no effect, I was amazed to learn that as soon as I had left him, he had left the house by the back door and vanished.[44] No-one knew what had become of him! It was now clear to me that he was concerned only with his own salvation and had tricked me.

I must admit that this behaviour annoyed me very much. If I had wished to follow his example, it would have been easy for me to look after myself, but I took it as my duty to maintain the post that I had been given.

In this situation, in which I was left entirely to my own devices, I decided to ignore everything else and to concentrate on saving the town and the troops that had been entrusted to me. It was now fully clear that the French authorities intended to sacrifice us to save their own army. It was also clear that in case the German states should change sides, their remaining armies should be destroyed here.

Marshal Marmont's account of the preparations for the city's defence reinforces that of Graf von Hochberg and refutes Marbot's version of events:

The defence of the city of Leipzig, which was totally unprepared, was utterly absurd. As soon as the enemy broke through at any one point, further defence was impossible. All the corps were mixed up together. The column leaving Leipzig got mixed up with those coming over the promenade, and the entire rearward movement was further held up by the artillery of III Corps [Souham] as this took up almost the entire width of the road.

The assault on the Halle Gate

Sacken opened the day's action here with another assault on Pfaffendorf by four regiments of Jägers. After a heavy fight, Durutte's much-reduced divi-

---

[44] This is taken from p.252 of the Markgraf's memoirs. Du Casse later wrote in his biography of Arrighi (*Le General Arrighi, Duc de Padoue*, vol.I, p.396) that the Duke was having breakfast in his quarters with his staff at midday, when the Russians burst into the square, and they all had to escape in a hurry. Only the Prince of Baden, 'a handsome young fellow of five feet six inches, respllendant in a uniform covered in embroidery and dripping with decorations, was left behind'.

sion abandoned the village's smouldering remains with its hundreds of charred corpses and fell back south over the Parthe. Langeron's corps then advanced to the left of Sacken's with Saint-Priest's corps in the front line. The intention was for Saint-Priest to cross the Parthe and take Durutte's division in the right flank, but the planners had forgotten that the Parthe was very swollen and without a bridging train could not be crossed. Langeron had no such train so the assault failed completely.

The Russian regiments Archangelsk and Alt-Ingermannland of Kapsewitch's X Corps of the Army of Silesia attacked the redoubt before the Parthe bridge but were beaten back by fierce fire from the French battery on the southern bank. Reinforced by five battalions of Jägers from the 20th, 37th and 45th Jägers, they advanced a second time but were again repulsed. A third attempt with added support from the regiments Jekaterinburg and Rylsk, with the regiment Polotsk in reserve, also failed.

The impasse at the Halle Gate – which was heavily barricaded – was finally broken when von Bülow's corps penetrated through the Georgen suburb into the French rear. At twelve o'clock Durutte retired from the Halle Gate and joined the general withdrawal around the north of the city and out to Lindenau on the fateful causeway.

Now the Russians of the Army of Silesia pushed forward again; the regiment Jekaterinburg (so distinguished at Borodino in 1812), under Major Bogdanowitsch, led the charge into the Halle suburb. There was bitter hand-to-hand fighting down the Gerbergasse in which no quarter was given and no prisoners taken. General Blücher was, as usual, in the thick of it, and Von Nostitz, his ADC, has left us the following impression of the courageous septuagenarian during the storming of the city:

The general did everything possible to be the first one inside the walls. He felt he owed it to his army to secure this trophy. Several assaults by General Sacken were repulsed, and with every hour Blücher's impatience to reach the coveted objective increased. He brought up troops from Langeron's corps and led them in person, shouting '*Vorwärts! Vorwärts, Kinder!* Forwards, forwards you brave Russians, hit them hard and keep on hitting!' – right up to within small arms' range.

A Russian general, of whose courage Blücher had no great opinion, protested about the personal danger to which Blücher was exposing himself; but Blücher paid no attention and renewed his shouts of '*Vorwärts!*', inspiring his troops to advance more rapidly still. At this moment my horse shied; it had been hit by a bullet. The Russian general, noticing this, drew Blücher's attention to the fact as proof of his earlier assertion that Blücher was in danger.

Blücher turned around peevishly and asked: 'Nostitz, is your horse wounded?' 'Not that I am aware of,' I replied. At the town gate Blücher remarked: 'That was clever of you, Nostitz, telling a lie about your horse's wound. If you had said "Yes", then our good friend would probably have gone to pieces.'

The Russian soldiers had not understood what the general had been shouting at them again and again, but when it was translated for them, they at once dubbed him '*Feldmarschall Vorwärts*'.

Nostitz continues his account of the assault on the Halle suburb:

I can still remember that a large house in the Gerbergasse was occupied by Polish soldiers who kept up a heavy fire on our men. A company of the regiment Archangelsk stormed towards the place with their bayonets levelled but in a trice they had lost their three officers so badly wounded that they were no longer capable of fighting. The leaderless soldiers fell back a little, regrouped and charged again, joining up with another company as they did so.

After some losses, the Russian sappers were able to break in the barricaded door; the soldiers rushed in. General von Sacken sent me into the house to prevent a massacre and to order the Russian soldiers, in his name, to spare any of the enemy who laid down his weapon. It took a lot of effort to get into the building as the lower floor was filled with Russians. The Poles had withdrawn to the upper floor and had blocked the stairs with furniture and were firing at us through the gaps in it.

Several enemy bodies lay in front of the house, in the lower room and out in the courtyard. Many of our soldiers too had been killed and wounded.

It took a lot of effort before I was able to have the Russian captain, who was in command, have his enraged men stop firing and I had to make him personally responsible to General Sacken for his further actions.

Waving a white cloth, I now climbed the stairs and called out to the officer commanding the Poles – he seemed to be an elderly major – that, in the name of General Sacken, he should surrender. 'I will never surrender to a Russian,' he shouted, 'Get out or I will shoot you!' I had jumped back only two steps when the Poles opened fire; a ball ripped the cap from my head and some Russian soldiers were hit.

There was no way I could now stop the fight. The enraged Russians stormed up the stairs and into the upper floor. After desperate hand-to hand fighting they bayoneted all the enemy.

I later learned from the captain of the Archangelsk regiment that thirty-five Poles were killed in this house for a cost of eleven Russian dead and seventeen wounded.

Major Bogdanowitsch's enraged Russians burst out of the southern end of the Gerbergasse and into the Holzmarkt square, through the inner Halle Gate, and westwards over the Fleischerplatz to the Ranstädter Gate. At the same time, other troops from Sacken's corps had crossed the Pleisse at Gohlis and worked their way southwards through the Rosenthal to the Jakobs-Hospital. They crossed the Elster mill race on a footbridge, pushed on to the northern side of the Ranstädter Steinweg – the single escape road for the unfortunate rearguard of the *Grande Armée* – and fired on the mass of fugitives just opposite the bridge across the Elster. This bridge had already been mined.

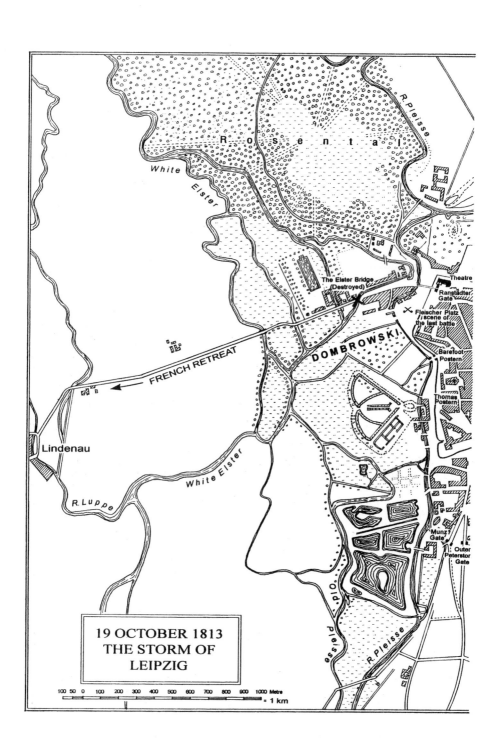

R.Pleisse

R o s e n t a l

White Elster

The Elster Bridge
(Destroyed)

Theatre

Ranstädter
Gate

Fleischer Platz
scene of
the last battle

DOMBROWSKI

Barefoot
Postern

FRENCH RETREAT

Thomas
Postern

Lindenau

White Elster

R. Luppe

Munz
Gate

Outer
Peterstor
Gate

Old Pleisse

R. Pleisse

**19 OCTOBER 1813
THE STORM OF
LEIPZIG**

100 50 0   100   200   300   400   500   600   700   800   900 1000 Metre

= 1 km

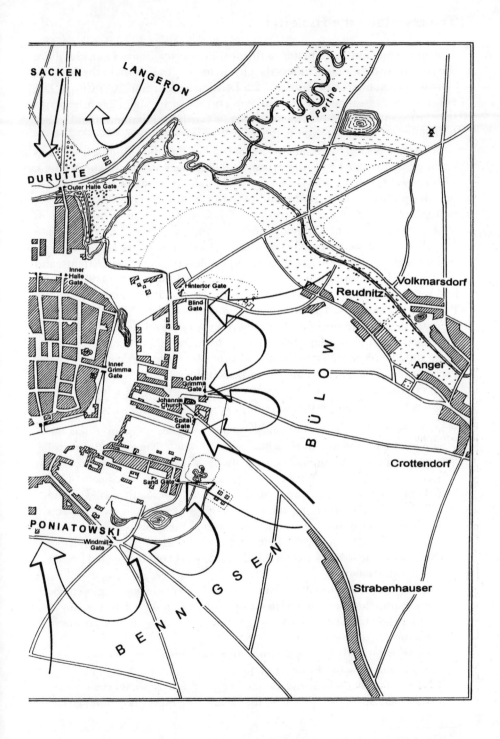

SACKEN

LANGERON

R. Parthe

DURUTTE

Outer Halle Gate

Volkmarsdorf

Inner
Halle
Gate

Hintertor Gate

Reudnitz

Blind
Gate

B
Ü
L
O
W

Inner
Grimma
Gate

Anger

Outer
Grimma
Gate

Johannis
Church

Spital
Gate

Crottendorf

Sand Gate

PONIATOWSKI

Windmill
Gate

B E N N I G S E N

Strabenhauser

The assault on the Hintertor

The Hintertor Gate was situated at the north-eastern corner of Leipzig where
the road from Schönefeld enters the city. It and the wall down to the Grimma
Gate were defended by Friedrichs' 22e Division of Marmont's VI Corps. The
Hintertor was assaulted by von Bülow's corps, led by Major Monsterberg's
East Prussian battalion together with Major Cardell's Pommeranian Fusilier
Battalion and Major Gleissenberg's East Prussian Battalion.

The initial assault was made by the Grenadier Battalion Romberg and was
repulsed by the 23e *Légère*, the Prussians falling back to the Milchinsel area.
This caused Cardell's and Gleisenberg's battalions to waver for a moment,
but they gathered their resolve and pushed on into the city. They could get
no further than the Neügasse (now the Poststrasse) and the great square on
which the divisions of Compans and Lagrange and Prinz Emil's Hessian
brigade were formed. The 23e *Légère* and the 142e *Ligne* were off to one side.
Major Cardell rushed back to General von Bülow to get reinforcements, and
the battalions of Hövell and Löwenfeld of the 2nd Reserve Infantry Regiment
and those of Linsingen and Podewils from the 2nd Pommeranian Infantry
Regiment came up just in time. In the ensuing melee Prinz Emil led the
Hessian Leib-Garde and Garde Fusiliers in a charge in which Major von
Linsingen was killed. Major von Donop took over Linsingen's battalions,
while the 70e *Ligne* (thirty officers and over 300 men) was captured by the
Prussian battalions of Löwenfeld and Beckendorf.

An eyewitness of these events was the Leipzig citizen Friedrich Hofmeister,
who has left us the following account of his experiences:

> My home was in the corner house of the Poststrasse. Opposite was the
> garden of the small inn, the Gasthaus zum Schwan.[45] The entire short road
> was packed with the ammunition waggons of the Saxon troops who had not
> been able to go over to the Allies the previous day. The bombardment of the
> town had been getting heavier all the time. At last, to the relief of the
> inhabitants of the street, the ammunition waggons began to move off and
> the dangerous cargo left us and moved out into the main column.
>
> From my roof I scanned the fields and saw columns of troops advancing.
> The nearest one – the assault on the Querstrasse – I couldn't see but I could
> hear it well enough.
>
> At twelve o'clock two Pommeranian fusilier battalions – deployed for
> skirmishing – came into view from the north. In my house, a half company of
> Badeners had blockaded the Torweg and were swearing to turn my house
> into a fort.
>
> At the first sound of the signal horns however, they cleared the barricades
> away and ran off towards the Grimma Gate.
>
> I opened my door and handed out food and drink as fast as I could to the
> powder-blackened liberators. With their increasing numbers it didn't go far;

---

[45] Where the post office now stands.

those who came later had to be satisfied with well water. Some demanded money and said that they wanted to buy food with it. Another hinted that I should hand over my pocket watch. This I refused to do, then he threatened me with force so I ran upstairs and locked the door. Some of them followed me, smashed open the door with their musket butts and ransacked the living room. I ran out of the back door and demanded that the two officers, that I saw there, gathering their men together, should come and help me. They followed me happily; went up the main stairway and met the last of the plunderers coming down. One of them offered to sell me my own blue coat! I answered that I didn't buy stolen goods, but these two officers would help me get my property back.

'Oh,' said one of them, 'we belong to the Russian army and may not give orders to Prussian soldiers.'

'But,' said the other, 'if you give us a couple of clean white shirts, you would be doing us a great service.'

What was I to do? I opened up the great laundry chest, picked out two white shirts and laughed at my bad luck.

The Russians changed quickly and were off. Their filthy, discarded shirts I picked up with the fire tongs and threw on the midden.

The Allies continued to chase the French down the avenue, south towards the Rossplatz. The noise of the battle receded. My market stall helper banged his fists on my window ledge full of joy and shouted: 'Thank God! The French have gone! 'But he rapidly pulled his hand away when a ball struck the ledge only an inch below it.

The Pommeranians were followed by the 2nd, 13th and 14th Russian Jäger Regiments, which were led by General Wintzingerode. They were attacked by some Baden infantry, French cuirassiers and Polish lancers under General Marchand, but the Allies counter-attacked and took the Johannisgasse from the Badeners, who were being fired on from the rear by their own comrades from the walls of the inner Grimma Gate, shooting blindly into the mass of men in the Johannisgasse.

The 2nd and 13th Russian Jägers did not join in the fighting here; they went off left [south] into Bosesgarten to the Bürgerschule.[46]

The Army of the North at the Outer Grimma Gate

This suburb on the eastern side of Leipzig was defended by Marchand's 39th Division of Macdonald's XI Corps, which consisted of the Hessian brigade and fifty men of the Baden brigade. The divisions of Albert and Charpentier were formed up on the Esplanade by the inner Grimma Gate. As we shall see, two Prussian units laid claim to the honour of having been the first Allied unit to storm through this gate: one was Major von Mirbach's Fusilier Battalion, while the other was Major Friccius' Königsberg *Landwehr* Battalion.

---

[46] On the south-east corner of the old town wall.

Now that the enemy was well and truly on the run, the Crown Prince of Sweden had suddenly blossomed into a spirited field commander. He ordered Major Mirbach, of Hessen-Homburg's 3rd Division of von Bülow's III (Prussian) Corps, to assault the Grimma Gate, and the battalion doubled forward to the gate set in the old city walls. Charpentier's 36th Division of XI Corps was charged with the defence of the gate and the section of the town wall southwards to the Windmühlentor Gate The gate was, of course, closed and barred and a mass of waggons, beams, planks, furniture and barrels had been piled up against the inside. The walls had been loopholed and each of the two houses flanking the gate was occupied by a French battalion, which had even knocked roof tiles off so as to create more firing points. Inside the gate, on the Johannes-Platz, were six battalions of French infantry. When the Prussians let out a great cheer as they ran forward, these six battalions doubled off along the Grimmär Steinweg westwards to the inner Grimma Gate.

The Prussians found a small postern gate that was locked but not barricaded, and Mirbach had his pioneers break it down with their axes and was, so he believed, the first to lead the way into Leipzig. His men flooded in behind him, and he stormed the houses to either side of the gate with one company each. A third company he gave orders to pile arms and to begin dismantling the jumbled barricade inside the gate. He also sent patrols left and right along the inside of the wall to make contact with other friendly units and to guard against the possibility of flank attacks on his battalion. A third strong patrol was sent forward along the Grimmär Steinweg into the city. They reported that the Johannis church, just inside and to the left of the outer gate, was full of enemy troops.

Mirbach was congratulated by the Crown Prince on his achievement and was presented with the Order of the Sword. The Swedish General Graf von Löwenhjelm also congratulated him and told him that he would surely become commandant of Leipzig, as it was the Swedish custom that the first field officer to enter a captured town automatically became the commandant. Mirbach had been wounded three times in the left leg and grazed on the head by musket balls during this gallant action. *Premierleutnant* von Platen of his battalion had died a hero's death at his side, and a further three NCOs and twenty-nine Fusiliers had been killed. Two officers, eleven NCOs and ninety-one men had been wounded.

Captain von Koss of Mirbach's battalion confirmed his commander's account of events:

On 19th October our battalion set out to march through the town as we had won the battle. None of us could believe that the place would still be full of enemy troops. We marched over the fields and then down the *chaussée* towards Leipzig without taking any security precautions. His Royal Highness the Crown Prince of Sweden rode beside the *chaussée*.

At about 500 paces from the city walls we were greeted by shots. His Royal Highness cried out: '*En colonne et en avant!*' which I clearly heard from my position at the head of my platoon. Major von Mirbach ordered: 'Deploy to right and left!' We held our muskets at the assault and with a 'Hurrah!' we ran forward. The gate was flanked with two massive stone pillars with a postern to each side. In the middle was a wide road. Everything was blocked with waggons, beams etc. We were taking a lot of enemy fire from the houses and the street and Lt von Platen (commander of the 5th Platoon) was shot dead at the barricade as were many Fusiliers; many others were wounded. I was commander of the 4th Platoon; I, my wing man, Mühlbrandt, and a lot of others were working to clear the right-hand gate so that we might at least creep into the town one-by-one. My wing man and I went in first, the whole of the 9th and 10th companies followed. The same thing happened at the other postern and soon the whole battalion was inside the walls. We deployed to attack the enemy in the houses. A short while later, an East Prussian *Landwehr* battalion came up and cleared the barrier away.

Von Mirbach states that his assault went in at ten o'clock.

Now for Major Friccius' account of events:

Our battalion was the only *Landwehr* battalion – not alone out of Bülow's corps but of all the Allied armies at Leipzig – which was involved in the fighting of the 19th. So today it was to be regarded as the representative of the entire *Landwehr*.

The Tirailleurs of the 1st Battalion of Krafft's Kolberg Regiment, which had attached themselves to Hessen-Homburg's brigade, advanced in front of the battalions on the right wing against the villages of Volkmarsdorf and Strassenhäuser; the other three battalions advanced against Krottendorf and Anger.

The latter three were initially preceded by light cavalry, which were soon recalled as they just got in our way.

The enemy fell back after brief resistance at all points and withdrew into the town. They thus abandoned the first line of defence of the town which could have been held for a long time. Our battalion advanced between Krottendorf and Anger. Benkendorf soon received orders to halt to protect the artillery, so that only four battalions of Hessen-Homburg's brigade – of which ours formed the left wing – took part in the ensuing combat.

When we had passed the villages, the Tirailleurs of our battalion were sent after the retreating enemy. They followed them with great boldness right up to the walls of the Boseschen Garten, which are also the walls of the suburb, and forced them to abandon two guns which were escorted by French hussars.

In order to avoid the enemy musket balls, they pressed their backs against the wall and, as soon as a French musket muzzle was poked through the loopholes, they grabbed it in order to capture or damage it. An odd contest which could not lead to anything.

As we advanced further, we came out onto a broad, open field on the east side of the town and were briskly bombarded by enemy guns which had been set up outside the outer Grimma Gate to good effect. But Bülow brought up the artillery belonging to the brigades of Hessen-Homburg and Borstell, under Glasenapp and Magenhofer, and a Russian battery on the main road from Dresden to Leipzig. These, and a battery of Langeron's on the far side of the Parthe, soon silenced the enemy artillery and dismounted some of the guns, of which we found many traces at the Grimma Gate.

Bülow stopped about 100 paces to our right and saw what a perilous position we were in. He sent an officer over to us who shouted loudly that, on the orders of the commanding general, the battalion was to lie down. Some of the men actually did so, but as more and more voices shouted 'We don't duck!' they got up again and everyone stood to attention as if on parade.

After we had stood under fire for a long time, Bennigsen arrived in front of the town with the [Russian] Polish army from the direction of Stötteritz where he had bivouacked. Bülow was on the left wing of our battalion, which was also the border of his responsibility, and received Bennigsen who, even though he was the senior general, saluted Bülow – who seemed to expect this – as he had reached the battlefield first. It was about nine o'clock.

Bennigsen's troops were very, impressive as was their marching; sixty heavy guns preceded them.

Convinced that there was nothing more for us to do, I wanted to fall back and halted as the Russians came past. Bennigsen, however, let me know through Major von Wedell – who was attached to him from the Prussian general staff – that I was to come up on his right wing. We thus advanced and took post close to the Russians.

Bennigsen's arrival, and that of officials from Leipzig at the Crown Prince of Sweden's location to negotiate the surrender of the town, caused there to be a short cease-fire. The Crown Prince showed the officials to Bennigsen and was inclined to negotiate. He considered the fighting to be over and said to General Borstell: 'You will enter the town of Leipzig first at the head of your fine troops. The enemy is in full retreat. You will meet none but the wounded. There is nothing to stop you marching in in parade formation.'

This opinion also took hold in Hessen-Homburg's brigade. They cleaned their weapons and uniforms and prepared to march in in style. I reminded the men of our battalion to live up to the honour of being some of the first to enter Leipzig. But Bennigsen – informed by Czar Alexander that there was no more time for negotiations and that force of arms must decide the day – told the Crown Prince that he would let his sixty heavy guns do the negotiating and sent von Wedell to order me to pull my Tirailleurs back from the town walls. As waving, shouting and horn signals didn't do the trick, our Adjutant Gäsebeck took the order to them at no small personal risk. They recognised his grey from a distance and followed him back. During this retreat from the wall, however, as could have been foreseen, some men were shot in the back and killed or wounded.

As it was now clear that the enemy was merely winning time with his negotiations, the cannonade began.

When the Crown Prince of Sweden saw that Bennigsen's troops were advancing against the town wall, he ordered Hessen-Homburg to storm the outer Grimma Gate with his nearest battalions at great speed. This was the most difficult spot on the eastern side of the town because the French had made the most preparations against an assault here. The three battalions of the left wing were selected for the job.

As soon as the gate had been stormed, our battalion was to go down the first street to the left, Müllenheim's battalion was to take the first street to the right and Gleissenberg's was to go straight ahead. That was the order that we received.

As our column approached the gate, they found the Tirailleurs of the 1st Battalion, the Kolberg Regiment, reinforced by the 3rd Company of that regiment, standing around in a confused mass with ordered arms and doing nothing to combat the enemy. They had been the outposts of the Reserve Brigade [Krafft's] and had advanced without orders on the responsibility of the regimental commander. The prince of Hessen-Homburg shouted to them that they should act as the *Avantgarde* that they thought themselves to be, and take the gate.

I halted to see what would happen. As the prince repeated his challenge two or three times and nothing happened, I advanced my battalion as quickly as possible past them towards the gate. It was about eleven o'clock.

The gate was heavily barred, set with anti-scaling spikes and was loop-holed. The guard and customs house on the right-hand side was empty but the houses in the walls were strongly held, particularly the house which, standing in the churchyard, is an extension of the churchyard wall and forms an acute angle with the gate. The assaulting troops were taking a lot of fire from the front and from both sides without being able to respond. Nothing had been prepared for a storm. We had no ladders and not even an axe, no crowbars, no pioneers, no carpenter. There was no cannon available to shoot in the gate. It was impossible to advance and to stand still meant certain death. Danger grew with each moment; they were even firing at us from the tower of the Johannis church.

At this moment my horse was hit in the chin by a bullet and became at once uncontrollable; I had to let it go. It galloped off. I had to continue on foot. Anyhow, it is no help to a staff officer to be mounted in a street fight; it just exposes him to greater danger as is proven by the many staff officers who were killed and wounded in Leipzig. Perhaps I owe my survival to the loss of my horse.

It was impossible to advance; to stand still meant certain destruction, but the target was so near that everyone dared death in preference to withdrawal. Finally, Adjutant Gäsebeck found a weak spot in the wall to the right of the gate, between the gatepost and the almshouses. I took the musket of the nearest soldier and smashed the thin wall down. It crumbled quickly as many were helping me. As soon as the hole was large enough I jumped through and shouted: 'You won't leave me alone!' In front of me was a short soldier, Gottlieb Maluga, who slipped under my arm and received a deep bayonet wound in the face which bled a great deal. The prince was so pleased with this rapid entry that he called out: 'Truly, the *Landwehr* is earning great fame this day and are outdoing my line troops!' and he looked towards the Tirailleurs of the line regiment who were still standing by the wall and were not joining in with us or doing anything. The best thing would have been to break through the churchyard wall.

The officers of the 2nd Company (*Hauptmann* Zieten and *Leutnant* Klebs) and of the 3rd Company (*Hauptmann* Motherby and *Leutnant* Stumpf) were with me. Motherby sprang forward with his sword in his hand and shouted: 'Follow me comrades!' but he was then shot in the head and fell into the arms of his friend Stumpf.

Everyone wanted to avenge their beloved leader; they overthrew every obstacle; everyone wanted to be first. The inside of the gate was blocked with waggons, gun carriages and beams. A few men at the breach with muskets and bayonets could have held us up for hours but little Maluga had scared them off and his bloody wound was their only resistance.

The enemy had fallen back 30–40 paces and then reformed in order to avoid a man-to-man melee and to keep us at bay with musketry. They fired continuously at us. As retreat was impossible for us, we gathered together and charged them with the bayonet. They at once fled and we – less than fifty in number – drove hundreds before us.

They ran straight ahead past the church, along the avenue towards the inner Grimma Gate; and the Grimmär Steinweg was clear of the enemy way past the square and the Johannis churchyard.

As the enemy were still firing at us from the houses in our rear, it was inevitable that groups of our men broke into these houses and terrible hand-to-hand fights took place. Some of the French were thrown out of the upper windows.

Many inhabitants – including old women – came out of the houses weeping with joy to thank us for their deliverance. After we had managed to extricate ourselves from these grateful hands, we pushed on, according to our orders, into the Totengässchen [now the Nürnberger Strasse] as it was the first lane on the left-hand side.

When we came back to the square in front of the Johannis Gate, where the happy inhabitants of Leipzig were just a few minutes ago, we were joined by other *Landwehr* men who had crawled through the hole by the gate after us. At the same time, however, the enemy advanced on us from the Esplanade in great numbers and wanted to force us into the Totengässchen, where we would have been lost.

After comparing these two accounts of the storming of the Grimma Gate, Seyfert says that it would appear that the first assault was made by Major von Mirbach and the Fusilier Battalion, 2nd Reserve Infantry Regiment. This battalion was with the Fusilier Battalion of the 1st Pommeranian Infantry Regiment under Major Cardell and was closest to the gate. Shortly after this, a second assault was made by three other battalions of Hessen-Homburg's 3rd Division (Friccius, Gleissenberg and Müllenheim), who had been on the left by the Johannis cemetery. They moved to the road and finished the fight at the outer Grimma Gate. The Prince of Hessen-Homburg was wounded here. He had given the order for the first battalion into the town to push along the first road to the left-hand side, the second to go straight ahead and the third to go to the right, along the Quergasse. Despite the evidence of Friccius' own account, Seyfert states that: 'Friccius went straight ahead along the Johannisgasse and into the large square in front of the inner Grimma Gate. Here they came upon a large force of French infantry and had to withdraw towards the Totengässchen.'

In the meantime, the French and the Badeners of Leipzig's garrison had advanced eastwards down the Johannisgasse and back to the Johannis church, where they became involved in a melee with the Prussians. The French General Marchand, of XI Corps, commandeered the 3rd Baden Infantry Regiment (which had just been ordered from the Rossplatz to the Peterstor Gate in the south of the city to support Poniatowski's Poles) and sent them back down to the Johannis churchyard to join the melee against the Prussians. The battalions of Friccius, Müllenheim and Mirbach fought in this melee.

The Fusilier Battalion Gleissenberg of the 3rd East Prussian Infantry Regiment came down the Quergasse and took the French and Badeners at the Johannis church in flank. The latter received reinforcements from the inner Grimma Gate, but the Prussians were also strengthened, as by now the outer Grimma Gate had been cleared.

Seyfert adds: 'Two Swedish guns under Major Edenhjelm were brought through the gate with two Swedish Jäger battalions under Major Lilljeström, then two Russian guns came up. These four guns were brought onto the Johannis-Platz square and fired into the men of Charpentier's division who broke and fell back through the inner Grimma Gate.'

But Friccius tells a different tale:

A dreadful melee now developed; a real slaughter. The muskets were used just as opportunity dictated; if there was a Frenchman to your front, you thrust your bayonet through him. A split-second later, you smashed the skull of the other enemy to your right-hand side with the butt. There were several places in the square where the dead were piled five or six deep.

One of our strongest and most deadly fighters was Johann Tiedke, the sweep; I asked him afterwards how many he had killed; 'I know of twelve,' was his answer.

In the face of our prolonged, furious attacks, a sort of panic gripped the enemy and they just stood there, frozen, and offered no resistance.

Suddenly a force of Frenchmen, with eight to ten officers at their head, burst out of the churchyard gate and attacked us in the right flank. It was probably two weak companies. It seemed that we were lost again. But they had seen the dreadful slaughter that had just taken place and the same panic that had paralysed their comrades now seemed to grip them. Instead of attacking us, the officers handed me their swords! What a scene! We had triumphed when we should really have been crushed.

The garrison in the churchyard ran back to the enemy troops on the Esplanade; this was a signal to those who had been frozen in inactivity before us. They all fled back to the inner Grimma Gate, and the officers who had just surrendered to me ran after them without their swords.

Just after this, the French General Pieret[47] came out of a side lane and was promptly captured by *Landwehrman* Leng. Although the battalion had been ordered not to allow themselves to be held up with taking prisoners, it seemed only fair, in view of the general's rank, and the fact that he was wounded, to make an exception. He was taken off to the rear but not by Leng – he was too strong and bold to be missing from this man-against-man fight. I sent him off under guard of young Hoppe, who was much more gentle. He was taken back to the headquarters of the Crown Prince of Sweden where, as they did not know what had gone on, they recommended his apparent captor for a decoration. That is why Hoppe got the Iron Cross instead of Leng.

As there were still French soldiers in the churchyard, part of our battalion went back there and another bloody melee took place. All the enemy were either killed or captured. *Landwehrman* Schwartz of the 2nd Company was surrounded by he enemy but he fought like a tiger and killed all seven of his foes.

Later we discovered a terrible atrocity which the French had carried out on one of our men; they had lowered him head first into a cesspit where he drowned. They left him with his legs sticking out.

The immediate fighting was now over and a terrible tiredness came over us; several men collapsed unconscious. But it was vital that we reorganised and pushed on as quickly as possible. Our battalion had been put at the head of the thrust and we had to stay there.

The enemy had regrouped and advanced against us from the inner Grimma Gate in great strength and with artillery, and forced us to fall back. Due to lack of support, we were about to lose everything that we had gained.

Meanwhile, thanks to the efforts of our tireless Gäsebeck and the worthy Major Müllenheim, it had been possible to clear the gateway. As soon as Gäsebeck and the Prince of Hessen-Homburg could get their horses through, they hurried up to us. We were at the wall of the Prinz Emilschen Garden. After only a few minutes, the prince was shot between the chest and the shoulder and – as none of his suite was with him – had to be evacuated by our *Landwehr* men. An officer wanted to escort him but he forbade it as his presence was needed more here. His last words to our battalion were: 'Boys, keep up the good fight!'

As Müllenheim had now joined us with his battalion, we advanced together to the next crossroads; but as the enemy were being continually reinforced, we were forced back again. But then Gleissenberg's battalion, which had finally driven the enemy out of the gardens to our right-hand side

---

[47] No such general is shown in Six or in Martinien; but General Pelleport of the 20th Division, VI Corps, was wounded on the 18th.

after a stiff fight, assaulted the enemy's left flank and we were able to advance again.

Both Müllenheim and Gleissenberg were mortally wounded in this fight; Müllenheim died that same day.

When the outer Grimma Gate was fully cleared, the Crown Prince of Sweden had two Swedish guns brought up into the Grimmär Steinweg. Already this day the Austrians (under Bubna) and the Russians (under Bennigsen) had supported us; now the other Allies, the Swedes, came up in their turn. The old Swedish chief of staff, General Adlerkreutz, commanded them himself with great bravery and took position in the middle of the road where the bullets were thickest. The Swedish gunners were also good and brave.

According to the Swedish report, Major von Döbeln was killed here and Major von Edenhjelm (commanding the artillery) was badly wounded here. Also according to this report, six battalions of Swedish infantry came up to help the Prussians. There were only two such battalions near the gate and only one of these – at the most two companies – entered the suburb. The others stayed outside the gate and took no part in the fighting.

Those Swedes that entered the town retreated again as soon as some bullets flew past their ears. General Adlerkreutz drove them back in again under a stream of abuse, but as soon as he took his eyes off them, they sneaked off back towards the gate.

The hope that the Swedish infantry (which had so far taken no part in any battle of the campaign) would crown the great achievement here, was bitterly disappointed and we now had a different opinion of them.

We fought through all the gardens between the Hintertor Gate and the Grimma Gate and every garden house had to be taken. Finally we drove the enemy back and we held the Quergasse. Borstell, who was everywhere in the thick of the fighting, was convinced however, that if we wanted to break through quickly, we would have to force our way down inside the left of the Grimma Gate. The Crown Prince of Sweden thus ordered some Russian battalions of Woronzoff's corps to advance through the Boseschen Garden where the sappers of the Russo-Polish [sic] army had made some openings.

A Swedish lieutenant, Wossido, who commanded the light company of the 'Swedish Pommeranian Life Guards'[48] in the 1st Brigade, gives another version of the dubious conduct of the Swedes here:

After daybreak all the infantry moved off in column towards Leipzig, then halted half a mile off and dressed off by brigades on the centre. We piled arms and several tents were pitched for the generals, and the troops were told to clean their muskets, inspect their ammunition, not to stray, and to await further orders.

At about ten o'clock we, the light infantry of the 1st Brigade, received orders to take up our weapons, load them and to go to the head of the

---

[48] This would appear to be a misnomer for the Pommeranian Legion.

brigade, which consisted of five battalions each of 800 men; the companies were 100–150 strong.

It must have been about quarter past ten when the Jägers of the 1st Brigade marched off under Lieutenant Baron Mellin of the 1st Guards. He had orders to report to General Adlerkreutz on the main Dresden–Leipzig road, out of artillery range, or to await him there. We now marched across the previous day's battlefield which was strewn with corpses, and after less than half an hour we reached the road. One of the general's ADCs was waiting for us. During our march we could clearly hear the sound of small arms fire in the Grimma suburb and also noticed how individual soldiers (no doubt Russian *Landwehr*) forced their way through openings in the white surrounding walls and then returned and disappeared from view.

The ADC led us on and we came to General Adlerkreutz and two Swedish guns a few hundred metres from the entrance to the suburb. He halted us, called the officers over and told us that we must carry the fight into the suburb as quickly as possible. He would follow us with the guns. At once the rifle company set off at the double in half columns, the guns rattling along behind us.

On reaching the suburb we found the street full of dead soldiers. Prussian troops stood nearby and in the houses and gardens but they were firing sparingly. We now encountered enemy small arms fire and case shot; this, and the many bodies lying about, soon hindered our progress and we had to slow down from a trot.

The head of our column opened fire. The order of march of our brigade was as follows: 1st Guards, 2nd Guards, King's Own Regiment, West Gotha Grenadiers, East Gotha Grenadiers. Here it was that I, at the head of my company during the slow advance, met a Prussian officer who was standing to one side, who called out: 'It's a good thing you have come my friend, because we have no cartridges left. Our buglers sound the advance but we cannot obey.'

The powder smoke was so thick that one could see nothing while standing, though if one bent right down one could see the legs of the enemy troops, to whom we came steadily closer. When the company had fired their way through and the 1st Guards company took the lead again, General Adlerkreutz galloped up and ordered us to move to the right into a garden so as to make room for the guns which almost immediately unlimbered between us and opened fire. We dashed into the garden and remained inactive there for a while, because it was shut in by tall houses. Behind our guns we spotted the rest of our riflemen: they were the Wärmland's Rifles and the rifle companies of the 3rd Brigade.

As these riflemen marched past the guns, the latter fell silent and we again joined the marching troops. The musket fire had largely stopped while the guns were firing and the smoke was no longer so thick. Consequently we noticed, as we went forward, that the enemy must have withdrawn into the inner town. The street was empty when our riflemen spread out across the square [before the Inner Grimma Gate] and began firing hard towards the town. Soon we could see nothing of the 1st Brigade or of how the battle was going, and for the time being, had too little room to take any part in it.

While we were standing idly by, a Russian militia battalion marched up in close column. On orders from General Adlerkreutz we had to squeeze up and let them past. Scarcely had the head of this Russian battalion reached the square, and while its rear was still in the street, than we were very amused to see the whole battalion raise their muskets and fire a volley from close column formation. Whereupon they wheeled left amid curses and knout blows from their officers and disappeared from view. This Russian battalion, probably Polish militia from Bennigsen's army, was a shabby-looking unit; they wore rough grey coats without a collar and dirty cloth caps. Because these Russians pushed their way through us, it seems likely to me that people took them for Swedes and blamed their running away on us.

Straight after this there emerged from a side-street or a garden an Austrian battalion. Both we and the Russians near us mistook them for French troops. As we prepared to open fire, we in turn were mistaken by them for Frenchmen or for troops of the Confederation of the Rhine, and a bloody encounter between Allies was only just avoided. Fortunately we recognised in time the double eagle on their shakos; several officers dashed forward to clear up the error.

While this was going on, the Wärmland rifles and those from the 3rd Brigade kept up a lively fire against the school building and the Grimma Gate. The Wärmland Jägers lost their commanding officer, Major Döbeln, and seven or eight other officers badly wounded, and, if I am not mistaken, lost eighty men killed and wounded. On orders from General Adlerkreutz they had to withdraw, and we, the Jäger Brigade of the 1st Division, were ordered to try a limited assault on the gate. Here I must mention that part of the open space was strewn with abandoned waggons and that the Prussian and Swedish riflemen were in disorder. As a result, we could hardly move forward and soon had to halt. Suddenly there came a shout from the gate: 'Cavalry! Cavalry!' For a moment we were so squashed by the troops withdrawing that we could scarcely keep on our feet. French cuirassiers rushed out of the gate and attacked us. There must have been forty or fifty of them. They were fired upon from all sides and these reckless horsemen, who made this desperate charge, were in an instant laid low beside their horses.

General Graf von Hochberg of Baden has also left us a brief account of this failed French counter-attack:

Marshal Macdonald had ordered General von Stockhorn to take his 1st Baden Brigade down to the Peterstor Gate where he would come under the orders of Marshal Augereau. But, as the outer Grimma Gate was soon stormed by the enemy, he ordered him to return there with the 3rd Baden Light Infantry Regiment and to retake the gate. A squadron of French cuirassiers and a detachment of Polish lancers accompanied him and he managed – for a short time – to take the gate from the enemy.

Lieutenant Wossido's account continues:

> We gave a great cheer, got our breath back, and ran to the gate, where we met no opposition. Here we were again joined by the Austrian battalion and we let them go ahead. Even so, once we entered the town we all had to halt because Prussians, Russians and Austrians were already there, pouring in from every direction. Hard by the gate, and to the left of the houses, stood Saxon [actually Hessian] and Baden soldiers, with piled arms.
>
> We moved quietly forward and passed the palace in which the king of Saxony was staying. Here a battalion of the Saxon Grenadier Guards stood behind their piled arms. A little further on, towards the Ranstädter Gate, we saw the end of the town. The Swedish bugler sounded 'Halt! Withdraw slowly!' Our task was done, so we marched back through the Grimma Gate to the suburb, where we found everything changed already. The dead had been cleared to one side, the windows were open, and whereas we had been welcomed with bullets, now we were showered with flowers and apples thrown by pretty hands.
>
> Of the ninety-two men I had taken into battle, I had lost nine killed, seven wounded and two missing, who made their way back to us a week later.

General Graf von Hochberg continues his own account of the day; it was now eleven o'clock:

> I thought that the time had now come to concentrate our troops together – an aim I had been pursuing for some time. For this purpose, I sent Major Pfnor to General von Stockhorn with the order that he was to bring his brigade into the town. In the meantime, the corps of Marshals Marmont, Macdonald and Poniatowski, which up to now had protected the town from attack, were rolled back more and more against the defile.
>
> While the enemy skirmishers spread out into the Esplanade and tried to climb the walls, the gates were shot in with artillery and the mass of refugees flooded back from them. The Italian battalion that was supposed to have defended the entrance by the theatre had already gone and the weak Baden detachment saw itself forced to withdraw, fighting, to the market square. Swedish artillery bombarded us from very close range.
>
> At this moment Prinz Emil von Hessen came up to me; I advised him to stay with me as it would be better to be captured at the front than in some corner, but he did not listen to me and went off to hide in one of the nearby houses. Soon after this, I saw some Prussians escorting him over the market square; one of them was carrying his sabre.

The capture of the southern part of the Grimma suburb and the Windmühlentor

The assault on the south-eastern sector of Leipzig was undertaken by Bennigsen's Reserve Army of Poland. Bubna's 2nd Light Division had been ordered to join in the chase after the retreating *Grande Armée* and had left the area of Stötteritz to march via Strassenhäuser and Connewitz to Pegau about twenty-three kilometres south of Leipzig, on the Weisse Elster River. Klenau's corps stayed with Bennigsen.

When the French abandoned Probstheida they set everything that was still standing ablaze, regardless of the hundreds of wounded – of both sides – who were lying in the remains of the village. Happily, Kleist's corps was quickly on the scene and was able to save most of these unfortunates.

On the left flank of Bennigsen's army were the 12th and 26th Russian divisions, up against the Pleisse. These advanced against Poniatowski's Poles, who were defending the Münz-Tor and the outer Peterstor Gate. The old town walls were not intact here as they were at the Grimma Gate, so the attackers had an easier task. They rapidly broke through the defences and advanced northwards to the Esplanade and the Königs-Platz in front of the inner Peterstor. The 13th Russian division, on Bennigsen's right wing, had meanwhile broken through the outer town wall at Boses Garten (in Marshal Macdonald's sector) and taken the Nikolai school. The regiments Galizien, Pensa, Saratow and Welikie-Luki were quickly through and, to their surprise, encountered no enemy troops. They advanced through Boses Garten to the Bürgerschule.

Blücher was now on the Holzmarkt in the north of the city, just outside the inner Halle Gate, with the corps of Langeron and Saint-Priest. The advanced elements of Sacken's corps were already firing on the crush of French fugitives at the fateful Elster bridge and his main body was in Lohrs Garten just north of the Ranstädter-Tor Gate. In addition to these troops, von Bülow's battalions filled the whole of the eastern area between inner and outer walls and Bennigsen's men flooded into the southern sector.

The enemy's escape route was about to be cut!

The storming of the inner city

From eleven o'clock in the morning of 19 October to one o'clock in the afternoon, the Allies had fought their way into and through the outer suburbs of Leipzig. Augereau's IX Corps, Albert's division of V Corps and Rothembourg's two-battalion brigade of the Old Guard were the last elements of the *Grande Armée*'s rearguard to leave. Dombrowski's division was in Richters Garten, between the Pleisse and the Elster and to the south of the single escape route. Durutte's division had escaped over the Holzmarkt (renamed Blücherplatz in 1913) and along the Ranstädter Steinweg.

The last defenders were deployed as follows:

– On the left or northern wing was the Hessian brigade under Prinz Emil (Garde Fusiliers, Liebgarde and 2nd Line Infantry Regiment). At 11:30 Prinz Emil gave the order for the brigade to withdraw into the inner city through the Georgenpförtchen at the north-eastern corner of the town. The Garde

Fusiliers were cut off, and surrendered to the Prussians at the Nikolai church just inside the inner Grimma Gate.

– In the market square were both battalions of the Saxon Leib-Grenadier-Garde and a battalion of the 1st Baden Line Infantry Regiment.

– On the south side of town, at the inner Peterstor Gate, was the 3rd Baden Line Infantry Regiment under General von Stockhorn, with Neapolitan troops from Macdonald's corps and Poniatowski's Poles.

As these troops held their positions they were suddenly confronted on their left flank by Chowanskoi's 12th Division, Paskiewitsch's 26th Division of Bennigsen's Reserve Army of Poland, and Prussians from von Bülow's Corps. In face of these overwhelming odds, the defenders were forced back through the southern half of the city, over the Pleisse at Thomas's mill and into Reichels Garten. Here, in the overgrown, swampy area between the two rivers, all control of their troops was lost and they disintegrated. With the only bridge gone, it was a case of every man for himself. In small groups they struggled and floundered westwards to the banks of the Elster and tried to cross, only to find that the recent rainfall had transformed the river into an impassable, fast-flowing barrier. However, the Russians at their backs provided the Poles with all the motivation they required to attempt the impossible. Hundreds tried their luck in the swift-moving river, and many actually managed to reach the far bank; but very few actually escaped, because the river bed and banks were of soft, clinging mud, the banks were steep, and the western one was about three feet above the surface of the water.

Prince Poniatowski, already wounded in the arm and the side, forced his horse into the dark waters and attempted to swim over with it. This he was able to do, but in his frantic efforts to mount the far bank his horse crashed over backwards on top of him and he drowned and was swept away like so many others. His corpse was found by Leipzig fishermen on 24 October, and he was interred temporarily in the Johanniskirche in the city. On 17 July 1817 Prince Sokolnicki removed his remains to Warsaw, and in 1820 he was finally interred in Krakau cathedral.

The last fight on the Fleischerplatz

The Elster bridge had been blown up just before twelve o'clock, at just about the same time that Podewil's Prussian battalion of the 5th Division of von Bülow's III Corps reached the outer Peterstor Gate in the south of Leipzig. Just after this, Langeron's Russians had flooded into the Holzmarkt in the north, inside the Halle Gate. Langeron tried to turn west around the inner city to the Fleischerplatz but found it impossible due to the incredible mass of abandoned guns, caissons and waggons of all descriptions which blocked the road leading to the Elster bridge. Only the 29th and 45th Jäger Regiments managed to worm their way, individually, through the tangle and at 12:30 they debouched onto the north side of the Fleischerplatz at the theatre, which was defended by a battalion of the Milan Guard.

In the south, Podewils was wounded and *Hauptmann* von Gayl took over in his place. Von Mirbach's Fusiliers, the Pommeranian Grenadiers and Löwenfeld's battalion came down from the Grimma Gate followed by the Russians of Chowanskoi and Paskewitsch, who came in through the Windmühlen suburb from the east. Gayl's battalion had pushed northwards and was now at the Thomaskirche, half way up the western side of the city. They went out through the Thomas Gate, turned north, and took the remaining defenders of the Fleischerplatz in the flank.

There was only one way over the Pleisse from the Fleischerplatz, and that was the footbridge into Richters Garten. The routed, panic-stricken mob flooded towards and across it, fighting one another to get onto the flimsy structure, which could not take the strain and collapsed under their weight, just as the 5th and 6th divisions of von Bülow's corps also joined the combat.

An eyewitness described the terrible scene:

Not more than twenty *Landwehr* men ran from the avenue onto the Fleischerplatz and the Ranstädter Steinweg. At the Anger mill they halted, fired one volley into the mass of fugitives and then charged with the bayonet, cutting and stabbing all they met and throwing them into the Pleisse. In the mill race at the Ranstädter Steinweg you could see everywhere the bodies of men and horses drifting along in hideous groups.

Friedrich Rochlitz was another eye witness:

It was quarter to one when there was an awful cry of 'Murder!' in the street. Directly in front of our window was the Barfüsspförtschen [Barefoot Postern], through which Hövel's Pommeranian battalion had come. A strong force of the victors [Russians who had come from the Peterstor Gate and turned left towards Reichel's Garden] ran through the swamps and meadows and through the streams in the garden, cheering as they went, heading for the town.

Whoever got in their way was either thrown into the Pleisse, into the city moat or rounded up into clumps of terrified captives screaming in heart-rending fashion for mercy.

At the same time, from the other side, I heard for the first time for years, the merry sound of the Prussian *Freiwillige-Jäger* hunting horns, which I had heard a thousand times before when I marched with my young friends Theodor Körner, Georg Göschen and others.

A great weight fell from my chest. I pulled the window open and let the bullets whistle past willy-nilly.

There was no real resistance any more. The victors pushed on in dense ranks.

The thirst for revenge and contempt for death of many of the Frenchmen who had become separated from their units was heroic but futile. In the garden under my windows not a few lurked behind trees and fired continually and blindly at the advancing victors, although they knew it served their cause no purpose and meant their own death. Four of them even hid in the little pavilion by the house and, when we called to them in a friendly way to save themselves, they took aim at us and swore to kill anyone who came nearer. We therefore left them to be dealt with. In the town moat by the Barefoot Postern many of the French stood in the water up to their armpits, held their weapons and whatever they needed to fire with high, and kept on loading and shooting. And whenever one of them was taken by the passing victors, like an isolated deer being hunted for pleasure, and, being hit sank below the surface, then all the others shouted over the prize as if they were the hunters.

An ADC of Czar Alexander clattered up and delivered an order making all corps commanders responsible for ensuring that their men did not plunder any houses or use any brutality against the inhabitants of Leipzig. It was very difficult to enforce this order as the units had become completely mixed up in the street fighting and their men were scattered all over the town. From the theatre, the Russian Jägers, who had overcome the Milan Guard, also poured onto the Fleischerplatz, and the bloody conflict gradually ebbed and died away.

The 2nd Battalion of the Pommeranian Reserve Infantry Regiment joined their compatriots through the Barfusspförtchen and their appearance was just too much for the last, demoralised defenders. They broke and fled across the footbridges over the Pleisse into the Reichels Garten and the Richters Garten, where Dombrowski's Poles constituted the last formed body of French troops. There followed a last vicious hand-to-hand melee which was soon decided in favour of the Allies, and Dombrowski surrendered at about one o'clock, although final, desperate struggles went on in scattered locations for about another hour.

Marbot's version of the closing stages of the fighting runs as follows:

The shameless Bernadotte, to whom the advance of his Allies to accomplish the destruction of his ex-compatriots and ex-comrades seemed to be too slow,[49] stormed the Taucha suburb with all his might, took it and pressed on to the city walls. Caught up in the wake of this example, the Prussians under Blücher, and the Russians and the Austrians now assaulted our column from all sides with great fury as it withdrew towards the great Elster bridge.

To make matters worse, there now developed heavy musket fire in the vicinity of this only bridge that was available to us for the retreat. This came from the battalions of the Saxon Guard[50] which had been left in the city with their king and who now used this opportunity to win favour with their brethren, who had gone over to the enemy, by shooting our troops in the back. That honourable prince is supposed to have roundly condemned the treacherous actions of his soldiers.

[49] Bernadotte's doubtful enthusiasm for the Allied cause has been adequately demonstrated in these pages to reveal the inaccuracy of Marbot's impassioned phraseology.
[50] This is incorrect. The initial fire came from Russian Jägers in the Rosenthal.

And, as with the Saxon Guard, a battalion of Badeners[51] heaped shame upon themselves by exploiting our terrible situation. This battalion, already notorious for its unreliability, had been left in the city during the battle to chop wood so that bread could be baked. They now bade farewell to us by firing the cartridges that they had saved into our densely-packed ranks from the safety of the windows and walls of the bakery. We were being kicked by the donkey.

Fighting raged in the streets and houses; the enemy had now reached the old town walls and was inside the city itself. It was total chaos, but despite this, our troops put up the most courageous resistance and withdrew only step by step.

General Graf von Hochberg recorded that:

At this time I learned that the bridge over the Elster in the Ranstädter suburb had been blown up. The city magistrate appealed to me for permission to send a deputation to the Allied monarchs to beg for the protection of the town. At this moment, an emissary from the Crown Prince of Sweden for the King of Saxony arrived and requested me to stop the bloodshed. It was the Comte de Noailles,[52] an *émigré* whom I later met as the French negotiator at the Congress of Vienna.

We were cut off by the destruction of the bridge and surrounded by the superior Allied forces. I had no alternative and was able at last to achieve my aim of saving what I could of my troops. They would be a vital help to the Grand Duke in the changed political situation which was soon to be expected.

I thus ordered 'Cease fire!' and had the men order arms. The Saxon Guards had already surrendered.

It was about twelve o'clock. General von Stockhorn later managed to join Graf Hochberg, but only with his own regiment; the Regiment Grossherzog was cut off from the town and formed part of the rearguard of the main French mob fleeing back towards the Pleisse. They consequently suffered heavy losses in killed and wounded, including many who drowned trying to swim the rivers. Even in the market square after the cease-fire, several Prussian soldiers took pot shots at General von Stockhorn.

***

Wichmann, the emissary of Leipzig city council, recounted his dramatic return to the city on the morning of the 19th:

---

[51] This slur is strenuously – and convincingly – denied by General Graf von Hochberg, commander of the Baden contingent. Anyway, the Baden brigade was part of the garrison of Leipzig, whose place of duty was in the city. Marbot repeats this calumny below. The fact that the entire Baden contingent were declared prisoners of war and were marched off to Prussia after the battle provides clear evidence of their participation in the fighting.

[52] Here, the Graf's memory has played him false; in his diary for 20 October, he noted that this emissary was Russian General von Toll.

We galloped across country to the Peterstor. On the Rossplatz stood artillery and cavalry. At the inner Peterstor we were held up at the barrier somewhat and then we galloped into the market square. The officers went up to the king and I went to the council chamber and relayed the Czar's promise to the councillors.

Shortly after this, the Prussians stormed the Grimma Gate. As the Allied troops spread into the city, all the populace went wild with joy; white cloths were waved from every window; everyone was cheering. It drowned out the noise of the musketry in the Peterstrasse and at the Thomas churchyard.

General von Toll's memoirs confirm this account of events. Von Toll and the Prussian *Oberstleutnant* von Natzmer went in to see the Saxon King and presented him with the Czar's ultimatum: 'Come over to us within thirty minutes or face the consequences!' However, the unhappy Friedrich August could not – or would not – acknowledge the seriousness of his situation. He still believed Napoleon's promise that he would return within a few days with a new army and destroy the Allies once and for all. Whenever he mentioned Napoleon's name in conversation he unwisely added 'my mighty ally', so it is small wonder that he was treated as a prisoner by the victorious Allies.

Von Natzmer then went down into the market square and addressed the assembled Saxon troops, urging them to turn their weapons on the fleeing French. While the Saxon officers refused to do this and left the square, their men eagerly took up their muskets – as did the Badeners – and followed von Natzmer to the Ranstädter Gate, where they engaged the French rearguard.

***

While Wichmann was hurrying back to Leipzig, another emissary was racing towards the city on a similar mission. As the Czar and his two Allies were berating the hapless Wichmann, Schwarzenberg turned to one of his ADCs, *Rittmeister* Graf von Schulenburg – an ex-Saxon officer known to King Friedrich August – and said: 'My dear Schulenburg, do as I now tell you as fast as you can – and before a Prussian beats you to it! Ride as quickly as possible to Leipzig and get to your king. Tell him that you come from Kaiser Franz of Austria, that Friedrich August is to regard himself as the Kaiser's prisoner of war and bring me his sword. I will await you at the gate of Leipzig!' Schulenburg rushed off. His account of events is as follows:

I at last managed to get through to the Thomas house in the market square. There was a company of the Saxon Leibgrenadiergarde in front of it. The company commander was an old friend of mine. 'Schulenburg! What are you doing here in Austrian uniform?' he asked me. I told him that I must see the king as quickly as possible and he showed me the way. As I entered the hall, I found it to be full of Polish officers. 'We want to be Austrian prisoners of war!' they said. 'Take our swords – don't let us be taken by the Russians!'

'Gentlemen,' I replied, 'I must go to the king. Lay your swords in a heap. You are my prisoners.'

I then ran up the stairs, entered the room in which the confused king was and introduced myself. 'Sire, I am a Saxon and come to you from his majesty, the Kaiser Franz of Austria. Please give me your sword so that you will not become a prisoner of the Russians or Prussians!'

There followed a long silence after which the king sent for a sword and handed it to me. I met Prince Schwarzenberg in the Grimmaischen Gasse and gave him the king's sword.

Schulenburg was with the king of Saxony at one o'clock that afternoon, when the Czar entered the market square; but von Toll and von Natzmer had spoken to Friedrich August at 10:30 that morning. The Austrian plot had failed.

Once again, we have an account by Graf Hochberg regarding the events which followed the cease-fire:

I now went to see the Crown Prince of Sweden whom I met on the Esplanade. He embraced me warmly as he remembered me from the battle of Wagram and was very charming. With him was the Russian General Bennigsen. The Crown Prince asked me to take him to the king of Saxony and we went to the Thomas house. We entered the king's quarters when, suddenly, there was a loud '*Vivat!*' from the square. At first I thought that Napoleon had returned, but it turned out that it was Czar Alexander. The Crown Prince of Sweden at once left the king of Saxony and hurried down to the square and I accompanied him.

The Crown Prince whispered something into the Czar's ear which I could not hear and then introduced me to him. The Czar was most friendly and gracious towards me. At this point, I saw the king of Saxony, who, however, due to the crush of spectators, could not get through to the Czar. I saw with pity how no-one would now make room for the dignified old man who had been abandoned by everyone as his luck had deserted him.

The Czar ignored the king, remounted his horse and, saying that he would speak to me again later, rode off with the Crown Prince.

Shortly after this, the Kaiser of Austria rode into the square. Our soldiers, who included many ex-subjects of his, shouted '*Vivat!*' which I was not pleased about.

The destruction of the Elster Bridge

The site of this dramatic event is totally unrecognisable today. The rivers have been canalised, the entire area is built up. There is a monument, but it is scarcely evocative of the drama that took place here on 19 October 1813.

General Dulauloy, commander of the reserve artillery of the Guard, had delegated command of the bridge's demolition to the legendary engineer Colonel Montfort,[53] with instructions that it was not to be detonated until the

---

[53] Montfort was supposed by some to have been promoted to general by the Bourbons in 1814; this is not confirmed by Six.

French rearguard had passed over and the enemy were about to seize it. Colonel Montfort was not informed of which exact French unit was to be the last across and sent messengers to imperial headquarters for this information. They did not return. As the morning of the 19th wore on, Colonel Montfort became more and more worried about the lack of information, so at last he set off himself to get the answer, leaving the unhappy Corporal Lafontaine of the sappers in command in his absence.

Montfort found that travelling westwards amidst the crush of the retreating army was bad enough; but getting back with the information once he had it, against the increasingly edgy flood, was impossible. Unfortunately, the Russian Jägers had begun firing at the tightly-packed mob around the bridge from the Rosenthal before he could get back, and Corporal Lafontaine, thinking that the moment had come to detonate the charge, lit the fuse before making good his own escape.

The bridge, of course, was packed at the time with soldiers trying to save themselves from the Allies, and when the charges exploded the effects were catastrophic. Men, horses, guns, waggons and blocks of stone were thrown high into the air and caused further havoc when they crashed back down to earth. Scores died in the explosion and the bridge was completely destroyed, thus sealing the fate of the vast majority now marooned on the eastern bank of the Elster.

The *Bulletin of the Grande Armée* laid the blame for the disaster at the Elster bridge very squarely on the humble Corporal Lafontaine: 'The corporal, a man without intelligence or understanding of his mission, panicked at the first shots from the walls of the town and fired the charge.' Marshal Marmont also blames the sapper NCO, as does Grabowski.

The last bonds of discipline now loosened among the thousands of fugitives trapped between the city and the river; generals and senior officers fought for survival like the common soldiery. The trappings of rank and status rapidly lost their significance in the mobs surging about in search of an escape route.

Marcellin de Marbot described the scene:

During this three-day battle, the Emperor's army had beaten off all the enemy attacks and had held the battlefield. There was great amazement and rage among the troops when it became known, on the evening of the 18th, that we would have to retreat due to lack of ammunition.[54]

We hoped at least, and it seemed to be the Emperor's plan, that we would pull back no further than behind the Saale to the area of the Erfurt fortress, replenish our ammunition, and renew the fight.

It was under this impression that we set off at eight o'clock on the night of the 18th and left the battlefield and all the dead comrades who rested on it.

Shortly after we left our bivouac we became very aware of a serious error on the part of our general staff[55] in the matter of the provision of crossing

---

[54] Marbot trivialises the hopeless situation into which Napoleon had led them.
[55] Of course, it was everybody's fault but that of the Emperor.

points. Not a minute went by without our march, particularly that of the artillery and cavalry, being interrupted by wide ditches, swamps and small streams, which could easily have been bridged beforehand. Horses and guns sank deep into the mud and, as the night was pitch black, there was delay after delay and much discontent.

Our progress to the city was thus extremely slow. But in the defiles of the city and its suburbs the delays reached new dimensions and we were often forced to halt for considerable periods. My regiment [the 23*e* Chasseurs à Cheval] was the point of Exelmans' division, the leading formation of the slow-moving column, and yet we reached the Elster bridge only at four o'clock on the morning of the 19th October. When we crossed it after a long halt, we little thought what disaster would soon take place here.

Dawn broke. The good, broad road was filled with troops of all arms whose interminable length gave us the reassuring feeling that the army would reach the Saale in considerable strength. During the march, the Emperor galloped past the column from the direction of Leipzig, but the cheers which usually greeted his appearance were not to be heard today. The troops were totally disillusioned by the total absence of any preparations for their withdrawal from the battlefield. What would they have said if they had known of the forthcoming bloody catastrophe, caused by the irresponsibility and lack of forethought of the senior army command, so soon to break over the bridge that they had just crossed?

We had a rest of some hours at Markranstadt, a little town about two hours from Leipzig. During this rest, we heard a dull explosion and assumed that the Elster bridge had been blown up. No-one had the slightest suspicion that the demolition was premature; just the opposite, everybody was pleased that the last of our troops must have passed over the bridge and that the enemy would not be able to follow us for a time.

Later, Marbot continued:

I have mentioned that we heard with satisfaction the demolition of the Elster bridge during our rest at Markranstadt. This satisfaction was soon to become the most terrible shock. The news suddenly arrived that the demolition had been premature and that the corps of Macdonald, Lauriston, Reynier and Poniatowski, and more than 200 guns that were still in Leipzig, were cut off. Thus a considerable portion of the army and almost all the artillery had been lost and the many thousands of our wounded had been sacrificed to the wild rage of the victorious *Soldateska*.

A silent horror, a deep depression took hold of us all. There was not one of us who did not have a friend, a relative or dear comrades to mourn.

The memoirs of Colonel Griois provide a glimpse of how news of the tragedy was received amongst the Imperial Guards:

At dawn a strong cannonade could be heard from the direction of Leipzig. It was our rearguard under violent Allied assault. Between eight and nine o'clock the bombardment grew very strong and then stopped suddenly. This was the point at which the bridge over the Elster was blown up, cutting the only means of escape for our troops left in Leipzig.

Utter chaos and panic now seized all those unfortunates trapped in the narrow space between the city and the River Elster. All resistance was useless. Many of those trapped tried to swim the river, which was not so wide but very deep and ran between steep, high banks. Many died in the attempt and the brave Poniatowski was among them.

The rest – some 10–12,000 men, including Generals Reynier and Lauriston, were captured.

It has not been possible to establish the exact cause of this disaster or who gave the order to detonate the charge. At any rate, Colonel Montfort of the Engineers was specifically placed in charge of this task. It seems probable that the charge was fired as the result of a misunderstanding when enemy tirailleurs appeared and began to fire on our men at the site of the bridge and precipitated the disaster.

The Prince de Neuchâtel issued orders directing the retreat of the numerous columns of the baggage and artillery. I received orders to go to Lützen with my artillery. The news of the fate of our rearguard spread like wildfire and our mood was extremely sombre on the march; many of us thought back to the retreat of the previous year.

***

There follows another of Marbot's 'ripping yarns', in which he plays the role of an avenging angel as the man who ensured that there was no Allied pursuit through Lindenau on 19 October – even if one had been planned. It is left up to the reader whether to believe him or not:

The Emperor was dumbstruck [by the news of the premature destruction of the Elster bridge] but he ordered General Sebastiani to return at once to the site of the bridge in order to gather up and to protect any individuals who may have crossed the river at other points. In order to be on hand with help as quickly as possible, my regiment and the 24th – as the two best mounted units – were ordered to ride at once. I had taken over command of the brigade in place of General Wathiez, who was ill, and I ordered them to move off at a sharp trot. About half-way there, we heard heavy musketry, and as we arrived, the desperate cries of our unfortunate comrades reached us. With no escape route and no cartridges, they were unable to fight the enemy. They were hunted from street to street, from house to house, and shamefully murdered by the superior Prussians, Badeners and Saxon guards.

My pen cannot describe the rage which gripped me and the men of my two regiments as we witnessed the unfair fight taking place before our eyes. We thirsted for revenge. What would we not have given at this moment for a chance to get at these murderers with our blades? But the intervening water rendered them unapproachable.

And our fury increased when we had to watch as crowds of our men, mostly unclothed and almost all already wounded, threw themselves into the river and attempted to save themselves by swimming to the safety of our bank under a hail of fire.

Among the swimmers I recognised Marshal Macdonald, who owed his survival to his great strength and agility as his horse had drowned. As he climbed out of the water I saw that he had taken off all his clothes so I at once gave him an overcoat and one of my spare horses. He rode to the Emperor in Markranstädt to report on what he had seen of the disaster including the death of Marshal Poniatowski, who had drowned in the Elster.[56]

All those who had swum over the river had had to leave their weapons behind and thus had nothing with which to defend themselves. They fled across country in terror of the 4–500 Prussians, Badeners and Saxons who, not satisfied with their slaughter in the town, had bridged the broken span of the bridge with planks and beams and crossed over so as to do as much damage to the fugitives as possible.

As soon as I saw this band of murderers, I resolved to destroy them. I spoke to the commander of the 24th, Colonel Schneit, and, as soon as we were ready, I had the charge sounded. It was terrible, horrible! The surprised enemy had scarcely time to react and attempt a feeble defence so quickly were we on them. Vengeance lent twice the normal strength to every stroke. There was, of course, no question of giving mercy. It was all over very quickly; our horses trampled the bodies of the fallen.

I was in such a rage at the start of the attack that I had sworn not to spare one of the scum. As I was in their midst, I saw that they were a drunken disorderly mob whose only leaders were two Saxon officers who were now frozen with terror. It was clear to me that this would not be a fight but an execution, to which I did not wish to lend my arm. I feared that once I started to kill, I would find a devilish pleasure in paying these villains back in their own coin. Thus I returned my sabre to its sheath and left the work of carrying out the sentence to my men. They had cut down about two-thirds of the mob and were chasing after the rest, who were fleeing back to the improvised bridge, led by the two Saxon officers. As this bridge was narrow, not all the refugees could get over in time, so some of them took refuge in a large inn on this side of the Elster and opened fire on us from there. They were supported by another enemy detachment on the far side of the river.

As it was clear that the noise of the firing would attract more enemy troops, who could then bombard us with impunity, I decided to bring matters to a quick close. I had part of my men dismount and take their carbines and surround the house and then set it and the attached stables alight. When those trapped inside saw the flames spreading, they tried to escape, but everyone who showed themselves was shot down by my Chasseurs.

---

[56] As we shall see below, this paragraph contains several embroideries of the truth.

In vain they sent one of the Saxon officers to me to negotiate; I knew no mercy, I had no pity. I was not going to treat as honourable soldiers these monsters who had slaughtered our captured comrades, after they had defended themselves bravely, in cold blood. None of the 4–500 Prussian, Saxon and Baden murderers that had crossed the bridge got back over it.

I reported what had happened to General Sebastiani who sent orders for the regiments which were following him to turn back.

The fire that we had started took hold of the adjoining houses and in a short time, a large part of the Lindenau suburb, on both sides of the road, was ablaze. This must have made the restoration of the bridge[57] and the pursuit of our army much more difficult for the enemy.

After I had gathered about 2,000 of our stragglers together, I returned to Markranstädt with them and my brigade. Among those we had saved were many officers of all ranks. The Emperor had them tell him what they knew of the explosion of the mine and of the slaughter in Leipzig. He must now have regretted not following the advice that he had been given – to secure the withdrawal of the army and to prevent the enemy interfering with it by firing the suburbs and, if necessary, the city of Leipzig itself, as this had been abandoned during the three-day battle by almost all the inhabitants.[58]

In order to explain the premature explosion that was so damaging to us, it was later said that the Badeners had opened the Halle Gate and let in Prussian and Swedish sharpshooters[59] who sneaked down towards the bridge, joined up with the Saxon Guard, and fired on the retreating troops from buildings near the bridge. The sapper in charge of the mine thought that the heavy firing signalled the approach of the enemy and that it was thus time for him to do his job; he thus fired the charge. Others lay the blame for this lamentable error on Colonel Montfort of the engineers, who is supposed to have given the order to blow the bridge himself when he saw these enemy troops. Napoleon believed this latter version and had the colonel court martialled, but the court found him to be innocent.

***

Marshal Marmont was one of those lucky enough to pass over the bridge just in the nick of time:

I had just been swept along by the fugitives through the gate by the bridge, when the [non-commissioned] officer commanding the demolition guard panicked, ordered the bridge to be blown and completed the chaos. No officer was directly responsible for this event as none was present.

---

[57] The bridge in question is two kilometres east of the Lindenau suburb!

[58] As we have seen from numerous accounts of Saxon civilian eyewitnesses, this is patently not true; the city was full of its own citizens and refugees from the surrounding villages. Marbot also conveniently forgets about the 20,000 sick and wounded that the French abandoned in various parts of the city and the suburbs, making no effort at all to evacuate them.

[59] The Prussians and Swedes were at the Grimma Gate and not the Halle Gate.

At eleven o'clock there were only a corporal and three men of the engineers at the bridge and these cannot be blamed for the catastrophe as they just did as they had been told; to blow up the bridge if the enemy seemed to be about to capture it.

Colonel of Engineers Montfort, second-in-command to General Rogniat – who had already left for Weissenfels – had orders to blow up the bridge as soon as the last French troops had crossed it. Colonel Montfort tried in vain to find out which would be the last French unit to come over and from which general he would receive the order to carry out the demolition. He even went to Berthier in Lindenau to get orders. Due to the flood of refugees, he could not get back to the Elster bridge. The sapper company at the Ranstädter bridge had also been pulled back to Lindenau.

Russian Jägers from Sacken's corps advanced through the Rosenthal to the Jacob's Hospital [which was unoccupied] and found a footbridge over the Elster which was intact. They crossed this and took post north of the Ranstädter Steinweg opposite the Ranstädter bridge.

There, not twenty paces away, they saw a flood of fugitives and fired into them. Corporal Lafontaine, the sapper NCO in charge of the demolition, thus lit the fuse to the charge, which was in a barge under the bridge.

A terrible explosion suddenly drowned out all the noises of the retreat: the shouts and cries and the rumbling of the waggons. Beams, planks, stone blocks, men, waggons, horses and equipment were hurled up into the air to crash down again. A huge cloud of smoke billowed up.

The column halted, but those in the rear pushed on again as the Russian Jägers poured their fire into them.

Marshal Macdonald was amongst those trapped by the destruction of the vital bridge. He recounted his adventures and lucky escape in his memoirs. Needless to say, they do not bear much similarity with Marbot's account of the same event:

I walked away [from the ruined bridge] with the clear aim of not being captured. I would have preferred suicide or drowning. Caught up in the mass of fugitives, I was carried over the two smaller arms of the Elster. On one footbridge I held on to the rails; my feet no longer touched the ground. The other arm I crossed on a horse given to me by an NCO. I was then in a great park [Reichels Garten[60]] and still in the midst of a great crowd. I wandered about looking for a possible crossing point. The soldiers followed me because they thought that I knew a way out, but my map showed me none. Lauriston had been with me but here we became separated. A little later an ADC of Poniatowski's came up and, amid tears, told me that the prince had drowned. During his tale, one of my adjutants, Buernonville, took my reins and said: 'Marshal! That doesn't matter any more. You must save yourself!' and pulled me with him at a gallop and told me that Colonel

[60] This lay some 600 metres south of Marbot's massacre of the 'murderers'.

Marion, commander of my engineers, had crossed the Elster. He had felled two trees at the river bank so that they fell across the river and had covered them with doors, shutters and planks.

We hurried to the site; it was full of troops. They told us that Augereau and Victor had insisted on riding over the flimsy structure before the decking had been nailed down. The trees had rolled apart and all the decking had fallen into the river. Only the two bare trees were left and no-one dared to try to cross. I decided to do it! I dismounted and shuffled over, one foot on each log. There was a high wind; I wore a heavy coat. I took it off. I was three parts of the way across when others tried to follow me; the logs rolled and I fell in.

Happily I could stand in the water but the banks were soft and steep and I could not climb out. I was soaked and sweating. On the far bank whole platoons threw themselves into the water and were swept to their deaths. They cried to me: 'Monsieur Marshal – save your soldiers! Save your children!' I could do nothing for them. I wept with rage and frustration.

I left the scene and made my way to Imperial Headquarters in Markranstädt. Napoleon wanted to see me. I was so furious that at first I refused, but then I went to him.

He was sitting at a table with a large map spread before him. Weeping, I reported to him. He listened without interrupting me. I told him that the losses of men and materiel were monstrous. If we wanted to save the remnants of the corps we had not a moment to lose. I was very tired.

Napoleon saw this and said coldly: 'Go and have a rest!'

I left, enraged at his equanimity. He did not give me one word of comfort. I had lost everything – all my possessions and carriages, 12–15,000 francs in gold and much silver!

* * *

Captain Coignet's eighth *Notebook* picks up the story of his own adventures in the early hours of the 19th:

About two o'clock in the morning we saw a fire on the battlefield; all the waggons were being burned and the caissons blown up. It was a frightful sight. On the 19th October, Napoleon, after a touching interview with the King of Saxony and his family, withdrew from Leipzig. He went by way of the boulevards which lead to the long bridge of the suburb of Lindenau, and ordered the engineer and artillery officers not to have the bridge blown up until the last platoon had left the city, the rearguard being obliged to remain twenty-four hours longer in Leipzig. But what with Augereau's sharpshooters on one hand and the Saxon and Baden troops[61] on the other, firing on the French, the sappers thought that the enemy's army was coming, and that the moment had come to fire the mine. The bridge was

---

[61] As we have already seen, this is wrong. It was the Russian Jägers who fired on the bridge from the Rosenthal.

destroyed, and all means of retreat was cut off for the troops of Macdonald, Lauriston, Reynier and Poniatowski. The last mentioned, though wounded in the arm, attempted to swim across the Elster and met his death in a whirlpool. Marshal Macdonald was more fortunate, and reached the opposite bank.

23,000 Frenchmen who escaped the slaughter that ensued in Leipzig till two o'clock in the afternoon were made prisoner. Two hundred and fifty pieces of artillery fell into the hands of the enemy.

The Emperor reached his headquarters greatly fatigued; he had passed the night without sleep, and was utterly worn out.

'Well, Monthion,' said he, 'where are my waggons and the treasure?'

'All are safe, sire. Your "Grouser"[62] stood a volley on the promenade.'

'Send him here; he had a serious affair with a colonel.'

'I know it,' said the general.

'Send them both here; let them explain the matter.'

I went into the Emperor's presence. The general related the affair.

'Where is your hat?'

'Sire, I threw it into one of the waggons and could not find it again.'

'So, you had some trouble on the causeway?'

'I wanted to share the road with the ambulances and the colonel told me that he would take no orders from me. I said to him: "In the name of the Emperor, move aside to the right." He had done this for the artillery, and he was not willing to give me half of the road. Then I threatened him; if he had been my equal, I should have sabred him.'

The Emperor turned to the colonel and said: 'Well, what have you to say? You have barely escaped being degraded. You shall be put under arrest for fifteen days for having started without my order, and, if you are not satisfied, my Grouser [Imperial Guardsman] will help you to see reason. As for you,' he said to me, 'you did your duty. Go and look for your hat.'

***

Colonel Saint-Chamans of the 7*e* Chasseurs recounted the fate which befell his party as the Allied troops spread through Leipzig:

Finally, at dawn on the 19th, we learned that the French army would commence a full retreat; I also heard what had happened to my regiment – it had been completely destroyed. Less than 100 men remained and of the twenty-two officers present on the morning of the 16th, thirteen had been killed or wounded. Killed: Bontin, Castel, Dubois, Duboismande, Grandin, Vangrasweld. Wounded: Boussi, Larderet, Mesplies, Michonnet, Veniere, Vieillageux and myself.

Marshal Augereau arrived and posted several companies around the house. Soon it became evident that I wouldn't be able to stay here much

---

[62] Napoleon's nickname for Coignet.

longer and I was carried by four grenadiers to the Hôtel Bavaria [in the Peterstrasse]; I was spitting blood.

I was in something of a stupor and things were happening so quickly that I was at the height of confusion. My cousin, Count Louis de Saint-Chamans, a lieutenant in my regiment, had not left me since my wound and Doctor Denoix was still with me, as was my valet.

It was now obvious that we were going to become prisoners of war. My companions in misfortune therefore busied themselves in hiding our money and valuables, leaving just one purse, containing 200 or 300 francs, in view; sufficient to satisfy the greed of the soldiers and spare us the abuse which was certain to follow if we didn't offer them anything. When everything was ready we awaited our first callers; just one thing worried me – that they might search under my mattress and, in so doing, move me and cause the pains to begin again.

Shooting broke out in the street under my window and from the 'Hurrahs' of the Russians, it became obvious that the Allies were now masters of the town. Just then, we heard a commotion in the corridor. The doctor went out to find the hotel owner being threatened by a French officer. The officer wanted bread and was about to run the hotelier through when the doctor intervened and the officer fled.

It was then that a party of Prussian grenadiers appeared; they came into the room with their bayonets lowered as though prepared to take the place by assault. One of them, some kind of NCO and their evident leader, demanded in German: 'Are there any French here?'

'We are all French.'

'Money?'

The doctor presented him with the purse prepared beforehand; he looked into it and seemed satisfied with what he saw. He put it into his pocket and said in French: 'Watches!'

The doctor gave him his; my cousin gestured that he didn't have a watch; my valet was shivering so much that he was incapable of speech or gesture.

They seemed satisfied with their small haul and they went out without having even touched our portmanteaus or our weapons. We were realistic enough to guess that this would not be our last set of visitors; we learned that a party of Russian generals had moved into the building and the doctor went off to see them in order to ask for their protection. 'Do not worry,' said the general, 'nothing will happen to you, I have issued strict orders to suppress looting and prisoners will be well treated.'

'But,' said the doctor, 'we have already been robbed!'

'That is impossible,' replied the general, 'because we have made such an offence punishable by death; please be reassured.'

They escorted him back to our room. We were, in fact, left in peace until around ten in the evening. My companions had just lain themselves down to rest when there was a loud banging on the door. We were obliged to open it and a Cossack officer, utterly drunk, staggered into the room. The Cossack and the doctor had the following conversation, in bad German, and I translated for the benefit of my cousin and valet.

'Give me money,' said the officer, 'I want money!'

'We've got nothing; the Prussians took it all this morning.'

'Those thieving Prussians! They're brigands! So, you have nothing for me?'

'Unfortunately we have nothing, and here is the colonel, wounded badly and deprived of everything.'

'Those thieves,' continued the Cossack, 'those bandits. But you must have something for us.'

'Look around for yourself. We have nothing but the clothes we are dressed in.'

'Prussian robbers! But,' finding my sabre, 'here is some gold.'

'That is the colonel's sabre.'

'The colonel is a prisoner and doesn't need it any more. It's a good sabre and I need one. Do you have anything I might like?'

'Nothing at all.'

'Those robbers!' said the Cossack, opening the door with difficulty, 'I'll find them and make them pay!'

The rest of the night passed without incident; nevertheless, we felt it necessary to place ourselves under the protection of someone with power and influence. We wrote a letter to some Austrian generals asking to become prisoners of their emperor and to be taken away to Bohemia or Moravia or Hungary. I don't know if they ever received it, but we never got a response. A few days later we heard that the Crown Prince of Sweden had arrived and I remembered that I knew his ADC, Noailles. We wrote to him and were overjoyed when he came to visit us, staying to chat. I put to him my idea of again writing to the Austrians; I knew too much about the Prussians to want to fall into their hands and the idea of being sent to Russia filled me with horror.

Noailles suggested that I join a convoy of prisoners that the Crown Prince was sending to Sweden; I was reluctant as I felt that I was still too weak but was persuaded in the end as it seemed the only option. I was added to the list and later joined the convoy, which, twenty days after the battle, set off for Stralsund and captivity.

***

Ludwig Hussel has left us this chilling account of the casualties left behind in Leipzig by the French:

The French hospitals, which we had had here since the beginning of the year, could, with every justification, be termed malignant, cancerous tumours. They were the cause of the outbreak of typhus in the unhappy city. This caused a fatality rate four or five times the norm among the population. Even before the battle it was bad enough in the poisonous caves, in these houses of suffering which became ever more crowded and more numerous.

Some of those who worked there, including the good doctors, carried the germs of death back into their own families. There was no hygiene to be found in them and one could not pass one by without feeling sick and holding one's nose. As Leipzig had been cut off from the outer world by the great ring of the contending armies for some time, like a stranded ship on a desert island, the desperate conditions in these hospitals worsened by the day. Now food was running short. The misery reached its high point when thousands from the battlefield sought help there. The unfortunates could not even be given enough bread. Many roamed the city homeless. One saw horrors that would make even the most hardened cannibal shudder and stand his hair on end. The eye can have seen nothing more hideous in Smolensk, at the Beresina, or on the road at Wilna; there at least, death had carried off his victims more speedily. Thousands of pitiful wretches staggered through the streets, begging at every door and window. There was rarely anything to be had. It was not at all rare to see one of these living skeletons picking up a dirty bone to gnaw hungrily at it, or pick up some filthy, tiny crust of bread from a rubbish heap, or apple peel, cabbage stalks or apple cores, and eat them. But their hunger did not stop at these revolting lengths. More than twenty eyewitnesses can confirm that French soldiers crawled up to dead horses, whose corpses were already rotting, and tore shreds of the flesh off with their bare hands or with blunt knives and ate it. Objects which ravens and vultures only turned to in hard times were their daily diet! It occurred that they even cut the flesh from amputated limbs and grilled it to sate their hunger! They even searched through excrement to look for undigested scraps! You know me and you would not expect me to tell you lies for which I could be punished by the whole city. So the hospitals were pestilential sores for the city which had to turn away in disgust from the hideous smells, sights and sounds. They were also like a great, terrible vampire that had sucked away so much of our blood and marrow and had now become destructive for the sick themselves. One also saw examples of extreme resignation and self-denial. Several times I saw young soldiers with missing legs or arms, lying on the bare ground or stone for three days without receiving any help, not a bit of bread nor a drop of water, without making any sound or changing the quiet, self-possessed air with which they regarded passers-by. They begged for nothing, they did not complain, and seemed to wish only that their meagre life spirit would ebb away as quickly as possible. Not one of these can have been saved.

As hard as the newly organised Allied authorities tried to alleviate the suffering that they found on all sides, it was beyond human endeavour to work through the hideous chaos. The French had left everything in too great a state of confusion. Everything was in short supply in the city, the villages far and wide were ruined and had been thoroughly plundered; in brief, we had nothing. The more than thirty hospitals were not enough to take in the sick who crawled and staggered around all over the place. Where were we going to find the necessary large houses, the palliasses, blankets, crockery, food and the great number of doctors which were needed to care for all these unfortunates? All remotely suitable premises and supplies had been requisitioned long ago; the Hospital Committee was no longer able to cope with the demands made upon it. Almost every barber's apprentice had already been forced into service dressing wounds in the hospitals with their amateur skills. It was impossible to buy the things that were needed even if there had been enough money – and even this well had dried up.

In the city were thousands of troops who had just arrived who were hungry and thirsty. Despite all our efforts it was impossible to even partially satisfy their needs. How would we not have loved to have been able to give each of them a feast, a strong drink, but there was not even a glass of the worst beer or brandy available. They often thought that it was ill will on our part because they were not French. How little they understood our position! Six Prussian footguards were quartered in the house in which I lived. They complained when we could give them nothing but dry potatoes. But they were modest enough and accepted our explanation. Quietly, four of them took their muskets and left. They came back in about an hour, and we were amazed to see that they had two cows with them that they had taken from the French. They gave them to their host and all started on the work of slaughtering them. In two hours, the household was so well provided with food that it was possible to help out some others and, as it was pickled, we had supplies for a long time.

The fate of Napoleon's German allies

The regimental history of the Hessian artillery contains an account of their participation in the fighting in Leipzig:

Marchand's 39th Division, Macdonald's XI Corps, was not involved in the fighting on the 16th October. That evening, it occupied the hills between Liebertwolkwitz and Seifertshain which the Austrians had been forced to evacuate with heavy loss. The battery set up its guns surrounded by dead and wounded Austrians; the night was very stormy. On the 17th October the battery remained in position and towards evening brought effective fire to bear on an approaching Austrian column which then moved off to a flank into a wood.

Before dawn on the 18th October, the division moved off in silence to the rear via Holzhausen and took post in Zuckelhausen. On the western side of the village, next to the road, they were soon engaged in a heavy artillery duel. *Kapitain* Müller was wounded here and *Leutnant* Scholl took over command. Later, the battery was ordered to withdraw through the village and to take up position on the heights of Stötteritz where the action stabilised.

They had lost some dead and wounded on this day and *Leutnant* Kühlmann's leg was smashed by a cannonball; he died in Leipzig on 12th November. *Oberfeürwerker* Schaffnit was wounded. The battery had fired heavily; some guns were damaged and others rendered unserviceable when the French-made shot, supplied to us in Leipzig, jammed in the barrels when being loaded.

In the end, the battery could only fire with three guns. The enemy fire was so heavy, that one driver of the train had four horses shot from under him.

Late that night, the battery withdrew into Leipzig under *Oberfeürwerker* Schaffnit to join the Reserve Park. *Leutnant* Scholl and Train *Leutnant* Vogel returned to Stötteritz with two repaired guns.

After untold difficulties the battery managed to fight its way over the Elster through the masses of panic-stricken French units. Many soldiers were pushed into the river to right and left of the bridge in the crush.

During the morning of the 19th October, the battery learned from a Hessian infantry NCO, that the Hessian brigade had been completely scattered in the fighting for the city. The battery thus joined in the retreat, which was in a state of incredible confusion. At every bridge there was a fight to get across as everyone sought to save his own skin. On the night of the 19th October, the battery bivouacked at Lützen in deep mud.

The two guns under *Leutnant* Scholl had a much worse time. On the evening of the 18th October they had rejoined the Hessian brigade at Stötteritz and remained there for the night. On the next morning, the whole brigade withdrew to Leipzig and halted in the suburb of the city by the Grimma Gate. This gate itself was occupied by Baden troops.

At nine o'clock a concentric assault was mounted by the Allies on Leipzig and soon the French had to yield ground. With the permission of the brigade commander, Prinz Emil, *Leutnant* Scholl threw one ammunition waggon into the moat and used the team for the guns. He was ordered to attempt to withdraw to the Lützen road via the Rossmarkt. After terrible difficulties, he reached to within 500 paces of the vital bridge over the Elster when it was prematurely blown up.

Leutnant Scholl took his guns along the Pleisse through some gardens, looking for a crossing point, but the banks were too steep and he could not get over. At this point, the enemy troops were shooting into the fugitives at the river so Scholl disabled both guns and told the crews to save themselves. Somehow, they managed to find a way over the Elster; the horses were abandoned but the men found a fordable point and waded over.

They gathered in Lindenau and marched to Lützen, which they reached that evening. On the 20th October they were reunited with the rest of the battery. Losses of the Hessian battery at Leipzig were two guns, two ammunition waggons, one limber; four killed, and five dead of their wounds. Fourteen horses had been killed. The battery had fired 697 six-pounder shot, fifty six-pounder canister rounds, 104 howitzer shells and twenty-four howitzer canister rounds.

Prinz Emil von Hessen-Darmstadt, commander of his nation's contingent in Marchand's 39th Division, wrote to his father regarding the day's events as follows:

At five o'clock on the morning of the 19th October, our division marched past Stötteritz and halted behind the village until it was fully daylight. All roads to Leipzig were filled with columns of all arms and with baggage trains. The streets in the city were all blocked with vehicles that had not been able to clear the town during the night.

The 39th Division now continued its withdrawal into the suburbs of Leipzig. The enemy saw us go and could follow us with impunity.

Leipzig had to be defended in order to prevent destruction. Several corps were used for this purpose. Our division was placed in front of the [inner] Grimma Gate, on the Esplanade, the Badeners to the right, the Hessians fairly far back on the left, in reserve. Other troops of our corps were in front of them. A battery of Württemberg artillery was set up opposite the bridge.

The Allies did not keep us waiting long. They sent their skirmishers in early and shot and shell cut down entire files.

Now the musketry came closer and the artillery fire stopped. The 1st Battalion, Garde-Füsiliere, and the Baden Regiment Grossherzog were sent out to the entrances to the town as the French there could no longer hold the enemy back and were fleeing into the city in large groups to save themselves. They had also been thrown out of the next gate to our left and fled back onto us in disorder, hotly followed by the enemy.

In order to give them time to regroup, and also to prevent disorder in our own ranks, I detached the 2nd Battalion of the Leib-Regiment to counter the enemy on this side, because we were now in danger of being cut off and crushed into a mass as the Allies had forced their way into the town through the Grimma Gate and we were being fired on from two sides.

And in fact, the Baden battalions were led forward twice, and twice repulsed, but they held up the enemy for a time. In the Wallgraben [the moat] there was a place where it was possible to climb onto the wall; I withdrew to that point. Those of the corps who could not follow me through this narrow defile ran to the Grimma Gate and reformed there under command of *Oberst* von Gall. The space on top of the wall was too narrow for us to deploy, and the trees on the Esplanade cut off all view of friend and foe. I thus withdrew the troops through a postern that had been found [the Zuchthauspförtschen] into the old city, had the entrance barricaded, and went down the so-called Rittegasse to rejoin the contingent that had come through the inner Grimma Gate.

But getting through the inner Grimma Gate was not so easy. The gate was still locked and guarded by Badeners of the Leipzig garrison, who had been given strict orders not to let anyone in. A large mob of fugitives, mostly French, rushed over the bridge to the gate, shouting and cursing, and tried to break it in. Now a Prussian *Landwehr* battalion appeared and advanced on the gate along the Grimmaschen-Steinweg. A Hessian soldier picked up a match and set it to one of the guns that had been abandoned by the Württembergers, and the murderous discharge caused the Prussians to halt; a second discharge sent them back in disorder.

Leutnant Hanesse quickly gathered some men and chased after them to drive them into the next side-street. But this success did not last long; two Swedish guns came up, unlimbered, and fired with canister into the mass of men in front of the locked inner Grimma Gate. The French and Hessian defenders fell back. Now there was another threat; the enemy were advancing along the glacis on both flanks from the Halle Gate in the north and the Peterstor Gate in the south.

In vain the defenders outside the locked gate pleaded, threatened and cajoled the commander of the Baden guard to open the gate, but he steadfastly refused to do so. At last, *Kapitain* von Bechthold, of the Hessian Leib-Garde-Regiment, had two pioneers break down the rotting old gate with their axes. The much-relieved mob rushed into the city.

The French dispersed in all directions; the Hessians, in contrast, rallied to their officers and formed up in front of the Baden gate guard to defend the gate. The gate was pushed shut again and barricaded. The men were allocated to the loopholes and *Bataillonstambour* Schulz, of the Garde-Füsiliere, beat the pas de charge continuously to overawe the enemy. But then an order arrived from Prinz Emil that they should fall back and join him at the next side-street (probably the Ritterstrasse). Scarcely had the detachment left the gate than it was opened to the enemy by the citizens of Leipzig and they poured in.

As armed resistance ended, most of the Hessian officers gathered around Prinz Emil. They broke open a shop on the Brühl and all went inside. At the same time, Prussian soldiers flooded into the backyard of the shop. Seeing the Hessian officers, they called their own officer; this officer took the swords of the prince and his officers and led them to General von Borstell, who gave them a house in the Grimma suburb to wait in.

Prinz Emil's report concludes:

> After beating off several enemy assaults on the Grimma Gate, the superior enemy masses finally became too strong for our weakened battalions there and at the barricaded postern. We fell back, in some disorder, in two detachments, the one down the Grimma Strasse to the Markt Platz and down the parallel lane, the Brühl.
>
> The other gates had been forced earlier and we met the Allies in all the streets, and the bridge on the defile to Lindenau had already been blown up. The game was up. The officers and soldiers who were with me did more than their duty; they showed pure dedication and devotion to Your Royal Highness' son right up to the last minute. Captivity was their fate as it was mine.

The exact losses suffered by the Hessian contingent on the 19th cannot be exactly determined; no officers were killed or wounded, but forty-five officers and 200 NCOs and men were captured. The rest escaped. No colours were lost.

On 21 October, Prinz Emil left to go to Berlin for the duration of his captivity. His officers and men were sent to Neu-Ruppin.

***

Like Prinz Emil, Graf Wilhelm von Hochberg also wrote a report to his father, the Grand Duke of Baden, describing the closing stages of the battle:

> I must report most humbly to Your Royal Highness, that yesterday was a most significant and tragic day for your contingent in that it brought about our total disbandment and resulted in us being in the hands of the Allied coalition.
>
> Only the artillery, the Dragoon Regiment von Freystedt and the divisional baggage, all of which left here prior to yesterday, still exist. All the infantry were captured here.
>
> Your majesty will have already learned of the serious situation of the French army from my last report and from the letter from General von Schäffer which accompanied it. This state of affairs deteriorated day by day. The lack of food became worse every day; the bad weather and the continuous marching and bivouacking exhausted the army and, at last, brought about the collapse of its morale.
>
> Added to this was the fact that the enemy's light cavalry swarmed all around us and cut off all supplies; made the communication between our corps very difficult and captured a lot of couriers and other prisoners. Anyone who ventured from the main road was taken.
>
> With his army thus much weakened and demoralised, the Emperor came to Leipzig, fought battles here in the area for days but was beaten on all fronts and suffered monstrous losses.
>
> Finally, on the evening of the 18th, he appeared to decide upon a retreat. He sent most of the baggage and the artillery back along the road to Lützen and followed them with the rest of his guard at ten o'clock on the morning of the 19th.
>
> To cover his withdrawal, and to defend the city, there were only the Poles, the corps of Marshal Macdonald and part of Augereau's corps. These troops, which included Your Majesty's 1st Brigade, were deployed in and before the suburbs. Within the city there was only our 2nd Brigade which included four companies of my regiment, which was heavily attacked by the Austrians at Lindenau on the 16th, and was reduced to eighty men.
>
> Ten officers were wounded, and of these, *Leutnant* von Freyberg died next day. Ninety-six NCOs and men have been killed and 150 wounded. They consisted of about 1,000 men of whom 800 were on duty in and before the town and 200 were in reserve.
>
> Leipzig was now assaulted from all sides, the suburbs quickly taken, and one gate was broken in by French fugitives and seized by the enemy.
>
> At this moment, a Russian emissary came to the king of Saxony and assured him, in the name of the Czar, of his protection and security. For this good man had been left behind by Emperor Napoleon to the generosity of the Allied powers together with 1,200–1,500 of his troops.
>
> Until this point, the Duke of Padua had been in command of the city. Upon hearing the news that the enemy had taken the suburbs and was about to enter the city, he sent me away to organise the defence. I was scarcely on

the street when a Russian general – the emissary previously mentioned – appeared with Russian and Prussian Jägers and demanded that I surrender. There was nothing else for me to do if I did not want to waste the lives of my men, for we were surrounded and cut off, and the Emperor himself had destroyed several bridges behind him.

I thus had the men in the square order their arms and sent messengers out to the groups still fighting to call them in. I also sent to General von Stockhorn, who was outside the Peterstor with his regiment, to join me as his retreat was also cut off. This he managed to do successfully.

Your Majesty's regiment was, however, closely engaged with the enemy and only a few managed to get into the city. The majority were killed or wounded and captured or scattered into the rivers.

All who came into the market place have retained their weapons and equipment up to now and have been well and respectfully treated.

After the city had been formally taken possession of, I was ordered to march the troops out of the town to a designated bivouac area. I had myself taken to the Crown Prince of Sweden, who apparently commanded the assault on the city. He received me very graciously and assured me that he would take care of me to Your Majesty's satisfaction. Later, Czar Alexander, Kaiser Franz and the King of Prussia arrived. I also wanted to approach the Czar but had only been able to arrange to see Grand Prince Constantine last night. His Majesty saw me this morning at nine o'clock. His Majesty was most gracious in this interview; assured me of his protection, and allowed me to send General von Schäffer and Major von Holzing back to Baden, and assured me that our troops would not be sent off into captivity as he hoped that we would soon be marching together.

Thus is our situation; General von Schäffer will give you a more detailed account of the events and will beg that you soon come to a decision and also send me a letter of credit as we are in urgent need of money and I have already had to take out a loan of 7,000 Florins in my name.

P.S. I have just heard that we are finally to be disarmed tomorrow and transported to the area of Berlin. Due to the flood of events, our men have suffered a great shortage of provisions; as of tomorrow we should be properly fed. Attached is a parade state of the corps; it is as accurate as possible.

***

Eduard Müller, a trooper of the Prinz Clemens Ulanen-Regiment of the 26th (Saxon) Light Cavalry Brigade, related his experiences during the battle thus:

On 16th October, a Saturday, we Saxons stood in the middle of the French line of battle in the area between Probstheida and Stötteritz. Even a common soldier could see that something big was about to happen. French couriers galloped back and forth over the field from a small hill nearby. Deafening gunfire made the earth shake. We Chevaulégers were in cover behind a large farm, ready to dash out at any time. Soon we were ordered to mount – and as quickly came the counter-order to dismount. Then a courier rushed up and ordered us to attack. We pulled the chains over the horses' heads, buckled our helmets tight, took our swords firmly in our right hands and dashed off into the storm of the battle. Our regiment rode like the wind over the fields towards the enemy. The rattle of the musketry volleys, the roar of the cannon, the shouted commands of the officers, the yells of the men, the thunder of the horses' hooves – it was terrible, like a scene from hell.

Then I felt my horse take a great blow; it reared up and crashed to the ground, dead. I was thrown to the ground.

When I awoke – as from a dream – my comrades had gone and I found myself, uninjured, in the midst of the groaning wounded, alone and unable to defend myself, behind the line of battle.

Night fell and the turmoil of the battle gradually ebbed away. I now looked about for somewhere to spend the night on the battlefield, which was lit by the burning villages that surrounded it. I came to a brickworks but all the rooms, and even the courtyard, were full of dead and dying. Some French sappers came up looking for firewood for their campfire, for the October night was wet and cold. Without pausing, they climbed up onto the roof and threw tiles and rafters down onto the wounded. The cries of those unfortunates that were hit were terrible; I could still hear them for weeks afterwards.

I was dead tired; I leaned into a corner of the wall and fell asleep. In the morning I was awakened by a feeling of icy cold; I had gone to sleep under the drainpipe!

I got up freezing; it was a Sunday; cold and dismal. There was no battle noise. I wandered about vainly looking for my squadron. Then I went towards Leipzig.

On the morning of 18th October I got to the Grimma Gate just as a French constable was about to shut it, for the retreat of the French army had begun. The sentry shouted to me: '*Tout de suite! Tout de suite!*' I understood his gestures better than his French gabble and hurried into Leipzig, to where Napoleon and his entourage had also fled shortly before. The gates slammed shut behind me.

Now I wandered through the streets of this city, which was unknown to me. At about evening time, I was walking through a side-street when a man took my arm and spoke to me: 'Listen to me, I see that you are a Saxon trooper; you could be the answer to my prayers! Please come into my house and hear what I have to say. I am a wine merchant and have a large wine cellar downstairs. If they find my wine, I am a ruined man. I'll make you the following offer: Stand in front of my gate as if you are a sentry. The plunderers will believe that a senior officer is staying here and will leave the house alone. You won't regret it!'

No sooner said than done! With a distinctly martial air, I marched back and forth in front of the gate and scared off several suspicious types. We found a few other comrades and soon had a smart guard assembled. We relieved one another every hour and spent the rest of the time in the house at a table loaded with expensive wines and tobacco, in peaceful revelry.

Whilst outside the retreat was in full swing and the French and their emperor had their hearts in their trousers and were full of terror, we drank a toast to their departure and to Germany's liberation. If a Frenchman had heard us singing we would have been in deep trouble!

When we got too merry and noisy, the merchant moved us into a back room and left us to it while he put on one of our uniforms and stood guard himself.

We went to sleep as Napoleon's thugs and woke up to a new day as free Germans.

As I wandered though the city on the 19th October, Napoleon's army was in full retreat. I came into the market square just as Napoleon, having spent a short time with our king, rushed off through Leipzig's streets and out of the Frankfurt gate.

It was dangerous to be on the streets as the first shells from the victorious Allies dropped in. I went back to my friendly wine merchant; after giving me another fine meal, he said goodbye with a warm handshake. I soon bumped into my Saxon comrades who had also gone over to the Allies.

Newly equipped as a trooper, I helped to chase the Frenchies back over the Rhine.

***

King Friedrich August of Saxony and his family were declared to be Prussian prisoners of war. Czar Alexander refused his requests for an interview, and Metternich, the Austrian chancellor, handed the unfortunate monarch a letter from Kaiser Franz which – in essence – said ' I told you so!'

Colonel the Honourable Lord Cathcart was present as the Allied monarchs entered Leipzig:

The Emperor of Russia and the King of Prussia rode down the hill, and placing themselves at the head of their guards, who were already at the gates, they entered the town about noon, and were no less anxious, by their presence and the good discipline of their reserve, to prevent those excesses that almost invariably follow the capture of a town by assault, than eager to ascertain and to secure the prize that had fallen into their hands. At the entrance of the town the Emperor and the King had to force their way through the streets that were crowded with the dejected and disarmed prisoners, the wounded and the inhabitants, who (some in consternation and to propitiate the victors; others in honest exultation at their happy deliverance) came out onto the streets and rent the air with their cheers and shouts of '*Vivat Alexander!*', '*Vivat der König von Preussen!*'

As we passed the house in which the King of Saxony had taken up his abode, the Saxon Guard was still there, formed on its post with its arms reversed. The King, with a few members of his court that were with him, had come down to the street and was standing on the steps of his house; but the

Emperor passed by him without notice and rode on through the market-place to the Markranstädt Gate. Finding that exit completely impassable, and learning that every possibility of the farther retreat of the French had effectively been cut off, he returned and took up his station in the centre of the great market place. A battalion of the Russian guard was placed for the protection and custody of the royal prisoners; and the proper officers of the several departments were charged, under the Emperor's immediate supervision, who sat there on horseback, to secure all arms and military stores, to re-establish order, and to prevent plunder or excess of any kind.

On 23 October the Saxon royal family left Leipzig with a retinue which included his cabinet minister Graf von Einsiedel, the Major Domo Graf von Vitzthum, generals von Bose and von Zeschau, Captain von Monthbe of the Swiss Guard, *Leutnant* von Lützerode of the general staff, the king's confessor, his surgeon Dr Kreyssig, and his legal advisor *Legationsrat* Breür. From the Allied side they were accompanied by the Russian privy councillor von Anstetten and General Prince Galizin. The escort consisted of sixty Cossacks commanded by Colonel Brendel.

In Aken these Cossacks were replaced by Prussian *Landwehr* cavalry and the column went on to Berlin, where the Saxon royal family were lodged in the palace at Friedrichsfelde on the eastern side of the city.

Baron Karl August von Hardenberg of the Prussian monarch's suite wrote an accompanying letter to Prince Wilhelm von Sayn-Wittgenstein, chief of the secret police in Berlin:

> Due to the fact that the king of Saxony remained faithful to the French cause to the end and was captured in a town that was taken by storm, he must be treated with the respect due to his high rank, but also with the security that his current situation demands. The guard of honour which he has, must also be his security guard who will watch the activities and correspondence of the king and his entourage, in a subtle manner...
>
> In addition, please ensure, in order to avoid public unrest, that the king enters Berlin after dark.

***

Following the removal of the king of Saxony to captivity in Berlin, both monarch and realm faced a very uncertain future. The victorious Allies let it be known that they expected some sign of enthusiasm for their cause from the newly-liberated country; and that the level of this enthusiasm might well influence their treatment of King Friedrich August.

Saxony was now governed by Russian General Prince Repnin. Together with the Prussian Minister von Stein and General von Thielmann (newly transferred from Saxon to Russian service), he urged the country's leading men to raise volunteer units for service with the Allies. One of those who responded was Wilhelm Traugott Krug, rector of the University of Leipzig, who volunteered for service in the *Banner der freiwilligen Sachsen* (Banner of Volunteer Saxons). He left an account of the early days of this organisation:

I decided to join up and went along to the recruiting office and signed on as a volunteer. After the last few days of indecision as to whether to go or not, I felt suddenly at peace. There was one very difficult task yet ahead of me: I had to go home and tell my wife what I had just done. But she was ill; the nervous strain of the war had taken its toll. I waited until she was a little better and then told her. She took it like a real trouper. 'I thought it would come to this,' she said with a tear in her eye. 'Go, in God's name!'

That is truly how it happened. It is wrong to say, as some did, that I joined up out of feelings of duty towards the *Tugendbund*.[63] The patriotism generated by French pressures and the general enthusiasm for Germany's freedom dragged me along with them.

Now the drilling and equipping began. The former gave me a lot of fun, the latter caused me much grief. I had volunteered to be a *Reitender Jäger* [a mounted rifleman, or Chasseur à Cheval]. I could already ride although I had now to learn to do the rising trot, which I found to be ridiculous. But there was a special reason why I wanted to join the light cavalry; I knew that they were used mainly to attack the enemy from all sides, to pursue him and to carry out all sorts of raids. Lady Luck, thought I, might well deliver Napoleon into your hands. This was no empty dream. How close did the Emperor come to being caught after Waterloo? He only saved himself by abandoning his coach in the darkness. In war, anything is possible. And if I had come so close to N, no pistol or sabre would have stopped me – and I am not bragging – from grabbing him by the scruff of the neck. The idea gave me a lot of pleasure. '*Voici le recteur de l'universite de Liepsic,*' I would have said, '*que vous avez si maltraite!*' ['I am the rector of the University of Leipzig, who you have ill-treated!']

But now we had to buy horses, weapons and uniforms – all out of our own pockets. Those were the rules. I didn't have a lot of cash. I sold the silverware and had to take out a loan as well, for the expenses were much higher than I had at first calculated. The Banner was to be an elite unit and someone had the bright idea of declaring it to be part of the Russian Imperial Guard. We had to swear an oath that we would lay down our lives to save Alexander's and we would certainly have done it.

This was a high honour, but it was bought at a high price in money and time. For now the uniform was to be as glamorous as possible and one of the main points of discussion was what hats we should wear. First the tricorne was favourite, then the Swedish hat (round but with the brim turned up at one side), then shakos and finally *Tschapkas* (high, square-topped Polish caps, all with lots of cords and other danglies). These various hats alone cost me over 100 Thaler. I complained about it once, but the answer was that a soldier must obey orders.

---

[63] The League of Virtue, originally a Prussian society, founded in Königsberg in 1808 to prepare for a national uprising against the French. The movement was copied in many other German states. Freemasons' lodges were frequently centres for the movement.

I received no pay; they said that I continued to receive my salary from the university. What they did not consider was that this had to go to my family, and that I, as a soldier on campaign, could not give lectures or write books. They gave me money to buy one horse; but, as an officer, I needed at least three – two for me and one for my groom.

The worst thing was that this messing about with uniforms held up the equipping and the march-out of the Banner. We left Leipzig soon enough, but then lay for a long time in Chemnitz, in a spinning mill. Here I was almost killed by a great comb wheel which caught my greatcoat and ripped it to shreds.

Then we went into Thuringia and had to hang about again, waiting for Prince Repnin, who wanted to carry out the first review of the entire Banner in order to see if we were well enough equipped and drilled to do duty as Russian bodyguards. We burned with impatience, but the harsh rules of obedience dictated silence.

In this manner so much time was wasted that the Banner never came into action:[64] Much ado about nothing!

The Allied victory

On the evening of 19 October, von Gneisenau wrote to his wife:

The great battle is won; the victory is decisive. Yesterday the monstrous masses battled with one another. It was a spectacle such as has not been seen for thousands of years. From a hill I could oversee both armies. A lot of blood has flown. Dead and dying lie spread for miles over the landscape. At last we pushed the French army into a small space near Leipzig; night brought an end to the fighting. This morning part of our army assaulted Leipzig. The attack was very bloody. After some hours our troops stormed the city. From all directions troops of the various armies met one another in the town. General Blücher and we were the first to enter. We were greeted by the cheers of the populace and of the victorious troops. We found a lot of prisoners, 20,000 wounded and many more sick; the dead lay everywhere. Many generals are in our hands. Ruined houses, upturned waggons, troops from all nations. The confusion is incredible. All measures have been taken to pursue the enemy as hard as possible. We want to destroy the remnants of his army.

On the 20th, Blücher wrote:

We have just had two great, beautiful days; during the 18th and 19th the Great Colossus fell like an oak tree in a storm. He, the Great Tyrant, has saved himself, but his henchmen are in our hands. Poniatowski was

---

[64] Though the Banner never came into action, several of its men drowned crossing the River Main in 1814.

wounded and has been drowned; we believe Augereau was as well. Reynier and Lauriston have been captured; the former is wounded. On the 19th, at the end of the battle, Leipzig was stormed with great bravery. Some wanted to set Leipzig afire but I stopped this and ordered the Russian batteries to use only ball.

The Russian infantry were first into the city on my side, on the other side it was the brave Pommeranians. It was an incomparable fight, 100 cannon were taken in Leipzig. Our monarchs, that is, the Austrian and Russian emperors and our king, thanked me on the market square. Alexander embraced me.

On the 16th I fought a battle alone in the village of Möckern and threw the French into Leipzig. Some forty cannon, some colours, an eagle and about 4,000 prisoners fell into my hands. This day was the lead-in to the next.

I am now marching off again, in order to attack the enemy again at Merseburg which is where he is headed for. My expedition is through Thuringia, the Great Army is headed for Würzburg.

The king of Saxony was captured here.

Goodbye. I am so tired that I am shaking all over.

Von Gneisenau – Blücher's chief of staff, who was not too popular with king Friedrich Wilhelm III – was less warmly received. He wrote to his wife:

When everybody in Leipzig was gathered in the market square, the king said some rather cold but friendly words of his satisfaction with the army to me. Nothing of me personally. I have still heard not one word of satisfaction about our crossing of the Elbe or the developments in the campaign following it. In comparison, Czar Alexander has said the most flattering things to me as has Kaiser Franz and Prince Schwarzenberg. But you can see how deep-rooted is the king's rejection of all those who do not share his political opinions. As soon as this holy war is over, I will resign from his army; I would sooner eat crusts than serve this unfriendly monarch.

On 23 October, he wrote to Marie von Clausewitz from Freiburg, giving a succinct account of the course of the three-day battle:

When I broke off my last letter, we were almost in a crisis. The French emperor was moving against us with his entire strength. Our headquarters was closer to the enemy than were our troops. The Cossacks had failed to cover a road. The enemy advanced along this road, unnoticed, close up to Bad Düben. Happily, we had decided to move to the Saale and to do it at once. The troops were already on the move. We ate earlier than usual and mounted up to follow them. We had scarcely left the place when the French entered it. We could easily have been captured. Our rapid decision had saved us.

Now began our battle with the Crown Prince. He did not want to get near the enemy. The enemy had made feints at Berlin and the Crown Prince fell for it. He wanted to withdraw over the Elbe and sent orders to us to join him and also to fall back over the Elbe. He told us an official lie, that Czar

Alexander had placed us under his orders. We did not believe him and we did not obey him. On the contrary, from Halle we moved on Leipzig. Finally, he decided to follow us and so saved himself from the infamy which would surely have befallen him had he held to his original plan.

On the 16th October we, the Army of Silesia, fought our fine battle of Möckern. I call it fine because the bravery of our troops came so to the fore in it. The fight for the village of Möckern was most bloody. Finally, it was taken and the enemy were thrown back on all points. We took fifty-four cannon.

On the same day, our main army was attacked. It suffered setbacks and lost terrain, and this was only regained with much trouble at the end of the day, so that one could speak of a drawn battle.

On the 17th, the armies stood quietly opposite one another, preparing for the renewal of the struggle. Only we, the Army of Silesia, attacked the enemy opposite us with part of our cavalry and horse artillery, and threw them back over the Parthe.

The Crown Prince of Sweden, despite all his promises, stayed well behind us – some miles, indeed – without taking any part in the fighting. His fine army was no use to us at all.

On the morning of the 18th, the old Field Marshal [Blücher] rode over to him to make him aware of his duty. I did not accompany my commander because I was too indignant already. Prince Wilhelm went with him. He acted as interpreter and did very well. What was said there was said in strong terms and had its effect; the Prince marched.

Our corps of General Langeron accompanied him and this corps made the first assaults while the Crown Prince kept his Swedes in the fourth line. Now our armies advanced against the enemy at all points and tightened the noose around him. It was a unique scene, to see half a million warriors fighting in such a small space.

We now attacked the suburbs of Leipzig with Sacken's very weak corps. They were taken, lost and retaken. The bloody struggle went on until nightfall: we could only hold part of our gains. Yorck's corps, which had been 19,000 strong on the 16th, had dwindled to 12,700 and needed a rest and only took a small part in the fighting.

When darkness fell, our armies had restricted the enemy to a very small space. We could hear the noise of waggons on the road from Leipzig to Weissenfels. We at once set Yorck's corps off that night to follow the enemy as quickly as possible on his retreat through Merseburg.

On the 19th, Sacken's corps attacked Leipzig again. The fight was very hard and very bloody for us. We had to throw Langeron's corps into the battle, and he also lost a lot of men. The French were covered by water obstacles. Finally, Bülow's corps assaulted from the other side. Favoured by the situation, the enemy put up desperate resistance. Finally, our Prussians broke through as did we at the same time. As the Field Marshal was close to the gate which was stormed, he and his staff were first as victors to enter the conquered city.

How can I describe, dear lady, my feelings as we were greeted by the tumultuous cheers of the victorious troops and of the inhabitants? Long columns of prisoners were marched by, with at their head, on foot, generals Lauriston, Reynier, Bertrand etc. An hour later the king and Czar Alexander arrived, and a little later Kaiser Franz and the generals of all the nations.

You are familiar with the beautiful walks around Leipzig. These were the battlefields of the 19th October. They were all littered with dead, wounded, wreckage, guns, ammunition waggons and muskets. The earth was soaked in blood.

The most admirable thing was that the soldiers, drunk with victory, stayed in their orderly ranks; there was no looting.

We took over 200 cannon, 6–700 ammunition waggons, perhaps 60,000 muskets. More than 40,000 prisoners are in our hands, including 15,000 healthy ones. These are days that are unprecedented in history. The Allies suffered between 40–50,000 dead and wounded. One may estimate the total loss of all the armies at about 100,000 dead and wounded.

Since then, we, the Army of Silesia, have been following the enemy and have taken about 4,000 prisoners from him, freed between 3–4,000 captured Russians and Austrians, and taken guns from him. All the roads are covered with ammunition waggons, many destroyed. At Freiburg, the enemy abandoned or destroyed over 400 ammunition waggons.

You may imagine how happy I am. There is no more happy feeling than the satisfaction of national revenge. We now advance, inexorably, on the Rhine in order to free this great national river from its bonds.

On 25 October, Blücher wrote to his wife from Weissensee:

My Dear Child, I cannot tell you of any great events this time, except that we are continuing our victorious advance, and I hope that in about twelve days the Great Army will be in Frankfurt am Main. I will probably march on Kassel, and then via Paderborn to Münster; if there is anything that you want from there, let me know.

Franz[65] is, I believe, still a prisoner in Dresden; that place will probably surrender soon and we shall have him back again; please God, just let him be healthy again, he probably won't be fit to be a soldier again.

Your brother has excelled himself and will surely be especially promoted and rewarded by the king; at this moment he is on the enemy's heels.

You will see a lot in the enclosures; as Mrs Field Marshall you will now have to conduct yourself very properly, and don't be greedy and lose some weight; I now receive a respectable salary, but, alas, none of us has received

---

[65] Franz was Colonel Friedrich von Blücher, the general's son, commander of the Blücher Hussars, who was captured (and slightly wounded) in a skirmish with the Polish Chevau-legers of the Guard at Pirna on 16 September. His captor, Corporal Wojciechowski, was rewarded by Napoleon with the Légion d'Honneur. There is some doubt as to whether he actually received the honour, however, as he had robbed his prisoner of his decorations after his capture, and General Krasinski took a dim view of this.

any pay for the last two months because no-one could get through to us from Berlin. Write to me soon. I have four fine greys for you and two mules – if only I could get them to you! Everyone here is fine and send their best regards; my best wishes to Heine and to Stössels.
Ever your best friend
Blücher.
P.S. I have no idea what to do with the decorations; I'm decked out like an old coach horse, but the best thing about it all is that it was I who humbled the haughty tyrant.

The cost of the battle

The haul of prisoners and booty that fell into Allied hands was immense. Zelle (p.476) described it as follows:

> The remnants of the Polish corps, 600 men – all that were left of seven regiments – laid down their arms. Their eagles and colours had been evacuated previously. Whole brigades and divisions surrendered. The commandant of Leipzig, General Bertrand [brother of the commander of IV Corps], went with seven other generals to the town hall to await his fate. A Pommeranian grenadier captured a heavily-bleeding General Lauriston. The 2nd Pommeranian Infantry Regiment accepted the surrender of eighteen colonels, 300 officers and 8,000 men. The 14th Prussian Infantry Regiment took Prinz Emil of Hessen, forty-seven officers and 2,170 men prisoner. Jäger Gauer accepted the sword of General Reynier.
>
> The booty included 800 waggons, 130,000 muskets, 323 guns [other sources say 200], thirty generals, 3,000 officers and about 130,000 men. These latter included 2,500 of III Corps, 300 Würzburgers, 600 Westfalians, 3,000 Poles, 600 Saxons, 1,200 Badeners, 2,000 Hessians and about 3,000 from V, VI, VII and XI Corps. The greater part of XI Corps was already over the Elster bridge when it blew up.
>
> Apart from this, there were over 20,000 sick and wounded in the town.

Again according to Zelle (p.477), the combat of 19 October cost the French 6,000 dead and wounded. III Corps lost 122 officers and 2,742 men dead and wounded and forty-seven guns; VI Corps lost 500 all ranks including twenty-four officers, of whom twenty were in Friedrich's division; XI Corps lost fifty-seven officers and 1,200 men; the Poles 1,000; Durutte 200; and Lauriston fourteen officers and 200 men. 'On the Allied side we know only that Borstell's 5th Division of von Bülow's III (Prussian) Corps, Army of the North, lost twenty-three officers and 860 men; Hessen Homburg's 3rd Division scarcely fewer; Langeron at least 2,000; Sacken about the same; and Bennigsen about 1,000. This brings the Allied loss for the 19th to 7,000.'
Zelle continues:

> As Napoleon had 309 guns and 120,000 men on 20 October, his total loss for the period from 14th–19th October (without counting the 20,000 sick and

wounded in Leipzig) was 70,000 men – of these 50,000 dead and wounded – and 400 guns. About 5–6,000 deserted, 14,000 were captured. French sources give 19,300 dead and 33,800 wounded.

One marshal [Poniatowski] had been killed, and two others wounded, as were four commanding generals; five generals of division had been killed, seven wounded; ten brigadiers killed, thirty wounded; five adjutant commandants were killed, eight wounded. Colonels – nine killed, thirty-four wounded; field officers – thirty-five killed, 125 wounded.

The following generals – some wounded – were captured after the Elster bridge was destroyed:

French: Reynier and Lauriston, Arle, d'Aubry, d'Augeranville, Bertrand, Bony, Charpentier, Chassot, Harlet, d'Henin, Mandeville, Oppeln, Pierrot, Valory and Vissot.

Confederation of the Rhine: Prinz Emil von Hessen, the Markgraf von Baden, the Saxons von Gersdorf, von Zeschau and von Bose; von Jett, von Rauchhaupt, von Scheffer and von Stockhorn.

Poles: Axamitowski, Bronikowski, Grabowski, Kaminiecki, Krasinski, Rautenstrauch and Uminski.

Croats: Slivarich.

The Prussians lost at least 20,000 (Kleist lost 9,500, Bülow certainly more than 2,000, Yorck 7,400).

I thus assess the real Allied loss from 14th–19th October at 72,000 men (not counting about 4,000 prisoners). A French source gives 32,509 dead and 45,000 wounded. Ten generals were dead, nineteen wounded, one captured.

In all, 120,000 lives must have been lost at Leipzig either directly or due to wounds [and sickness?].

One thing is sure, 40–50,000 bodies lay on the battlefield.

Official Allied lists show the following losses from 16–19 October (after the Austrian Kriegs-Archiv, Quistorp, and Plotho) and speak volumes for the relative efforts of the nations involved:

	Officers	Men
Russians	865	21,740
Prussians	498	15,556
Austrians	419	14,541
Swedes	12	203
Totals	*1,794*	*52,040*

Expressed by armies, the losses were as shown below:

	Officers	Men
Army of Bohemia	1,114	36,469
Army of Silesia	487	9,779
Army of Poland	70	3,000
Army of the North	123	2,792

The raging flood of the war now ebbed quickly away to the west, leaving sorely-tried Saxony and its capital – in the centre of a wide belt of nearly total devastation – to lick its wounds and try to recover from the trauma. Firstly there were the wounded and the sick of the armies that filled the city and every surrounding village; to these were added, very rapidly, thousands of civilians sick from weakness and from disease resulting from the presence of so many corpses, the lack of food and shelter, and the absence of hygiene, medical facilities, doctors and medicine.

Allied pursuit was not as energetic as it might have been. The vital Elster bridge had to be repaired and the Allied armies needed to regroup following the capture of the city, which had thrown their corps into complete confusion. Gyulai's weak corps and some cavalry from Bennigsen's Reserve Army of Poland were initially the only Allied formations on the heels of the *Grande Armée* as it hurried westwards to the great depot at Erfurt.

At Lützen on 20 October, Bennigsen's cavalry caught up with and captured about 2,000 stragglers, and next day there occurred two sharp actions, at Frieburg on the Unstrut and Kösen on the Saale, as Napoleon sought to make a clean break from his tormentors. At Freiburg, the advanced guard of Yorck's I Prussian Corps came up just too late to block the river crossing for Napoleon's main body, but did cause him about 2,000 casualties and captured eighteen guns. Gyulai managed to save the bridge at Kösen which the French IV Corps had been sent to destroy in order to seal off the southern flank of the *Grande Armée*'s withdrawal.

Next day, at Eckartsberga, Napoleon gave Gyulai a smart check in a clash about twenty kilometres north of Jena, and then marched on to reach Erfurt in safety. According to Grabowski, the French army reached Erfurt with 70,000 men fit for duty with the colours and some thousands of stragglers.

After hastily regrouping and re-equipping his army in the depot at Erfurt, the Emperor was off again, racing for the safety of the Rhine and his reserves in France. He inflicted a check on Blücher with Yorck's corps at the Hörselberge mountain barrier on the road between Weimar and Eisenach on 26 October and hurried on to seize the defile at Gelnhausen on the 29th before the Austro-Bavarians[66] under the Bavarian General Graf von Wrede could block him there. Wrede refused to believe that he was facing Napoleon's main body at Hanau on 30 October, and his dispositions for the action were pitiful. He had left his artillery train in Uffenheim (120 kilometres away to the south) and he completely underestimated his enemy, well deserving the defeat that followed. As Napoleon said when he saw Wrede's troops drawn up with the river Kinzig at their backs: 'Well, I made him a count, but I could not make him a general.'

The Austro-Bavarians were pushed aside on 30 and 31 October with heavy loss. Napoleon passed Frankfurt/Main on the 31st and reached and crossed

---

[66] Austria and Bavaria had signed the Treaty of Ried on 8 October, whereby Bavaria declared war on France.

the Rhine into the safety of the fortress of Mainz. He had won his race. According to Grabowski his army crossed the Rhine with about 40,000 men with the colours and a further 40,000 stragglers. There was a rearguard action at Hochheim on 9 November, but the 1813 campaign was to all intents and purposes over. The several French garrisons in the fortresses on the Vistula and the Elbe fell into Allied hands as all hope of relief faded. The most spectacular was the surrender of Dresden on 11 November, when Marshal Gouvion Saint-Cyr and two whole corps went into captivity. Hamburg, Magdeburg, Mainz and Wesel held out until Napoleon's abdication ended the war.

Blücher opened the 1814 campaign on New Year's Day, when he crossed the Rhine at Kaub to carry the war into France.

***

The effects of the Allied victory at Leipzig were truly momentous. It had smashed Napoleon's stranglehold on Europe for good, opened up European markets for external international trade for the first time since the Berlin Decrees six years earlier, destroyed the Confederation of the Rhine, liberated Germany, catapulted Prussia into the ranks of the Continent's leading powers, and laid the basis for the final defeat and dethronement of Napoleon and the restoration of the Bourbons.

The blind faith which thousands had previously placed in the Emperor also began to fade. On 22 October, Murat, his own brother-in-law, had a secret meeting with the Austrian General Graf Mier near Erfurt, to sound out the possibility of changing sides and retaining his crown. Napoleon learned of this, but only after Murat had left to return to Naples.

In his memoirs, written on Elba, Napoleon's account of these momentous events has little in common with the actual events of October 1813:

> In October I left Dresden in order to go to Magdeburg, on the left bank of the Elbe, in order to deceive the enemy. My plan was to cross to the right bank again at Wittenberg and to advance on Berlin. Various army corps had already arrived at Wittenberg, and the enemy's bridge at Dessau had been destroyed, when a letter from the king of Württemberg warned me that the king of Bavaria had suddenly changed sides and, without a declaration of war or any announcement, the Austrian and Bavarian troops on the Inn had joined together to form an army of 80,000 men[67] under the command of General von Wrede and was marching on the Rhine, and that soon 100,000 men would besiege Mainz.
>
> On receipt of this unexpected news, I felt obliged to change my plan of campaign which I had developed over two months ago and for which I had prepared fortresses and magazines. It had been my aim, under the protection of the fortresses and magazines of Torgau, Wittenberg, Magdeburg and Hamburg, to move the war into the zone between the Elbe and the Oder

---

[67] The total was actually 30,000.

(the French army held the fortresses of Glogau, Küstrin and Stettin on the latter's banks) and, according to circumstances, to relieve the Vistula fortresses of Danzig, Thorn and Modlin.

From this grand plan, one might have expected such a success that the coalition would have fallen apart and the German princes would have been confirmed in their loyalty and in their alliance with France. I had hoped that Bavaria would have waited fourteen days before she made a decision, and at that time, I calculated that she would not change her mind.

The armies clashed on the fields of Leipzig on the 16th October. The French army was victorious. The Austrians were defeated and thrown out of all their positions. A commander of one of the enemy corps, the Graf von Meerveldt, was captured.

On the 18th October, the victory was won by the French, despite the defeat suffered by the Duke of Ragusa [Marmont] on the 16th. Then the entire Saxon army, with sixty guns, went over to the enemy at one of the most vital points in the army's position and turned their guns on the French. Such base treachery was bound to bring about the ruin of the French army and to give all the honours of the day to the Allies. With half my guard I rushed up, defeated the Saxons and the Swedes and threw them out of their positions.[68]

The day of the 18th came to an end. The enemy fell back along the entire battle field, which remained in French hands. During the night, the French army moved to place itself behind the Elster and to open up direct communications with Erfurt, from whence it awaited the ammunition resupply which it needed. In the days from the 16th to the 18th it had fired over 150,000 cannon shots.

The treachery of various corps of the Confederation of the Rhine,[69] who had been contaminated by the example of the Saxons on the previous day, and the accident at the Leipzig bridge, which was demolished too soon, caused the still-victorious army extremely heavy losses.

The French army crossed the Saale at Weissenfels, where it was to reorganise itself and await ammunition resupply from Erfurt, which was available in adequate quantities, when we heard news of the Austro-Bavarian army. This had made forced marches and had reached the Main. I had to move against them. On 30th October they made contact with the French army, and fought a battle in front of Hanau, on the way to Frankfurt. Although the Austro-Bavarian army was strong and was in a good position,[70] it was completely defeated and thrown out of Hanau, which was occupied by Count Bertrand. The French army continued its withdrawal over the Rhine and crossed this river on the 2nd November.

---

[68] The reader will now know how exaggerated and untrue this claim is.

[69] Presumably Graf Normann and his 560 men and one gun.

[70] The Allies had 30,000 men to oppose 60,000 French, and the Allied deployment was tactically extremely weak and faulty.

Appendices

A: List of abbreviations

ADC   aide de camp; a personal assistant to a general.

Adj   adjutant; administrative assistant.

AdjC   adjutant-commandant; rank in the general staff equating to colonel.

AdjG   adjutant general; rank in the general staff equating to brigade commander.

Bde/bde   Brigade; a tactical formation of infantry or cavalry, usually consisting of three or more infantry battalions or two or more cavalry regiments. As will be noticed, the Prussian 'brigades' which took the field in 1813 were more the size of divisions.

Bn/bn   *Bataillon* (battalion); a tactical unit of from 600 to 1,000 infantry consisting of four or more companies.

Brandb   Brandenburg; a Prussian provincial designation.

Bty/bty   Battery.

Capt   captain.

Cav   cavalry.

ChaChR   *Chasseurs à Cheval* regiment; nominally mounted rifles but in fact light cavalry armed with smoothbore carbines.

ChaP   *Chasseurs à Pied*; rifles or light infantry.

ChBn   *chef de bataillon*; commander of an infantry battalion.

ChdE   *Chevalier de l'Empire* (Knight of the Empire).

Chef   the proprietor of a regiment; the regiment would bear his name.

ChEs   *chef de escadron*; commander of a cavalry squadron.

Chev   *chevalier* (knight).

ChLR   *Chevau-Léger*; light horse regiment.

ChLLR   *Chevau-Léger-Lanciers*; light horse lancer regiment.

Cie/cie   *Compagnie* (company); a tactical unit of infantry consisting of about 100 men, or half a squadron of cavalry, about 50 men.

Cmdr   commander.

Cmdt   commandant; usually of a static installation such as a depot, garrison, or fort.

Col   colonel; the most senior field officer below the rank of general.

CoS   chief of staff; an officer who manages the general staff of a formation in his commander's best interests.

Coy/coy   Company. See *Cie*.

CuirR   Cuirassier regiment.

DBde   *Demi-Brigade*, a term used in Revolutionary French armies of 1792–1803 to describe the tactical infantry equivalent of the old royalist 'Regiment'. It had three battalions. The term was also used in 1809 and 1813–15, usually to describe provisional or ad hoc units.

DBdeLe   *Demi-Brigade de Infanterie Légère*, a French tactical term used in the period 1792–1803 to describe a regiment of light infantry. Also encountered in 1809 and 1813–15.

DBdeLi	*Demi-Brigade de Infanterie de Ligne,* a French tactical term used in the period 1796–1803 – and in 1809 and 1813–15 – to describe a line infantry regiment.
Div/div	Division; a tactical formation consisting of two or more brigades.
Div Mil	*Division Militaire.*
DragR	*Dragon* or Dragoon regiment.
Eh	*Erzherzog* (Archduke).
en 1er	*en premier,* senior.
en 2e	*en seconde,* deputy.
FAB	foot artillery battery.
FM	field marshal or *feldmarschall.*
FML	*feldmarschall-leutnant,* an Austrian rank equating to the French GdD.
FZM	*feldzeugmeister,* an Austrian rank equating to French general.
GdB	*général de brigade.*
GdC	*general der cavalerie,* a rank in Austria, Prussia and Russia above the French GdD.
GdD	*général de division.*
GdI	*general der infanterie,* a rank in Austria, Prussia and Russia above the French GdD.
GdK	*general der kavalerie,* a rank in Austria, Prussia and Russia above the French GdD.
GdN	*Garde Nationale.*
Gen	General.
Gen Adj	General Adjutant; a high-ranking ADC to a General.
GFM	*general-feldmarschall,* a Prussian rank equating to field marshal.
GL	*generalleutnant,* equivalent to GdD.
GM	*generalmajor,* a rank in Austria, Prussia and Russia equating to the French GdB.
GoI	General of Infantry.
GQM	General Quartermaster.
GraCh	*Grenadiers à Cheval,* horse grenadiers.
GraP	*Grenadiers à Pied,* foot grenadiers.
Gren	grenadier.
GrenR	Grenadier regiment.
GS	general staff; a military management organisation designed to assist the commander.
GzIR	*Grenz-Infanterie-Regiment,* Austrian regiments raised in the areas of present-day Romania and what was Yugoslavia.
HA	horse artillery.
HAB	horse artillery battery.
Haupt	*Hauptmann.*
HC	heavy cavalry.
HusR	Hussar regiment.
IG	Imperial Guard.
Inf	infantry.
Insp Gen	Inspector General.
IR	infantry regiment.
JgBn	Jäger battalion.

JgR	*Jäger-Regiment*; rifle regiment.
K	killed.
Kapt	*kapitän* (captain).
Kurmk	Kurmark; a Prussian provincial designation.
KürR	*Kürassier-Regiment*; the equivalent of Cuirassiers.
LC	light cavalry.
Le	*Légère.*
LG	*Leib-Garde*, Life Guards.
Li	*Ligne.*
LI	line infantry.
LIR	line infantry regiment.
Lt	lieutenant; a junior commissioned officer, below the rank of captain but above that of *sous lieutenant.*
LtCol	lieutenant-colonel; a field officer above the rank of major but below that of colonel.
LtGen	lieutenant-general; a rank above GdD.
LW	*Landwehr.*
LWCR	*Landwehr-Cavallerie-Regiment*; Prussian cavalry regiments of the 'Territorial Army'.
LWIR	*Landwehr-Infanterie-Regiment*; Prussian infantry regiments of the 'Territorial Army'.
LWKR	*Landwehr-Kavallerie-Regiment*; Prussian cavalry regiments of the 'Territorial Army'.
M	*Maréchal* or Marshal.
Maj	major; a field officer below the rank of lieutenant-colonel.
MG	major-general; the most junior grade of general.
MtdRR	Mounted Rifle Regiment; Russian equivalent of the French Chasseurs à Cheval.
MuskR	Musketeer Regiment; Russian designation for line infantry.
MW	mortally wounded.
NCO	non-commissioned officer (*sous-officier* in French).
NCR	National Cavalry Regiment.
Neum	Neumark; a Prussian provincial designation.
NR	number.
Obst	*Oberst*; German equivalent of colonel.
ObstLt	*Oberstleutnant*; German equivalent of lieutenant-colonel.
OG	Old Guard.
Olt	*Oberleutnant*; German equivalent of lieutenant.
OOB	order of battle.
OstPr	*Ostpreussisch* (East Prussian); a provincial regimental designation.
pdrs	pounders; refers to the weight of shot fired by a gun.
Pomm	Pommeranian; a provincial regimental designation.
Prlt	*premierleutnant*; a Prussian rank equating to lieutenant.
Pv	provisional.
PW	prisoner of war.
QM	quarter master; a senior NCO or officer appointed to manage logistics.
QMG	Quartermaster General.
RAM	*Régiment Artillerie de la Marine.*
Regt	regiment.
ResIR	*Reserve-Infanterie-Regiment.*

RIdLi	*Régiment Infanterie de Ligne.*
RILe	*Régiment Infanterie Légère.*
Rttm	Rittmeister; cavalry captain.
Schl	Schlesisch; Silesian, a Prussian provincial designation.
Sklt	*sekondeleutnant;* second lieutenant, a Prussian rank equating to French *sous-lieutenant.*
Sqn	squadron.
Stkapt	*stabskapitän;* junior captain, a Prussian infantry rank.
Strttm	*stabsrittmeister;* junior captain, a Prussian cavalry rank.
Tirs	*Tirailleurs;* skirmishers or light infantry.
UlR	*Ulan-Regiment;* lancer regiment.
Vol	volunteers.
Volts	*Voltigeurs* (literally 'vaulters'); light infantry soldiers.
WestPr	*Westpreussisch* (West Prussian); a Prussian provincial designation.
YG	Young Guard.

B: The French order of battle at Leipzig

This is based on a combination of two highly detailed sources, one compiled by George Nafziger, based on French archive documents, Fabry, Rousset, Quistorp, and the *Spectateur Militaire* of 1827; the other compiled by Herr Peter Ihbe of Dessau and based on Aster, Bleibtreu, Kerchnawe, the Raddatz collection, Quistorp, von Stön, and a very detailed but anonymous listing. The reader will note the numerous differences between the two resultant OOBs. To highlight these, whereas the Nafziger data is shown in normal type, where the Ihbe data differs it is shown in **bold type**. It is very doubtful that either version reflects the actual situation on the ground on 16 October with total accuracy, but no better sources are known.

IMPERIAL HEADQUARTERS

PETIT QUARTIER GENERALE
Cmdr: **The Emperor Napoleon I.**
Personal Adj: **Col Bernard; Imperial interpreter: Chev Lelerque d'Ideville; Imperial pages: Devienne, Ferreri, Martarieu, St Perne.**
General Adjs: GdDs Baron Corbineau (commanded a cavalry division in the I Cavalry Corps), **Baron Dejean, Baron Drouot, Lebrun, Duc de Piacenza; GdBs Baron Flahaut, Baron Gucheneux, Kirsakowski, Pac,** Col Bernard (Engineers).
Emperor's Cabinet: **Baron Fain, Baron Mounier, ChdE Jouanne, ChdE Prevost.**
Chief of the Secret Police: **Capt Wasowicz (two Saxon officers).**
Topographical Bureau: **Col Bacler d'Albe, Capts Duvivier, Lameau.**
Orderly officers: **Maj Baron Gourgoud, Capts Baron Athalin, Baron Caramon, Baron Dessaix, von Grabowski, ChdE Lamezan, Baron Laplace, Baron Lauriston, Baron de Mortemart, Pailhou, ChdE Protet, Reytan, ChdE de St.Marsan.**

QUARTIER GENERALE DU MAJOR GENERALE
CoS: **M Alexander Berthier, Prince of Neufchatel, Duc de Wagram.**
Staff of the CoS: **Aide: MG Count Bailly de Monthion; 1st Adj: GdB Durieu.**

Cabinet of the CoS: **Troop movements: Capt Salamon; Commissar for Payments: Secretary Le Duc; Inspectors of Reviews: Dufresne, Denniée; Commissar: Guillabert; Assistants: Belle, Huguet, Latran, Lechantre, Riancey.**
Adjs to the GS: **Cols Beaugard, Denzel, Fodras, Fontenille, Gablois, Lazinski, Lecouteaux, Lejeune, Le Pernet, Mondreville.** Other sources add Cols Falkowski, Lacsinski 'and others'.
Orderly Officers to the GS: **Cmdr: Col Paris.** The orderly officers were very numerous and included six Poles and several from the Confederation of the Rhine.
Generals à la suite of the Imperial Headquarters: **GdDs Cassagne, Decouz, Games-Frayre; GdBs Dellard, Esteve, Latour, Thomas.**
Cmdr of the Artillery: GdD Count Sorbier.
GS of the Artillery: **CoS: Col Chauveau;** *Insp Gen*: **GdD Drouot;** *General Director of the Park*: **GdB Neigre.**
Cmdr of the Engineers: GdD Baron Rogniat; *Insp Gen*: **GdD Dejean;** *CoS*: **Col Montfort;** *Cmdr of the Engineer Park*: **Maj Finod.**
Cmdr of the GHQ: GdD Durrieu.
Cmdr of the GHQ Train: **GdD Guillemeriot.**
Cmdr of the Bridging Train: **GdB Bouchu.**
Insp Gen of the Baggage Train: **GdB Picard.**

QUARTIER GENERALE DE L'INTENDANT
Administration Director: **Count Daru.**
General Intendant: **Gen Count Dumas.**
Army Chief Paymasters: **Joinville, Marchand, Martellière.**
Chief Inspector of Reviews: **Gen Lambert.**
Chief Inspector of Depots and Hospitals: **GdD Sahuc.**
Medical Services: *Insp Gen of Medicine and Chief Doctor*: **Baron Desgenettes;** *Insp Gen of Surgery and Chief Surgeon*: **Baron Larry;** *Insp Gen of Pharmaceuticals and Chief Chemist*: **Baron Laubert.**
Master of Horse: **GdD Caulaincourt, Duc de Vicence.**
Cmdr of the Escort, Relay and Courier Service: **Gen Guyot.**
Cmdt of the Gendarmerie: **GdB Badet.**
Cmdr of the Lifeguards of the Guides: **ChEs Bessières jnr.**
Cmdr of security services: **Col Nequenen, Cmdt of the Gendarmerie d'Elite.**
Court officials: *Major-domo*: **Baron Yvan;** *1st Chamberlain*: **Count de Turenne;** *Palace Prefect*: **Count de Beausset;** *Palace QM*: **Baron de Banouville, Barons de Mesgriny, Mentarau, van Lenneps;** *Imperial Paymaster*: **Peyrousse.** There were four doctors appointed to the court.

Southern Front (Right Wing) Cmdr: M Murat, King of Naples; *Adj*: **Col Vantier;** *CoS*: **GdD Count Belliard;** *Orderly officer*: **Capt Malczawski.**

Northern Front (Left Wing) Cmdr: M Ney, Prince de la Moskwa, Duc d'Elchingen; *CoS*: **GdD Count Bechet de Levcour.**

THE IMPERIAL GUARD

THE OLD GUARD
Cmdr of the Guard Foot Artillery: Col Griois
Cmdr of the Guard Horse Artillery: Col Duchand.

1*re* Div, GdD Count Friant.

1*re* Bde, GdB Christiani (actually **Michel**): 1*er* GraP, 2*e* GraP (2 bns each).

2*e* Bde, GdB Baron Michel (actually **Christiani**): 1*er* ChaP, 2*e* ChaP (2 bns each).

Artillery: 1*er* and 2*e* OG FABs (6 × 6-pdrs [**only 1 × FAB of 8-pdrs**), 6 × 12-pdrs, 2 × 6-inch and 2 × 5.7-inch howitzers) & Artillery Train.

Total: 6,255 men, 16 guns.

2*e* Div, GdD Baron Curial.

1*re* Bde, GdB Rousseau: Fusilier-Chasseurs, Fusilier-Grenadiers (2 bns each); Velites de Florence, Vélites de Turin (1 bn each).

2*e* Bde, GdB Rothembourg: Saxon Leib-Grenadier-Garde, Polish Guards, West-falian Guards (1 bn each). (**The Westfalian Guard Bn consisted of the Garde-Füsilier-Regt and the elite companies of the 2nd and 3rd LIRs. This Bn was attached to the Reserve Artillery of the Guard as escort. Bleibtreu reckons that the Old Guard had only 8,000 men on 14 October.**)

Artillery: 10*e* and 14*e* YG FABs (12 × 6-pdrs and 4 × 5.7-inch howitzers) & Artillery Train.

Total: 4,664 men, 16 guns.

I CORPS OF THE YOUNG GUARD

M Oudinot, Duc de Reggio.

1*re* Div, GdD Pacthod (**originally GdD Dumoustier**).

1*re* Bde, GdB Lacoste: 1*er* and 2*e* Volts (2 bns each) (**1*er*, 2*e*, 3*e* & 6*e* Volts, 2 bns each**).

2*e* Bde, GdB Couloumy: 3*e* and 4*e* Volts (2 bns each) (**7*e* & 11*e* Volts, 2 bns each**).

3*e* Bde, GdB Gros: 11*e* Tirs, 11*e* Volts (2 bns each) (**No 3*e* Bde**).

Artillery: 1*er*, 2*e* & 8*e* YG FABs (18 × 6-pdrs, 6 × 5.7-inch howitzers) & Artillery Train.

Total: 6,044 men, 24 guns.

3*e* Div, GdD Decouz.

1*re* Bde, GdB Boyer de Rebeval. 5*e*, 6*e* & 7*e* Volts (2 bns each) (**4*e*, 5*e* and 8*e* Volts, 2 bns each**).

2*e* Bde, GdB Pélet: 8*e*, 9*e* & 10*e* Volts (2 bns each) (**9*e*, 10*e* & 12*e* Volts, 2 bns each**).

Artillery: 9*e*, 11*e* & 13*e* YG FABs (18 × 6-pdrs, 6 × 5.7-inch howitzers) & Artillery Train.

Total: 4,731 men, 24 guns.

II CORPS OF THE YOUNG GUARD

M Mortier, Duc de Treviso.

CoS: **Col Lapointe.**

Adj: **Capt Kierskowski.**

2*e* Div, GdD Barrois.

1*re* Bde, GdB Poret de Morvan: 1*er*, 2*e* & 3*e* Tirs (2 bns each).

2*e* Bde, **GdB Dulong**?: 4*e*, 5*e* & 6*e* Tirs (2 bns each).

Artillery: 3*e*, 4*e* & 12*e* YG FABs (18 × 6-pdrs, 6 × 5.7-inch howitzers) & Artillery Train. **1 cie sappers.**

Total: 5,470 men, 24 guns.

4*e* Div, GdD Roguet.

1*re* Bde, GdB Flamand: Flanquer-Grenadiers, Flanquer-Chasseurs, 7*e* Tirs (2 bns each) (**4*e* & 5*e* Tirs instead of 7*e*, 2 bns each**).
2*e* Bde, GdB Marguet (**Marquet**): 8*e*, 9*e* & 10*e* Tirs (2 bns each).
Artillery: 5*e*, 6*e* & 7*e* YG FABs (18 × 6-pdrs, 6 × 5.7-inch howitzers) & Artillery Train.
Total: 5,521 men, 24 guns.

RESERVE ARTILLERY OF THE GUARD
GdD Dulauloy.
3*e*, 4*e*, 5*e* & 6*e* OG FABs (24 × 12-pdrs, 8 × 6-inch howitzers), 1*re* & 2*e* OG HABs (8 × 6-pdrs, 4 × 7-inch howitzers), Grand Duchy of Berg HAB (4 × 6-pdrs, 2 × 5.7-inch howitzers) & Artillery Train.
Total: 3,911 men, 50 guns.

Sappeurs: 2 cies; *Génie:* 12 cies (1*re*–12*e* cies); Guard Equipage Train Bn; Guard Engineering Train Cie. No manpower given.

Total, II Corps, Young Guard: 14,902 men (**16,966 infantry, 2,500 artillery & sappers**), *98 guns.*

ARTILLERY OF THE IMPERIAL GUARD
Cmdr: **GdD Dulauloy.**
CoS: **GdB Lallemand.**

Reserve Artillery, Col Griois: 4 × 12-pdr FABs (32 guns), 1 × 8-pdr FAB (8 guns). GdB Baron Desvaux de St-Maurice: 2 × French HABs (12 guns), 1 × HAB (6 guns) of the Grand Duchy of Berg.
Foot Artillery of the Young Guard, GdB Henrion: 2 × FABs (16 guns); Westfalian Guard Battalion.
Total: 10 batteries, 2,750 men.

Génie, **Col Boisonnet** (no such colonel in the French army according to Six): **2 cies sappers, 12 cies** *Gendarmerie.*
Total: 1,161 men.

Total, Artillery of the Imperial Guard: 3,911 men.

Aster, Quistorp and FML von Stön all give the overall strength of the Young Guard as 20,000 men; on 16 October Bleibtreu has them with 17,000, which must be only the infantry.

GUARD CAVALRY CORPS
GdD Count Nansouty.
CoS: ?
Cmdr of the Artillery: **GdB Desvaux.**

1*re* Div, GdD Count Ornano.
1*re* Bde, GdB Colbert: Grand Duchy of Berg ChLR (5 [**6**] sqns), 2*e* (Dutch) ChLLR (**Col Dubois**) (10 [**4**] sqns).
2*e* Bde, Col (**GdB**) Pinteville: DragR 'YG' (2 sqns).
Artillery: 6*e* OG HAB (4 × 6-pdrs, 2 × 5.7-inch howitzers) & Artillery Train.
*Total: 1,518 (**1,861**) men, 6 guns.*

2*e* Div, GdD Lefebvre-Desnouëttes.

1*re* Bde, GdB Krasinski: 1*er* (Polish) ChLLR (4 [**10**] sqns) (**ChaCh 'YG', 4 sqns**).
2*e* Bde, GdB Castex: GraCh 'YG' (2 sqns), ChaCh 'YG' (4 sqns).
Artillery: 5*e* OG HAB (4 × 6-pdrs, 2 × 5.7-inch howitzers), 1 cie Artillery Train.
Total: 1,618 (1,585) men, 6 guns.

3*e* Div, GdD Count Walther.
1*re* Bde, GdB Baron Lyon: 1*er* (Polish) ChLLR 'OG' (**Col Prince Radziwill**) (3 sqns), 4*e* Regt Gardes d'Honneur (**Col Count de Clermont-Tonnère**) (1 [**4**] sqn), ChaCh 'OG' (**with the Mamelukes**) (6 sqns), 1*er* Regt Gardes d'Honneur (**Col de Castellane**) (2 [**4**] sqns).
2*e* Bde, GdB Letort (**Lefort**): Drag de l'Imperatrice 'OG' (4 sqns), 2*e* Regt Gardes d'Honneur (2 sqns).
3*e* Bde, GdB Lafferière: GraCh 'OG' (4 sqns), 3*e* [**2e**] Regt Gardes d'Honneur (**Col d'Ambrugeac**) (1 [**4**] sqn).
Artillery: 3*e* & 4*e* OG HABs (**1 × HAB**) (8 × 6-pdrs, 4 × 5.7-inch howitzers), 2 cies Artillery Train.
Total: 4,457 cavalrymen, 450 artillerymen, 12 guns (3 × batteries).

Quistorp gives Guard cavalry strength as 9,800 men, Bleibtreu as 8,000; von Stön gives 61 sqns and 3 × HABs = 7,903 men.

Total, Imperial Guard: 44,499 men, 218 guns.

II CORPS
M Victor, Duc de Belluno.
CoS: **GdB Château.**
Cmdr of the Artillery: **GdB Mongenet.**
Cmdr of the Engineers: **Maj Bron.**

4*e* Div, GdD Dubreton.
1*re* Bde, GdB Ferrière: 24*e* RILe & 19*e* RIdLi (**Col Trupel**) (1*er*, 2*e*, 4*e* Bns each).
2*e* Bde, GdB Brun: 37*e* & 56*e* RIdLi (1*er*, 2*e*, 4*e* Bns each).
Artillery: 2 × FABs (12 × 6-pdrs, 4 × 5.7-inch howitzers), 2 cies Artillery Train.
Total: 5,618 men, 16 guns.

5*e* Div, GdD Dufour.
1*re* Bde, GdB D'Etzko: 26*e* RILe & 39*e* RIdLi (1*er*, 2*e*, 4*e* Bns each).
2*e* Bde, GdB ?: 46*e* & 72*e* RIdLi (1*er* Bn of each). **These regiments were reduced from 3 to 1 bn each after Kulm; they also lost their artillery in this battle.**
Artillery: 1 × FAB (6 × 6-pdrs, 2 × 5.7-inch howitzers), 1 cie Artillery Train.
Total: 4,235 men, 8 guns.

6*e* Div, GdD Vial.
1*re* Bde, GdB Valory: 11*e* RILe (**Col Triburzio Sebastiani**), 4e RIdLi (1*er*, 2*e*, 4*e* Bns each).
2*e* Bde, GdB Bronikowski: 2*e* (**Col Materre**) & 18*e* (**Col Sausset**) RIdLi (1*er*, 2*e*, 4*e* Bns each).
Artillery: 2 × FABs (12 × 6-pdrs, 4 × 5.7-inch howitzers), 2 cies Artillery Train.
Total: 6,325 men, 16 guns.

The corps' light cavalry bde (1st & 2nd Westfalian Hussars) had gone over to the Allies on 23 August.

Total, II Corps: 16,178 men, 40 guns.

As losses since 1 October had been few, and as reinforcements had been received with Lefol's column, the corps still had 16,500 men on 14 October. Friedrich gives 16,731. But he gives GdB D'Etzko's Bde as being 26*e* RILe & 96*e* RIdLi, and Valory's Bde as 11*e* RILe & 2*e* RIdLi.

III CORPS
GdD Count Souham (as of 5 October).
CoS: **GdB Tarayre.**
Cmdr of the Artillery: **GdB Chabronnel.**
Cmdr of the Engineers: **GdB Valaze.**

8*e* Div, GdD Baron Brayer.
1*re* Bde, GdB J. Fournier: 6*e* RILe (2*e*, 3*e* Bns), 16*e* RILe (2*e*, 3*e* Bns), 40*e* RIdLi (3*e*, 4*e* Bns).
2*e* Bde, GdB Bony: 28e RILe (1*er*, 3*e* Bns), 22*e* RIdLi (1*er*, 3*e*, 4*e* Bns), 59*e* RIdLi (2*e*, 3*e* Bns), 69*e* RIdLi (3*e*, 4*e* Bns).
1*re* Bde, GdB Boney: 6*e* Pv Regt (6*e* & 25*e* RILe, 2 bns), 10*e* Pv Regt (16*e* & 28*e* RILe, 2 bns), 14*e* Pv Regt (34*e* & 40*e* RIdLi, 2 bns), 19*e* Pv Regt (32*e* & 58*e* RIdLi, 2 bns).
2*e* Bde, GdB Baron Charrière: 21*e* Pv Regt (59*e* & 69*e* RIdLi, 2 bns), 24*e* Pv Regt (88*e* & 103*e* RIdLi, 2 bns).
Artillery: 2 × FABs & Artillery Train.
*Total: 5,491 (**4,442**) men, 16 guns.*

9*e* Div, GdD Delmas.
1*re* Bde, GdB Esteve (**d'Anthing**): 2*e* Pv Regt (2*e* RILe & 4*e* RILe [3*e* Bn each], 136*e* RIdLi [1*er*, 2*e*, 3*e* Bns]) (**Col d'Aubreme**).
2*e* Bde, GdB Maran (**Vergez des Brareaux**): 138*e* (**Col Maran**) & 145*e* (**Col Delisie**) RIdLi (1*er*, 2*e*, 3*e* Bns each).
Artillery: 2 × FABs & Artillery Train.
*Total: 4,800 (**4,235**) men, **13 guns.***

11*e* Div, GdD Ricard.
1*re* Bde, GdB Charrière (**Vandedem van der Gelder**): 9*e* RILe (3*e*, 4*e*, 6*e* Bns), 50*e* (2*e*, 3*e*, 4*e* Bns) & 65*e* (3*e*, 4*e* Bns) RIdLi, **17*e* Pv Regt (43*e* & 75*e* RIdLi, 1 bn each).**
2*e* Bde, GdB Vergez (**Dumoulin**): 142*e* & 144*e* RIdLi (1*er*, 2*e*, 3*e* Bns each).
Artillery: 2 × FABs & Artillery Train.
*Total: 5,280 (**4,357**) men, 12 guns.*

23*e* Light Cavalry Bde, GdB Baron Buermann.
10*e* HusR (**Col Curely**) (6 sqns), Baden Light DragR (**LtCol von Degenfeld**) (5 sqns).
Artillery: 1 × French HAB (6 guns) & Artillery Train.
Total: 1,065 men, 6 guns.
Artillery: $\frac{1}{2}$ HAB (3 guns), $\frac{1}{2}$ cie Artillery Train.
Total: 1,078 men, 3 guns.

Light Cavalry Bde, GdB Aximatowski (attached from IV Corps): 4*e*, 5*e*, 12*e*, 14*e*, 24*e* DragRs (1 sqn each).
Total: 722 men.

Corps Artillery Park: 2 × FABs, 1 × HAB (**HAB not shown by Ihbe**) (18 [**16**]) guns), 3 cies Artillery Train, 3 cies Spanish Sappers, 1 cie Gendarmerie, a detachment of Train d'Equipage.
Total: 3,791 men, 18 (16) guns.

Total, III Corps: 20,783 (17,168) men, 78 (63) guns.
According to Ihbe, the 10e Div had been transferred to V Corps.

IV CORPS
GdD Count Bertrand.
CoS: **GdB Baron Delort.**
Cmdr of the Artillery: **GdD Tavel or Col Mervon.**
Cmdr of the Engineers: **Col Izoard.**

12e Div, GdD Count Morand.
1re Bde, GdB Belair: 8e RILe (**Col Guyard**) (1er–4e Bns).
2e Bde, GdB Toussaint: 13e RIdLi (**Col Lucas**) (1er–4e Bns).
3e Bde, GdB Hulot: 23e (1er, 2e, 4e Bns) & 137e (**Col Gaillard**) (1er, 2e, 3e Bns) RIdLi.
Artillery: 2 × FABs, 2 cies Artillery Train.
Total: 5,705 men, 12 guns.
According to Bleibtreu the 2e Bn 13e RIdLi was captured at Dahme on 7 September. The 137e RIdLi came from the disbanded XII Corps.

15e (Italian) Div, GdD Count Fontanelli.
1re Bde, GdB St Andrea: 1st LIR (**Col Moretti**) (2 bns), 6th LIR (**ChBn Varese**) (1 bn).
2e Bde, GdB Martel (**GdB Moroni**): 1st & 4th LIRs (1 bn cach) (**1st, 4th [Col Ceccopieri], 6th [Col Ferru] & 7th [Col Rossi] LIRs, 1 bn each**).
3e Bde, GdB Moroni: Milan Guard (1 bn), 7th LIR (1 bn) (**No 3e Bde and no Milan Guard. According to Bleibtreu most of the Milan Guard were captured at Luckau in mid-September**). Luckau actually took place on 4 June, and the Italians were not involved; however, they were in the French defeat at Dennewitz (Juterbog) on 6 September so probably suffered the losses intimated by Bleibtreu and by Ihbe's data then.
Artillery: 1 Italian FAB & Artillery Train.
Total: 1,859 men, 6 guns.

38e (Württemberg) Div, GL Count von Franquemont.
1re Bde, GM von Stockmayer: 1st Combined Light Bn, 1st (**LtCol von Stumpe**), 2nd (**Col Prinz Hohenlohe**) & 3rd (**Col von Misani**) Combined Line Bns. **Light Bn not shown by Ihbe.**
24e (Württemberg) Light Cavalry Bde, GM von Jett: 1st ChLR 'Prinz Adam' (LtCol von Bismark), 3rd ChLR 'Herzog Ludwig' (Col von Gainsberg) (1 sqn each). *Total: 125 men.*
Artillery: 1 Württemberg HAB (6 guns) & Artillery Train coy.
On 19 October 41 men, 22 horses & 1 gun of this battery went over to the Allies.
Total: 1,168 (1,043) men, 6 guns.

29e Light Cavalry Bde, GM von Wolff: Westfalian ChLR (**Col von Berger**), Hessen-Darmstadt Garde-ChLR (**Capt von Boyneburg**) (1 sqn each).
Total: 221 men.

Reserve Artillery: 1 × French FAB (8 guns), 1 cie Artillery Train, 1 (**3**) cie sappers, 1 cie Gendarmerie.
Total: 871 men, 6 guns.

Total, IV Corps: *10,444 (9,824) men, 34 guns.*

V CORPS
GdD Count Lauriston.
CoS: GdB **Baillot.**
Cmdr of the Artillery: GdB **Canas.**
Cmdr of the Engineers: **Col Lamar.**

Parade states as of 1 October.

10*e* Div, GdD Albert.
1*re* Bde, GdB Bachelet: 4*e* Pv RILe (5*e* & 12*e* RILe, 4*e* Bns each), 139*e* RIdLi (1*er*, 2*e*, 3*e* Bns). (12*e* RILe left this Div on 10 October to return to main body of 12*e* RILe in 42*e* Div.)
2*e* Bde, GdB Bertrand: 140*e* RIdLi, 141*e* RIdLi (1*er*, 2*e*, 3*e* Bns each).
Artillery: 2 × FABs (8 × 6-pdrs, 2 × 5.7-inch howitzers) & Artillery Train.
Total: 3,721 (3,250) men, 10 guns.

16*e* Div, GdD Maison.
1*re* Bde, GdB Mandeville (**Montevalle**): 152*e* & 153*e* RIdLi (1*er*, 2*e*, 3*e* Bns each).
2*e* Bde, GdB Simmer (**Montesquieu**): **153*e* &** 154*e* RIdLi (1*er*, 2*e*, 3*e* Bns **each**).
Artillery: 2 × FABs (8 × 6-pdrs, 2 × 5.7-inch howitzers) & Artillery Train.
Total: 3,928 (3,627) men, 10 guns.

19*e* Div, GdD Rochambeau.
1*re* Bde, Lafitte (**Harlet**): 135*e* & 149*e* RIdLi (1*er*, 2*e*, 3*e* Bns each) (**149*e* not in Ihbe**).
2*e* Bde, Harlet (**Lafitte**): 150*e* & 155*e* RIdLi (1*er*, 2*e*, 3*e* Bns each).
Artillery: 2 × FABs (8 × 6-pdrs, 2 x 5.7-inch howitzers), 1 cie Artillery Train.
Total: 3,818 (3,656) men, 10 guns.

6*e* Light Cavalry Bde, GdB Dermoncourt or GdB Boyer (**Both are shown by Six to have commanded this brigade at Leipzig, but an eye-witness asserts that Boyer was commanding on 16 October**): 2*e* ChaChR (1*er*, 2*e*, 3*e* Sqns [**2 sqns**]), 3*e* ChaChR (1*er*, 2*e* Sqns), 6*e* ChaChR (1*er*, 2*e*, 3*e* Sqns).
Total: 700 (761) men.

Reserve Artillery & Park: 3 (**2**) × FABs (11 × 12-pdrs, 4 howitzers), 2 (**1**) × HABs (6 × 6-pdrs, 2 howitzers), 5 cies Artillery Train, 1 cie artillery artisans, 3 cies sappers.
Total: 872 men, 23 guns.

Total: V CORPS *13,039 (13,332) men, 53 guns.*
10*e* Div was transferred from III Corps after Puthod's [17th] Div of V Corps was reduced to 250 men in clash at Plagwitz [River Bober] on 29 August. Puthod's Div had consisted of 134*e*, 146*e* (Col Falcon), 147*e* (Col Sibuel), 148*e* RIdLi (3 bns each) and the Irish Regt (2 bns), and had totalled about 7,850 men.
As V Corps had a clash and forced march on 13 October, its strength would have dropped to 10,000 infantry, 700 cavalry, and 1,800 artillery, train etc.
Quistorp, in his *Geschichte der Nordarmee*, gives the following strengths for 15

October: 10*e* Div 11 bns, 3,966 men; 16*e* Div (Maison) 9 bns, 4,274 men; 19*e* Div (Rochambeau) 12 bns, 3,728 men.

Ihbe also shows the following OOB for V Corps for 14 October, taken from Bleibtreu's *Die Völkerschlacht bei Leipzig*:

16*e* Div, GdD Maison: 1*re* Bde GdB Penne, 139*e* (Col Genevay) & 140*e* RIdLi; 2*e* Bde GdB Reynaud, 152*e*, 153*e* & 154*e* RIdLi.

19*e* Div, GdD Rochambeau: 1*re* Bde GdB Baillot, 135*e* & 149*e* RIdLi; 2*e* Bde GdB Mandeville, 141*e* (Col Piguet), 150*e* (Col Dereiz) & 155e RIdLi (Col Jennegon). 6*e* Light Cavalry Bde, GdB Dermoncourt: 7 sqns of ChaCh (500 men).

VI CORPS
M Marmont, Duc de Ragusa.
CoS: **GdB Richemont.**
Cmdr of the Artillery: **GdD Foucher.**
Cmdr of the Engineers: **Maj Constantin.**

Parade states as for 1 October.

20*e* Div, GdD Count Compans.
1*re* Bde, GdB Baron Pelleport: 32*e* RILe (**Maj Cheneser**) (2*e*, 3*e* Bns), 1*er* RAM (**Col Maréchal**) (1*er*–5*e* Bns).
2*e* Bde, GdB Baron Joubert: 3*e* RAM (**Col Bormann**) (1*er*, 2*e*, 3*e* Bns), 20*e* Pv Regt (**Maj Druault**) (66*e* [5*e* Bn] & 122*e* RIdLi [3*e* Bn]), 25*e* Pv Regt (**Col Bochaton**) (47*e* & 86*e* RIdLi [3*e* Bn each]).
Artillery: 2 × FABs (12 × 6-pdrs, 4 × 5.7-inch howitzers), 2 cies Artillery Train. *Total: 4,846 (5,079) men, 16 guns.*

21*e* Div, GdD Count Lagrange.
1*re* Bde, GdB Baron Jamin: 37*e* RILe (**Col Jaquet**) (1*er*–4*e* Bns), 4*e* RAM (**Col Rouvroy**) (1*er*, 2*e*, 3*e* Bns), Regt Joseph Napoleon (**Maj Dimpre**) (1*er* Bn).
2*e* Bde, GdB Baron Buquet: 2*e* RAM (**Col Deschamps**) (1*er*–6*e* Bns).
Artillery: 2 × FABs (12 × 6-pdrs, 4 × 5.7-inch howitzers), 2 cies Artillery Train. *Total: 5,877 (5,543) men, 16 guns.*

22*e* Div, GdD Baron Friedrichs.
1*re* Bde, GdB Baron von Coehorn: 23*e* RILe (**Maj Jeannin**) (3*e* & 4*e* Bns), 11*e* Pv Regt (**Col Goujon**) (1*er* [4*e* Bn] & 62*e* RIdLi [2*e* Bn]), 13*e* Pv Regt (**Maj Cogne**) (14*e* [3*e* Bn] & 16*e* RIdLi [4*e* Bn]), 15*e* RIdLi (**Col de Rouge**) (3*e* & 4*e* Bns).
2*e* Bde, GdB Choisy: 16*e* Pv Regt (**Col Verbois**) (26*e* & 82*e* RIdLi [6*e* Bn each]), 70*e* (**Col Maury**) & 121*e* (**Maj Prost**) RIdLi (3*e* & 4*e* Bns each).
Artillery: 2 × FABs (12 × 6-pdrs, 4 × 5.7-inch howitzers) & Artillery Train. *Total: 5,891 (4,720) men, 16 guns.*

25*e* (Württemberg) Light Cavalry Bde, GM Count Normann (**He went over to the Allies on 18 October with 556 men & 1 gun**).
2nd **Leib-ChLR (Col Prinz Wallerstein)** & 4th **ChLR König (LtCol von Mylius)** (4 sqns each).
Artillery: Württemberg HAB (Lt von Fleischmann) (6 guns).
Total: 898 (935) men, 6 guns.

Reserve Artillery & Park: 3 (**2**) × FABs (18 × [**12-pdr**] guns, 6 × howitzers), 2 × HABs (8 × guns, 4 × howitzers), 5 cies Artillery Train, 1 platoon artillery artisans, 4 cies sappers, **38 Gendarmes**.

Total: 1,346 (2,553) men, 36 (28) guns.
In his memoirs, Marmont states that Col Marion commanded his engineers, but Six does not confirm this.

Total, VI Corps: 18,858 (19,304) men, 76 (68) guns.
According to Bleibtreu, three 'Naval Infantry Regiments' were detached and took no part in the battle; VI Corps strength thus fell to 17,700 men for Leipzig. Exactly which units are meant by this remark is unclear, but Martinien's lists show heavy officer casualties for all *Régiments Artillerie de la Marine* **at Leipzig.**

VII CORPS
GdD Count Reynier.
CoS: **GdB Baron Gressot.**
Cmdr of the Artillery: **GdB Baron Le Noury (or Col Verpau).**
Cmdr of the Engineers: **ChBn Bertard.**

13e Div, GdD Count Guilleminot.
1re Bde, GdB Gruyer: 1er (**Maj Fayard**) (4e Bn) & 18e RILe (**Col Bertrand**) (1er & 2e Bns), 7e (**Maj Georges**) (3e Bn) & 156e RIdLi (**ChBn Latolie**) (1er Bn).
2e Bde, GdB Baron Lejeune: 52e (**Maj Limouzin**) (3e Bn), 67e (**Col Tripoul**) (3e Bn) & 101e (**Col Robillard**) RIdLi (2e & 3e Bns), Regt Illyrian (2e Bn).
Artillery: 1 × FAB (6 × guns) & Artillery Train.
Total: ? men, 6 guns.
On 3 October 13e Div received 1er Bn, 18e RILe, from Pirna. On the same day, 4e Bn, 42e [sic] RIdLi (Col Pierre, 520 men) left for Torgau with the Park.
This new 13e Div consisted of the remnants of the divs of Guilleminot and Pacthod of the disbanded XII Corps, whose 17 bns were reorganised into 12, while 137e RIdLi (3 bns) went to Morand's 12e Div, IV Corps.

32e Div, GdD Baron Durutte.
1re Bde, GdB Baron Devaux: 35e RILe (1er Bn), 131e (**Col Maury**) (3e Bn) & 132e RIdLi (**Col Tridoulat**) (3e Bn).
2er Bde, GdB Baron Jarry: 36e RILe (**Col Baume**) (4e Bn), 133e RIdLi (**Col Menu**) (3e Bn), Würzburg IR (**Col Moser**) (3rd Bn).
Artillery: 1 × FAB (6 guns) & Artillery Train.
Total: ? men, 6 guns.

24e (Saxon) Div, GL von Zeschau.
CoS: **Maj von Cerrini.**
Cmdr of the Artillery: **LtCol von Raabe.**
1st Bde, GM (**Col von**) Brause: 1st LI Bn (**1st LIR von Lecoq [Maj von Rade]**), 1st Gren-Bn von Spiegel, LIR Prinz Friedrich **August (Maj von Brandt)** (1 bn), **LIR von Rechten (Maj von Hausen) (1 bn), LIR Steindel (Maj von Larisch) (1 bn).**
2nd Bde, GM von Ryssel: 2nd LI Bn (**LIR von Sahr [1 bn]**), 2nd Gren-Bn **Maj** von Anger, **LIR Prinz Anton (Maj von Holleuffer) (1 bn),** LIR von Niesemüschel (**Maj von Bose**) (1 bn), **Feld-**Jägers (1 coy).
Artillery: 1st × 12-pdr Saxon FAB (**Capt Dietrich**) (**8 guns**), **2nd** × 6-pdr Saxon **FAB (Capt Zandt),** 1 × HAB (**8 guns**) & Artillery Train.
Total: 4,547 men, 16 guns.
The LIR von Low (1 bn) under Capt Roos had left the Div and gone to Torgau with the main park. The Leib-Grenadier-Garde (1 bn) was attached to the

Imperial Guard. On 23 September, at Dessau, the LIR König (1 bn) had gone over to the Swedes.

26*e* (Saxon) Light Cavalry Bde, Col von Lindenau: Prinz Clements UlR (**Maj von Trotha I**) (5 sqns), HusR (**Maj Feilitsch**) (3–8 Sqns) (**8 sqns**).
Artillery: 1st HAB Birnbaum, 2nd HAB Grosshayn (**Capt Probsthain**) (4 guns).
Only 1 × HAB given by Ihbe, but both these HABs were in action at Paunsdorf on 18 October.
Total: 684 men, 4 guns.

Saxon Reserve Artillery: HAB (Capt von Birnbaum) (4 guns), 12-pdr FAB (Capt von Rouvroy I) (6 guns), 1 × French 12-pdr FAB (6 guns), 1 coy Saxon sappers.

Total, VII Corps: 12,637 men, 48 guns.
At ten o'clock on 18 October the 26*e* Light Cavalry Bde went over to Langeron's Russians at the Heiteren Blick; shortly after this, the LIR von Sahr went over to Platoff's Cossacks. At about two o'clock in the afternoon the Saxon artillery and most of the infantry went over to the Russians at Paunsdorf. The Leib-Grenadier-Garde, LIRs Prinz Friedrich August and Niesemüschel and the 1st Gren Bn von Spiegel remained with the French.

VIII (POLISH) CORPS
GdD Prince Poniatowski.
Adjs: Capts Kicki, Skorzewski, Lt Szydlowski.
CoS: GdD Rozniecki; *Deputy*: GdB Rautenstrauch.
Adjs to GS: Braun, Brodowski, Kostkowski, Potoulicki.
Cmdr of the Artillery: Col Redel.
Cmdr of the Engineers: Col Mallet.

26*e* Div, GdD Kamieniecki.
1st Bde, GdB Sierawski: Vistula Legion Regt (**Col Malcewski**) (1st & 2nd Bns), 1st (**Col Piotrowski**) & 16th LIRs (1st & 2nd Bns each).
2nd Bde, GdB Malachowski: 8th & 15th (**Col Strazewski**) LIRs (1st & 2nd Bns each).
Artillery: 3 × Polish FABs (14 guns).
Total: ? men, 14 guns.

27*e* Div, GdD Krasinski.
3rd Bde, GdB Grabowski: 12th & 14th LIRs (1st & 2nd Bns each).
Artillery: $4\frac{1}{2}$ ($1\frac{1}{2}$) × Polish FABs (? guns) & Artillery Train.
Total: ? men, ? guns.

27*e* Light Cavalry Bde, GdB Uminski: 14th CuirR (1st & 2nd Sqns), Krakus Regt (1st–4th Sqns).
Total: 700 men.

Polish Reserve Artillery: 2 × FABs with Artillery Train coys, 1 coy sappers, 1 Equipment Train detachment.
Total: ? men, 16 guns.

Total, VIII Corps: 5,000 men, ? guns.
On the evening of 16 October, Prince Poniatowski was promoted to Marshal of the Empire in recognition of the bravery of the Polish troops.
Zoltowski's bde and 1 FAB of the 27*e* Div had been detached to Dombrowski's

div. After the battle of Dresden 3,000 Austrian deserters of Polish nationality were taken into the corps; thirty to each company. Many of them continued to wear their old uniforms. At Leipzig, Aster reckons VIII Corps at 5,500 infantry and 1,300 artillery etc, Bleibtreu as 7,500. Since the end of September the Poles had been in several clashes and at Borna, on 10 October, they suffered some loss. A roll call of the infantry and artillery of VIII Corps on the evening of 18 October showed only 2,430 men present. On 19 October Col Rybinsky surrendered at the Peterstor with the remnants of the corps – about 500 men.

IX CORPS
M Augereau, Duc de Castiglione.
CoS: **GdD Monthion.**
Cmdr of the Artillery: **GdB Pellegrin.**
Cmdr of the Engineers: **GdB Dode.**

51*e* Div, GdD ?.
1*re* Bde, GdB Lagarde: 32*e* Pv DBde (2*e* Bn 25*e* RILe & 4*e* Bn 32*e* RILe), 63*e* RIdLi (2e Bn).
2*e* Bde, GdB Aymard: 34*e* Pv DBde (3*e* Bn 10e RILe & 2*e* Bn 21*e* RILe), 35*e* Pv DBde (3*e* Bn 32*e* RIdLi & 2*e* Bn 58*e* RIdLi).
Artillery: 3 × FABs (? guns) & Artillery Train cies.
Total: 4,350 men, 18 guns.

52*e* Div, GdD Semelle.
1*re* Bde, GdB Bagneris: 37*e* Pv DBde (2*e* Bn 17*e* RILe & 4*e* Bn 29*e* RILe), 39*e* RIdLi (1 bn).
2*er* Bde, GdB Godard: 2*e* Bn 86*e*, 6*e* Bn 121*e* & 6e Bn 122*e* RIdLi.
Total: 4,297 men, ? guns.

Reserve Artillery: 2 × FABs (? guns) & Artillery Train cies, 1 cie sappers, 1 Engineering Train cie.
Total: 539 men, ? guns.

Total, IX Corps: 9,186 men, 12 guns.
GdD Tharreau had been detached to Würzburg with the 52*e* Div (8 bns) and 2 bns of the 53*e* Div. The corps had only been in action at Weissenfels on 10 October, as had Milhaud's cavalry, which was marching with it; hence their strength being so high on 16 October. Bleibtreu reckons the 52*e* Div at 6,000 men and 14 guns for Leipzig; FML von Stön says 9,186 men.

XI CORPS
M Macdonald, Duc de Tarent.
CoS: **GdB Baron Grundeler.**
Cmdr of the Artillery: **Col Lautereau.** Six shows GdB Baron Aubry de la Boucharderie as artillery cmdr at Leipzig.
Cmdr of the Engineers: **ChBn Marion.**

31*e* Div, GdD Ledru des Essarts.
Adj: **Cmdt Hugues.**
1*re* Bde, GdB Bourment (**Fressinet**): **13*e* Pv Regt** (5*e*, 11*e* & **79*e*** RIdLi [2 bns (**1 bn**) each]), 11*e* Pv DBde (6*e* Bn 20*e* RIdLi [**27e RILe**] & 4*e* Bn 102*e* RIdLi).
2*e* Bde, GdB **O'Henin** [this is incorrect]: 4th (Westfalian) LI Bn (**LtCol Gauthier**), 8th (Westfalian) LIR (**Col von Bergeron**) (1st & 2nd Bns).

Neapolitan Bde, GdB Macdonald: Neapolitan Elite Regt (**grens & volts of 5th, 6th & 7th LIRs**), 4th LIR (2 bns).
Artillery: 1 × French (**8 guns**) & 2 × Westfalian FABs (**Capts Schleenstein & Schultheiss**) (**12**? guns) & Artillery Train cies.
Total: 5,023 men, 20? guns.

35*e* Div, GdD Baron Gerard.
Adj: **Cmdt Thomas.**
1*re* Bde, GdB D'Henin (Ihbe incorrectly gives **Le Senecal**): 6*e* (**Maj Frossart**) (3*e*, 4*e*, 7*e* Bns) & 112*e* (**Col Labedoyere**) (1*e*–4*e* Bns) RIdLi.
2*e* (Italian) Bde, GdB Zucchi: 2nd (**Maj Jabin**) (3rd Bn [**2 bns**]) & 5th (**Col Peri**) (1st & 2nd Bns [**4 bns**]) LIRs.
Artillery: 1 × French (**Italian**) FAB (**8 guns**), 1 × Italian HAB (**6**? guns), 1 French & 2 Italian cies Artillery Train.
Total: 3,551 men, 14? guns.

36*e* Div, GdD Count Charpentier.
Adj: **Cmdt Baron Lejeune.**
1*re* Bde, GdB Charras (**Simmer**): 22*e* RILe (**Col Charras**) (1*er*–4*e* Bns), 10*e* RIdLi (**Maj Emion**) (4*e*, 6*e* Bns).
2*e* Bde, GdB Meunier: 3*e* (**Maj Tissot**) (3*e* & 4*e* Bns) & 14*e* (**Col Tripp**) (3*e*, 4*e*, 7*e* Bns) RILe.
Artillery: 2 × **French 6-pdr** FABs (**16 guns**) & Artillery Train cies.
Total: 4,229 men, 16 guns.

39*e* Div, Count GdD Marchand.
Adj: **Cmdt Richard.**
Baden Bde, GM von Stockhorn: 1st (**Col von Brandt**) & 3rd (**Col Brückner**) LIRs (1st & 2nd Bns each).
Hessen-Darmstadt Bde, GM Prinz Emil von Hessen-Darmstadt: Garde-Füsilier Bn (**Col von Schönberg**) (1 bn [**2 bns**]), LG Regt (**Maj von Steinling**) & Leib-Regt **2nd LIR** (**Col von Gall**) (2 bns each).
The history of the LG Regiment confirms the following units present at Leipzig: LG (2 bns), Leib-Regt (2 bns), Garde-Füsilier-Bn, & the artillery.
Artillery: 1 × Baden (**4 guns**) and 1 × Hessian (**3 guns**) FABs & Artillery Train coys.
Total: 4,602 men, 7 guns.

28*e* Light Cavalry Bde, GdB Chev Montbrun: 4th Italian ChaChR (**Col Erculei**) (1st & 2nd Sqns), 2nd Neapolitan ChaChR (**Col Regnier**) (1st–4th Sqns), Würzburg ChaChR (**Col Hermetz**) (1st Sqn).
Total: 446 men.

Reserve Artillery & Park. 1 × **French HAB (6 guns)**, 2 × French (**16 guns**) & 1 × Neapolitan FABs (**no Neapolitan FAB**) & Artillery Train, 2 French & 1 Italian (Capt Alietto) coys sappers, 65 Gendarmes.
Total: 2,612 men, 22? guns.

Total, XI Corps: 20,533 men, 79 guns.

INDEPENDENT DIVISIONS
GdD Lefol's **Div de Marche**: 1*er* & 2*e* 'Erfurt Bns' (**formed from stragglers and convalescents in the French depot in Erfurt**), 54*e* RIdLi (2*e* Bn), 1½ Bns de Marche (detachments of 29*e* RILe, 25*e* & 33*e* RIdLi).

Artillery: 1 × FAB (6 guns).
Total: 2,229 *men,* 6 guns.
On 4 October this formation had consisted of 7,116 infantry, 933 cavalry, 1,800 *Gardes d'Honneur,* **336 artillery, and 6 guns. By 13 October the cavalry and** *Gardes* *d'Honneur* **had left to join their divisions and many of the Erfurt Bns had left to rejoin their parent regiments or had deserted.**

27*e* (Polish) Div, GdD Dombrowski.
GdB Zoltowski: 2nd (**Col Szymanowski**) & 4th (**Col Cichocki**) LIRs (1st & 2nd Bns each).
18*e* Light Cavalry Bde, GdB Krukowiecki: 2nd ChLLR (**Col Simialkowski**) (1st–4th Sqns), 4th ChaChR (**Col Kostanski**) (1st–4th Sqns).
Artillery: 1 × FAB (**Lt Szwan**) (**4 guns**), 1 × HAB (**Capt Swiecicki**), (**4 guns**) & Artillery Train, 1 coy sappers.
Total: 2,850 *men,* 8 guns.

GdD Margaron's Div (Garrison of Leipzig).
GdB Bertrand (**Mario d'Isle**): 4*e* Bn 35*e* & 1 combined bn 36*e* RILe, 1*er* Bn 132*e* & 1 bn 138*e* RIdLi (**138e not in Ihbe**), 1*er* Pv Regt (96*e* & 103*e* RIdLi [2*e* Bn each]).
Baden Bde, GM Graf von Hochberg: Jäger (**Leichtes**) Bn von Lingg, 2nd LIR (1 combined bn).
Cavalry Bde, **GdB Baron Quinette de Cernay**: 1*er* (**Col Lepic**) & 2*e* (**Col Saviot**) Pv Cav (**Drag**) Regts (**3 sqns each**). From 2*e* **Bde, 4***e* **Cavalry Div, III Cavalry Corps; consisted of 1 sqn each of 16***e*, **17***e*, **21***e*, **26***e* **& 27***e* **Drag, and 1 sqn of 13***e* **CuirR.**
Total: ca 700 *men.*
Artillery: 1 (**2**) × French HAB (**12 guns**), 1 × Baden FAB (**4 guns**) & Artillery Train, 16 artisans, 19 Gendarmes.
Total: 4,820 *men,* 16 guns.

I CAVALRY CORPS
GdD Count Latour-Maubourg.
CoS: Col Mathieu.
Cmdr of the Artillery: Col Lavoye.

1*re* Light Cavalry Div, GdD Baron Berckheim.
2*e* Light Cavalry Bde, GdB Count Montmarie: 16*e* ChaChR (1*er*, 2*e* Sqns), 1*er* (1*er*, 2*e* Sqns) & 3*e* (1*er*, 2*e* Sqns) ChLLR.
3*e* Light Cavalry Bde, GdB Baron Piquet: 5*e* (1*er*, 2*e* Sqns) & 8*e* (1*er*, 2*e* Sqns) ChLLR, 1st Italian ChaChR (**not show by all sources**) (1st–4th Sqns).
Total: 1,850 *men.*

Half 1*re* **Light Cavalry Div, GdD Corbineau.**
1*re* Light Cavalry Bde, GdB Baron Pire: 6*e* HusR (Col De Carignan) (2 sqns), 7*e* HusR (3 sqns), 8*e* HusR (Col De Coetlosquet) (3 sqns). Artillery: $\frac{1}{2}$ × French HAB (3 guns). *Total:* 750 *men,* 3 guns.
Half 1*re* **Light Cavalry Div, GdD Baron Berckheim.**
2*e* Light Cavalry Bde, GdB Count Montmarie: 16*e* ChaChR (Col Foissac la Tour) (2 sqns), 1*er* (2 sqns) & 3*e* (Col Hatry) (2 sqns) ChLLR. 3*e* Light Cavalry Bde, GdB Baron Piquet: 5*e* (Col Chabert) & 8*e* (Col Count Lubienski) (2 sqns) ChLLR.
Artillery: 1 × French HAB (6 guns).
Total: 1,100 *men.*
Total: 1,850 *men,* 9 guns.

2*e* Light Cavalry Div, GdD Corbineau.
1*re* Light Cavalry Bde, GdB Du Coetlosquet (**GdB Baron Pire**): 6*e* (1*er*, 2*e* Sqns), 7*e* (1*er*, 2*e*, 3*e* Sqns) & 8*e* (1*er*, 2*e*, 3*e* Sqns) HusR.

3*e* Light Cavalry Div, GdD Baron Chastel.
4*e* Light Cavalry Bde, GdB Baron Vallin: 8*e* (**Maj Planzeaux**) (1*er*, 2*e* Sqns), 9*e* (**Col Dukermont**) (1*er*, 2*e* Sqns) & 25*e* (1*er*, 2*e* Sqns) ChaChR (**25*e* ChaChR not shown by all sources**).
5*e* Light Cavalry Bde, GdB Vial (some sources give van Merlin): 1*er* (**Col Hubert**) (1*er*–3*e* Sqns), 19*e* (**Col Vincent**) (1*er*–4*e* Sqns) & 25*e* (**2 sqns) ChaChR**.
Artillery: 1 HAB (6 × 6-pdrs), 1 cie Artillery Train.
Total: 1,910 men, 15 guns.

1*re* Heavy Cavalry Div, GdD Count Bordessoulle.
1*re* Bde, GdB Sopranski (**from 16 October Col de Lacroix**): 1*er* (**not in Ihbe**) (1*er*, 2*e* Sqns), **2*e* (Col Baron Rollaud) (2 sqns)**, 3*e* (**Col de Lacroix**) (1*er*–3*e* Sqns), 6*e* (**Col ChdE Martin**) (1*er*–3*e* Sqns) & **9*e* (3 sqns) CuirR**.
2*e* Bde, GdB Bessières: 9*e* (1*er*–3*e* Sqns), 11*e* (**Col Duclas**) (1*er*–3*e* Sqns) & 12*e* (**Col Daudies**) (1*er*, 2*e* Sqns) CuirR.
3*e* (Saxon) Bde, GM Lessing: Leib-Kürassier-Garde (**Col von Berger**) (1st–4th Sqns), von Zastrow-Kürs (**Maj von Metzradt**) (1st–4th Sqns).
Artillery: 1 French HAB (6 × 6-pdrs) & Artillery Train.
*Total: 1,350 men, **6 guns**.*

3*e* Heavy Cavalry Div, GdD Baron Doumerc.
1*re* Bde, GdB Baron de Lalaing d'Audenarde: 4*e* (**Col Baron Dujon**) (1*er*–3*e* Sqns), 7*e* (1*er*–3*e* Sqns) & 14*e* (**Col Tripp**) (1*er*, 2*e* Sqns) CuirR, Italian Dragoni Napoleoni (**Col Gualdi**) (1st–4th Sqns).
2*e* Bde, GdB Baron Reiset: 7*e* (**Col Sopranzi**) (1*er*, 2*e* Sqns), 23*e* (**Col Martique**) (1*er*–3*e* Sqns), 28*e* (1*er*, 2*e* Sqns) & 30*e* (**Col Ordener**) (1*er*, 2*e* Sqns) DragR.
Artillery: 1 × Italian HAB & Artillery Train coy.
*Total: 540 men, **6 guns**.*

Total, I Cavalry Corps: 6,480 men, 24 (27) guns (**but some sources show two more French HABs as Corps Reserve Artillery, which would bring total to 39 guns**).

II CAVALRY CORPS
GdD Count Sebastiani.
CoS: Col De Lascours.
Cmdr of the Artillery: Col Colin.
Adj: Marquis de Lavoestine.

2*e* Light Cavalry Div, GdD Baron Roussel d'Hurbal.
7*e* (**8*e***) Light Cavalry Bde, GdB Baron Dommanget: 4*e* ChLLR (**Col Deschamps**) (1*er*, 2*e*, 3*e* Sqns), 5*e* (**Col Fournier**) (1*er*, 2*e*, 3*e* Sqns) & 9*e* (**Col ChdE Maigret**) (1*er*, 2*e*, 3*e* Sqns) HusR.
8*e* (**7*e***) Light Cavalry Bde, GdB Lagrange (**GdB Baron Gerard**): 2*e* ChLLR (**Col ChdE Berruyer**) (1*er*, 2*e*, 3*e* Sqns), 11*e* (**Col Nicolas**) (1*er*, 2*e*, 3*e* Sqns) & 12*e* (**Col Ghingy**) (1*er*, 2*e*, 3*e* Sqns) ChaChR.
Artillery: $\frac{1}{2}$ × French HAB & $\frac{1}{2}$ cie Artillery Train.
Total: 5,679 men, 3 guns.

4*e* Light Cavalry Div, GdD Baron Exelmans.

9*e* Light Cavalry Bde, GdB Baron Maurin: 6*e* ChLLR (**Col Perquit**) (**2 sqns**) (1*er*, 2*e*, 3*e* Sqns), 4*e* (**Col Count de Vence**) (**2 sqns**) (1*er*, 2*e*, 3*e* Sqns), 7*e* (**Col ChdE St-Chamans**) (**3 sqns**) (1*er*–4*e* Sqns) & 20*e* (**Col Baron Sourd**) (1*er*–4*e* Sqns) ChaChR.

10*e* Light Cavalry Bde, GdB Wathiez: 23*e* (**Col Marbot**) (1*er*–4*e* Sqns) & 24*e* (**Col ChdE Schneidt**) (1*er*, 2*e*, 3*e* Sqns) ChaChR, 11*e* HusR **ex-Dutch** (**Col Liegeard**) (**2 sqns**) (1*er*, 2*e*, 3*e* Sqns).
Artillery: $\frac{1}{2}$ French HAB & $\frac{1}{2}$ cie Artillery Train.

2*e* Heavy Div, GdD Baron St-Germain.
1*re* Bde, GdB Baron Davrange d'Haugeranville: 1*er* (**Col Baron Laroche**) & 2*e* (**Col Baron Blancard**) Carabiniers (**2 sqns each**), 1*er* CuirR (**shown by Ihbe in 2*e* Bde**) (**Col Baron Clerc**) (**2 sqns**) (1*er*, 2*e*, 3*e* Sqns each).
2*e* Bde, GdB Thiry: 5*e* (**Col Christophe**) (1*er*, 2*e*, 3*e* Sqns), 8*e* (**Col Lefaivre**) & 10*e* CuirR (1*er* & 2*e* Sqns each).
Artillery: 1 × French HAB & Artillery Train cie.

Total, II Cavalry Corps: 5,679men, 12 guns.
Quistorp shows II Cavalry Corps strength on 15 October as 5,680 men and 12 guns. Bleibtreu gives only 4,500 sabres on 16 October, even though they received a march regiment of 600 men on the 5th.

III CAVALRY CORPS
GdD Arrighi, Duc de Padoue.
CoS: Col Salel.
Cmdr of the Artillery: Col Chevau.

5*e* Light Cavalry Div (attached to VI Corps), GdD Baron Lorge.
CoS: Col Dastorg.
12*e* Light Cavalry Bde, Col Baron Shea (**GdB Baron Jacquinot**): 5*e* (**Col Beugnot**) (**2 sqns**) (1*er*, 3*e*, 4*e* Sqns), 10*e* (**Cmdt Duhamel**) (**2 sqns**) (1*er*, 3*e*, 4*e* Sqns) & 13*e* (**Col Baron Shea**) (**2 sqns**) (5*e*, 6*e* Sqns) ChaChR.
13*e* Light Cavalry Bde, GdB Merlin: 15*e* (**Maj Rougeot**) (4*e* Sqn), 21*e* (3*e* Sqn) & 22*e* (**Maj de Bourbel**) (3*e*, 4*e* Sqns) ChaChR.
Artillery: $\frac{1}{2}$ × HAB (3 guns).

6*e* Light Cavalry Div (attached to III Corps), GdD Baron Fournier-Sarlovese.
14*e* Light Cavalry Bde, GdB Baron Mouriez: 29*e* (**Cmdt Montailleur**) & 31*e* ChaChR (4*e* Sqn each), 1*er* HusR (**Col Clary**) (4*e* Sqn).
15*e* Light Cavalry Bde, GdB Baron Amiel: 2*e* (**1 sqn**) (3*e*, 4*e* Sqns), 4*e* (5*e* Sqn) & 12*e* (4*e* Sqn) HusR.
Artillery: $\frac{1}{2}$ × HAB (3 guns).

4*e* Heavy Cavalry Div, GdD Count Defrance.
CoS: Bylandt.
1*re* Bde (attached to III Corps), GdB Aximatowski (**GdB Baron Avice**): **4*e*, 5*e*, 12*e*, 14*e* & 24*e* DragRs (1 sqn each).**
2*e* Bde, GdB Baron Quinette de Cernay (attached to IV Corps) (**attached to Margaron's independent Div**): **16*e*, 17*e* (Col Lepic), 21*e* (Col Saviot), 26*e* & 27*e* DragRs (1 sqn each), 13*e* CuirR (1 sqn).**
Artillery: $\frac{1}{2}$ × French HAB & Artillery Train cie.

Total, III Cavalry Corps: 4,000 men, 9 guns.

IV (POLISH) CAVALRY CORPS

GdD Sokolnicki (commanding for GdD Kellermann who was absent [**either sick or**] commanding both IV & V Cavalry Corps).
CoS: Col Tancarville.
Cmdr of the Artillery: GdB ?.

7*e* (Polish) Light Cavalry Div, GdD Sokolnicki.
17*e* Light Cavalry Bde, GdB Tolinski: 1st ChaChR (**Col Turnakowski**) (1st–4th Sqns), 3rd ChLLR (**Col Oberski**) (1st–4th Sqns).
Artillery: 1 × Polish HAB (**4 guns**) & Artillery Train coy.

8*e* (Polish) Light Cavalry Div, GdD Prince Sulkowski.
19*e* Light Cavalry Bde, GdB Krustowski: 6th & 8th ChLLR (1st–4th Sqns each).
Artillery: 1 × Polish HAB (**4 guns**) & Artillery Train cie.

Reserve Artillery: 2 × French HABs & Artillery Train cies.

Total, *IV Cavalry Corps*: 3,000 *men, 12 [8] guns.*
2*e* Bde (13th Polish HusR & 16th Polish ChLLR) & 1 × HAB of 7*e* Light Cavalry Div had been left in Dresden. Bleibtreu reckons that on 16 October IV Cavalry Corps stood at 1,200 lancers, 400 ChaCh, 300 gunners & 8 guns. The commander of the corps, Kellermann, was sick.

V CAVALRY CORPS

GdD Pajol (**wounded on 16 October; GdD Milhaud took over**).
CoS: Not known.

9*e* Light Cavalry Div, GdD Pire (**GdD Subervie**).
32*e* Light Cavalry Bde, GdB Klicki: 3*e* HusR (1*er*, 3*e*, 4*e* Sqns), 27*e* ChaChR (1*er*–4*e* Sqns).
33*e* Light Cavalry Bde, GdB Vial: 14*e* (**Col Lemoyne**) & 26*e* ChaChR (1*er*, 3*e* & 4*e* Sqns each), **13*e* HusR (4 sqns)**.
Total: 1,700 men, no guns.

5*e* Heavy Cavalry Div, GdD L'Heretier.
Bde, GdB Quenot: 2*e* (1*er*, 2*e*, 3*e* Sqns), 6*e* (**4 sqns**) (1*er*, 3*e*, 4*e* Sqns) & 11*e* (1*er*–4*e* Sqns) DragRs.
Bde, GdB Collaert. **11*e* (4 sqns)**, 13*e* (1*er*, 3*e* Sqns) & 15*e* (1*er*, 2*e*, 3*e* Sqns) DragRs.
Artillery: $\frac{1}{2}$ × HAB (3 guns) & Artillery Train cie.
Total: 1,700 men, 3 guns.

6*e* Heavy Cavalry Div, GdD Milhaud.
Bde, GdB Lamotte: 18*e*, 19*e*, 20*e* (**3 sqns**) DragRs (1*er* & 3*e* Sqns each).
Bde, GdB Montelegier: 22*e* & 25*e* (**4 sqns**) DragRs (1*er*, 2*e* & 3*e* Sqns each).
Artillery: 1 × French HAB & Artillery Train cie.
*Total: **1,600** men, 6 (0) guns.*

Total, *V Cavalry Corps*: 5,000 *men, 6 (3) guns.*

SUMMARY OF THE *GRANDE ARMEE* AT LEIPZIG (after Ihbe)

	Bns	Cies	Sqns	FABs	HABs	Men
Imperial Guard	66	16	61	27	3	44,499
II Corps	32	3	–	8	–	17,292
III Corps	38	4	11	9	$\frac{1}{2}$	17,168
IV Corps	24	3	4	5	$1\frac{1}{2}$	9,824
V Corps	29	3	7	9	1	13,332
VI Corps	42	4	8	11	3	19,304
VII Corps	24	2	13	8	2	12,837
VIII Corps	14	1	6	$6\frac{1}{2}$	–	5,000
IX Corps	13	1	–	2	–	9,186
XI Corps	46	3	7	12	3	20,533
Margaron's Div	6	–	–	$2\frac{1}{2}$	2	4,820
Lefol's Div	$4\frac{1}{2}$	–	–	1	–	2,229
Dombrowski's Div	4	1	8	2	1	2,850
I Cavalry Corps	–	–	75	–	$4\frac{1}{2}$	6,480
II Cavalry Corps	–	–	52	–	2	5,679
III Cavalry Corps	–	–	27	–	$1\frac{1}{2}$	4,000
IV Cavalry Corps	–	–	16	–	4	3,000
V Cavalry Corps	–	–	47	–	$\frac{1}{2}$	5,000
Total:	*$342\frac{1}{2}$*	*41*	*342*	*103**	*$29\frac{1}{2}$**	*203,033*

* = 729 guns.

SUMMARY OF THE *GRANDE ARMEE* DURING THE RETREAT TO ERFURT (after Kerchnawe)

	Bns	Cies	Sqns	Btys	Guns	Men
Imperial Guard	67	9	65	19	138	32,800
II Corps	32	3	–	7	16	9,400
III Corps	38	4	10	12	16	10,200
IV Corps	30	3	2	8	33	8,500
V Corps	33	3	7	9	16	7,200
VI Corps	39	4	–	?	16	10,000
VII Corps	$22\frac{1}{2}$	1	–	4	16	5,600
VIII Corps*	8	2?	3?	?	?	2,200
IX Corps	22?	1	–	2	6	5,000
XI Corps	33	3	7	8	16	8,800
Margaron's Div	5	–	–	2	10	2,000
Lefol's Div	$4\frac{1}{2}$	–	–	1	6	2,300
I Cavalry Corps	–	–	70	–	10	4,650
II Cavalry Corps	–	–	52	–	6	3,200
III Cavalry Corps	–	–	23	–	?	2,300
IV Cavalry Corps	–	–	16	–	–	800
V Cavalry Corps	–	–	47	–	6	3,900
Total:	*334*	*33*	*301*	*?*	*301†*	*118,850*

* = Dombrowski's Div is included in VIII Corps' totals.

† = Calculated by subtracting from those known to have been with the *Grande Armée* before the battle minus the 380 lost to the enemy and the 38 which fell under enemy control when the Saxons and Württembergers went over to the Allies. It thus seems that Kerchnawe calculated the manpower losses of the *Grande Armée* to have been 84,243.

C: Order of battle of the Army of Bohemia

This order of battle for the main Allied army is based on Aster, Friedrich, Herbstfeldzug, Kerchnawe, Plotho, and Quistorp. Where Kerchnawe's data differs significantly the differences are shown in **bold type**. Kerchnawe's data seems to be dated about 20 October. Most Russian infantry units were reduced to one battalion after the battle. A note in a document in the Austrian archives states that the figure of eight guns per battery quoted in Kerchnawe is wrong, and that the correct figure was six.

The following full headquarters organisation is taken from Vitzthum von Eckstädt. It is valid for the period after the armistice.

Cmdr in Chief: FM Fürst Carl zu Schwarzenberg.
Chief of the GS: FML Graf Radetzky von Radetz.
Secret Office of the Cmdr: 5 officers, 2 senior and 3 junior officials.

Operations Chancellery
QMG: GM Baron Langenau.
QMG's staff: 10 officers with 3 infantry or cavalry officers attached.

General Staff Departments
Auditors: 1 Field Auditor, 1 Actuary (attached from the Army General Commando).
Provosts: 1 Provost Marshal, 4 Assistant Provosts.
QM's Office: 1 QM, 1 Vice QM, 6 QM NCOs.
Transport Office: 5 train and civilian officials.
Guides Office: 5 military and civilian officials.
Courier Service: Capt Herbert and 32 messengers.
Army Police Service: Russian LtGen von Oertel with 1 field officer and 2 officers from each Allied army; 1 commissary official, 1 senior doctor, 2 junior doctors, 1 superintendent, *Platzkommandant* Maj Büttner (attached from the *Platzkommando*).

Detail Chancellery
Directing AdjG: MG Baron Koller.
AdjGs: Col Pausch, LtCol Graf Paar, LtCol Fialla.
ADCs: Maj Graf Woyna, Maj Böhm, Maj Graf Chotek, Maj Wenzel Fürst Liechtenstein.
Orderly officers: Rttm Graf Szechenyi and others as required.

Army General Commando
Cmdr: FML Baron Prochaska with adjs.
War Commissariat: 1 *Oberkriegskommisar* with commissars and adjs and *Hofrat* Witzmann.
'Secretarial Headquarters': *Hofkriegskonzipist* and officials.
Ration Office: *Hofrat* Graf Baltazzi and officials.
Paymaster's Office: Paymaster and officials.
Auditor's Office: Auditor General and officials.
Medical Chancellery: Commissar with doctors and officials.
Field Post Office: 1 Post official and staff.
Field Transport Office: In 1814 this consisted of 1 officer 146 men and 252 horses.

1813: Leipzig

Transport Directorate: no details given.
Garrison Command: no details given.
Headquarters Protection Unit: 1 coy *Stabsinfanterie*, $\frac{1}{2}$ sqn of *Stabs-Dragoner* or *Landwehr-Dragoner*.

Artillery Directorate
FML Reisner von Lichtenstern, GM Frierenberger, Col Graf Künigl, Col Stwortnik and adjs. Attached: GM Baron Smola.

Engineering Directorate
1 general, several officers.

Military Liaison Officers
Prussia: GM von Hacke, Haupt von Brandenstein.
Russia: GM Baron von Toll.
Britain: General Sir Robert Thomas Wilson.

AUSTRIAN TROOPS

I CORPS
FZM Hieronymus Graf Colloredo-Mansfeld.

1st Light Div, FML Moritz Prinz zu Liechtenstein.
1st Bde, GM Gustav Prinz von Hessen-Homburg: 1st & 2nd JgBns, ChLR Kaiser Nr 1 (6 sqns).
Artillery: 1 × HAB (6 guns) & Train coy.
2nd Bde, GM Heinrich Freiherr von Schiether: GzIR Broder Nr 7 (1st Bn), 7th JgBn, DragR Levenehr Nr 4 (4 sqns), ChLR Vincent Nr 4 (6 sqns).
Artillery: 1 × 3-pdr HAB (6 guns) & Train coy.

2nd Light Div, FML Ferdinand Graf Bubna.
This division was detached until the morning of 18 October and took no part in the fighting of the 14th–17th.
1st Bde, GM Theophile Freiherr Zechmeister von Rheinau: GzIR Peterwardeiner Nr 9 (1st Bn), 6th JgBn (5 coys; 1 coy was at Dresden with Seethal's Bde, see below), HusR Liechtenstein Nr 7 (6 sqns).
Artillery: 1 × 6-pdr HAB (6 guns) & Train coy.
2nd Bde, Col Georg Freiherr von Wieland: IR Eh Rainer Nr 11 (3rd Bn), IR Würzburg Nr 7 (1st LW Bn), **HusR Blankenstein Nr 6 (4 sqns).**
Artillery: $\frac{1}{2}$ × 3-pdr bty (6 guns) & Train coy.
3rd Bde, GM von Seethal: 6th JgBn (1 coy), IRs Kaiser Nr 1, Eh Ludwig Nr 8, Kaunitz Nr 20, Kollowrath Nr 36 (1 LW Bn each), HusR Blankenstein Nr 6 (2 sqns), DragR Levenehr Nr 4 (1 sqn).
The 3rd Bde was detached to blockade Sonnenstein fortress on the Elbe between Dresden and Pirna and took no part in the battle of Leipzig.

Div of FML Ignaz Graf Hardegg.
1st Bde, GM Adam Graf Neipperg: 5th JgBn, HusR Kaiser Nr 1 (6 sqns).
Artillery: 1 × HAB (6 guns) & Train coy.
According to the ÖMZ of 1839 (vol.II, *Heft* 5, p.169) this brigade was attached to FML Bubna's 2nd Light Div from at least 5–19 October and thus did not fight at

Leipzig until the 18th. Seyfert (p.193) confirms that it did fight at Paunsdorf on the 18th.

2nd Bde, GM Karl Graf Raigecourt: GzIR Deutsch Banater Nr 12 (2 bns), HusR Hessen-Homburg Nr 4 (5 sqns; 1 was detached to Mensdorf's *Streifkorps*), DragR Riesch Nr 6 (5 sqns; 1 was detached to the mobile column of GM Herzogenberg). Artillery: 1 × 6-pdr HAB (6 guns) & Train coy.

Div of FML Maximilian Freiherr von Wimpffen.
1st Bde, GM Samuel von Giffing: IR Froon Nr 54, IR de Vaux Nr 25 (3 bns each).
Artillery: 1 × FAB (6 guns) & Train coy.
2nd Bde, GM Josef Czerwenka: IR Argentau Nr 35 (3 bns including the 1st LW Bn), IR Erbach Nr 42 (2 bns).
Artillery: 2 × 6-pdr FABs (16 guns) & Train coys.

Div of FML Karl von Greth.
1st Bde, GM Franz von Mumb (**Col Jacardowsky**): IR de Ligne Nr 30 (3 bns), IR Czartoryski Nr 9 (2 bns).
Artillery: 1 × FAB (6 guns) & Train coy.
2nd Bde, GM Karl von Quosdanovich: IR Albert Gyulai Nr 21 (2 bns), IR Reuss-Plauen Nr 17 (3 bns; 1 bn was with Mensdorff's *Streifkorps*).
Artillery: 2 × 6-pdr FABs (16 guns) & Train coys.

Corps Reserve Artillery: 2 × 12-pdr & 1 × 6-pdr Position Btys (18 guns).

Total, I Corps: 32 bns, ? coys, 46 sqns, $11\frac{1}{2}$ btys, 33,564 men, 6,000 horses, 68 guns (**Kerchnawe says 86 guns**).

II CORPS

GdK Maximilian Graf Meerveldt (following his capture on 16 October, FML Alois Prinz zu Liechtenstein took over).

Div of FML Ignaz Freiherr von Lederer.
1st Bde, GM Graf Ferdinand Sorbenburg (**Kerchnawe incorrectly states Gen Maj Prinz von Sachsen-Koburg**): GzIR Gradiskaner Nr 8 (1st Bn), HusR Kienmayer Nr 8 (5 sqns; 1 sqn was with Thielmann's *Streifkorps*), DragR Eh Johann Nr 1 (4 [**6**] sqns).
Artillery: 1 × FAB (6 guns) & Train coy.

2nd Bde, GM Johann von Longueville: IR Strauch Nr 24 (2 bns), IR Bellegarde Nr 44 (2 bns) **& IR Eh Rainer Nr 11 (LW Bn).**
Artillery: 1 × 6-pdr FAB, **1 × 3-pdr HAB** (6 [**16**] guns) & Train coys.

Div of FML Alois Prinz zu Liechtenstein.
1st Bde, GM Josef Freiherr von Ennsbruck (**Gen Maj Klopstein**): IR Kaunitz Nr 20, IR Wenzel Colloredo Nr 56 (3 bns each).
Artillery: 1 × 6-pdr FAB (8 guns) & Train coy.

2nd Bde, GM Karl Freiherr von Mecsery: IR Reuss-Greitz Nr 18 (2 bns), IR Vogelsang Nr 47 (3 bns including 1st LW Bn), IR Eh Rainer Nr 11 (1st LW Bn).
Artillery: 1 × 6-pdr FAB (8 guns) & Train coy.

Corps Reserve Artillery: 1 × 12-pdr & 2 × 6-pdr Position Btys (18 guns).

Total, II Corps: 17 bns, ? coys, 9 sqns, 3 btys, 14,129 men, 1,092 horses, 42 guns (**50 guns**).

III CORPS
FZM Ignaz Graf Gyulai.

Div of FML Karl Graf Crenneville.
1st Bde, GM Josef Hächt: GzIR Warasdin-Kreuzer Nr 5 (1st Bn), GzIR Warasdin-St Georger Nr 6 (1st Bn), ChLR Klenau Nr 5 (7 sqns [**6 sqns; 1 sqn with Thielmann's** *Streifkorps*]), ChLR Rosenberg Nr 6 (6 sqns; **1 sqn in Weissenfels, 1 sqn to Army GHQ**).
Artillery: 1 × 3-pdr HAB (8 guns).

Div of FML Franz Graf Murray de Melgum (FML Murray).
1st Bde, GM Josef Graf Lamezan-Salins (GM Salins): IR Eh Ludwig Nr 8 (3 bns), IR Würzburg Nr 7 (3 bns; 3rd Bn joined regt on 17 October).
Artillery: 1 × 6-pdr FAB (6 [**8**] guns) & Train coy.
2nd Bde, GM Josef Weigel von Löwenwarth. IR Mariassy Nr 37, IR Ignaz Gyulai Nr 60 (2 bns each).
Artillery: 1 × 6-pdr FAB (6 [**8**] guns) & Train coy.
On 14 October 1 bn Eh Ludwig, 1 bn Würzburg & $\frac{1}{2}$ FAB of 1st Bde were detached as garrison of Weissenfels; and 2 bns Eh Ludwig, 1 sqn ChLR Rosenberg & 2 guns of 1st Bde as garrison of Naumburg. The strength of Murray's div at Leipzig was 15 weak bns & 11 sqns plus the reduced artillery.

Div of FML Philipp Prinz von Hessen-Homburg.
1st Bde, GM Martin von Csollich: IR Kottulinsky Nr 41 (3 bns), IR Kaiser Nr 1 (2 bns).
Artillery: 1 × 6-pdr FAB (6 [**8**] guns) & Train coy.
2nd Bde, GM Anton Grimmer von Riesenburg: IR Kolowrat Nr 36 (2 bns), IR Frelich Nr 28 (3 bns; 3rd Bn joined regt on 17 October).
Artillery: 1 × 6-pdr FAB (6 [**8**] guns) & Train coy.

Corps Reserve Artillery: 1 (**2**) × 12-pdr & 2 (**1**) × 6-pdr Position Btys (18 guns).

*Total, III Corps: 22 bns, ? coys, 13 sqns, 7 btys, 20,526 men, 1,707 horses, 42 guns (**58 guns**).*

IV CORPS
GdK Johann Graf Klenau.

Div of FML Josef Freiherr von Mohr.
1st Bde, GM Maximilian Ritter von Paumgarten: GzIR 1st Wallachen Nr 16 (1st Bn), GzIR Wallachisch-Illyrisch Nr 13 (2 bns), ChLR Hohenzollern Nr 2 (6 sqns, of which 2 were with Thielmann's *Streifkorps*), HusR Palatinal Nr 12 (6 sqns).
Artillery: 2 × HAB (10 guns) & Train coy.

Div of FML Prince Ludwig Hohenlohe-Bartenstein.
1st Bde, GM Josef von Schäffer: IR Josef Colloredo Nr 57 (2 bns), IR Zach Nr 15 (3 bns).
Artillery: 1 × FAB (6 guns) & Train coy.
2nd Bde, GM Franz Spleny de Mihaldy: IR Württemberg Nr 40, IR Lindenau Nr 29 (3 bns each).
Artillery: 1 × FAB (6 guns) & Train coy.

Div of FML Anton Ritter Mayer von Heldensfeld.
1st Bde, GM Franz Freiherr von Abele: IR Alois Liechtenstein Nr 12, IR Koburg Nr 22 (3 bns each).

Artillery: 1 × FAB (6 guns) & Train coy.
2nd Bde, GM Albrecht de Best: IR Eh Karl Nr 3, IR Kerpen Nr 49 (2 bns each).
Artillery: 1 × FAB (6 guns) & Train coy.

Cavalry Bde of GM Franz Graf Desfours (attached from Army Reserve): KürR Kaiser Nr 1, ChLR O'Reilly Nr 3 (6 sqns each).

Corps Reserve Artillery: 1 × 12-pdr Position & 1 × 3-pdr Btys (10 guns).

Total, IV Corps: 24 bns, ? coys, 30 sqns, 8 btys, 24,544 men, 3,285 horses, 46 guns.

ARMY RESERVE CORPS
GdK Erbprinz Friedrich von Hessen-Homburg.

Div of FML Nikolaus von Weissenwolff.
1st Bde, GM Karl Freiherr von Fürstenwärther: Gren Bns Czarnotzay, Obermayer, Berger & Oklopsia (4 bns).
Artillery: 1 × 6-pdr FAB (6 [8] guns) & Train coy.
2nd Bde, GM Watzl: Gren Bns Habinay, Portner, Fischer & Call (previously Rüber) (4 bns).
Artillery: 1 × 6-pdr FAB (6 [8] guns) & Train coy.

Div of FML Friedrich Ritter von Bianchi.
1st Bde, GM August von Beck: IR Hiller Nr 2, IR Heironymus Colloredo Nr 33 (2 bns each).
Artillery: 1 × 6-pdr FAB (6 [8] guns) & Train coy.
2nd Bde, GM Eugen Graf Haugwitz: IR Hessen-Homburg Nr 19, IR Simbschen Nr 48 (2 bns each).
Artillery: 1 × 6-pdr FAB (6 [8] guns) & Train coy.
3rd Bde, GM Karl von Quallenberg: IR Esterhazy Nr 32, IR Davidovich Nr 34 (2 bns each).
Artillery: 1 × 6-pdr FAB (6 [8] guns) & Train coy.

Cavalry Div of FML Johann Graf Nostitz.
Wing of GM Johann Graf Klebelsberg.
1st Bde, GM Leopold Freiherr von Rothkirch: KürR Eh Franz Nr 2, KürR Kronprinz Ferdinand Nr 4 (4 sqns each).
2nd Bde, GM Maximilian Graf Auersperg: KürR Hohenzollern Nr 8, KürR Sommariva Nr 5 (6 sqns each).
Wing of GM Karl Graf Civalart.
3rd Bde, GM Ferdinand Kuttalek von Ehrengreif: KürR Herzog Albert Nr 3, KürR Lothringen Nr 7 (4 sqns each).
4th Bde, GM Desfours: KürR Kaiser Nr 1, ChLR O'Reilly Nr 3 (6 sqns each).

There was no Corps Reserve Artillery.

Total, Army Reserve Corps: 20 bns, ? coys, 28 (40) sqns, 5 btys, 19,739 men, 3,390 horses, 30 guns.

THE 'EXTRA CORPS'
The army's Reserve Artillery and Technical Troops.
FML Anton von Reisner.
Col Frierenberger, Col Künigl, Col Swortnik.

Artillery: 20 (**25**) coys; 18 (**22**) btys (2 × 3-pdr 'Bde', 2 × 6-pdr, 6 [**8**] × 12-pdr, 2 × 16-pdr [**18-pdr**] 'Position', 4 × 6-pdr HABs): 2,029 men, 112 [**142**] guns); Artillery assistants: 21 (**23**) coys (3,331 men); Pioneers: 3½ coys (763 men); Pontoniers: 3 coys (340 men); Medical troops: 1 bn (689 men); *Stabsinfanterie:* 1 bn (139 men); *Stabsdragoner:* 2 sqns (139 men); LW-*Stabsdragoner:* 1 sqn (129 men).

THE MOBILE COLUMN
GM August Freiherr von Herzogenberg.
IR Erbach Nr 42 (LW Bn, 1,152 men), 2nd Schl LWKR (2 sqns) (attached from Kleist's II [Prussian] Corps).

*Total, Austrian contingent of Army of Bohemia: 120 (**91 5/6**) bns, 44½ (**55**) coys, 132 (**102**) sqns, 56½ (**49**) btys, 121,599 men, 15,645 horses, 340 (**348**) guns (guns per bty have been reduced from 8 to 6 in accordance with an annotation to this effect in the Austrian archives).*

RUSSO-PRUSSIAN TROOPS
Cmdr: GdC Count Barclay de Tolly.
CoS: GM Baron Diebitsch (**GM Sabanjew**).
QMG: **GM Diebitsch.**
Cmdr of the Artillery: **LtGen Prince Yaschwill.**
Cmdr of the Engineers: **GM Count Siewers.**
Army General Commissariat: **GM Cancqerin; Attached troops: Little Russia, Tschernigoff & 2nd Poltawa LW Cossack Regts.**
GHQ Guard Detachment: **Kirejeff, Platoff IV, Rebrkoff III & Tabuntschikoff Don Cossack *Pulks*, 3rd Bug Cossack *Pulk*, 1st Tula LW Cossack Regt.**

Wing of GdC Count Wittgenstein.
Cavalry Div, LtGen Count P.A. Pahlen **III**.
Bde of MG Rüdiger: HusR Sum (6 [**5**] sqns), HusR Grodno (6 [**5**] sqns).
Bde of MG Lisanevitsch (**Col Schuwanoff**): HusR Lubno (4 sqns), UlR Tschugujeff (8 [**6**] sqns).
Bde of MG Illowaiski XII (**MG Knorring**): Grekow VIII, Illowaiski XII, Radjanoff II & Eupatoria Tartar Cossack *Pulks.*
Artillery, MG Nikitin: 6th & 7th HABs (20 guns).
*Total: 24 (**27**) sqns, 4 pulks, 2,600 (**2,900–3,100**) men.*

I CORPS
LtGen Prince Gortschakoff II.

5th Div, MG Mesenzieff.
Bde of MG ? (**Lukoff**): IR Perm, IR Siewsk (2 bns each).
Bde of MG ? (**Wlastoff**): IR Mogilew, IR Kaluga (2 bns each).
Bde of MG ?: JgR Nr 23 & Nr 24 (2 bns each), Militia Bn of Grand Princess Katharina Pawlowna, Duchess of Oldenburg (1 bn).

14th Div, MG von Helfreich.
Bde of MG ? (**Ljallin**): IR Tenginsk, IR Estland (2 bns each).
Bde of MG ? (**Roth**); IR Tulsk, IR Nowaginsk (2 bns each).
Bde of MG Winstoff (**Wustoff**): JgR Nr 25 & Nr 26 (2 bns each).
Artillery: **3rd** Heavy FAB, **6th & 7th** Light FABs (36 guns).
Total: 25 bns, 5,700 men, 36 guns.

II CORPS
LtGen Prince Eugen von Württemberg.

3rd Div, MG Schachafskoi.
Bde of MG ? (**Col Schalnitzky**): IR Murom, IR Reval (2 bns each).
Bde of MG ?: IR Tchernigow, IR Selenginsk (2 bns each).
Bde of MG ?: JgR Nr 20 & Nr 21 (2 bns each).

4th Div, MG Pueschnitzki.
Bde of MG ?: IR Tobolsk, IR Wolhynien (2 bns each).
Bde of MG ?: IR Krementchuk, IR Minsk (2 bns each).
Bde of MG ?: JgR Nr 4 & Nr 34 (2 bns each).
Artillery: **5th** Heavy FAB, 2 (**27th**) × Light FABs & 2 × HABs (60 guns).
Total: 24 bns, 5,200 men, 60 guns.

Attached troops: Pioneers (1 coy), DragR Ingermannland (1 sqn), 2nd Bug Cossacks (1 sqn), LW Infantry Bns Olonetz & Wologda (450–500 men).

THE RESERVE CORPS
Grand Prince Constantin of Russia.

THE GRENADIER CORPS
LtGen Rajewski.

1st Gren Div, MG Pisareff.
Bde of MG Kniasnin: GrenR Araktchejeff, GrenR Jekaterinoslav (2 bns each).
Bde of Col Ocht: GrenR Tauride, GrenR St Petersburg (2 bns each).
Bde of Col Jemiljanoff: GrenR Kexholm, GrenR Bernau (**Perm**) (2 bns each).

2nd Gren Div, MG Tchoglokoff.
Bde of MG Levin: GrenR Moscow, GrenR Kiev (2 bns each).
Bde of Col Dumas: GrenR Astrakhan, GrenR Fanagoria (1 bn each).
Bde of MG ? (**Col Hesse**): GrenR Siberia, GrenR Little Russia (2 bns each).
Artillery: **33rd** Heavy FAB, **13th & 14th** Light FABs (36 guns).
Total: 22 bns, 9,100 men, 36 guns.

THE RUSSIAN IMPERIAL GUARD
LtGen Yermoloff.

Div of LtGen Rosen.
Bde of MG **Prince** Potemkin: Preobraschenski Life Guards, Semionowski Life Guards (3 bns each).
Bde of MG Bistrom: Ismailoffski Life Guards, Guards JgR (2 bns each).

Div of MG Udom I.
Bde of MG Kryschanoffski: Lithuanian Life Guards, Gren Guards (2 bns each).
Bde of MG Scheltuchin: Finnish Life Guards, Pawloffski Life Guards (2 bns each).
Artillery: **2nd** Heavy FAB, **1st & 2nd** Light FABs (36 guns).
Total: 18 bns, 8,070 men, 36 guns.

1st Kür Div of LtGen Depreradowitsch.
Bde of MG Arsenjeff (**Arsenius**): Chevalier Guards Regt, Horse Guards Regt (6 sqns each).

Bde of MG ? (**Prince Koburg**): Leib-KürR of the Czar, Leib-KürR of the Czarina (4 sqns each).

2nd Kür Div of MG Kretoff.
Bde of MG Leontieff: KürR Pskoff, KürR Glochoff (5 sqns each).
Bde of MG Karatschjeff: KürR Jekaterinoslav, KürR Astrakhan (4 sqns each).

3rd Kür Div of LtGen Count Duka II.
Bde of MG Lewaschoff: KürR Staroduboff, KürR Novgorod (4 sqns each).
Bde of MG Gudovitsch: KürR Little Russia, KürR Military Order (4 sqns each).

Light Cavalry Div of LtGen Schewisch (**MG Tschaklikoff**).
Hussars of the Guard, Dragoons of the Guard, Ulans of the Guard (6 sqns each), **Cossacks of the Guard (4 sqns)**.

Artillery: 3 × HABs (36 guns), **1st & 2nd Guards HABs (16 guns)**.

Total: 72 sqns, 7,200 men, 36 guns.

THE PRUSSIAN ROYAL GUARD
Foot Guards, Col von Alvensleben: 1st & 2nd Garde-Regiment zu Fuss (3 bns each), Garde-Jäger-Bn ($\frac{1}{2}$ bn).
Horse Guards, Col Laroche von Starkenfels (**Col von Werder**): Garde-du-Corps (5 sqns), Garde-Dragoon-Eskadron, Garde-Ulan-Eskadron, Garde-Hussar-Eskadron, 1st & 2nd Garde-Volontär-Jäger-Eskadrons, Garde-Cossacken-Eskadron (6 sqns).
Guard Artillery. 1 × HAB, 1 × FAB (16 × 6-pdr guns).
Total: 8 bns, 11 sqns, 6,680 men, 16 guns.

THE DON COSSACK CORPS
Ataman Count Platoff.
Col Bergmann: **GorinI** *Pulk*, **Grekoff I** *Pulk*, Kostine *Pulk*, Schaltanowka *Pulk*, Elmurusin *Pulk*, 1st Black Sea *Pulk*.
MG Prince Schtscherbatoff: Ataman *Pulk*, **Gorin II** *Pulk*, **Jagodin II** *Pulk*, **3rd Orenburg Regt, 2nd Teptjaerisch Regt**, Tschilikeff *Pulk*, Tchernobusoff *Pulk*, Grekoff V *Pulk*, Platoff V *Pulk*, **3rd Ural Regt**, Wlassoff V *Pulk*, **Wlassoff X** *Pulk*.
Total: 10 pulks, 3,800 men.

ARMY ARTILLERY RESERVE
MG Stime (killed in the battle).
$7\frac{1}{2}$ Btys (94 guns), 3 coys Pioneers.
1st Guards FAB, 1st, 14th, 29th & 36th Heavy FABs, 3rd & 23rd HABs, 10th HAB (6 guns), 1st HAB (2 guns), Guards Marine Equipage (2 guns).

Total, Russo-Prussian contingent of Army of Bohemia: 95 bns, 3 coys, 107 sqns, 10 pulks, 48,650 men, 314 guns.

II (PRUSSIAN) CORPS
LtGen von Kleist.
CoS: LtCol von Grolmann.
Prince Frederick of Orange (attached).

9th Bde, GM von Klüx.

Schl Schützen Bn ($\frac{1}{2}$ bn), 1st Westpr IR (3 bns), 6th ResIR (3 bns), 7th Schl LWIR (2 bns), 1st Schl LWCR (2 sqns), 1 x HAB (**7th FAB**) & Train coy.
Total: 8$\frac{1}{2}$ bns, 2 sqns, 5,833 men, 382 horses, 8 guns.

10th Bde, GM von Pirch I.
2nd Westpr IR (3 bns), 7th ResIR (2 bns), 9th LWIR (2 bns), 1st Schl LWCR (1 sqn), **16th** FAB & Train coy.
Total: 7 bns, 1 sqn, 4,551 men, 168 horses, 8 guns.

11th Bde, GM von Ziethen.
Schl Schützen Bn ($\frac{1}{2}$ bn), 1st Schl IR (3 bns), 10th ResIR (2 bns), 8th Schl LWIR (2 bns), Neum DragR (6 sqns), **1st Schl HusR (2$\frac{1}{2}$ sqns, with *Freiwillige-Jäger* detachments)**, 2nd Schl LWCR (1 sqn), **9th FAB** & Train coy.
Total: 7$\frac{1}{2}$ bns, 7 sqns, 5,363 men, 1,058 horses, 8 guns.

12th Bde, GM Prinz August von Preussen.
2nd Schl IR (3 bns), 11th ResIR (3 bns), 10th Schl LWIR (2 bns), Schl UlR (4$\frac{1}{2}$ sqns, **with *Freiwillige-Jäger* detachments**), **1st Schl HusR (2 sqns)**, 2nd Schl LWCR (1 sqn), 1 × FAB & Train coy.
Total: 8 bns, 5 sqns, 5,419 men, 646 horses, 8 guns.

Cavalry Bde, GM von Röder.
Ostpr KürR, Brandb KürR, Schl KürR (4$\frac{1}{2}$ sqns each, **with *Freiwillige-Jäger* detachments**), **7th & 8th HABs** & Train coys.
Total: 12 sqns, 2,350 men, 2,372 horses, 16 guns.

Cavalry Bde, Col von Mytius.
1st, 7th & 8th Schl LWCRs (5 [**6**]sqns in all).
Total: 5 (6) sqns, 650? men, 650? horses.

Corps Reserve Artillery, **LtCol von Braun**: 1 × 6-pdr FAB (**9th, 14th & 21st FABs**), 1 × 12-pdr FAB (**3rd & 6th FABs**), 1 × HAB (**9th & 10th HABs & 1st 7-pdr Howitzer Bty**) & Train coys, 2 × pioneer coys.

Total, II (Prussian) Corps: 31 bns, 2 coys, 32 sqns, 10 (14) btys, 24,251 men, 5,182 horses, 80 (112) guns.

STREIFKORPS

The Allies formed several *Streifkorps* (small corps of light cavalry and horse artillery) to operate deep in the enemy's flanks and rear, cutting up foraging detachments, capturing couriers and despatches, gathering intelligence from the inhabitants and spreading false rumours about Allied strengths and movements. Such corps had been used to no small effect in Russia in 1812 and had been modelled on the operations of the Spanish guerrillas.

RUSSIAN *STREIFCORPS* OF LtGen von THIELMANN

Bde of LtCol Freiherr von Gasser: ChLR Hohenzollern Nr 2 (2 sqns, 210 men), ChLR Klenau Nr 5 (1 sqn, 140 men), HusR Kienmayer Nr8 (1 sqn, 100 men).
Bde of GM Prinz Biron von Kurland: Schl HusR Nr 2 (2$\frac{1}{2}$ sqns, 200 men), **2nd** Schl NCR (2 sqns, 250 men), **Neum DragR (*Freiwillige-Jäger* Sqn).**
Don Cossack Bde of Col Count Orloff-Denissoff: Gorin II & Jagodin II *Pulks* (600 men in all).
Artillery. 2 × Austrian HA howitzers, 2 × Cossack HA guns (**unicorns**).
Total: 8$\frac{1}{2}$ sqns, 2 pulks, 1,500 men, 4 guns.

AUSTRIAN *STREIFKORPS* OF Col COUNT MENSDORFF-POUILLY

HusR Eh Ferdinand Nr 3 (2 sqns, 260 men), HusR Hessen-Homburg Nr 4 (1 sqn, 130 men), Gorin I & Illowaiski X Don Cossack *Pulks* (400 men in all).
Total: 3 sqns, 2 pulks, 790 men.

RUSSIAN STREIFKORPS OF MG ILLOWAISKI XII

Grekoff I, Grekoff VIII & Illowaiski XII Don Cossack *Pulks* (850 men in all).

SUMMARY OF THE ARMY OF BOHEMIA

	Bns	Coys	Sqns	Btys	Guns	Men
Austrians	120	$44\frac{1}{2}$	132*	$56\frac{1}{2}$	388	121,599
Russians	95	3	107*	$26\frac{1}{2}$	314	48,650
Prussians	31	2	$36\frac{1}{2}$*	10	80	24,251
Total:	246	$49\frac{1}{2}$	271*	$92\frac{1}{2}$	782	194,430

* *+18 pulks, including those with Thielmann and Mensdorff.*

DETACHED TROOPS

Escort to Kaiser Franz I of Austria: KürR Sommariva Nr 5 (2 sqns), 1 Gren Bn (600 men).
Total: 802 men.

Escort to Czar Alexander I and King Friedrich Wilhelm III: Cossacks (2 sqns), various duty bns from the Russo-Prussian Reserve Corps.

Mobile Column of MG Freiherr von Herzogenberg: IR Reuss-Greitz Nr 18 (LW Bn), DragR Riesch Nr 6 (1 sqn), ChLR Rosenberg Nr 6 (1 sqn), 2nd Schl LWCR (2 sqns), Russian UlR Serpuchoff (4 sqns).
Total: 1,151 infantry, 960 cavalry.

Prisoner of War Escorts: 2nd & 11th Baschkir Regiments.

D: Order of battle of the Army of Silesia

Cmdr: **Prussian General der Kavallerie von Blücher.**
ADC: Rttm Graf von Nostitz.

The following headquarters organisation is taken from Vitzthum von Eckstädt.
CoS: Generalquartiermeister (Prussian equivalent of CoS) GM Neithardt von Gneisenau.
ADC: Prlt von Fehrentheil; Attached: LW-Prlt von Stosch.

The General Staff

Chief of the GS Office for Tactical Operations.
QM: Obst von Müffling.
ADCs: Sklt von Gerlach (attached from the infantry), Maj Rühle von Lilienstern, Kapt von Knackfuss, Prlt von Oesfeld, Sklt von Scharnhorst.
Intelligence Office: Maj von Oppen; Attached: *Oberjaeger* Roth, Jägers and cartographers.

Adjutantur

For army orders and personnel matters: *1st Adj*: Obst Graf von der Goltz; *Chef der Kanzlei*: Strttm Graf von Moltke (drowned in the upper Elbe at end of August), Kapt von Unruh.

For reinforcements and parade states: Kapt von Brünneck, Stkapt von Kezewsky. Attached: 1 vice auditor, 1 clerk and several Jäger couriers.

General Commanding the Artillery, Engineers, Ammunition and Equipment Resupply, and the Silesian Fortresses: GM von Rauch.
Attached from the *Adjutantur*: Kapt von Liebenroth of the engineers.
Attached from the artillery: Prlt von Bock.

Commissary General: State Councillor von Ribbentrop with 1 official.

Generalwagenmeister (transport manager).

Generalchirurg (staff surgeon).

Headquarters Cmdt: Maj von Wedell (until mid-September), Maj Graf Hardenberg, *Volontairoffizier* von Harlem (attached from Intelligence Office).

Security Guard: a detachment of Don Cossacks.
Headquarters Police: 1 officer and 20 mounted gendarmes.

Attached Prussian officers: GL Prinz Wilhelm von Preussen, Lt Graf von Brühl, LW-*Offiziere* von Raume and Eichhorn, *Jägeroffizier* Häckel (of Lützow's Jägers), *Volontairoffiziere* Focke, Steffens and several others. Personal physician to the commander: *Stabschirurgus* Bieske.

Attached Russian officers: MG Baron Teils, Col Baron Tuyll-Serooskerken, Col (and ADC) Bartholomay.

Austrian Military Attaché: Maj von Marschall.

I (PRUSSIAN) CORPS

The OOB of battle of Yorck's corps is taken from his biography by Droysen. This differs greatly from the other sources quoted but seems to reflect the actual groupings as mentioned for 16 October by Seyfert, whose account is highly regarded and very detailed. After the heavy losses suffered at Möckern on the 16th, Yorck's corps was slightly reorganised from the details shown here.

NB All totals include the detached troops; actual strengths at Leipzig were thus much lower than shown here. Throughout this listing, * indicates an officer wounded on 16 October, and † an officer killed on 16 October.

GL von Yorck.
CoS: Col von Zielinski; *Adj*: Capt Delius.
Oberquartiermeister: LtCol Freiherr von Valentini.
GS: Maj Wilhelm von Schack, Maj von Klitzling, Capt von Dedenroth, Capt von Lollhöfel, Lt von Wussow; *Adjs*: Maj Graf Brandenburg, Maj von Diedrich, Capt von Selasinsky, Rttm Ferdinand von Schack, Lt von Below, Lt von Röder.
Kriegskommissar: von Reiche.
Corps medical officer: Dr Völtze.
Headquarters medical officer: Dr Hohenhorst.
Padre: Divsprediger Schultze.

1st Bde, Col von Steinmetz*.
Staff: Capt von Kaufbergt.
Adjs: Capt von Lützow, Lt Henkel von Donnersmark.
1st Gren Bde, Maj Hiller von Gärtringen*: 1st Ostpr Gren-Bn (Maj von Leslie*),
Leib-Grenadier-Bn (Maj von Carlowitz*), Schl Gren Bn (Maj von Burghof),
Westpr Gren-Bn (Maj von Schon*).
2nd LW Bde, Col von Losthin*: 5th Schl LWIR (Maj von Maltzahnt) (3 bns, Maj
von Mumm*, Maj von Seydlitz*, Maj von Koseckyt; 2nd Bn was in Görlitz), 13th
Schl LWIR (Maj von Gödiket) (4 bns, Maj von Larisch, Maj Walter von Cronegk,
Maj von Rekowskyt, Maj von Martitz).
Cavalry: 2nd Leib HusR (Maj von Stöffel) (4 sqns).
Artillery: 2nd 6-pdr FAB (Lt Lange) (8 guns).
Total: 11 bns, 4 sqns, 9,270 men, 8 guns.

2nd Bde, Gen Maj Prinz Karl von Mecklenburg*.
Staff: Maj von Schütz*, Lt von Riesenburg.
Adjs: Maj von Folgersberg, Capt von Heinzmann.
1st Line Bde, LtCol von Lobenthal*: 1st Ostpr IR (3 bns, Maj von Schleuset, Maj
von Kurnatowsky*, Maj von Pentzig*), 2nd Ostpr IR (LtCol von Sjöholm) (3 bns,
Maj von Dessauniers*, Maj von Krauthof, Maj ?).
2nd LW Bde: 6th Schl LWIR (Maj von Fischer*) (1 combined bn).
Cavalry: Mecklenburg-Strelitz HusR (LtCol von Warburg) (4 sqns).
Artillery: 1st 6-pdr FAB (Capt Huet) (8 guns).
Total: 7 bns, 4 sqns, 7,673 men, 8 guns.

7th Bde, Col von Horn.
Staff: Maj von Rudolphi, Lt von Manstein.
Adjs: Capt Graf Kanitz, Lt von Barfuss*, Lt von Reibnitz*.
1st Line Bde, Col von Zepelin: Leib-Regiment (Col von Zepelin) (3 bns, Maj von
Oertzen, Maj von Hagen, Maj von Ledebur), Thüringian Bn (Maj von Linker),
Gardejaeger (Capt von Bock) ($\frac{1}{2}$ bn).
2nd LW Bde, Col von Welzien: 4th Schl LWIR (Maj Graf Herzberg) (2 bns; 1st Bn
was in Wartenburg, 2nd & 4th Bns had been combined into one in September);
Maj Graf Reichenberg, 15th Schl LWIR (Col von Wollzogen*) (3 bns, Maj von
Sommerfeld, Maj von Pettinger, Maj Graf Wedell; 3rd Bn was in Wartenburg).
Cavalry: 3rd Schl LWCR (Maj von Falkenhausen) (2 sqns), Brandb HusR (Maj
von Sohr*) (3 sqns).
Artillery: 3rd 6-pdr FAB (Capt Ziegler*) (8 guns).
Total: 8$\frac{1}{2}$ bns, 5 sqns, 8,686 men, 8 guns.

8th Bde, GM von Hünerbein.
Staff: Capt von Arnaud, Lt von Unruh.
Adjs: Lt von Unruh, Lt von Sellin.
1st Line Bde, LtCol von Borcke*: Brandb IR (Maj von Bülow) (3 bns, Maj von
Othegraven*, Maj von Krosigkt, Maj ?), 12th ResIR (Maj ?) (3 bns, Maj von
Hermann, Maj von Zepelin, Maj von Laurens*).
2nd LW Bde: 14th Schl LWIR (Col von Gotze) (2nd & 3rd Bns, Maj von Thile*,
Maj von Brixen; 1st & 4th Bns were in Wartenburg).
Cavalry: Brandb HusR (Maj von Knaublauch), 3rd Schl LWCR (Maj von Kani-
lowsky) (2 sqns each).
Artillery: 15th 6-pdr FAB (Lt Anders) (8 guns).
Total: 8 bns, 4 sqns, 7,447 men, 8 guns.

Corps Reserve Cavalry, Col Freiherr von Wahlen-Jürgass.
Staff: Rttm Freiherr von Canitz, Lt von Briesen.
Adjs: Maj von Palusdorf, Graf Reuss LXIII, Graf Ingenheim.
1st Bde, Col Graf Henkel von Donnersmark: Lithuanian DragR (LtCol von Below) (4½ **sqns including** *Freiwillige-Jägers*), 1st Westpr DragR (LtCol von Wuthenow) (4 sqns).
2nd Bde, LtCol von Katzeler*: Brandb UlR (Maj von Stutterheim), Ostpr NCR (Maj Graf Lehndorf) (4 sqns each).
3rd Bde, Maj von Bieberstein: 5th Schl LWCR (Maj von Ozorowsky), 10th Schl LWCR (Maj von Sohr), 1st Neum LWCR (Maj von Sydow) (4 sqns each).
Artillery: 1st (Capt von Zinken) & 3rd (Lt von Barowsky) HABs (16 guns).
Total: 28½ sqns, 3,896 men, 16 guns.

Corps Reserve Artillery, LtCol von Schmidt.
Staff: Maj von Fiebig, Maj von Rentzell, Maj von Graumann.
Adjs: Lt Erhard, Lt von Peucker.
Engineers: Maj Markoff, Lt von Hülsen, Lt von Poser.
1st (Lt Witte) & 2nd (Lt Simon) 12-pdr FABs, 12th (Lt Bully) & 24th (Lt Varenkampf) 6-pdr FABs, 1st 3-pdr FAB (Lt von Oppen), 3rd (Lt Fischer) & 12th (Rttm von Pfeil) HABs. *Total: 973 men.*
Park: *Parkkolonnen* Nrs 1, 3, 5, 11 & 13, *Handwerkercolonne* Nr 2. *Total: 126 men.*
Pioneers: 2 coys (149 men).
Total: 1,248 men, 56 guns.

Total, I (Prussian) Corps: 34½ bns, 1 coy, 45½ sqns, 38,220 men (including 1,576 volunteers & 15,236 LW), 13 btys, 104 guns.

SACKEN'S RUSSIAN CORPS
GL Baron Osten Sacken.
CoS: Col Count Rochechouart.
Cmdr of Avantgarde and Cavalry: GL Wasilltschikoff.

10th Div of MG Count Lieven III.
Bde of MG ? (**Agatin**): IR Jaroslav (2 bns).
Bde of Col Baron Sass: IR Crimea, IR Bialostock (2 bns each).
Bde of Col Achlesticheff: JgR Nr 8 & Nr 39 (2 bns each).
Total: 3,259 men, 0 guns.

16th Div of MG Repninski (part).
Bde of Col Rachmanoff: IR Ochotsk, IR Kamtchatka (2 bns each).
Total: 787 men, 0 guns.

27th Div of LtGen Nevjerowski.
Bde of Col Stawicki (**LtCol Lewandowsky**): IR Odessa, IR Wilna (1 bn each).
Bde of Col Alexejeff: IR Simbirsk, IR Tarnopol (1 bn each).
Bde of Col Kologriboff: JgR Nr 49 (2 bns) & Nr 50 (1 bn).
Total: 3,093 men, 0 guns.

Cavalry: LtGen Wasilltschikoff.
3rd Drag Div of MG Pantschulitcheff II (part).
Bde of MG Uschakoff: DragR Smolensk (2 sqns), DragR Kurland (5 sqns).
Total: 501 men, 0 guns.

2nd Hus Div of MG Lanskoi.

Bde of MG Yurkowski: HusR Aleksandria (5 sqns), HusR Mariupol (6 sqns).
Bde of Col Wasilltchikoff (**II**): HusR White Russia (4 sqns), HusR Achtyrsk (6 sqns).
Total: 2,637 men, 0 guns.

Cossack Div of MG Karpoff II.
4th Ukrainian Cossacks (3 sqns), St Petersburg (**Volunteer**) Cossacks (4 sqns).
Don Cossacks: Grekoff I (**III**), Illowaiski IX, Karpoff II, Kuteinikoff IV, Lukowkin II, **Popoff XIII**, Sementchikoff IV *Pulks.*
2nd (**9th**) Baschkir Regt, 2nd Kalmuck Regt (1 *pulk* each), **4th Ukrainian Cossack Regt (3 sqns)**.
Total: 2,449 men, 0 guns.

Corps Reserve Artillery, Cmdr unknown.
18th HAB, 10th (**20th**) & 13th Heavy FABs, 24th & 35th (**25th**) Light FABs, 1 pioneer coy (87 men).
Total: 1,072 men, 60 guns.

Total, Sacken's Corps: 19 bns, 1 coy, 35 sqns, 8 pulks, 13,798 men, 5 btys, 60 guns.
The very low number of guns with this corps is not explained.

LANGERON'S RUSSIAN CORPS GROUP
GdI Count Langeron.
CoS: Col von Neidhardt.

AVANTGARDE
LtGen Rudzewitch.

LtGen Korff's Div
DragR Kargopol (4 sqns), DragR Kiev (4 sqns), DragR Kinburn (2 sqns), MtdRR Dorpat (2 sqns), MtdRR Livland (2 sqns), 1st & 3rd Ukrainian Cossacks (3 sqns each), Kutainikoff VIII & Selivanoff II Don Cossack *Pulks.*
Total: 20 sqns, 2 pulks, 3,194 men.

9th Div, MG Udom II (detached from IX [Russian] Corps).
Bde of Col Poltaratzki: IR Nascheburg (1 bn), IR Apscheron (2 bns).
Bde of MG Juschkoff II: IR Rjesk (2 bns), IR Jakutsk (1 bn).
Bde of MG Grimblatt: JgR Nr 10 & Nr 38 (1 bn each).
Total: 8 bns, 3,322 men, 0 guns.

Artillery (detached from IX [Russian] Corps; see below): 15th Heavy FAB, 8th HAB (24 guns), 1 pioneer company. *Total: 444 men.*

Total, Avantgarde: 8 bns, 1 coy, 20 sqns, 2 pulks, 6,960 men, 2 btys, 24 guns.

VIII (RUSSIAN) CORPS
LtGen Count Saint-Priest.

11th Div of MG Gurjaloff.
Bde of MG Karpenko: IR Jeletz, IR Polotzk (1 [**2**] bn each).
Bde of Col Turgenjeff: IR Rylsk (1 bn), IR Jekaterinburg (2 bns) (**2 bns each**).
Bde of Col von Bistrom II: JgR Nr 1 (1 [**2**] bns) & Nr 33 (**38**) (2 bns).
*Total: 8 (12) bns, 3,602 (**4,200**) men, 0 guns.*

17th Div of MG von Pillar (**or Z.D. Olsuvieff**).
Bde of Col Kern: IR Rjasan, IR Bielosersk (2 bns each).
Bde of Col Tschertoff I: IR Brest, IR Wilmannstrand (2 [**1**] bns each).
Bde of Maj Charitanoff: JgR Nr 30 & Nr 48 (2 [**1**] bns each).
*Total: 12 [8] bns, 4,072 (**2,800**) men, 0 guns.*

Combined Cavalry Div of LtGen Borosdin II.
Not shown as part of Saint-Priest's corps in Kerchnawe's table.
Bde of MG **Dawidoff**: DragR New Russia, DragR Mitau, DragR Charkoff (4 sqns each, 1,139 men).
Bde of MG Kaissaroff: Greckoff XXI & Jeschoff II Don Cossack *Pulks* & Stawropol Kalmucks (809 men).
Total: 12 sqns, 3 pulks, 2,118 men, 0 guns.

Reserve Artillery: 32nd Heavy FAB, 32nd & 33rd Light FABs (601 men, 36 guns).

*Total, VIII (Russian) Corps: 20 bns, 12 (**0**) sqns, 3 (**0**) pulks, 10,393 (**7,000**) men, 3 btys, 36 guns.*

IX (RUSSIAN) CORPS
LtGen Olsuvieff (elsewhere given incorrectly as **LtGen Kapsevitch**).

15th Div of MG Korniloff.
Bde of Col Torn: IR Witebsk, IR Koselsk (1 bn each).
Bde of Col Mensur: IR Kolywan (1 bn), IR Kursk (2 bns).
Bde of Col Tichanowski I: JgR Nr 12 (2 bns) & Nr 22 (1 bn).

Total, IX (Russian) Corps: 2,892 men, 0 guns.

X (RUSSIAN) CORPS
LtGen Kapsevitch (elsewhere given incorrectly as **LtGen Olsuvieff**).

8th Div of MG Prince Urusoff.
Bde of Col Schenschin: IR Archangel, IR Old Ingermannland (2 bns each).
Bde of Col Rehren: IR Schlüsselburg (1 bn), JgR Nr 7 (2 bns) & Nr 37 (1 bn).
Total: 6 bns, 2,921 men, 0 guns.

22nd Div of MG Turtschaninoff.
Bde of MG Schkapskoi: IR Wiatka, IR Staroi Okolsk (2 bns each).
Bde of Col Durnoff: JgR Nr 29 & Nr 45 (2 bns each).
Total: 8 bns, 3,036 men, 0 guns.

Attached from 1st MtdR Div, I Cavalry Corps, **MG Denissieff**: Sjewersk & Arssamas MtdRRs (2 sqns each).
Total: 4 sqns, 383 men, 0 guns.

Attached from 2nd MtdR Div, I Cavalry Corps, MG Count Pahlen II (Other sources show MG E.A. Emanuel commanding these 2 regts on 18 October):
Lifland & Dorpat MtdRRs (2 sqns each).
Artillery: 8th HAB (12 guns).

Reserve Artillery: 2nd, 18th, 34th, 39th Heavy FABs, 3rd, 19th, 29th Light FABs, 2nd Don Cossack HAB.
2 pioneer coys, 2 Pontonier coys, 1 Naval Equipage coy.
Reserve Artillery: 10th Heavy FAB, 29th Light FAB.

1 pioneer coy, 4th & 5th Pontonier coys, 75th Naval Equipage coy.
Total: 3 coys, 2,319 men, 8 btys, 86 guns.

Total, X (Russian) Corps: 14 bns, 3 coys, 4 [8] sqns, 8,686 men, 8 btys, 86 (98) guns.

Total, Langeron's Russian Corps Group: 53 (52) bns, 6 (7) coys, 36 (41) sqns, 5 (6) pulks, 28,914 (23,600) men, 13 btys, 146 (156) guns.

STREIFKORPS

PRUSSIAN *STREIFKORPS* OF Maj VON BOLTENSTERN
Prussian Garde-Jäger Bn (1 coy & *Freiwillige-Jäger* detachment), Neum LWCR ($\frac{1}{2}$ sqn), 1st Ukrainian Cossack Regt ($\frac{1}{2}$ sqn).
Total: 250 infantry, 80 cavalry.

PRUSSIAN *STREIFKORPS* OF Capt COUNT PUCKLER
Brandb HusR (*Freiwillige-Jäger* detachment), 3rd Ukrainian Cossack *Pulk* ($\frac{1}{2}$ sqn).
Total: 100 men.

PRUSSIAN *STREIFKORPS* OF Maj VON COLOMB
2 combined sqns from II (Prussian) Corps.
Total: ca 170 men.

SUMMARY OF THE ARMY OF SILESIA

	Bns	Coys	Sqns	Pulks	Btys	Guns	Men
I (Prussian) Corps	$33\frac{1}{2}$	1	42	–	13	104	21,149
Sacken's Russian Corps	19	1	35	8	5	60	13,798
Langeron's (Russian) Corps	53	6	36	5	13	146	28,914
Total:	$105\frac{1}{2}$	8	113	13	31	310	63,861
Total:	$96\frac{1}{2}$	9	$115\frac{1}{2}$		27	288	48,266

E: Order of battle of the Army of the North

The following full organisation of the headquarters is taken from Vitzthum von Eckstädt.

Headquarters of the Army of the North (after the armistice).
Cmdr: Carl Johann, Crown Prince of Sweden.
ADC: General von Carlheim-Gyllenskjöld.
Adjs: LtCols von Camps, von Holst, Wirsen & Graf Montrichard, Majs Hierta & Forsell, Rttms Baron Stierncrona, Baron von Essen, Baron Adlerkreutz, Capts Pählman, Forselles von Thun & Graf von Noailles.

Prussian Adjs: LtCol Graf Kalkreuth (chief of the secret police and intelligence gathering), Maj von Kleist (from Wallmoden's Corps), Maj von Brause & Rttm Graf von Hacke (from III Corps), Capt von Gädicke & Lt Graf Schlieffen (from IV Corps).
Prussian orderly officers: Lts Caesar & von Rapin.
Russian Adj: Capt Krasnokockii.

Crown Prince's Suite
Chamberlain: Graf Brahe; *Prussian Chamberlain:* von Podewils; *Master of the Horse:* Maj Flichet; *Royal Surgeon:* Coholm & 1 assistant surgeon; *Major-domo:* Chapell, various butlers, chefs, scullions, hunters & other servants; Rough Rider Ahrntz, 19 drivers, postilions & grooms.

Political Officials
Court Chancellor: Baron Wetterstedt; *Cabinet Secretaries:* Schultzenheim, Baron Stjerneld, Hartmannsdorf & 2 secretaries; *War Adviser:* Gyllenkam with secretary Ullric; *Administrative Adviser:* Schlegel; *State Secretary for War:* Wirsen; 4 secretaries, 1 printer with 4 assistants.

Chief of GS: General of Cavalry Baron Adlerkreutz.
Deputy Chiefs: MGs Baron Tawast & Graf Löwenhielm.
Senior Adjs: LtCol von Peyron, Maj Akrell, Rttm Baron Engeström, Capts von Heykenskjöld & von Pantzerhielm, Lt Graf von Rosen.
Headquarters Cmdt: initially Col Bergencreutz, replaced a few days after end of the armistice by Prussian Maj von Ciriacy.
Staff Adj: Lt Hederstierna.

Headquarters Guard: 1 field officer, 13 junior officers, 300 men of Swedish Guard Infantry, 50 men of Swedish Horse Guards, and a Russian 'escort'.

Commissar General: *Geheime Kriegsrat* Crelinger and 15 Prussian commissars.

Headquarters domestic staff: 78 servants, 115 horses including 36 for the Crown Prince.

Ambassadors and Military Attachés
Austria: FML Baron Vincent (as of early September), Rttm Graf Bellegarde.
Britain: Minister Thornton, LtCol Cooke & (as of early October) General Sir Charles Stewart.
Prussia: MG von Krusemarck (as of 28 August).
Russia: MG Freiherr von Suchtelen, Col Graf Pozzo di Borgo, Lt Marquis de la Maisonfort.

III (PRUSSIAN) CORPS
GL von Bülow.
CoS: Col von Boyen.
Since 2 October the following Austrian officers had been attached to the Headquarters: Maj V. Augustin & Capt Franz Ritter von Hannekarl of GQM's staff & Col Franz Freiherr von Hacker, Capt Graf Bernhard Caboga & Lt Graf E. Auersperg of Engineer Corps.

3rd Div of GM Prinz Ludwig von Hessen-Homburg.
Bde of LtCol von Sjöholm II: 2nd Ostpr Gren Bn, 3rd Ostpr IR (2 bns; 3rd Bn was in Bernburg), 4th ResIR (3 bns), 4th Ostpr LWIR (4 bns), 1st Leib HusR (4 sqns).
Artillery: 5th 6-pdr FAB (8 guns).
Total: 7,168 men, 8 guns.

5th Div of GM von Borstell.
Bde of LtCol von Schoon: Pomm Gren Bn, Pomm IR (3 bns), 2nd ResIR (3 bns), 2nd Kurmk LWIR (4 bns).

Bde of Col von Hobe: Pomm HusR, Westpr UlR (4 sqns each).
Artillery: 10th 6-pdr FAB (8 guns).
Total: 7,767 men, 8 guns.

6th Div of Col von Krafft.
Bde of Maj von Zastrow: Colberg IR, 9th ResIR, Neum LWIR (3 bns each), Pomm NCR (3 sqns).
Artillery: 16th 6-pdr FAB (8 guns).
Attached from 4th Div: Ostpr JgBn (2 coys, 322 men).
Total: 6,017 men, 8 guns.

Reserve Cavalry Div of GM von Oppen.
Bde of Col von Treskow: DragR Königin, Brandb DragR, 2nd Westpr DragR (4 sqns each).
Bde of Col von Sydow: 2nd Kurmk LWCR, 4th Kurmk LWCR, 2nd Pomm LWCR (4 sqns each).
Artillery: 5th & 6th HABs (16 guns).
Total: 2,761 men, 16 guns.

Attached from the Russians:
Bde of Col Dietrichs III: Bychalow II & Illowaiski V Don Cossack *Pulks* (440 men).
Artillery: 7th & 21st Heavy FABs (453 men, 22 guns).

Reserve Artillery, LtCol von Holtzendorf.
19th 6-pdr FAB, 4th & 5th 12-pdr FABs, 11th HAB (753 men, 32 guns).
2 pioneer coys (153 men).

Total, III (Prussian) Corps: 30 bns, 2 coys, 39 sqns, 2 pulks, 24,619 men, 11 btys, 94 guns.

RUSSIAN CORPS OF LtGen BARON VON WINTZINGERODE
CoS: MG von Rönne.

Avantgarde, LtGen Woronzoff.
Bde of MG Kniper: 2nd JgR (1 bn), 13th JgR (2 bns), 14th JgR (2 bns).
Bde of MG Benkendorf: Pawlograd HusR (6 sqns), Wolhynia UlR (3 sqns), Djatschkin Cossack *Pulk.*
Bde of Col Melnikoff IV: Melnikow IV & Melnikoff V Cossack *Pulks.*
Bde of MG Staal: Andrejanoff II Cossack *Pulk* & 1st Baschkir Regt.
Bde of Col Brändel: 1st Bug & 3rd Ural Cossack *Pulks.*
Artillery: 11th HAB (12 guns).
Total: 5 bns, 9 sqns, 7 pulks, 6,298 men, 1 bty, 12 guns.

21st Div of MG Lapteff.
Bde of Col Rosen: IR Petrowsk, IR Lithuania, IR Podolia (1 bn each).
Bde of Col Rüdiger: IR Newa (1 bn), JgR Nr 44 (2 bns).
Artillery: 31st Heavy FAB, 42nd Light FAB (24 guns).
Total: 6 bns, 4,049 men, 24 guns.

24th Div of MG Wuitsch.
Bde of Col Zwarykin: IR Schirwan, IR Ufa (2 bns each).
Bde of Col Macnew: IR Butyrsk, 19th JgR (2 bns each).
Bde of Col Bukinski: IR Tomsk & JgRNr 40 (1 bn each).
Artillery: 46th Light FAB (12 guns).
Total: 4,355 men, 12 guns.

Temporary Div of MG Harpe.
Bde of MG ?: IR Tula (2 bns), IR Nowaginsk (2 bns), Grens (3 bns).
Artillery: 21st & 26th Heavy FABs, 1 × HAB (24 guns).
Total: 4,506 men, 24 guns.

Cavalry Div of MG Manteuffel.
DragR St Petersburg (4 sqns), HusR Jelisawetgrad (6 sqns), St Petersburg
Volunteer Cossacks (2 sqns).
Artillery: 4th HAB (8 guns).
Total: 1,576 men, 8 guns.

Cavalry Div of MG Magnus Pahlen.
DragR Riga (3 sqns), DragR Finland (2 sqns), HusR Iszum (4 sqns).
Artillery: 1st & 5th HABs (16 guns).
Total: 1,282 men, 16 guns.

Cavalry Bde of MG ?.
Njeschin MtdRR (2 sqns), Polish UlR (6 sqns).
Total: 925 men.

Cossack Bde of MG ?.
Barabantschikoff II, Grekoff IX, Illowaiski IV & Lotschilin I Cossack *Pulks.*
Total: 1,748 men.

Total, Wintzingerode's Corps: 28 bns, 38 sqns, 11 pulks, 24,739 men, 10 btys, 96?
guns.

SWEDISH ARMY CORPS
FM Count Stedingk.
CoS: Col Björnsterna.
The available documentation on this corps is extremely vague and partially
contradictory.

1st Div of MG Posse.
1st Bde of MG Schulzenheim: Svea LG Regt (1 bn), 2nd LG Regt (1 bn), Grens of
the LG (1 bn), Leib-Gren Regt (2 bns).
2nd Bde of MG Lagerbring: Upland IR (2 bns), Södermanland IR (2 bns),
Nordschonen IR (1 bn), Pomm Legion Inf (1 coy).
Cavalry Bde of MG ?: LG DragR (5 sqns), Pomm Legion Cav (1 sqn).
Artillery, Maj Endenjelm: 2 x 6-pdr FABs (? guns).
Total: ? men, ? guns.

2nd Div of LtGen Sandels.
3rd Bde of Col Brändström: Westgotha IR, Westmanland IR, Nerike IR (2 bns
each).
4th Bde of MG Kasimir Reuterskjöld: Skaraborg IR (2 bns), Elfsborg IR (2 bns),
Wermland Feld Jg (1 bn).
6th Bde of MG Boije: Kronoberg IR, Calmar IR (1 bn each).
Artillery, Maj Geist: 2 × 6-pdr FABs (? guns).
Total: ? men, ? guns.

Cavalry Div of LtGen Sköldebrand.
Leib-KürR (4 sqns), Schonen HusR (6 sqns), Mörner HusR (5 sqns), Småland
DragR (6 sqns).

Artillery: 1 × HAB (? guns).
Total: ? men, ? guns.

Reserve Artillery, Col Cardell: 1 × 12-pdr & 1 × 6-pdr FABs (? guns).

Attached Troops.
Rebrejeff Don Cossack *Pulk* (362 men).
1 × British Rocket Battery (32 rocket launchers, 151 men).

Total, Swedish Army Corps: 23 bns, 1 coy, 27 sqns, 1 pulk, 17,165 men, 8 btys, 46 guns, 32 rocket launchers.

SUMMARY OF THE ARMY OF THE NORTH

	Bns	*Coys*	*Sqns*	*Pulks*	*Btys*	*Guns*	*Men*
III (Prussian) Corps	30	4	39	2	11	94	25,512
Wintzingerode's Russian Corps	28	–	38	11	10	86	24,739
Swedish Army Corps	23	1	27	1	8	46*	17,165
Totals:	*81*	*5*	*104*	*14*	*29*	*226**	*67,416*

* + 32 rocket launchers.

F: Order of battle of the Reserve Army of Poland

Cmdr: GdC Count Bennigsen.
CoS: LtGen Oppermann.
GQM: MG Count Berg.
Cmdr of the Artillery: MG Reswoy.
Austrian Col Josef Freiherr von Rosner was attached to this GHQ.

AVANTGARDE DIV
LtGen Stroganoff.
Bde of MG Gljeboff: 6th & 41st JgRs (2 bns each), 1 coy of sappers.
Artillery: 10th HAB (2 guns), 56th Light FAB (12 guns).
Light Cavalry Bde of MG ? (**Prince Bagration**): 1st Combined HusR (5 sqns), 1st Combined UlR (5 sqns), Andrejanoff III, Platoff V & Wlassoff III Don Cossack *Pulks* (Platoff V & Wlassoff III detached to Platoff's Cossack Corps), 4th Ural Cossack *Pulk*, 2 × Baschkir *Pulks*.
Cossack Bde of MG Tenischeff: Penza & Simbirsk LW Cossack *Pulks*.
Total, Avantgarde Div: 4 bns, 1 coy, 10 sqns, 8 pulks, 8,257 men, 2 btys, 14 guns.

CORPS OF GdI DOKTOROFF
GdI Doktoroff.

12th Div of MG Prince Chowanskoi.
Bde of MG Sanders: IR Smolensk, IR Narwa (2 bns each).
Bde of MG Scheltuchin: IR Alexopol, IR New Ingermannland (2 bns each).
Artillery: 45th Heavy FAB, 1st Light FAB (24 guns).
Total: 6,210 men, 24 guns.

26th Div of MG Paskiewitsch.
Bde of MG Sawoina (some sources put Paskiewitsch in command of both the div and this bde): IR Ladoga, IR Poltawa (2 bns each).
Bde of Col Schemtschuschnikoff: IR Nischni-Nowgorod, IR Orel (2 bns each).
Bde of MG ? (**Col Kowrigin**): JgR Nr 5 & Nr 42 (**Nr 12**) (2 bns each).
Artillery: 26th Heavy FAB, 47th Light FAB (24 guns).
Total: 7,195 men, 24 guns.

13th Div of MG Lindfors.
Bde of MG Rossi: IR Galizien (2 bns), IR Weliki-Luki (3 bns).
Bde of MG Ivanoff: IR Penza (2 bns), IR Saratoff (3 bns).
Total: 6,711 men, 0 guns.

Cavalry Div of LtGen Tschaplitz.
Bde of MG Repninski Combined DragR (5 sqns), 1st & 2nd Combined MtRR (4 sqns each).
Bde of MG Kreutz; 2nd Combined UlR (4 sqns), Siberian UlR (2 sqns), Taganrog UlR (4 sqns), Zhitomir UlR (2 sqns).
Artillery: 2nd HAB (12 guns).
Total: 3,532 men, 12 guns.

Cavalry Bde of MG Knorring (attached from Wittgenstein's Corps).
Tartar UlR (6 sqns), Radjanoff Don Cossack *Pulk*, Poltawa Cossack *Pulk*, 14th Baschkirs.
Total: 800 men.

Reserve Artillery, Col Kotolinski 18th, 48th & 53rd Light FABs, 22nd Heavy FAB, 9th HAB, 1 coy miners, **1st & 7th** coys Pontoniers.
Total: 1,170 men, 60 guns.

Total, Reserve Army of Poland: 34 bns, 4 coys, 41 sqns, 11 pulks, 33,875 men, 12 btys, 134 guns.

G: Overview of the combined Allied armies

	Bns	Coys	Sqns	Pulks	Btys	Guns	Men
Army of Bohemia	246	49½	271	18	92½	782	194,430
Army of Silesia	105½	8	113	13	31	310	63,861
Army of the North	81	5	104	14	29	226	67,416
Reserve Army of Poland	34	4	41	11	12	134*	33,875
Total:	*466½*	*66½*	*533½*	*56*	*165½*	*1,452**	*359,582*

* + 32 rocket launchers.

	Bns	Coys	Sqns	Pulks	Btys	Guns	Men
Army of Bohemia	196½	61	259	23	91⅓	742	137,617
Army of Silesia	96½	9	115	16	31	288	48,270
Reserve Army of Poland	34	2	31	6	12	134*	27,900
Total:†	*327*	*72*	*405*	*45*	*134½*	*1,164**	*213,787*

* + 32 rocket launchers.

† Kerchnawe gives no details of the Army of the North.

Please note that, as a result of conflicting sources, many of these figures do not tally with those given for the same armies in the preceding appendices.

H: Losses of Klenau's IV (Austrian) Corps at Liebertwolkwitz on 14 October

	Dead		Wounded		PW		Missing		Total	
	Offs	*Men*	*Offs*	*Men*	*Offs*	*Men*	*Offs*	*Men*	*Offs*	*Men*
Generals	–	–	1*	–	–	–	–	–	1	–
GzIR 1st Wallachen Nr 16	–	7	–	57	–	–	–	–	–	64
GzIR Wallachisch-Illyrisch Nr 13	–	4	1	83	–	67	–	54	1	208
HusR Palatinal Nr 12	–	2	1	8	–	–	–	5	1	15
HausR Eh Ferdinand Nr 3	–	5	1	9	–	1	–	–	1	15
ChLR Hohenzollern Nr 2	1	4	1	15	–	–	–	–	2	19
IR Eh Karl Nr 3	1	37	2	194	1	21	–	–	4	252
IR Lindenau Nr 29	1	66	15	303	–	40	–	38	16	447
IR Württemberg Nr 40	–	20	–	114	1	5	–	72	1	221
IR Kerpen Nr 49	–	4	1	28	–	–	–	–	1	32
ChLR O'Reilley Nr 3	–	11	–	16	–	–	–	–	–	27
KürR Kaiser Nr 1	–	1	–	5	–	–	–	–	–	6
Artillery†	–	31	–	22	–	–	–	3	–	56
Total:	*3*	*192*	*23*	*854*	*2*	*134*	*–*	*172*	*28*	*1,362*

* GM Defours.

† 5 guns dismounted.

Bibliography

Anon, *Denkwürdigkeiten des Mecklenburg-Strelitzschen Husaren-Regiments in den Jahren des Befreiungskampfes 1813–1815*, Neubrandenburg, 1854.

Anon, *Der k. k. österreichische Feldmarschall Graf Radetzky*, Stuttgart and Augsburg, 1858.

Apel, Dr Theodor, *Tabellarische Zusammenstellungen der Kriegsereignisse bei Leipzig im Oktober 1813*, Leipzig, 1866.

Aster, Heinrich, *Die Gefechte und Schlachten bei Leipzig im Oktober 1813*, Dresden, 1856.

– *Schilderung der Kriegsereignisse in und vor Dresden vom 7. März bis 28. August 1813*, Leipzig, 1857.

Beck, Fritz, *Geschichte des 1. Grossherzoglich Hessischen Infanterie (Leibgarde) Regiments Nr 115*, Berlin, 1899.

– and Hahn, Karl von, *Geschichte des Grossherzoglich Hessischen Feldartillerie-Regiments Nr 25*, Berlin, 1899.

Belhomme, Lieutenant-Colonel, *Histoire de l'Infanterie en France* (6 vols), Paris, 1899.

Bernhardi, Theodor von, *Der Herbstfeldzug 1813*, Leipzig, 1866.

Bigge, Generalmajor W., *Geschichte des Infanterie-Regiments Kaiser Wilhelm (2. Grossherzoglich Hessisches) Nr 116*, Berlin, 1903.

Biereye, Professor Dr, *Die Befreiung Erfurts von der Napoleonischen Zwingherrschaft*, Erfurt, 1913.

Börner, Karl-Heinz, *Tage nach der Völkerschlacht*, Berlin, 1988.

– *Vor Leipzig 1813*, Berlin, 1988.

Brauer, Hans M., 'Die Feldzüge der Badischen Infanterie-Regimenter', *Zeitschrift für Heereskunde*, nos.20–1, 1930.

Brett-James, Anthony, *Europe Against Napoleon: The Leipzig Campaign 1813*, London, 1970.

Campbell, Major-General Sir Neil, *Napoleon at Fontainebleau and Elba, being a Journal of Occurrences in 1814–1815, with Notes of Conversations, with a Memoir of the Life and Services of that Officer by his Nephew Archibald Neil Campbell Maclachlan*, London, 1869.

Chandler, David, *The Campaigns of Napoleon*, New York and London, 1966.

Coignet, J., *Les Cahiers du Capitaine Coignet (1799–1815)*, Paris, 1894.

Dedem van der Gelder, Baron Antoine-Baudoin-Gisbert van, *Memoires du Général Baron de Dedem der Gelder, 1744–1825*, Paris, 1900.

Droysen, Johann Gustav, *Das Leben des Feldmarschalls Graf Yorck von Wartenburg*, Leipzig, 1890.

Duvernoy, Noon von, 'Die Württembergische Kavalleriebrigade Normann im Feldzuge 1813', *Militär Wochenblatt*, no.10, 1907.

Friccius, Major Carl Friedrich, letter to his wife Rike on 19 October 1813, reproduced in *Leipziger Kalendar*, Leipzig, 1914.

Friedrich, R., *Geschichte des Herbstfeldzuges 1813*, Berlin, 1906.

Grabowski, Joseph von, *Errinerungen eines Ordonnanzoffiziers Napoleon I aus den Freiheitskriegen*, Berlin, 1910.

Hirtenfeld, Dr J., *Der Miltär-Maria-Theresien-Orden und Seine Mitglieder*, Vienna, 1857.

Hoffmann, General-Leutnant von, *Zur Geschichte des Feldzugs vom Jahre 1813*, Posen, 1838.

Hollander, O., *Nos Drapeaux et Etandards de 1812 à 1815*, Paris, 1902.

Hussel, Ludwig, *Leipzig's Schreckenstage Während der Völkerschlacht*, Leipzig, 1863.

Keim, Generalmajor A., *Geschichte des Infanterie-Regiments Grossherzogin (3. Grossherzoglich Hessisches) Nr 117*, Berlin, 1903.

Kerchnawe, Hugo, *Von Leipzig bis Erfurt*, Leipzig, n.d.

– and Veltze, Alois, *Feldmarschall Karl Fürst zu Schwarzenberg der Führer der Verbündeten in den Befreiungskriegen*, Vienna, 1913.

Kraft, Heinz, *Die Württemberger in den Napoleonischen Kriegen*, Stuttgart, 1953.

Krimer, Wenzel, *Errinerungen eines alten Lützower Jägers, 1795–1819*, Stuttgart, 1913.

Krug, Wilhelm Traugott, *Krugs Lebensweise in sechs Stationen*, Leipzig, 1846.

Lanrezac, Colonel, *La Manoeuvre de Lützen*, Paris, 1904.

Londonderry, Charles William Vane, Lord, *Narrative of the War in Germany and France in 1813 and 1814*, London, 1830.

Marbot, General Marcellin de, *Memoirs*, London, 1892.

Martinien, A., *Tableaux par Corps et par Batailles des Officiers Tués et Blessés Pendant les Guerres de l'Empire (1805–1815)*, Paris, 1890.

Marx, Karl, *Geschichte des Infanterie-Reiterregiments Kaiser Friedrich (7. Württembergischen) Nr 125 1809–1895*, Berlin, 1895.

Mitteilungen des K und K Kriegsarchivs, Dritte Folge, vol.IV, Vienna, 1906.

Müller, Herbet, *Geschichte des 4. Württembergischen Infanterie-Regiments Kaiser Franz Joseph von Österreich, König von Ungarn*, Heilbronn, 1906.

Nafziger, George, *Leipzig*, Chicago, 1994.

Nostitz, August Ludwig Ferdinand, Graf von, 'Tagebuch des Generals der Kavallerie Grafen von Nostitz', *Kriegsgeschichtliche Einzelschriften*, vols.5–6, Berlin, 1884–5.

Nübling, H., *Geschichte des Grenadier-Regiments König Karl (5. Württembergisches) Nr 123*, Berlin, 1911.

Obser, Karl, *Denkwürdigkeiten des Markgrafen Wilhelm von Baden, vol I*, Heidelberg, 1906.

Odeleben, Otto von, *Napoleons Feldzug in Sachsen im Jahr 1813*, Dresden, 1816.

Österreichische Militärische Zeitschrift, Vienna, 1834 and 1836.

Pascale, Adrian, *Histoire de l'Armée et de tous les Régiments* (6 vols), Paris, 1847–58.

Petersdorff, Hermann von, *General Johann Adolf Freiherr von Thielmann*, Leipzig, 1894.

Petre, F. Loraine, *Napoleon's Last Campaign in Germany – 1813*, London and New York, 1992.

Pflugk-Harttung, Julius von, *Das Befreiungsjahr 1813*, Berlin, 1913.

– *1813–1815 Illustrierte Geschichte der Befreiungskriege*, Stuttgart, 1913.

Plotho, Carl von, *Der Krieg in Deutschland und Frankreich in den Jahren 1813–1814*, Berlin, 1817.

Priesdorf, Kurt von, *Soldatisches Führertum, Die Preussischen Generale 1792–1815*, Hamburg, 1837.

Quintin, Danielle and Bernard, *Dictionnaire des Colonels de Napoleon*, Paris, 1996.

Quistorp, Barthold von, *Die Kaiserlich Russisch-Deutsche Legion*, Berlin, 1860.

Rau, Ferdinand, *Geschichte des 1. Badischen Leib-Dragoner-Regiments Nr 20*, Berlin, 1878.

Rehtwisch, Thedor, *Die Grosse Zeit 1813–1815*, Leipzig, 1913.

Röhrig, Johann Jakob, *Unter der Fahne des ersten Napoleons*, Altenburg, no date.

de Saint-Chamans, Colonel, *Memoires du Général Comte de Saint-Chamans, Ancien Aide-de-Camp du Maréchal Soult*, Paris, 1896.

Seyfert, Friedrich, *Die Völkerschlacht bei Leipzig vom 14. bis 19.Oktober 1813*, Dresden, 1913.

Six, Georges, *Dictionnaire Biographique des Généraux et Amiraux Français de la Révolution et de l'Empire 1792–1814*, Paris, 1934.

Smith, Digby, *The Greenhill Napoleonic Wars Data Book*, London, 1998.

– *Napoleon's Regiments*, London, 2000.

Stadlinger, L.J. von, *Geschichte des Württembergischen Kriegswesen von der frühesten bis zur neüsten Zeit*, Stuttgart, 1856.

– *Militär-Handbuch des Königreiches Württemberg*, Stuttgart, 1836.

Starklof, R., *Geschichte des Königlich Württembergischen Vierten Reiterregiments Königin Olga 1805–1866*, Stuttgart, 1867.

Strack von Weissenbach, Major, *Geschichte der Königlich Württembergischen Artillerie*, Stuttgart, 1882.

Susane, General Louis Augustine, *Histoire de l'Artillerie Française*, Paris, 1874.

– *Histoire de la Cavalerie Française* (3 vols), Paris, 1874.

– *Histoire de l'Infanterie Française* (5 vols), Paris, reprinted 1985.

Toll, C.F. Graf, General der Infanterie, *Denkwürdigkeiten*, Leipzig, 1866.

Thielen, Maximilian Ritter von, *Errinerungen aus dem Kriegerleben eines 82-jährigen Veteranen der österreichischen Armee, mit besonderer Bezugnahme auf die Feldzüge der Jahre 1805, 1809, 1813, 1814, 1815*, Vienna, 1863.

Tulard, J., *Dictionnaire Napoleon*, Paris, 1989.

Veltze, Major Alois, *Die Politik Metternichts*, Leipzig, 1911.

Vitzthum von Eckstädt, Graf Karl, *Die Hauptquartiere im Herbstfeldzuge 1813 auf dem Deutschen Kriegsschauplatze*, Berlin, 1910.

Voigt, Günther, *Deutschlands Heere bis 1918*, Osnabrück, 1983.

Wolzogen, Ludwig von, *Memoiren des Königlich Preussischen Generals der Infanterie Freiherr von Wolzogen*, Leipzig, 1851.

Wrede, Alphons Freiherr von, *Geschichte der K. u. K. Wehrmacht*, Vienna and Leipzig, 1911.

Zelle, Dr W., *1813 Preussens-Völkerfrühling, Part II*, Leipzig, no date.

Zimmermann, Rittmeister, *Geschichte des 1. Grossherzoglich Hessischen Dragoner-Regiments (Garde-Dragoner-Regiments) Nr 23*, Darmstadt, 1878.

Index